REMEMBERING TRAUMA

REMEMBERING TRAUMA

Richard J. McNally

THE BELKNAP PRESS OF
HARVARD UNIVERSITY PRESS

Cambridge, Massachusetts, and London, England

2003

Library of Congress Cataloging-in-Publication Data

McNally, Richard J.
Remembering trauma / Richard J. McNally.
p. cm.
Includes bibliographical references and index.
ISBN 0-674-01082-5 (alk. paper)
1. Psychic trauma. 2. Post-traumatic stress disorder.
3. Recovered memory. I. Title.

RC552.P67 M396 2003
616.85′ 21–dc21
2002028143

For my wife, Peggy

CONTENTS

REMEMBERING TRAUMA

I

THE POLITICS OF TRAUMA

How victims remember trauma is the most divisive issue facing psychology today. Some experts believe that rape, combat, and other horrific experiences are engraved on the mind, never to be forgotten. Others believe that the mind protects itself by banishing traumatic memories from awareness, making it difficult for many people to remember their worst experiences until many years later.

This is not an ordinary academic controversy. It has spilled out of the clinics and psychology laboratories, capturing headlines, provoking legislative change, and determining outcomes in criminal trials and civil suits. The question of sexual abuse and how it affects people's lives has been especially contentious. Attempts to understand how people are affected by abuse can lead scientists into conflict with powerful political forces. Indeed, in 1999, in an unprecedented event, the United States Congress issued a formal condemnation of three psychologists who published an article synthesizing the results of many studies on the psychological effects of sexual abuse.

Contemporary debates about trauma—how it is defined, how it is remembered, how it affects its victims—have been shot through with politics ever since the Vietnam war. Concerns about the psychological adjustment of returning veterans inspired the formal recognition of posttraumatic stress disorder by American psychiatry in 1980. While many applauded the new diagnosis as finally giving voice to survivors of trauma, others questioned its validity, seeing it as a political artifact of the antiwar movement.

The field of traumatic stress became engulfed in controversy in the mid-1980s as suspicions of widespread molestation of children in daycare centers proliferated and adults in psychotherapy began recovering memories of their own long-forgotten abuse. The circumstances surrounding the investigation of allegations of abuse in daycare centers and the recovery of allegedly repressed memories of trauma in adults sparked claims that reports of trauma were not based on genuine events and were perhaps inadvertently fostered by law enforcement investigators and therapists.

Until the mid-1990s, debates about trauma and memory were hampered by vitriolic accusations issuing from both sides and by the scarcity of clinically relevant scientific data. During the last few years, matters have improved dramatically. An outpouring of research has clarified many of the most contentious issues. Now it is time to take stock of what we have learned.

The evidence points to three conclusions. First, people remember horrific experiences all too well. Victims are seldom incapable of remembering their trauma. Second, people sometimes do not think about disturbing events for long periods of time, only to be reminded of them later. However, events that are experienced as overwhelmingly traumatic at the time of their occurrence rarely slip from awareness. Third, there is no reason to postulate a special mechanism of repression or dissociation to explain why people may not think about disturbing experiences for long periods. A failure to think about something does not entail an inability to remember it (amnesia). The purpose of this book is to lay out the evidence that supports these conclusions.

A WORD ON TERMINOLOGY

Questions of terminology immediately arise for anyone grappling with issues of trauma. For example, what shall we call individuals who have experienced terrible events? The traditional term is *victim*. It has its advantages. It implies that those exposed to rape, earthquakes, child abuse, and so forth are not to blame for their misfortunes. Moreover, *victim* tends to direct attention to perpetrators and to the damage they have inflicted on others. But some people dislike this term, preferring *survivor*. *Survivor* implies resilience and strength in overcoming adversity. Then again, others argue that *survivor* should be reserved for those who have undergone life-threatening traumatic events, such as combat, serious earthquakes, or confinement in concentration camps. The phrase *Holocaust survivor* was among the first uses of *survivor* in the trauma field; the word later came to be applied broadly, as in *survivor of childhood sexual abuse*. Following contemporary usage, I have opted to use both *victim* and

2

survivor to denote anyone who has been exposed to traumatic events, including events that were not life-threatening.

The other contested term is *recovered memory therapy*. As far as I can tell, no one practicing psychotherapy today endorses this term as descriptive of what they do. However, although there are no self-described recovered memory therapists, there have certainly been many therapists who believed that repressed (or dissociated) memories of early trauma contribute to psychological symptoms, and that remembering and working through these traumatic experiences can foster psychological healing. Thus the term *recovered memory therapy* undeniably applies to a set of assumptions and techniques about how to treat people who are presumed to be unable to remember their terrible experiences. Of course, even recovered memory therapists do much more than help people remember and emotionally process the past; they help people cope with problems in the here and now as well as with the lingering effects of the past. Because not all therapists who work with survivors of abuse and other trauma endorse these beliefs or use these methods, one cannot refer simply to *trauma therapists* when discussing a very specific approach to psychotherapy.

A Word on Bias

Anyone endeavoring to interpret the evidence on trauma and memory runs the risk of being charged with bias. People too often hurl this charge—especially when their opponents seem to be winning the argument. A charge of bias is appropriate only when one systematically ignores relevant data, misinterprets it, or applies different standards of evidence depending on whether the results are favorable or unfavorable to one's theoretical position. Having a strong opinion is not equivalent to being biased—as long as the opinion is warranted by the evidence.

It is important to keep in mind another crucial point about highly polarized debates such as those abounding in the field of traumatic stress. Consider the debate about recovered memory. Some argue that people rarely, if ever, repress and then recover memories of childhood sexual abuse, whereas others argue that it happens frequently. An apparently judicious resolution might be to split the difference between these views. Yet the truth about recovered memory may lie at either end of this continuum; nothing requires us to assume that it must constitute a compromise between these sharply contrasting views. Analogously, one person may believe the earth is round while another believes it is flat, but a "balanced" view of the matter does not compel us to conclude that the earth must therefore be oblong. An unbiased approach requires only that our conclusions be supported by the evidence. We cannot decide in advance where the truth about trauma and memory must lie.

THE REEMERGENCE OF TRAUMA

Political, social, and clinical attention to trauma waxed and waned throughout the twentieth century, as the historian Philip Jenkins (1998) has shown. Concerns about sexual endangerment were widespread during the Progressive era (roughly 1890–1920), as exemplified by lurid newspaper coverage about horrific sex crimes and legislation designed to protect women and children against these criminals. But these concerns subsided as the media turned their attention to other topics such as Prohibition-era gangsterism. Worries about sexual psychopaths rose again during World War II, when many women worked in factories, leaving their children with caretakers, while their husbands fought overseas. These concerns persisted throughout much of the 1950s, but declined markedly in the 1960s, when the sex offender transmuted into a semi-humorous figure of fun (or pity). Noting that mores have fluctuated wildly, Jenkins points out that Eric Clapton and his band Blind Faith featured a topless preadolescent girl on the cover of their 1969 album; although this album is sold today as a compact disc, a white band now covers the girl's chest.

The current historical upswing began in the early 1960s following the publication of Henry Kempe and his colleagues' landmark article describing the battered-child syndrome (Kempe et al. 1962). Its authors documented what pediatricians had long been reluctant to believe: that children's seemingly inexplicable injuries were far too often inflicted by their parents. Since the publication of that article, abuse and neglect of children have never ceased to be urgent social concerns.

Concerns about the sexual abuse of children intensified during the 1970s as feminists heightened public awareness of domestic violence and rape. The initial focus was on incest, traditionally defined as sexual intercourse between biological relatives. This narrow legal definition soon broadened to include touching and fondling. Incest, in turn, was subsumed under the category of *sexual abuse,* a term covering diverse experiences, including being flashed by an exhibitionist and being "forced to listen to sexual talk," as Ellen Bass and Laura Davis asserted (1988: 21). Researchers conducted large surveys designed to measure the extent of the problem. They arrived at widely discrepant estimates of the prevalence of sexual abuse, in large part because what counted as sexual abuse varied from study to study. Depending on the study and its definition of abuse, anywhere from 3 to 62 percent of the population of American adults were classifiable as survivors of sexual abuse in childhood.[1]

THE RISE OF RECOVERED MEMORY THERAPY

Therapists writing in the early 1980s observed that adult incest survivors were often reluctant to disclose their abuse to others (Gelinas 1983; Herman 1981). By the end of the decade, reluctance to disclose became inability to remember. Influenced by the writings of the feminist psychoanalyst Alice Miller, many therapists now believed that many women harbored repressed memories of early abuse. Synthesizing Freud's nineteenth-century ideas about total repression of sexual trauma with contemporary feminist critiques concerning the prevalence of incest in a patriarchal society, Miller and others argued that many successful but distressed women suffered from complete amnesia for their "brutal abuse during childhood" such "that their illusion of a good childhood can be maintained with ease." Miller asserted: "For some years now, it has been possible to prove, thanks to the use of new therapeutic methods, that traumatic experiences in childhood are stored up in the body and, although remaining unconscious, exert their influence even in adulthood" (Miller 1997: 2, 6, 131). Therapy designed to recover these memories was how one healed from trauma.

Following Miller's lead, many therapists now believed that many women were wholly unaware of having been sexually abused as children, because of what Judith Herman and Emily Schatzow called "massive repression" (1987: 12). Hence as Daniel Brown and his colleagues asserted, "approximately a third of sexually abused victims report some period of their lives where they did not remember anything about the abuse and later recovered the memory of the abuse" (Brown, Scheflin, and Hammond 1998: 196).

These therapists believed that memories of abuse, blocked from awareness by defensive mechanisms of the mind, silently poisoned the mental health of survivors. Repressed memories, which lay at the root of diverse psychological problems, needed to be remembered, emotionally processed, and cast into narrative form. Of course, this was not the only goal of an integrated trauma treatment; therapists also endeavored to enhance the patient's emotional stability and social functioning. Nevertheless, leading professional authorities emphasized that healing requires remembering. Thus Karen Olio affirmed that recovering memories of sexual abuse is "crucial to successful resolution of the trauma" (1989: 99), and Christine Courtois stressed that healing from "sexual abuse trauma requires the retrieval of memory and the working through of associated affect" (1992: 15).[2]

Because memories of abuse often do not surface spontaneously in therapy, these authors recommended special techniques for triggering recollection (see Person and Klar 1994). As Olio put it: "Once sexual abuse is considered a possibility, therapeutic modalities can be included which provide the necessary triggers. Trance work, dreamwork, bodywork, and/or group work with other survivors are some preferred options" (1989: 96). Interpreting pains, panic attacks, and other bodily sensations as possible indicators of abuse was justified by assuming that the body "remembers" even when the mind cannot.[3] Courtois recommended guiding patients through imagery exercises requiring them to visualize hypothetical scenarios of abuse. Herman and Schatzow urged female patients to join incest recovery groups; hearing the voices of survivors would presumably trigger recollection in those whose memories were blocked from awareness. Finally, hypnosis was accorded special status as a retrieval method. As Brown, Scheflin, and Hammond wrote: "Because some victims of sexual abuse will repress their memories by dissociating them from consciousness, hypnosis can be very valuable in retrieving these memories. Indeed, for some victims, hypnosis may provide the only avenue to the repressed memories" (1998: 647).

The emphasis on recovering repressed memories of abuse emerged from the core of the trauma field, not from its paraprofessional fringe. Beliefs about trauma and memory, expressed by renowned therapists in the professional literature, were soon echoed in best-selling books written for women who suspected they might be abuse survivors. Addressing a lay audience, the social worker E. Sue Blume estimated that "more than half of all women are survivors of childhood sexual trauma." But many incest survivors, perhaps half of them, were entirely unaware of their abuse histories, because amnesia was "the most common feature of Post-Incest Syndrome." Recovering these memories of abuse was crucial for "healing the inner child" (Blume 1990: xiv, 81, 280).

In *The Courage to Heal*, a book that has sold approximately half a million copies since its publication in 1988, Ellen Bass and Laura Davis informed readers that "many adult survivors are unaware of the fact that they were abused," owing to the mind's "tremendous powers of repression." Hidden abuse, they said, could be revealed in many ways, including feeling "different from other people" and feeling a need to be "perfect." Bass and Davis reassured readers: "If you don't remember your abuse, you are not alone. Many women don't have memories, and some never get memories. This doesn't mean they weren't abused." For those who questioned the authenticity of their memories, they wrote: "So far, no one we've talked to thought she might have been abused, and then later discovered that she hadn't been. The progression always goes the other way, from suspicion to confirmation. If you think you were abused and your life shows the symptoms, then you were" (1988: 42, 35, 81, 22).[4]

Also addressing a lay audience, the clinical psychologist Renee Fredrickson asserted that "profound disbelief is an indication that memories are real," noting that second thoughts about memories' authenticity merely reflect attempts to repress them once again. To guard against doubt, she advised readers to affiliate with "people who believe your repressed memories are real," and she warned them not to be deceived by the apparent normality of their families; 99 percent of all abusive families, she said, exhibit no outward signs of dysfunction. Fredrickson stressed the centrality of memory work: "The bulk of your repressed memories need to be identified, retrieved, and debriefed for healing to occur" (1992: 171, 12, 224, 71, 223).

Panic in the Daycare Center

While trauma therapists throughout the 1980s were helping adults recover memories of molestation, child welfare workers were claiming to have discovered widespread current abuse of children in daycare centers. The alleged victims seldom disclosed any abuse, nor were they symptomatic. But their occasional odd remarks and behavior convinced their parents that something sinister was afoot. Frightened parents contacted the police, and investigations began. When first questioned, most children denied any abuse. Their denials, however, were interpreted as reflecting either fear of reprisal by the abusers or dissociative amnesia for horrors suffered. Convinced that crimes had occurred, mental health and law enforcement professionals subjected the children to relentless interrogations, marked by suggestive, leading questions, until they disclosed their abuse. The most spectacular allegations concerned physical and sexual tortures occurring during satanic rituals. The children became increasingly disturbed as they recounted these crimes, and their pervasive anxiety, nightmares, sexualized behavior, and conduct problems were interpreted as confirming the allegations. Juries, informed by mental health professionals that children rarely fabricate reports of abuse, convicted many alleged abusers solely on the basis of preschoolers' testimony. Physical evidence of crimes was scarce to nonexistent.[5]

POSTTRAUMATIC STRESS DISORDER

The new diagnosis of posttraumatic stress disorder (PTSD) provided a framework for conceptualizing the problems of survivors of abuse and other trauma. PTSD was first recognized by the American Psychiatric Association in 1980 in the third edition of its *Diagnostic and Statistical Manual of Mental Disorders* (DSM-III). The DSM specifies the criteria for diagnosing each mental disorder officially recognized by American psychiatry. DSM-III heralded a sharp break from psychiatry's psychoanalytic past. The authors of DSM-III declined to speculate about the causes of mental disorders; they sought merely to achieve reliable criteria for diagnosing them. PTSD, however, was an exception to this rule because it specified a causal factor in its definition: exposure to a traumatic "stressor that would evoke significant symptoms of distress in almost everyone" and "that is generally outside the range of usual human experience" (APA 1980: 238, 236).

DSM-III described three clusters of symptoms caused by exposure to trauma. The first cluster comprised reexperiencing symptoms, such as having recurrent intrusive recollections and dreams about the trauma and suddenly acting and feeling as if it were happening again ("flashbacks"). Rather than merely remembering the trauma, sufferers seemed to relive it again and again as if it were happening in the present. The second cluster comprised numbing symptoms, such as blunted emotion, feelings of estrangement from others, and loss of interest in formerly enjoyable activities. The third cluster comprised miscellaneous symptoms, including hypervigilance for threat, enhanced startle response, sleep disturbance, memory and concentration impairment, avoidance of distressing reminders of the trauma, and guilt about having survived when others did not.

Posttraumatic stress disorder, then, was fundamentally a disorder of memory. Most important, terrifying events from the past were remembered all too well, producing emotional distress in the present. A secondary memory problem was increased forgetfulness in everyday life, perhaps resulting from preoccupation with the past.

Psychiatrists had long recognized that exposure to horrific events could produce symptoms of stress in previously well-adjusted individuals. Syndromes such as shell shock and combat fatigue had been observed in soldiers following World Wars I and II. But most doctors believed that these reactions dissipated soon after the stressor was removed, unless preexisting vulnerabilities or psychopathology was present. The conventional wisdom about traumatic stress reactions changed during the Vietnam war (Young 1995). In retrospect, this is surprising, because psychiatric casualties were extremely rare in Vietnam, and most had nothing to do with combat. The rate of psychiatric breakdown was only 12 cases per 1,000 men compared to 37 per 1,000 during the Korean war and 28–101 per 1,000 during World War II (Dean 1997: 40). However, antiwar psychiatrists such as Robert Lifton (1973) argued that emotional problems often emerge only after combatants return to civilian life. Because stress reactions that were delayed, chronic, or both could not be accommodated within the existing diagnostic framework, these psychiatrists proposed that a "post-Vietnam syndrome" be included in DSM-III.[6]

Initially skeptical, DSM-III committee members were reluctant to include a diagnosis so closely tied to the war. Advocates for the diagnosis replied that symptoms reported by veterans in informal counseling groups were strikingly similar to those reported by people exposed to other traumatic events, such as rape (Burgess and Holmstrom 1974), natural disaster (Rangell 1976), and confinement in concentration camps (Chodoff 1963). Evidence that exposure to a diverse range of horrific events produced a common syndrome clinched the argument, and PTSD, not "post-Vietnam syndrome," appeared in DSM-III. The ratification of PTSD as an official psychiatric diagnosis stimulated an outpouring of research and prompted the founding of the International Society for Traumatic Stress Studies (ISTSS) and the establishment of the *Journal of Traumatic Stress* in 1988. Treating survivors of traumatic stress became a mental health specialty, and many clinical scientists conducted studies to understand the psychopathology of PTSD and its treatment.

Clinical experience and research on trauma motivated changes in the diagnostic criteria for PTSD in DSM-III-R and in DSM-IV, published in 1987 and 1994, respectively. DSM-III acknowledged that PTSD sufferers complain about everyday forgetfulness, adding the diagnostic criterion "memory impairment or trouble concentrating." Although DSM-III-R retained "difficulty concentrating" as a symptom, it replaced everyday memory impairment with "inability to recall an important aspect of the trauma (psychogenic amnesia)" (APA 1987: 250–251). This was a radical change. No longer was PTSD only about having excruciatingly vivid memories of trauma; it was now about inability to remember parts of the trauma. The notion that people are incapable of remembering significant aspects of their traumatic experience was retained in the DSM-IV criteria for PTSD, and the definition of what counts as a traumatic stressor was expanded to include "developmentally inappropriate sexual experiences without threatened or actual violence or injury" (APA 1994: 427–429). Sexual abuse in childhood was now formally recognized as a stressor akin to combat, rape, torture, and other traumas capable of triggering PTSD.[7]

Appearing for the first time in DSM-IV was a new diagnosis, acute stress disorder (ASD). Like PTSD, ASD is triggered by traumatic stressors, and it is characterized by many of the same symptoms (APA 1994: 429–432). The symptoms must last at least two days but no longer than one month. If symptoms persist longer than a month, the person may qualify for PTSD. To qualify for ASD, a person must experience at least three of five dissociative symptoms during or immediately after the trauma: emotional numbing, being in a daze, derealization, depersonalization, and inability to remember aspects of what happened. Advocates of the ASD diagnosis urged its inclusion in DSM-IV because they believed that people who experience dissociative symptoms during the trauma and meet criteria for ASD are those most likely to develop PTSD.

ASD has been controversial (for the definitive scholarly work on the topic, see Bryant and Harvey 2000). Because so many people experience stress symptoms immediately after horrific events, some critics believe that diagnosing these people as mentally ill amounts to pathologizing the normal human response to such events (Wakefield 1996). Reviewing the literature on ASD, Randall Marshall, Robert Spitzer, and Michael Liebowitz (1999) conclude that many people who develop chronic PTSD do not experience dissociative symptoms during the trauma and thus do not first qualify for ASD. In any event, the rationale for defining a set of acute stress responses as a disorder in itself (ASD) merely because it was supposedly a risk factor for another disorder (PTSD) was never logically compelling.

Trauma and Multiple Personality Disorder

Another stress-related diagnosis introduced in DSM-III was multiple personality disorder or MPD (APA 1980: 257–259). MPD was defined by at least two distinct, complex, and integrated personalities within the same person, each of which assumed control over the person's behavior at different times. MPD was classified as one of the dissociative disorders—syndromes marked by severe *dissociation*, disruptions in consciousness or personal identity. As the psychiatrist Frank Putnam and his colleagues affirmed, the fracturing of the normally integrated sense of self and consciousness characteristic of MPD was believed to begin "as a childhood response to overwhelming sexual, physical, and psychological trauma" (1986: 292). Histories of severe sexual and physical abuse during childhood were uncovered in more than 95 percent of patients diagnosed with MPD (see Putnam et al. 1986; Ross et al. 1990). MPD specialists believed that patients develop alternative personalities ("alters") to accommodate dissociated memories of abuse that are too painful for the main ("host") personality to experience consciously. According to this posttraumatic theory of MPD, the syndrome is very much a disorder of memory. Memories of terrible experiences are sealed off from awareness, accessible only to those personalities capable of coping with trauma.

The belief that severe childhood trauma causes MPD became popular only after the appearance of the best-selling book and film about Sybil, a woman who had developed 16 personalities after having been brutalized throughout childhood by her mother (Schreiber 1973). Child abuse rarely figured in the histories of previous "multiples," including that of the patient depicted in the film *The Three Faces of Eve*. Unlike Sybil, Eve never remembered abuse, despite her therapists' extensive hypnotic probing of her childhood memories (Thigpen and Cleckley 1954).[8]

Before the 1980s, MPD had been one of the rarest disorders in the history of psychiatry. The first documented case may have been that of a sixteenth-century French nun who was "diagnosed" as demonically possessed and suc-

11

cessfully treated through exorcism (van der Hart, Lierens, and Goodwin 1996). Few cases had appeared in the literature since then. But diagnoses of MPD skyrocketed in the post-Sybil era. Writing in 1986, Putnam and his colleagues observed that "more cases of MPD have been reported within the last five years than in the preceding two centuries" (285). As many as six thousand patients may have received the diagnosis by 1986, most in North America (Hacking 1995: 8). Whereas MPD, fugue, and other dissociative disorders had long been considered rare and exotic syndromes, the therapists Bessel van der Kolk and Onno van der Hart proclaimed "that between twenty and fifty percent of psychiatric inpatients suffer from dissociative disorders" (1991: 432).

How was it possible for such a severe and supposedly common disorder to have been missed by psychiatrists for so many decades? How could an extremely rare illness suddenly reach epidemic proportions almost overnight? According to Putnam (1991a), most doctors were unfamiliar with the bewildering symptoms of MPD, often confusing it with schizophrenia, a common psychotic illness characterized by delusions and hallucinations. Moreover, unlike people with depression, panic disorder, and other familiar syndromes, most "multiples" were unaware that they suffered from the illness. Self-diagnosis was rare. Most patients sought help for other problems, and their multiplicity often became apparent only after weeks or months of therapy. Once the diagnosis was made, certain therapeutic tactics came into play. Applying psychodynamic psychotherapy and hypnosis (Putnam and Loewenstein 1993), therapists elicited and identified alter personalities, fostered communication among them, recovered dissociated memories of childhood abuse, and endeavored to integrate alters into a single functional personality (Kluft 1991). Hypnotic elicitation of alter personalities was easy, as the psychiatrist Eugene Bliss affirmed: "To enter the domain of the personalities is childishly simple, for the key to the door is hypnosis and these patients are excellent hypnotic subjects. This is the world of hypnosis. Personalities hidden for decades may be accosted and interviewed or forgotten memories can be encountered and relieved [sic] by the subject with all the emotional intensity of a contemporary event" (1980: 1394).

The epidemic of multiple personality disorder was accompanied by the founding of the International Society for the Study of Dissociation and Multiple Personality in 1990. Shortly thereafter, the society launched its journal, Dissociation. Hospitals throughout the United States opened specialized inpatient units for treating dissociative disorders. The disorder, however, acquired a new name with the publication of DSM-IV in 1994. Patients formerly diagnosed with MPD were now diagnosed with dissociative identity disorder or DID (APA 1994: 484–487). The notion of dozens of distinct personalities inhabiting the same body was abandoned in favor of the view that the real problem was that these patients lacked even a single coherent identity. Apart from the new name, little changed in terms of theory or practice. DID was still assumed to result from a person's attempt to prevent horrific memories of early abuse from entering awareness.

Traumatic Memory in the Courtroom

Throughout the 1980s and 1990s, increasing numbers of adults, most of them women, recovered memories of abuse during the course of psychotherapy. Many received diagnoses of PTSD or MPD. Most had sought treatment for other problems, such as depression, eating disorders, or relationship difficulties, and had discovered their histories of abuse only during treatment. Four beliefs held by therapists drove this process: that sexual abuse was far more widespread than anyone had imagined; that the mind protects itself by blocking awareness of abuse memories; that these hidden but toxic memories are expressed in diverse psychological problems; and that recovering the memories is vital to overcoming psychological problems.

Yet recovered memory therapy would have had little impact beyond the consulting room had it not been for two developments. First, after recalling abuse, many patients accused their fathers and others of sex crimes and severed ties with their families. Most alleged parental abusers vehemently denied any wrongdoing, but their denials were dismissed by the accusers as the prevarication to be expected from sex offenders.

Second, some patients sought to file suit against alleged abusers. Therapists sometimes encouraged legal action as an empowering step toward healing. At first, patients encountered insurmountable legal barriers due to statutes of limitations. Most states required that plaintiffs file suit no later than two years after reaching adulthood. So a 30-year-old woman could not sue her father for abuse she had suffered at the age of 12. However, some lawyers argued that the statute of limitations should be "tolled" (extended) for those who had either repressed their memory of abuse or only belatedly recognized its negative impact on their lives. Many courts were sympathetic to this argument. Beginning in the mid-1980s, laws were changed in 37 states to permit adult survivors to sue perpetrators long after the statute of limitations would otherwise have expired (see Williams 1996). For example, Massachusetts state law extends the statute of limitations because "a child may repress all memory of the abuse, lack understanding of the wrongfulness of the conduct, or be unaware of any harm or its cause until years after the abuse" (quoted in Behnke and Hilliard 1998: 67). But some courts have been reluctant to toll the statute of limitations for plaintiffs who always remembered their abuse and who only belatedly recognized its negative impact on their lives. Hence, those who claim to have repressed all memories are those most likely to have their day in court. Some states, however, require corroboration of such memories for extension of the statute of limitations (Reagan 1999).

Most adults who have recalled being molested in childhood have not initiated legal action against alleged perpetrators. Surveys indicate that suits are filed in only 6–14 percent of cases (False Memory Syndrome Foundation 1995; Gudjonsson 1997). As of July 1998, 803 claims filed in the United States on the basis of recovered memories had led to litigation (Lipton 1999). These included 633 civil suits, 103 criminal actions, and 67 miscellaneous actions (such as restraining orders). Most concerned recovered memories of sexual abuse, but 7 concerned recovered memories of having witnessed homicide. In 79 percent of the civil and criminal suits, memories surfaced while the complainant was in psychotherapy, and 69 percent of all claims concerned adults who recovered memories of having been abused by their parents; alleged perpetrators in the other cases were usually other relatives, clergymen, or teachers.

The False Memory Syndrome Foundation

In response to the flood of allegations, a group of accused parents in the United States founded the False Memory Syndrome Foundation (FMSF) in 1992. The purposes of the FMSF were to provide support and advice to accused family members and to disseminate scientific information about trauma and memory to its members and to the public at large. To accomplish its educational aim, the FMSF assembled a Scientific and Professional Advisory Board including eminent representatives from psychology, psychiatry, sociology, and the law. The FMSF claimed that therapeutic techniques designed to recover hidden memories of trauma often result in the inadvertent creation of psychologically compelling but false memories of abuse. According to the FMSF, "recovered memory therapists" were producing an epidemic of "False Memory Syndrome," destroying families and harming patients while attempting to heal them. Similar societies formed in the United Kingdom and Australia shortly thereafter.[9]

Many cognitive psychologists—experimentalists who study memory, attention, and other mental processes—shared these concerns (e.g. Ceci and Loftus 1994; Lindsay and Read 1994; Read and Lindsay 1994). Certain techniques for memory recovery resembled methods known to create memory distortion in laboratory studies, heightening worries that at least some abuse memories were false. Among these techniques were guided imagery, dream interpretation, and hypnosis.

Researchers were especially critical of using hypnosis as a memory recovery method. Contrary to beliefs held by many therapists and laypersons, there is no convincing evidence that hypnosis enhances memory. In fact, not only does hypnosis fail to improve accuracy of recollection, it fosters false memories while significantly increasing confidence that they are genuine (Steblay and Bothwell 1994). Likewise, hypnotic "age regression"—a method designed to reinstate a developmentally early mode of psychological functioning—does not enable adults to remember otherwise inaccessible events of early childhood (Nash 1987). "Age-regressed" adults do not return to an early mode of cognitive functioning; they merely behave like adults pretending to be children. Summarizing the science, the cognitive psychologist and hypnosis researcher John Kihlstrom stated: "Because the risks of distortion vastly outweigh the chances of obtaining any useful information, forensic investigators and clinical practitioners should avoid hypnosis as a technique for enhancing recollection" (1997a: 1731).[10]

MPD therapists received the most intense criticism, because of their extensive use of hypnosis and the often bizarre memories their patients retrieved during treatment. Some MPD patients remembered being exposed to sexual abuse, torture, human sacrifice, and cannibalism in satanic cults. Because most MPD patients had been unaware of these atrocities until after they sought help for mundane problems, critics accused the therapists of unwittingly fostering false memories of trauma, thereby creating the disorder they thought they were treating. MPD, charged the critics, was the ultimate False Memory Syndrome.[11]

Not all clinicians believe that MPD results from severe abuse during childhood. Some endorse an alternative "sociocognitive" theory. According to this theory, MPD is a socially shaped idiom of distress that develops in response to certain therapeutic practices (such as hypnosis) and to cultural expectations about how people with multiple personalities are supposed to behave. Indeed, public pronouncements by MPD experts unmistakably underscore the glamour of the diagnosis. Cornelia Wilbur, Sybil's therapist, characterized MPD patients as heroic creative geniuses who have applied their autohypnotic gifts to surmount grotesque and horrific abuse (in Mulhern 1997). Advocates of the sociocognitive model note that bizarre dissociative phenomena are rarely evident before intensive therapy conducted by MPD specialists. By eliciting, identifying, and conversing with alters, therapists help shape, if not create, the syndrome. These theorists do not deny that distressed individuals can develop symptoms that fulfill diagnostic criteria for MPD—the disorder is "real" in this sense—nor do they deny that experts can diagnose it reliably, nor do they deny that MPD patients suffer psychological distress. But they are deeply skeptical of the syndrome's alleged traumatic etiology. These horrific abuse histories are often first detected, and perhaps suggested, during hypnotic treatment, and they seldom receive independent corroboration.[12]

Ironically, some of the sharpest critics of the MPD epidemic were the clinicians familiar with the two most famous cases, Eve and Sybil. Eve's therapists, Corbett Thigpen and Hervey Cleckley (1984), argued that MPD was being grossly overdiagnosed by psychiatrists specializing in dissociative disorders. Indeed, they reported, they had encountered only one other genuine case of multiple personality among the tens of thousands of patients they had seen since their treatment of Eve. But the crowning irony of the MPD controversy was the revelation that Sybil was not a multiple personality after all. According to the distinguished psychiatrist Herbert Spiegel, who had assessed her many years earlier, Sybil was a highly hypnotizable classic hysteria patient. Spiegel said Sybil's therapist had believed that a book based on Sybil's life would never sell unless she carried the exotic diagnosis of multiple personality disorder (in Borch-Jacobsen 1997).

Even Pierre Janet—the great early twentieth-century French psychiatrist who popularized the concept of dissociation and is deemed the godfather of the field of dissociative disorders—became a critic of multiple personality disorder. He came to regard those with the diagnosis as actually suffering from manic-depressive illness (folie circulaire) (Hacking 1998: 76).

Despite having been recognized in DSM for more than 20 years, MPD continues to provoke divided reactions among psychiatrists. Although, in the mid-1990s, approximately two-thirds of Canadian psychiatrists endorsed MPD as a valid diagnosis, two-thirds of them believed its prevalence was affected by publicity and by the belief systems of psychiatrists (Mai 1995). A survey of 367 randomly sampled board-certified American psychiatrists—300 of whom responded—indicated diverse opinions regarding DID. Only 21 percent endorsed the view that science has strongly confirmed the validity of DID (Pope et al. 1999). Even Allen Frances, the chairman of the DSM-IV committee, joined the critics, asserting that "the current over-diagnosis of multiple personality is an illusory fad that leads to misdiagnosis and mistreatment and does a disservice to the vast majority of patients who fall under its sway" (Frances and M. B. First quoted in Slovenko 1999: 229).

Apparently in response to critiques of "recovered memory therapy" and publicity about "False Memory Syndrome," the number of lawsuits against alleged abusers filed on the basis of recovered memories plummeted after 1994, having peaked the previous year (Lipton 1999). By the late 1990s most such lawsuits were being dismissed, and most appellate courts have prohibited tolling of the statute of limitations and have refused to admit testimony based on recovered memories (Piper, Pope, and Borowiecki 2000).

Moreover, increasing numbers of patients began to question the authenticity of their recovered memories, and some of these "retractors" sued their former therapists for malpractice. They accused their therapists of having negligently "implanted" false memories of abuse, causing them psychological harm and damaging their family relationships. As of October 1998, 139 such malpractice claims had been filed against therapists by their former patients. Another 70 retractors were planning to follow suit. Some former patients have been awarded large settlements, $10.6 million in one case. Most suits have been settled out of court, many on the evening before the trial was to begin. By 1998, 152 malpractice suits had been filed by third parties against therapists. Instead of the patient filing a malpractice claim against the therapist for implanting false memories, the relatives of the patient are doing so on the grounds that they have been damaged by false allegations (see Lipton 1999).[13]

While the FMSF publicized the dangers of "recovered memory therapy," some psychologists became deeply concerned that professionals investigating reports of abuse in daycare centers were subjecting children to suggestive and coercive interviewing techniques likely to result in false allegations of abuse (Bruck and Ceci 1995). During the 1990s these concerns motivated further research that altered interviewing practices, bringing to a sudden halt the apparent epidemic of abuse of preschoolers. One case involving more than 100 children who had allegedly been sexually molested and physically brutalized at the McMartin preschool in suburban Los Angeles became the longest criminal trial in American history and resulted in not a single conviction for any of the alleged satanic perpetrators (see Nathan and Snedeker 1995: 92). Many people convicted on the apparently coerced testimony of young children had their convictions overturned, although some still languish in prison.

THERAPISTS RESPOND TO THE BACKLASH

In response to these developments, therapists specializing in the treatment of sexual abuse launched a counterattack against their critics. The psychologist Laura Brown observed that "the tactics of the false memory movement have shown remarkable parallels to those of sexual abusers who attempt to silence their victims" (1998: 191). The clinical psychologists Judith Alpert, Brown, and Christine Courtois speculated that the ascendance of the FMSF implied that "people need to repress and deny that sexual abuse happens or that even they themselves may be capable of committing abuse" (Alpert 1997: 987). Still others interpreted critiques as reflecting a reactionary backlash against feminism designed to buttress the forces of patriarchy and silence the voices of survivors.[14]

Alpert, Brown, and Courtois dismissed critiques of recovered memory therapy as reflecting "a gross misunderstanding of what actually happens in psychotherapy" (1998c: 1062), and the clinical psychologist John Briere (1995) reframed them as wholesale attacks on the practice of psychotherapy in general. Alpert and her colleagues (1998b) warned that criticism of recovered memory therapy would lead to legislative prohibition of any kind of treatment for trauma survivors.

Although Alpert, Brown, and Courtois conceded that some instances of incompetent trauma therapy had occurred, they blamed these rare cases on "a number of poorly informed therapists, untrained lay counselors, and self-help books" (1998b: 1013). Indeed, according to Brown (1995b), so-called recovered memory therapy was little more than an inflammatory caricature bearing scant resemblance to the therapeutic work of Judith Herman, Christine Courtois, and other leaders of the trauma field. Especially controversial was the claim that someone could forget years of abuse, thanks to a mechanism of "robust" or "massive" repression. Yet Alpert and her colleagues attributed this controversial concept to allies of the FMSF, claiming never to have encountered it in the scholarly literature on repression. This attribution is surprising: Alpert (1994) herself had used the term "massive repression," and Herman and Schatzow (1987) had done so years before the FMSF was founded. Clearly, the idea of repressing and then later remembering years of trauma did not originate with the FMSF camp. Others claimed that recovering dissociated memories of sexual abuse was merely an optional goal of trauma treatment, not a central one (van der Hart and Steele 1999).

Some therapists claimed that the alleged epidemic of False Memory Syndrome was a product of FMSF propaganda, not of negligent practice by therapists treating trauma survivors. As Karen Olio stated, "Currently, there is no scientific evidence to indicate that false memories of sexual abuse have been or can be implanted in people who do not have trauma histories" (1994: 442). Similarly, the psychiatrist Colin Ross asserted, "There is not a single scientific study showing that a False Memory Syndrome created in therapy exists" (1995: 186). And, asked the clinical psychologist Kenneth Pope (1996), how could critics "diagnose" False Memory Syndrome in patients they had never met or interviewed? How could the critics of trauma therapy be so sure that the memories were false, especially when the critics had apparently confined their informal interviews to the alleged perpetrators? Moreover, this "syndrome" was nowhere to be found in DSM-IV.[15]

Others asked why the recovered memories of survivors were questioned while the memories of the alleged perpetrators, who denied having abused anyone, were believed. Why should perpetrators be exempt from memory distortion? Perhaps they had repressed all memory of their crimes. Or perhaps they could not remember having abused their children because they had done so during alcoholic blackouts (Rubin 1996).

Therapists also asked why patients were believed when they retracted their memories of abuse, but not believed when they recovered them during therapy. They cited reasons for doubting the veracity of these retractions. Pressured by skeptical family members in denial, bombarded by FMSF "propaganda," and enticed by the prospect of lucrative lawsuits against their former therapists, many patients might falsely claim that their recovered memories of abuse were not genuine. Any post-retraction improvement in mental health might be more apparent than real, merely signifying denial (Brown, Scheflin, and Hammond 1998: 398–399). Furthermore, added Daniel Brown and his colleagues, any lawsuits directed against therapists for practicing hypnosis with MPD patients were wholly without merit. Hypnotherapy had long been the standard of care in the field of dissociative disorders; if experts in the field endorsed hypnotic treatment of multiple personality, how could it possibly constitute malpractice (Brown, Frischholz, and Scheflin 1999)? (If we accept Brown's assertion that only those clinicians who assess and treat multiple personality are permitted to criticize MPD treatment, then surely we have to disqualify astronomers from criticizing astrology.)

Critics responded to this counterattack by trauma therapists. Attempts to dismiss the concept of False Memory Syndrome because it was not listed in DSM-IV, they said, were disingenuous. After all, the trauma field abounds with informal "syndromes" that do not appear in the DSM-IV (Kihlstrom 1998).[16] The main issue, they contended, was not whether False Memory Syndrome appeared in the DSM but whether the beliefs and practices of a nontrivial number of therapists had led to the phenomena that this "syndrome" was meant to describe. Some studies suggested that this concern was warranted.

In a landmark study, Debra Poole and her colleagues (1995) surveyed random samples of licensed psychotherapists in the United States and Great Britain about their beliefs, practices, and experiences regarding memories of childhood sexual abuse in their adult female patients. Most respondents (71 percent) had used at least one technique to help patients recover suspected memories of abuse (for example, dream interpretation, guided imagery, hypnosis), and 25 percent endorsed a constellation of beliefs and practices indicating an emphasis on memory recovery. More specifically, these "abuse-focused" respondents emphasized the importance of recovering abuse memories during therapy, claimed they could tell whether a patient was an abuse survivor during the first session, and reported using at least two techniques to help patients recover memories of abuse. Respondents generated a total of 85 different symptomatic indicators of a possible history of abuse (such as relationship problems, panic attacks, sexual dysfunction), but agreement among the respondents was limited.[17]

In a survey of therapists belonging to the American Psychological Association, Melissa Polusny and Victoria Follette (1996) found that respondents estimated that 22 percent of adult patients harbor repressed memories of childhood sexual abuse. The respondents were asked which memory-retrieval techniques they used for adults whom they strongly suspected had been sexually abused as children but who denied having any specific memories of abuse. The percentages of therapists who reported using these techniques for uncovering such memories were: dream interpretation, 47 percent; body memory interpretation, 15 percent; guided imagery, 27 percent; hypnosis or trance induction, 20 percent; bibliotherapy regarding sexual abuse, 33 percent; and referral to sexual abuse survivors' group, 29 percent.

Surveying more than 860 psychotherapists about their beliefs regarding trauma, memory, and hypnosis, the clinical researcher Michael Yapko (1994a, 1994b) found that 54 percent agreed that hypnosis enables individuals to recover accurate memories that date from birth and 28 percent agreed that hypnosis enables people to recover accurate memories of their past lives. These findings suggest that mental health professionals practicing hypnosis are unaware of the hazards of the method.

In response to the controversy over recovered memory therapy, some leaders of the field have recently revised their views. For example, in an article written with several colleagues, Christine Courtois stated, "we recommend that therapists avoid the use of hypnosis for memory retrieval" (Enns et al. 1998: 249). Moreover, these authors warned, books written for known survivors of sexual abuse should not be used to help patients recover presumably repressed memories of abuse. However, they also claimed that "there is little evidence for the creation of false memories" (250). And in a 1998 book, which won a prestigious award from the American Psychiatric Association, Daniel Brown, Alan Scheflin, and D. Corydon Hammond said that hypnosis may be the only way to recover repressed memories of trauma (647). So it remains unclear how much attitudes and practices have changed.

THE AMERICAN PSYCHOLOGICAL ASSOCIATION TASK FORCE

In 1993 the American Psychological Association formed a six-member working group to evaluate the evidence about recovered memory. This group comprised three eminent psychotherapists experienced in the treatment of survivors of sexual abuse, Judith Alpert, Laura Brown, and Christine Courtois, and three eminent experimental psychologists experienced in the study of memory, Stephen Ceci, Elizabeth Loftus, and Peter Ornstein. Despite several years' effort, the members were unable to reach consensus, except on several uncontroversial points. For example, they agreed that it is possible to forget and then later remember being abused, and that it is possible to develop "memories" for abuse that never occurred. But the three clinicians and the three experimentalists remained sharply divided on the most important issues, forcing the two sides in 1998 to issue their conclusions in different publications in a point-counterpoint exchange.[18]

The well-worn claim that "trauma is a political issue" has been meant to be taken metaphorically, not literally. Because trauma so often involves a perpetrator's abuse of power over his victims, many have remarked that PTSD is inevitably political in ways that other anxiety disorders are not. However, the controversy over childhood sexual abuse reached such a fever pitch that it spilled over into the halls of Congress—making trauma political in a literal sense.

THE CONGRESSIONAL CONDEMNATION

On July 12, 1999, members of the United States Congress unanimously voted to condemn a scientific article published in one of psychology's most prestigious journals. Congress denounced it for its alleged moral and methodological flaws. The article, written by Bruce Rind, Philip Tromovitch, and Robert Bauserman (1998), contained a meta-analysis of 59 studies that had addressed the long-term psychological correlates of childhood sexual abuse (CSA). Subjects in the original studies were college students who had filled out questionnaires about sexual experiences they might have had during childhood and adolescence, and about any psychological symptoms they might be experiencing in the present. Consistent with professional consensus, 73 percent of the studies defined CSA broadly, from being "flashed" by an exhibitionist to being raped by one's father. Childhood was likewise defined broadly; only 25 percent of the studies confined CSA to events occurring before adolescence.

The results flew in the face of professional opinion. The meta-analysis revealed that students who had been sexually abused were nearly as well-adjusted as their counterparts who had not been abused. Less than one percent of the variance in psychological adjustment could be attributed to CSA. Having been reared in a generally dysfunctional family was ten times more predictive of subsequent maladjustment than was CSA. Contrary to widespread belief, early sexual experience was seldom traumatic. Lasting psychological harm was the exception, not the rule.

Because the association between broadly defined CSA and later maladjustment was so weak, the authors advised researchers to avoid conflating the sexual experiences of adolescents with those of prepubescent children. Indeed, the long-term psychological consequences for a 16-year-old who has intercourse with her 21-year-old boyfriend are likely to differ dramatically from those of a 10-year-old who is raped by her father. Classifying both as CSA may obscure any relation between abuse and subsequent psychiatric symptoms. They also suggested that the term *abuse* should be confined to distressing, unwanted sexual contacts between adults and minors. Definitional issues notwithstanding, the authors emphasized that the *wrongfulness* of adult-child sexual contact must not be confused with its *harmfulness*. An act does not become morally permissible merely because it fails to produce lasting harm.[19]

The article sparked outrage among political conservatives, religious fundamentalists, and psychotherapists convinced that early sexual experience causes lasting psychological damage. Rather than interpreting the article as documenting the resilience of children, they saw it as a defense of pedophilia. The North American Man-Boy Love Association likewise misread it as authorizing sex between men and boys, seemingly confirming the worst suspicions of the critics.

Although scientists had rigorously reviewed the article before publication, the critics assumed it must be flawed because it ran counter to the opinions of many people. Accordingly, they endeavored to attack it on scientific as well as moral grounds. The politically conservative radio personality Dr. Laura Schlessinger raged against Rind and his colleagues and against the American Psychological Association for publishing the article in one of its most influential journals, claiming that "the point of the article is to allow men to rape male children." Denouncing it as "junk science at its worst," she urged Congress to take formal action against the Association (quoted in Lilienfeld 2002a: 178). Responding to the call, Arizona Republican Matt Salmon characterized the article as "the emancipation proclamation of pedophiles" (ibid.: 180). Salmon and his fellow conservatives began organizing bipartisan support for a formal condemnation of the Association should it refuse to denounce the article. A group called the Leadership Council for Mental

Health, Justice and the Media joined the fray, advising Congress on how to debunk the meta-analysis on methodological grounds.[20]

Raymond D. Fowler, the chief executive officer of the American Psychological Association, defended the scientific quality of Rind, Tromovitch, and Bauserman's work, and the integrity of peer review, against the critical onslaught. But when it became apparent that Congress was poised to condemn the Association as well as Rind and his colleagues, he abruptly reversed himself in a letter written to the House majority whip, Tom DeLay. Fowler expressed regret that the article's policy implications had not been considered during its review. He promised that potentially controversial manuscripts would undergo special scrutiny in the future. Moreover, he emphasized that the official position of the Association was that sexual contact between children and adults should never be "labeled as harmless." Fowler also promised that the Association, for the first time in its history, would "seek independent expert evaluation of the scientific quality" of the disputed article, and would encourage "refutations from researchers and practitioners with expertise in child sexual abuse in an upcoming issue of one of our premier journals" (Fowler 1999).

Fowler's repudiation of the article did not save its authors from the wrath of Congress. Passed unanimously, House Congressional Resolution 107 stated that "Congress condemns and denounces" their "severely flawed" study for concluding that sexual contacts between children and adults "are less harmful than believed and might even be positive for 'willing' children." The resolution called for "competent" research on the effects of childhood sexual abuse that would enable policymakers to act on the basis of "accurate information." The United States Senate unanimously approved the resolution on July 30, 1999.[21]

While religious fundamentalists, political conservatives, and some mental health professionals celebrated the congressional condemnation as a ringing defense of children, others saw it as a serious threat to scientific freedom. Many psychologists were outraged that leaders of the American Psychological Association had capitulated to political pressure. As the social psychologist Carol Tavris observed, "the APA missed its chance to educate the public and Congress about the scientific method, the purpose of peer review, and the absolute necessity of protecting the right of its scientists to publish unpopular findings. Researchers cannot function if they have to censor themselves according to potential public outcry or are silenced by social pressure, harassment, or political posturing from those who misunderstand or dis-approve of their results" (2000: 17).

Keeping his promise to Congress, Fowler asked the American Association for the Advancement of Science (AAAS) to provide an independent evalu-ation of Rind, Tromovitch, and Bauserman's work. But after a preliminary evaluation uncovered "no clear evidence of improper application of method-ology or other questionable practices on the part of the article's authors," the AAAS committee declined to conduct a full-scale review, noting that it saw no reason to second-guess an article that had already undergone expert scientific scrutiny prior to publication. Writing to the American Psychologi-cal Association, the AAAS committee expressed grave concern about the politicization of the issue. The AAAS sharply rebuked the critics for misrep-resenting the article in the media and for failing to understand the meta-analytic methods they had attacked (Lerch 1999).

The congressional resolution was purely symbolic. Neither Rind and his colleagues nor the American Psychological Association was penalized in any way. Nevertheless, this unprecedented act provoked widespread worry about the censorship of science. In addition to highlighting the hazards of conduct-ing politically controversial research, this incident illustrated just how explo-sive the topic of trauma had become in American society.

Taking a less political approach than advising Congress on how to con-demn psychology articles, members of the Leadership Council (among oth-ers) published critiques of Rind's meta-analysis in the same journal in which it had appeared. Although moral condemnation occasionally leaked into these critiques, they chiefly discussed alleged methodological problems with Rind's statistics. Rind and his colleagues thoroughly discredited these cri-tiques, showing them to be entirely specious. Even the editors who published the critiques agreed that the critiques had little merit. But the wisdom of their publishing them was unassailable; it is better to have scientific disputes aired in the professional literature than in the halls of Congress.[22]

Although Rind, Tromovitch, and Bauserman's meta-analysis seemed to suggest that sexually abused children were more resilient than anyone had expected, their article was far from the final word on the topic. After their meta-analysis had been published, new studies began to appear that painted a less sanguine picture of resilience among abuse survivors. Avoiding biases in-herent in clinical samples, these investigators examined the relation between self-reported histories of childhood sexual abuse and risk for psychiatric disorders in large community samples. In one study numbering more than 1,000 subjects, women who reported having been sexually abused as children experienced greater risk for depression, suicide attempts, social anxiety, and alcohol dependence (Nelson et al. 2002). In another study numbering more than 7,000 adults, self-reported history of childhood physical abuse as well as sexual abuse increased risk for a range of psychiatric disorders in men as well as in women (MacMillan et al. 2001). These studies show that we still do not know for sure which variables predict vulnerability and which predict resilience among children exposed to these adverse experiences.

The debate about recovered memories of sexual abuse is unresolved, but not irresolvable. The issues and evidence have become increasingly clear since the 1990s. Moreover, the attention to childhood sexual abuse has obscured the fact that there is much more to trauma and memory than recollections of incest. Clinical researchers have studied people exposed to combat, rape, natural disasters, and terrorism. They have endeavored to understand how trauma affects memory, and how people remember trauma, across a wide range of circumstances. PTSD researchers have increasingly applied the methods of cognitive psychology and cognitive neuroscience to answer questions that have preoccupied their clinical counterparts for decades.

This book began with three assertions about what we have learned about how people remember trauma. The remainder of the book provides the evidence that supports these conclusions.

2

HOW WE REMEMBER

UNDERSTANDING HOW PEOPLE remember trauma requires familiarity with the science of human memory. Yet most laboratory research concerns how people remember lists of words and other innocuous material. Seldom have psychologists studied memory for anything like the horrors that haunt survivors of trauma. Accordingly, some psychotherapists question the relevance of this research. They wonder whether knowing how someone remembers a list of words has anything to tell us about how someone might remember a brutal rape. They suspect that the psychobiological mechanisms enabling someone to remember terrifying experiences may differ dramatically from those enabling someone to remember ordinary events. And they wonder whether traumatic memory is exempt from the principles governing ordinary memory. As the psychotherapist Daniel Brown and his colleagues put it, "we are not in a position to generalize the findings from laboratory studies on normal memory to memory for traumatic experiences" (Brown, Scheflin, and Hammond 1998: 98).

These issues cannot be resolved by armchair speculation. Whether or not the mechanisms of traumatic memory differ from those of ordinary memory, and whether the differences are more important than the similarities, can only be determined by research. The findings and principles emerging from the laboratory are essential for evaluating claims about the special status of traumatic memory. Only when we are confident that we understand everyday memory can we determine whether memory for trauma requires distinct explanatory mechanisms.

THE INFORMATION-PROCESSING MODEL

Memory means several things. Most generally, it means our capacity for acquiring, retaining, and using information. It can also refer to the neuro-cognitive mechanisms mediating these processes, to the content of the information itself, or to the subjective experience of reliving our past, which is essential to our sense of personal identity.

Scientists have likened memory to a computer that receives, transforms, stores, and retrieves information (Atkinson and Shiffrin 1968). This information-processing model has three components: a sensory register, a short-term memory store, and a long-term memory store. Physical input that stimulates sensory receptors first enters a register where it remains for about one second. Unless selected for further processing, information in this *sensory register* vanishes without a trace, thanks to the ceaseless flow of incoming stimulation. Evidence for a sensory register emerged from experiments in which subjects read letters of the alphabet that were flashed on a screen for extremely brief durations. Subjects could still read the letters for up to 150 milliseconds after they had disappeared, thus confirming that the vanished letters must have left behind a lingering sensory trace (Sperling 1960).

If the person attends to information in the sensory register, that information is transferred to *short-term memory*, a limited-capacity buffer that retains about 7 chunks of information for about 25 seconds before new input bumps it out. Further processing of information in short-term memory may enable its transfer to *long-term memory*, a functionally unlimited store that retains facts, experiences, and skills.

Dramatic evidence confirming the distinction between short-term and long-term memory emerged from studies done on a single patient, "H.M.," who had undergone a bilateral temporal lobectomy to treat his intractable epilepsy. Surgeons removed his amygdala and about two-thirds of his hippocampus, structures located deep within the brain's temporal lobes. H.M.'s epilepsy improved, but he became almost entirely incapable of remembering any new facts or events. He would read the same magazine over and over again without recognizing its content, and people he met one day would be strangers to him the next. His memory for most information stored before his surgery was intact, and he could retain new information for about 30 seconds.

But once his attention shifted to another topic, he immediately forgot everything that had just been on his mind. That is, H.M. was incapable of transferring the contents of short-term memory into long-term memory.[1]

Psychologists have since reconceptualized short-term memory as *working memory* to emphasize its active processing tasks. Working memory comprises three subsystems: the central executive, the phonological loop, and the visuospatial sketchpad. Its contents correspond to the contents of conscious awareness (Baddeley 2000; Baddeley and Hitch 1974).

The *central executive* subsystem coordinates operations in working memory, including selecting information from the sensory register and retrieving information from long-term memory. It is the site of conscious reflection, problem solving, reasoning, and manipulation of information. Control processes directed by the central executive subsystem include attention, encoding, and retrieval. *Attention* refers to the selection of information in the sensory register for further processing in working memory; *encoding* refers to the transfer of information from working memory to long-term memory; and *retrieval* refers to the selection of information from long-term memory for further processing in working memory.

In addition to the central executive subsystem, working memory includes a *phonological loop* enabling short-term maintenance of verbal information and a *visuospatial sketchpad* enabling short-term visual imagery. The phonological loop allows us to retain a telephone number long enough to dial it. By repeating and "hearing" the number in our heads, we prevent it from fading from working memory. The visuospatial sketchpad comes into play when someone asks us how many windows there are in our living room. If we are in the living room at the time, we may simply look at the windows and count them. But if we are elsewhere, we answer the question by creating a visual image of the room that enables us to count the windows. This component of working memory is very much involved in posttraumatic stress disorder. Trauma survivors often suffer from graphic, disturbing images that monopolize the visuospatial sketchpad.

Scientists have modified the information-processing model in many ways, and this sketch does not do justice to the complexities of contemporary theorizing (see Tulving and Craik 2000). Nevertheless, the model remains useful as an expository device, and its core concepts (such as *encoding* and *retrieval*) are indispensable for interpreting the literature on trauma and memory.[2]

Memory: A Multifaceted Mental Ability

Psychologists once viewed memory as a single, unitary mental ability enabling us to recollect facts and the events of our lives. The ability enabling us to remember the capital of France was presumably the same one enabling us to remember our high school graduation day. Having a "good memory" presumably permitted a person to remember all sorts of things with relative ease. But there is more to memory than just recollecting facts and the experiences from one's life (see Tulving 1999). The past leaves its mark on behavior as well as on thought. Remembering how to ride a bicycle reflects memory, as does the visceral reaction of fear experienced by a person who gets behind the wheel after having recently survived a terrible automobile accident. Memory—the effects of experience on thought, action, and feeling—is expressed in diverse ways. Whether distinct expressions of memory reflect distinct systems in the brain remains a matter of debate (Foster and Jelicic 1999; Schacter, Wagner, and Buckner 2000). But few psychologists today question memory's diverse expression.

Scientists conceptualize long-term memory in two ways. One way distinguishes between declarative and nondeclarative forms of memory (Squire 1994). *Declarative memory* provides the basis for the conscious recollection of events and facts. It corresponds to the everyday sense of the term *memory*. As its name implies, declarative memory can be "declared"—expressed in language.

Declarative memory, in turn, comprises episodic memory and semantic memory (Tulving 1985a). *Episodic memory* denotes conscious recollection of one's personal experiences—the episodes of one's life. Examples include remembering words learned 30 minutes ago in a psychology experiment and remembering an earthquake experienced many years ago. *Semantic memory* refers to knowledge about facts devoid of the circumstances of their acquisition. One may remember that Thomas Jefferson was the third president of the United States without recalling where or when one learned this fact.

Nondeclarative memory is expressed in behavior rather than declared in language. It comprises a diverse group of capacities whose only common feature is that they do not require conscious recollection for their expression. The subtypes of nondeclarative memory include procedural memory, simple Pavlovian (classical) conditioning, nonassociative learning, and priming.

Expressed in skilled performance, *procedural memory* concerns knowing *how* rather than knowing *that*. It can be manifested cognitively (as in reading French) or motorically (as in riding a bicycle). Although we can sometimes provide a how-to description for a skill, the ability to do so plays no role in its performance. A child may know how to tie his shoelaces without being able to describe how he does it. Procedural memory usually develops gradually through practice. But acquisition of a skill need not require conscious recollection of previous practice sessions. H.M., for example, mastered several new motor tasks over the course of a few days even though he could not remember having practiced them the day before.

Nondeclarative memory can also be expressed in responses established through *Pavlovian conditioning*. For example, an experimenter might turn on a light for several seconds before following it with a very brief but startlingly loud noise that triggers an emotional response in the research subject, such as an increase in heart rate. After experiencing several of these light-noise pairings, a subject may begin to have the emotional response to the light itself. Hence an originally neutral cue, such as a light, can become a conditioned stimulus (CS) if it predicts the occurrence of an unconditioned stimulus (US), such as a loud noise. The conditioned emotional response (CR)—an increase in heart rate, in this example—reflects nondeclarative memory of the light-noise sequence. Obviously, in subjects who lack language (such as laboratory rats), Pavlovian conditioning procedures establish only nondeclarative memories of CS-US pairings. But these procedures can also establish declarative memories in human subjects capable of describing the CS-US sequence ("First a light would come on for a few seconds, and as soon as it went off, there'd be a loud noise").

CS-US pairings usually generate declarative as well as nondeclarative memories in normal human subjects—those without brain damage. In fact, the ability to describe the circumstances of conditioning may be *necessary* for any conditioned emotional responses to emerge. But as Antoine Bechara and his colleagues seem to have shown, these types of memory can be dissociated in certain brain-damaged patients. Following an aversive conditioning procedure—one involving an uncomfortable US, in this case, a loud boat horn—a patient with hippocampal damage acquired a conditioned emotional response, but could not describe the CS-US sequence, whereas a patient with amygdala damage failed to acquire a conditioned emotional response, but could describe the CS-US sequence. A patient with damage to both structures exhibited neither a CR nor CS-US awareness. Therefore, emotional responses occurred even when the subject with hippocampal damage was incapable of recalling why the stimuli provoked these reactions (Bechara et al. 1995; see also Weiskrantz and Warrington 1979).

Bechara's study may tempt some to suggest that stimuli associated with trauma might evoke intense emotion in survivors who cannot consciously remember what happened to them. Might these stimuli elicit nondeclarative memories of trauma—physiologic reactions, such as rapid heart rate—without the person knowing why? This scenario is unlikely. When neurologically intact people acquire a conditioned emotional response, they almost always acquire declarative knowledge as well. For example, a rape survivor who responds physiologically to cues associated with the assault will almost always know why she is responding this way. Her nondeclarative memory of the assault, expressed in physiologic reactions, will be accompanied by declarative, conscious knowledge about why these stimuli provoke fear.

Moreover, in a penetrating critique of the literature, the experimental psychologists Peter Lovibond and David Shanks (2002) argue that there is little or no convincing evidence that people can acquire Pavlovian conditioned responses in the absence of awareness. For example, even Bechara's results are more ambiguous than they first appear to be. Bechara's group assessed CS-US awareness only after a delay, so it is possible that the patient with hippocampal damage was aware that the loud horn followed a certain stimulus, but then forgot this information before the researchers administered the test of CS-US awareness. Conditioning without awareness would only have been convincingly demonstrated had Bechara's group shown that the hippocampal patient was unaware of what stimulus predicted the loud noise during the conditioning procedure itself. At the very least, as Lovibond and Shanks concluded, "the idea that unconscious conditioning is commonplace is clearly contradicted by our review" (22).[3]

Nonassociative processes, such as sensitization and habituation, are additional forms of nondeclarative memory. *Sensitization* refers to increased responsivity arising from repeated exposure to a stimulus, whereas *habituation* refers to decreased responsivity arising from repeated exposure to a stimulus. The physical intensity of the stimulus, among other variables, usually determines whether repetitive stimulation produces sensitization or habituation. Soldiers who startle at any noise after having withstood days of artillery bombardment exhibit sensitization, whereas those who scarcely notice distant gunfire anymore exhibit habituation. Neither sensitization nor habituation involves new associations between stimuli, but both count as forms of memory because they reflect experience-dependent changes in responsivity to stimuli.

Priming refers to facilitated processing of a stimulus that results from previous exposure to it or to a related stimulus (Tulving, Schacter, and Stark 1982). For example, in stem-completion tasks, subjects first study a list of words and then complete three-letter stems (such as COF_____) with the first word that comes to mind (Bowers and Schacter 1990). Priming is revealed when subjects disproportionately complete stems with words they saw on the study list relative to other appropriate solutions. Subjects need not remember what words appeared on the study list for the priming effect to occur: a subject might respond with COFFIN to the stem COF_____ despite having forgotten that COFFIN had been on the list. Indeed, brain-damaged patients with amnesia exhibit this priming effect even though they have extreme difficulty remembering having seen the study list at all (Warrington and Weiskrantz 1970).

Priming is also demonstrated in perceptual identification experiments (Jacoby and Dallas 1981). In this kind of experiment, subjects view a list of words and shortly thereafter are shown another list that includes "old" words from the original list intermixed with "new" ones not previously seen by the subjects. Each word on the second list is flashed for a few milliseconds, and the subject attempts to identify each word immediately after it appears. Priming is revealed when subjects can read more old words than new ones.

The second way scientists conceptualize long-term memory is by distinguishing between *explicit* and *implicit* expressions of remembering (Graf and Schacter 1985). Most traditional memory tests, such as tests of *recall* and *recognition*, concern explicit memory. In a typical recall test, subjects learn a list of words and later attempt to retrieve them from memory. In a typical recognition test, subjects are shown words and asked which ones they remember having seen or heard earlier in the experiment. In contrast, priming tests, such as those requiring subjects to complete three-letter stems with the first appropriate word that comes to mind or to identify briefly flashed words, do not require any conscious recollection of the study phase of the experiment. As the cognitive psychologist Daniel Schacter summarizes: "Implicit memory is revealed when previous experiences facilitate performance on a task that does not require conscious or intentional recollection of those experiences;

explicit memory is revealed when performance on a task requires conscious recollection of previous experiences" (1987: 501).

It is important to be clear about what is and is not "unconscious" about implicit memory. Obviously, when subjects complete a stem with the first word that comes to mind, they are conscious of what the word is. But they are unaware of having seen the word earlier in the experiment. This is not a matter of material having been "repressed into the unconscious mind." Indeed, the concept of the unconscious of contemporary cognitive science must not be confused with the psychodynamic unconscious of Freud, with its buried memories of childhood trauma and its forbidden sexual and aggressive urges struggling to burst through into awareness. The two are entirely different concepts. The unconscious of cognitive science, exemplified by research on implicit memory, simply refers to information processing that occurs outside awareness (Kihlstrom 1987).

Involuntary Explicit Memory

In a typical explicit memory experiment, subjects intentionally search memory for words they saw earlier on a study list. If successful, they have a conscious recollection of having seen the words before. Implicit memory is different on both counts. In his classic paper on the topic, Schacter specified two criteria for implicit memory: unintentionality and unconsciousness. That is, words come to mind without any deliberate search, and subjects are not aware of having seen them earlier.

As it turns out, intentionality and consciousness do not always covary; sometimes subjects unintentionally rely on conscious memory during implicit memory experiments. Consider a subject who, while performing a stem-completion task, suddenly remembers having seen a solution to a stem on an earlier study list. Completion of the stem is "implicit" in that it did not result from effortful search, yet "explicit" in that he became aware of having seen it earlier. Schacter (1987) calls this phenomenon *involuntary explicit memory*.

The idea that memory can operate unconsciously has fascinated psychologists. But researchers studying implicit memory have found it difficult to prevent subjects from becoming aware of having seen target items before, prompting the cognitive researchers Laurie Butler and Dianne Berry to bemoan "the lack of genuine evidence regarding implicit memory in normal participants" (2001: 196). They interpret involuntary explicit memory as a nuisance—implicit memory "contaminated" by awareness. But involuntary explicit memory is highly relevant to posttraumatic stress disorder, more so than "genuine" implicit memory. People with posttraumatic stress disorder suffer from involuntary explicit memory as exemplified by unbidden, intrusive recollection of horrific events from their past. Involuntary explicit memory deserves more attention from psychologists interested in how people remember trauma.

Autobiographical Memory

Autobiographical memory is personal memory. Bridging the episodic/semantic distinction, it includes the experiences of one's life and the facts about one's self (Conway 1996; Conway and Pleydell-Pearce 2000). Thus remembering a firefight in Vietnam requires autobiographical episodic memory, and remembering one's name, rank, and serial number requires autobiographical semantic memory. Strictly speaking, remembering having seen a word earlier in an experiment counts as an autobiographical episodic memory. But psychologists working in this area are not especially interested in such things. They want to know how people remember in the real world outside the laboratory.

Autobiographical recollection is a reconstructive, not a reproductive, process (Bartlett 1932). Recalling one's past is not like replaying a videotape of one's life in working memory. When we remember an event from our past, we reconstruct it from encoded elements distributed throughout the brain. There are very few instances in which remembering resembles reproducing. These include reciting poems, prayers, telephone numbers, and other material memorized by rote.

The reconstructive character of autobiographical memory is especially evident for repeated episodes of the same type. Consider someone who has traveled by air only once versus someone who has flown many times. The first person is likely to retain a reasonably specific memory of that single, memorable flight. The second person, for whom memories of many flights will tend to blend together into a generic memory of "flying on airplanes," will find it tough to remember the details of any particular flight unless something unusual happened during it. But even though this generic memory does not correspond to any particular flight, it will be just as vivid as the memory of the person who has flown only once (Linton 1986). The frequent flyer's vivid memory is what the cognitive psychologist Ulric Neisser (1981) calls a *repisodic memory*—a memory constructed from repeated episodes of the same type. The more episodes of a certain type we experience, the harder it becomes to distinguish among them.

While repetition makes it harder to retrieve any specific episode, it strengthens overall memory for the entire class of event. Frequent flyers are highly unlikely to forget having flown on airplanes even though their memories for individual flights may blur together. Likewise, a person who suffered many beatings as a child will find it difficult to recall details from any particular attack—unless something unusual occurred during it—yet will never forget what it was like to be subjected to such violence. This point warrants emphasis because some psychotherapists actually believe that the more frequently a person is traumatized, the *less* likely the person is to remember having been traumatized. The psychiatrist Lenore Terr, for example, claims that children are more likely to experience amnesia for repeated traumas than for single traumas. She holds that single-impact ("type I") traumas, such as a terrible accident, are remembered vividly, whereas repeated, prolonged traumas ("type II"), such as chronic incest, are not. According to Terr: "Children who experience type II traumas often forget. They may forget whole segments of childhood—from birth to age 9, for instance" (1991: 16). This notion flies in the face of everything we know about how repetition affects memory.

Once a specific episode blends into a generic repisodic memory, is it ever possible to retrieve it again? Can we pluck specific episodes from generic memories? Occasionally we can, if relevant reminders are available. Using HMO records, Barbara Means and Elizabeth Loftus (1991) queried subjects about their visits to the doctor during the previous year. Means and Loftus distinguished between visits prompted by a nonrecurring event, such as a single bout with the flu, and visits prompted by a recurring chronic condition, such as an allergy. Just as we would expect, subjects recalled more visits associated with unique illnesses than visits associated with chronic illnesses. Visits for chronic illness tend to blend together, reducing the distinctiveness of any particular visit. But when Means and Loftus provided retrieval cues for these forgotten visits, subjects were often capable of recalling them. For example, they prompted subjects for details about their most recent visit—what the weather was like that day, how long they had to wait to see the doctor, and so forth. Given adequate hints, people can sometimes recollect a specific episode that had apparently been irretrievably blended into a generic memory.

Even though autobiographical memory does not operate like a video recorder, it often seems to do so. This popular misconception about the mind gained credence from the work of Wilder Penfield, a Montreal neurosurgeon who in the 1950s claimed to have discovered the "anatomical record of the stream of consciousness" (1955: 68). Prior to performing surgery on epilepsy patients to cure their intractable seizures, he electrically stimulated their temporal cortex to identify where their convulsions originated. Much to his surprise, some of his patients reported remarkably vivid "experiential flashbacks from the past" (1969: 150). He concluded that the brain contains a neuronal record akin to "a strip of cinematographic film, on which are registered all those things of which the individual was once aware" (1955: 68).

Penfield exaggerated his claims. Only 40 of his 520 patients reported any experiential responses, and only 12 had both visual and auditory perceptions (Loftus and Loftus 1980). The rest experienced only sensory fragments, such as hearing someone talking, a dog barking, or a toilet flushing. Penfield thought these events were "reproductions of past experience" (Penfield and Perot 1963: 686), and because they were so trivial, he concluded that the brain must retain everything that was once in awareness. But what his patients termed "flashbacks" were actually little more than sensory fragments accompanied by a feeling of familiarity, and even when entire scenes unfolded, some could not have happened in the way they were remembered. For example, one woman saw herself, from the perspective of an observer, as a 7-year-old girl walking through grass. Other researchers have since obtained higher rates of experiential responses by electrically stimulating the amygdala and other limbic ("emotional") structures of the brain (Gloor et al. 1982). However, the fragmentary character of these responses makes it unlikely that they replayed a literal record of the past.

Finally, Penfield himself (1955, 1969) stressed that ordinary autobiographical memory—the conscious recollection of one's past in the absence of electrical stimulation—does not function like a video recorder. The neuronal record of the stream of consciousness was permanent, accurate, and unchangeable, he argued, but conscious efforts to retrieve details always amounted to a selective reconstruction of only a small portion of what had been stored.

As the cognitive psychologist Endel Tulving (1985a) has noted, autobiographical recollection is accompanied by autonoetic (self-knowing) awareness, a form of consciousness unique to human beings. Lacking a sense of self, nonhuman animals possess only noetic (knowing) awareness, as revealed by their adaptive responding to the immediate environment. But people are aware that they are aware, and the sense of self that emerges in early childhood allows us to recollect our experiences as having happened to ourselves. Autonoetic awareness, as Tulving says, permits mental time travel, enabling people to relive the past and envision the future.

Autonoetic awareness also distinguishes merely *knowing* from *remembering* (Tulving 1985b). A woman may *know* that her parents celebrated her fourth birthday, or that she locked the door after leaving the house this morning, or that she encountered a certain word on a study list during a psychology experiment. But her knowledge may arise from inference, from other evidence, or from mere feelings of familiarity. In contrast, she may *remember* each of these episodes, autonoetically reliving them by recollecting the sights, sounds, thoughts, and feelings that accompanied each event. Likewise, a woman may *know* that she was molested as a very young child, having been informed of this fact by reliable sources, yet she may not *remember* this event because she was too young when it occurred. Autobiographical episodic memory is about remembering—not merely knowing—one's personal past.

Remembering the personal past is guided by one's current concerns, goals, and self-concept (see Greenwald 1980), as illustrated by a study of how 48-year-old men recalled themselves as adolescents. Daniel Offer and his colleagues (2000) interviewed these subjects at age 14 about their home lives, parental discipline, sexuality, religion, and other emotional topics, then interviewed them again 34 years later, asking them to remember how they had responded as 14-year-olds. Remarkably, the men's ability to guess what they had said about themselves in adolescence was no better than chance. Some remembered themselves as bold, outgoing teenagers, though at age 14 they had described themselves as shy. How they saw themselves in adulthood seemed to shape how they remembered their younger selves. They were no better at remembering their home atmosphere. At age 14, 82 percent said that their parents used corporal punishment, but only 33 percent remembered having been physically punished when asked about it 34 years later.

Studies like Offer's can make us despair about remembering anything accurately about our past. But even when we garble the details about the past, we often get the essence right. Memory for the gist of many experiences is re-tained with essential fidelity, and this is especially true for events having per-sonal, emotional significance. The paradox of memory, as Daniel Schacter has said, lies in its "fragile power" (1996: 1). Although subject to distortion, memory usually serves us well. It provides the core of personal identity and the foundation of cognition.[4]

CAN MEMORY IMPROVE OVER TIME?

Ever since Hermann Ebbinghaus published his classic work on remembering in 1885, psychologists have agreed that memories tend to fade over time. As events recede into the past, they become harder to recall. To be sure, other factors play a role, too. Distinctive, emotionally salient events fade less than banal ones, and well-practiced skills may be retained undiminished for years. But all else being equal, time tends to erode our memories.

Are there ever circumstances in which memory gets better over time? The answer is yes, as the cognitive psychologist David Payne (1987) has shown in an article on reminiscence and hypermnesia. *Reminiscence* refers to recall of previously unrecalled items (words, pictures) over repeated testing. For ex-ample, a person might learn a list of 20 words and then attempt to recall them. The person might recall 11 words on the first try, an additional 3 words on a second try, and another 2 words on a third try. The recall of these addi-tional items on the second and third tries is reminiscence. *Hypermnesia* refers to the *net* increase in amount recalled over increasingly long intervals. That is, over repeated testing, subjects may recall previously unrecalled items, but forget to recall ones they had recalled before. A voluminous literature docu-ments that repeated recall attempts produce hypermnesia for pictures, but less often for words (Erdelyi and Becker 1974). (Unfortunately, the term *hypermnesia* is also used in psychiatry to refer to extremely vivid autobio-graphical memories, often of traumatic events. The two types of hypermnesia must not be confused.)

At first glance, hypermnesia in the laboratory seems consistent with recov-ery of forgotten memories of abuse in the clinic. Over the course of repeated attempts to remember, patients often report recollecting more and more hitherto forgotten abuse episodes (or more details of these episodes). But as the cognitive psychologists Henry Roediger and Erik Bergman (1998) point out, there are important differences between the two. Most laboratory hypermnesia studies concern repeated attempts to recall well-encoded pictures and words that were learned only minutes earlier. In contrast, recovered memories of abuse concern presumably poorly encoded, dissociated autobiographical episodes from years or decades earlier. As Roediger and Bergman point out, hypermnesia does not occur when there are long gaps between recall attempts. Also, defensive mechanisms such as repression, which are presumably operative in the abuse cases, are irrelevant to studies of hypermnesia in the laboratory, where the material seldom has much emotional significance for the subject.

How Context Affects Remembering

What we remember sometimes depends on the context of recollection. Certain memories may pop into mind only in certain situations. All else being equal, we are more likely to recall something when the context of remembering resembles the context of encoding. This idea is embodied in Endel Tulving and Donald Thomson's (1973) *encoding specificity principle*, which states that information is most accessible when encoding conditions are reinstated at retrieval. Information may be *available* in memory, but not *accessible*, because of the absence of potent reminders (see Tulving and Pearlstone 1966). Yet seemingly long-forgotten events may immediately come to mind when cues present at encoding are present once again, as when we experience a rush of memories upon returning to our childhood neighborhood.

Research designed to test the validity of the encoding specificity principle entails having subjects learn material in one context before testing them in either the same context or a different one. In a remarkable demonstration of this principle, D. R. Godden and Alan Baddeley (1975) had scuba divers memorize lists of words while either underwater or on land, then tested their recall in one of the two contexts. Those who learned words underwater recalled more of them when tested underwater than when tested on land; those who learned words on land recalled more of them when tested on land than when tested underwater. These findings suggest that the context of encoding, if reinstated at retrieval, enhances recall of information. Note, however, that subjects merely recall fewer items when retrieval context differs from that at encoding. Changes in context seldom result in complete amnesia for material learned in a different situation.

The physical environment rarely affects retrieval as strikingly as it did in Godden and Baddeley's research. Nor, for that matter, do the contexts of encoding and retrieval usually differ so dramatically. Few of us have to remember things in everyday life after learning them underwater. In fact, most subsequent research has shown that people can usually recall material despite shifts in environmental context. For example, students who take examinations in classrooms different from the ones where they attend lectures do no worse than do students who take their examinations in their regular classrooms (Saufley, Otaka, and Bavaresco 1985). This is reassuring. If material mastered during lectures were inaccessible outside the classroom, what would be the point in teaching?[5]

Most psychologists have thought about the encoding specificity principle in terms of physical features of the environment. But as the cognitive psychologist Gordon Bower (1981) pointed out, emotion or mood might also serve as a context for encoding and retrieval. According to Bower's *mood-state-dependent-memory hypothesis*, recall works best when mood at retrieval matches that at encoding. Conversely, material should be harder to recall if the mood at retrieval differs dramatically from that at encoding.

Early work confirmed his hypothesis (Bower, Monteiro, and Gilligan 1978: Experiment 3). In one study, subjects learned two lists of words, one while feeling happy and one while feeling sad. (The moods were induced via hypnosis.) Subjects recalled the most words from a given list when mood during retrieval was the same as that during encoding, and the least when retrieval and encoding moods differed. But most subsequent attempts to replicate the effect failed, including those by Bower himself (Foa, McNally, and Murdock 1989; Bower and Mayer 1989). Eventually he concluded that the original findings were attributable to chance and that mood-state-dependent memory was little more than "an evanescent will-o'-the-wisp" (Bower and Mayer 1985: 42).

Undaunted by these negative results, Eric Eich and his associates renewed efforts to isolate the critical variables responsible for the elusive effect of mood on memory. They discovered that this fragile effect is most likely to occur when subjects experience a mood of at least moderate intensity, when it persists throughout the experimental session, when the target information is self-generated, such as a personal memory prompted by a cue word, and when both mood and degree of arousal change. For example, subjects who recall a personal memory in response to a cue word during a high-arousal, positive mood (joy) are less likely to recall it later if tested during a low-arousal, negative mood (sadness) than if joy is reinstated at retrieval (Eich 1995).

Two points about mood-state-dependent memory warrant emphasis. First, as Eich has stressed, the effect is fragile and occurs "only within a restricted range of circumstances or conditions" (1995: 74). Second, even when it does occur, it does not result in outright amnesia. At most, subjects are slightly less able to recall information when mood at retrieval differs from that at encoding. These points require emphasis because some psychotherapists believe that mood-state-dependent effects may be relevant to remembering trauma. Because trauma occurs during states of extreme emotional arousal, they suspect that survivors may be incapable of recalling terrible experiences while in normal moods. Perhaps, they conjecture, the difference between the emotional state during the trauma and subsequent emotional states leads survivors to experience complete amnesia for traumatic events.

This amnesia hypothesis was seemingly confirmed by the case of Sirhan Sirhan, the assassin of Robert Kennedy. Despite claiming that he could not recall shooting the senator, Sirhan recounted the murder in graphic detail when a psychiatrist hypnotically reinstated the agitated state in which Sirhan had killed Kennedy. After emerging from hypnosis, he once again claimed that he could not remember the murder. Bower (1981) cited this famous case as an instance of extreme mood-state-dependent memory—but it later became apparent that Sirhan had been faking his amnesia for the crime all along (Schacter 1996: 226–227).

Reality Monitoring

People sometimes wonder whether an event they remember actually happened or was merely a dream or fantasy. The process whereby people decide if a mental experience arose from perception ("reality") or from imagination is what Marcia Johnson and Carol Raye (1981) termed *reality monitoring*. Reality monitoring, in turn, is a subset of *source monitoring*: the process whereby people judge the origins of mental experiences (Johnson, Hashtroudi, and Lindsay 1993; Mitchell and Johnson 2000). Not all source judgments concern the discrimination between imagined and perceived events. For example, a person may recollect hearing some important news, but forget whether she saw it on television or read about it in the newspaper.

Source monitoring is relevant to controversies concerning memories for childhood sexual abuse. An abuser who molests a child at night may tell the child it was "only a dream," thereby fostering subsequent source confusion about the origins of her memories of abuse. Also, psychotherapy patients who have retracted their recovered "memories" of abuse appear to have mistaken imaginings emerging during hypnosis for genuine recollections of trauma (Goldstein and Farmer 1993).

To ascertain how people identify the origins of their mental experiences, psychologists have compared memories of perceived events and memories of imagined events. Memories of imagined events usually contain fewer perceptual and sensory details and less information about spatial and temporal context. In a longitudinal diary study, Martin Conway and his colleagues (1996) asked subjects to record both events that had actually happened and events that they fabricated. Conway wanted to know whether subjects would be able to recognize which of their recorded events were true and which were false several months later. True memories were usually accompanied by feelings of recollective experience, whereas false memories were usually accompanied by mere feelings of familiarity.

Recent genuine memories contain more vivid visual details than do those from childhood. Thinking or talking about memories of both imagined and perceived events prevents their details from fading. The more someone thinks about an imaginary event, the more likely the person is to confuse it with an event that really happened. Individuals scoring high on measures of imagery ability and dissociation are especially prone to confuse imagined with real events, and a focus on one's own emotional response fosters confusion among external sources of information.[6]

MEMORY IN INFANCY AND EARLY CHILDHOOD

Many adults report recovering memories of early childhood abuse, and all too many children are exposed to trauma. Interpreting reports of early abuse, and understanding how children remember trauma, requires familiarity with basic research on how adults remember their earliest years and how memory develops in children.

Childhood amnesia refers to the inability of adults to recall the earliest events of their lives. Most adults are incapable of recalling any experiences they had before the age of 3 or 4. The cognitive psychologist David Rubin

(2000) found that about 90 percent of the childhood episodes recalled by adults occurred after their fourth birthday, and many adults remember hardly anything from before the age of 7 (Eacott and Crawley 1998). Earliest memories usually contain visual imagery, and are often little more than fragmentary "snapshots" devoid of narrative structure. Many are colored by emotions, especially joy, fear, and anger, but rarely shame or guilt. Samuel Waldfogel (1948) found that approximately 50 percent of early childhood (before the age of 8) memories were rated as pleasant, 30 percent were rated as unpleasant, and 20 percent were rated as neutral. Joy and fear were the two most commonly cited specific emotions associated with early childhood memories, occurring in approximately 30 percent and 15 percent of the memories, respectively.

Some adults, however, do report remembering very salient events, such as the birth of a sibling, that occurred when they were as young as two and a half years of age. However, it is difficult to determine whether the "memory" is based on direct recollection (autobiographical memory) or on other sources, such as family stories or photo albums (Loftus 1993). For example, older children who hear family stories about the birth of a sibling will generate visual imagery of this exciting event. As they grow older, they may have trouble distinguishing memories of such imagery from direct memories of the event. That is, problems of reality monitoring can complicate interpretation of these reports of early recollection.[7]

Scientists disagree about the causes of childhood amnesia (see Eacott 1999). The developmental psychologists Sheldon White and David Pillemer (1979) believe that autobiographical, episodic memories acquired prior to language acquisition are unlikely to survive into later childhood. Once children acquire language, their style of encoding and retrieving memories changes dramatically, making it difficult for them to remember and describe experiences that occurred earlier. Children whose immature language skills prevent them from describing an event as it occurs are unlikely to be able to do so later.[8]

The developmental psychologists Mark Howe and Mary Courage (1993) attribute childhood amnesia to the slow maturation of a sense of self, essential for the emergence of autobiographical memory. The behavioral neuroscientists Lynn Nadel and Stuart Zola-Morgan (1984) speculate that immaturity of the hippocampal system accounts for the scarcity of early memories. Although recent research on human and nonhuman primates indicates that the hippocampus itself matures early (McDonough et al. 1995), this structure is only one element of the system that supports declarative memory, and it is unclear when the entire system becomes functionally mature.

Although the period of childhood amnesia is marked by a striking paucity of autobiographical memories, children encode and recall a tremendous amount of semantic information during this period. Few early episodic memories survive into later childhood, let alone adulthood, yet semantic memory—language being the most striking example—is established and retained for life (Newcombe et al. 2000).

The mystery of childhood amnesia has been deepened by mounting evidence of preschoolers' episodic memory capabilities. Although adults can seldom recall events from the first few years of their life, very young children apparently can. For example, preschoolers can often remember experiences they had many months earlier, but as they get older they have a harder time remembering them.[9] In one of the most systematic investigations, Nina Hamond and Robyn Fivush (1991) studied recollection of a trip to Disney World in two groups of 24 preschoolers. At the time of their visit, one group ranged in age from 33 to 42 months and the other from 43 to 54 months. Half of the children in each group were asked about their visit 6 months later; the other half were questioned after 18 months. All children provided accurate accounts of the trip, as verified by parental report. The amount of information provided did not vary as a function of either retention interval or age, although older children gave more elaborate responses than their younger counterparts. Only about 20 percent of the information reported across both groups was furnished spontaneously; the rest was provided in response to specific questions about the trip. These data indicate that preschoolers accurately encode information about memorable emotional events, but that specific prompts are often required to reveal the full extent of their knowledge.

Other studies have revealed similarly impressive memory abilities in young children. Psychologists have discovered that kindergartners can retain their memory of touring an archeology museum one year after their visit, that 4-year-olds can describe the circumstances surrounding the birth of a sibling just as accurately as school-age children, and that children between 2 and 3 years of age can recount distinctive events that had occurred three to six months earlier (such as Christmas or a trip to SeaWorld).[10]

Verbal report may underestimate how much information about an event children encode. That is, memory may be more adequately reflected in nondeclarative measures than in declarative ones. Brenda Smith and her colleagues had kindergartners follow a step-by-step recipe for making clay and then recount the steps immediately thereafter. Memory for the procedure was tested two weeks later. Children were able to verbalize only about 20 percent of the steps in the presence of the utensils and ingredients, but were able to reenact 80 percent of the steps when allowed to remake the clay (Smith, Ratner, and Hobart 1987). Hence verbal report alone underestimated the knowledge they had acquired. Very young children know more than they can say.

If motor behavior can reflect memory, then it may provide a means for testing retention of events that children experience before they acquire language. Nancy Myers and her associates had five children who had undergone a distinctive experimental procedure 15–19 times when they were very young (6–40 weeks) return to the laboratory for retesting when they were nearly 3 years old. During the original experiment, designed to assess perceptual ability, the children had gazed into a darkened chamber that would occasionally light up, illuminating colorful objects and toys. Upon their return to the laboratory, the children exhibited motor behavior similar to that they had exhibited two years earlier (for example, grasping for luminous objects in the darkened experimental chamber). Remarkably, one child verbally recollected that a "whale" decal had been hidden behind a screen during the original study. Apparently, re-exposure to the original context prompted the child's visual memory of the whale decal for which the child now had a verbal label (Myers, Clifton, and Clarkson 1987).

Andrew Meltzoff's research with the *deferred imitation task* provides the strongest evidence of episodic memory capability in preverbal children. It requires infants to view an adult performing a simple action sequence, such as dismantling a novel toy. The adult may repeat the sequence more than once, but the entire demonstration rarely lasts longer than one minute. After an interval, the adult provides the child with the props and records whether the child reproduces the action sequence. Children who have not witnessed the original demonstration serve as control subjects.

Using this method, Meltzoff (1985, 1995) has documented impressive event memory in preverbal infants: 45 percent of 14-month-olds who had witnessed a simple motor sequence correctly reproduced it 24 hours later, whereas only 7.5 percent of control infants performed the same sequence. In later work, Meltzoff found that infants ranging from 14 to 16 months of age were more likely than control infants to reproduce as many as four action sequences after having witnessed them two months earlier. Those who had merely watched the adult demonstrate the sequences were just as accurate as those who had performed the sequence immediately after witnessing it. Visual information encoded during the demonstration enabled infants to recreate the sequence later even though they had never performed it themselves.

Does the deferred imitation task provide a nonverbal analogue of explicit, episodic memory? Does it reflect conscious recollection of the original demonstration? Or does it merely tap unconscious, implicit memory? Psychologists disagree about the answers to these questions. Verbal report of conscious recollection of the original event has always been the hallmark of episodic, explicit memory. As the child psychologist Katherine Nelson (1994) has argued, there is no convincing evidence that infants at testing are aware of having been in the experimental context before or of what the adult did with the props. Accordingly, she argues, the deferred imitation task reflects implicit procedural memory, not episodic recollection. That is, infants know *how* to perform the sequences, but they may not remember *that* they have learned them.

But if one suspends the requirement about verbal report, behavior in the deferred imitation task is more akin to explicit than to implicit memory. Implicit procedural memory tasks, such as habit or skill learning, require practice, whereas behavioral reproduction in the deferred imitation task does not (Squire 1994). Other implicit tasks are sensitive to variations between study and test conditions. Thus priming effects for perceptual identification of words diminish for words appearing in lowercase when they previously appeared in uppercase (Jacoby and Hayman 1987). Yet the modality (vision versus motor action) differs drastically in Meltzoff's deferred imitation task. The infant views the model, and then matches the action sequence motorically. Finally, adults with organic amnesic syndromes that spare implicit memory (but not explicit memory) fail to reproduce age-appropriate action sequences after a mere 24 hours (McDonough et al. 1995). Because amnesic adults perform so poorly, the deferred imitation task must require that the brain structures affecting explicit memory, damaged in these patients, be intact. Hence infants who reproduce action sequences after long delays exhibit an early capacity for long-term explicit memory.[11]

Although recent research has revealed impressive memory abilities in young children, few episodic memories from these years persist beyond toddlerhood. Preschoolers exhibit procedural memory and perhaps declarative memory for events that occurred even earlier in their young lives, but hardly any of these memories persist into later childhood, let alone into adulthood. An event that is salient for a 3-year-old may no longer be memorable for a 10-year-old whose language capabilities and ways of accessing memory have developed over the ensuing years. So the impressive memory abilities of very young children do not conflict with the amnesia for early childhood exhibited by older children and adults.

How Emotional Stress Affects Memory

How does intense emotion affect memory? Does extreme stress enhance or impair memory for traumatic events? Answers to these questions are fundamental to determining how people remember (or forget) trauma. For obvious ethical reasons, traumatic levels of stress cannot be induced and studied in the laboratory. But there are ethical ways of addressing these issues short of experimentally traumatizing subjects. Psychologists have used three approaches to study emotional stress and memory: laboratory simulation experiments, flashbulb memory studies, and nonexperimental field studies of trauma.

In laboratory simulation studies, some subjects view an emotionally stressful videotape, slide sequence, or staged event, whereas others witness the same situation, but with the stressful elements replaced by neutral ones. For example, a stressful video might depict a bank robbery, whereas the nonstressful version would depict the same bank activities, minus the holdup. In some studies, physiological measures, such as heart rate, verify that subjects in the stress condition are more emotionally aroused than those in the neutral condition. The advantage of simulation studies is that the experimenter knows precisely what the subjects witnessed, thereby enabling valid assessments of memory for the witnessed events. Of course, stress levels never approach those of genuine traumatic events, leaving open the possibility that results might differ if subjects were extremely stressed.

In flashbulb memory studies, researchers assess subjects' memories about how they heard news of a momentous public event, such as a presidential assassination. Memories for these events tend to be more emotionally intense than anything occurring in the laboratory. Unfortunately, researchers can never be certain about the accuracy of memory reports because they were not present when subjects received news of the event. At best, psychologists have compared memory reports obtained long after the event with those obtained soon after the event. Consistency of reports over time has served as a proxy measure for memory accuracy.

Finally, in nonexperimental field studies, researchers assess memory for directly witnessed events, such as serious crimes. Although studies on memory for "real-life" events avoid artificial aspects of laboratory studies, they too have their methodological shortcomings. Certainty about what happened is often impossible, and researchers usually lack a neutral control event, witnessed by all subjects, that might serve as a baseline against which to measure memory accuracy for the target event. Lack of control over other variables further complicates matters; witnesses may vary in their proximity to the crime scene, for example. Nevertheless, their stress level is much higher than anything that researchers can ethically produce in the laboratory. Field studies can answer questions about extreme stress and memory that remain forever unanswerable in simulation experiments.

Akin to field studies are investigations of how children remember naturally occurring stressful events, such as painful medical procedures. Sometimes investigators are present to observe the event, and sometimes they are able to compare memory for the stressful event with memory for a control, neutral event.

Two hypotheses have guided research on the effects of emotional stress on memory. One holds that stress improves memory, but only up to a point of optimal arousal, after which it begins to impair memory. Invoking the work of Robert Yerkes and John Dodson (1908), who studied the effects of stress on learning in mice, advocates of this view hold that memory is impaired when arousal is either very low or very high. The effect of stress on memory, they believe, is best described by an inverted-U function (see Deffenbacher 1983).

The evidence, however, does not fit a Yerkes-Dodson formulation. Very high levels of stress do not produce general impairments in memory. In fact, the evidence best fits the second hypothesis, one based on J. A. Easterbrook's cue-utilization theory (see Christianson 1992). According to Easterbrook (1959), increasing levels of arousal direct attention to the central features of the arousing event at the expense of the peripheral features. Accordingly, an extremely stressed person will encode and remember central aspects of the experience while failing to encode trivial details. For example, a robbery victim may vividly recall the robber's weapon and perhaps his face but fail to encode, and therefore to recall, the kind of shoes he was wearing. Emotional stress does not always impair encoding of peripheral details; sometimes minor things are remembered as well as the important ones. But emotional stress does not prevent encoding and memory for the central, important aspects of the experience.

Laboratory Simulation Studies

Several studies suggest that shocking stimuli are easily remembered, but that their presentation can block encoding (and therefore memory) of associated neutral stimuli. Sven-Åke Christianson and Lars-Göran Nilsson (1984) had subjects view 18 slides of faces, each accompanied, on an adjacent screen, by 4 words describing the person in the slide. All faces seen by the control group were normal, whereas the middle 6 seen by the "trauma" group were horribly disfigured. Words accompanying the disfigured faces were recalled less often than those accompanying the normal faces. Subjects attended so closely to the shocking faces that they failed to encode the accompanying words.

T. H. Kramer's research team also found that traumatic slides impaired memory for subsequent nontraumatic material. Subjects viewed a series of emotionally neutral travel slides. For one group of subjects, a gruesome slide depicting a homicide victim appeared in the middle of the series. Relative to subjects who saw only neutral slides, those exposed to the gruesome slide were less able to recall neutral slides that appeared after the traumatic one. Subjects easily remembered the traumatic slide, but they often failed to encode and remember the neutral slides that followed it (Kramer et al. 1991).

This effect is not confined to traumatic stimuli. Stephen Schmidt showed subjects a series of slides, each depicting a person. When a nude suddenly appeared in the middle of the series, subjects exhibited impaired memory for the slides that followed. As Schmidt observed, the nude "was quite memorable" (2002: 353). Subjects seldom encounter pictures of naked people in the middle of cognitive psychology experiments, and when they do, they rarely forget them. These studies indicate that distinctive, emotional stimuli are often encoded, and therefore remembered, at the expense of other stimuli, regardless of whether the stimulus is negative or positive.

Brian Clifford and Jane Scott (1978) had subjects view one of two videotaped versions of an encounter between a police officer and a citizen, and then asked them about what they had just witnessed. Subjects who saw a nonviolent version were more accurate than those who saw a violent one. A later study by Clifford and Clive Hollin (1981), featuring a simulated mugging, yielded similar results.

Elizabeth Loftus and Terrence Burns (1982) had subjects view either a violent or a nonviolent videotape of a simulated bank robbery and then take a memory test about aspects of the film. Over 90 percent of the subjects in each group provided correct answers to 7 of 16 questions. However, for 14 of 16 questions, rates of correct answers were higher among those who saw the nonviolent version than among those who saw the violent one. When asked to recall the number on the football jersey of a boy playing in the parking lot, a much larger proportion of those who watched the nonviolent version (27.9 percent) than of those who watched the violent one (4.3 percent) gave the correct anwswer. Loftus and Burns concluded that emotional shock may impair eyewitness memory. But consistent with the Easterbrook hypothesis, subjects failed to encode and remember a peripheral, not central, detail of the witnessed scene. They remembered the violence very well, at the expense of encoding the jersey number.

During a traumatic event, people often experience the illusion of time slowing down (Noyes and Kletti, 1977). This effect also occurs in the laboratory. In the first of two studies, Loftus and her colleagues had subjects view a 30-second film of a simulated bank robbery. Two days later, subjects estimated it to have been four times longer than it was. Their second study revealed that time overestimation was more pronounced for high-stress videotapes than for low-stress ones (Loftus, Schooler, et al. 1987).

These studies show that exposure to a shocking event does not produce "amnesia" for the event itself. Indeed, simulated traumatic events themselves are easily remembered, but sometimes they capture attention so well that subjects fail to encode related neutral information.

Other studies have further clarified how people encode and remember emotional events. Sven-Åke Christianson (1984) had subjects view a slide sequence forming a story whose traumatic version depicted a boy being struck by a car. Two weeks later, subjects who had viewed this version recalled the central features of the slides better than did subjects who had seen the neutral version. In addition to confirming that emotional events are retained better than neutral ones, subsequent slide experiments by Christianson and Loftus (1987, 1991) documented that central details of emotional events are better retained than those of neutral events, and that peripheral details of neutral events are better retained than those of emotional events.

Robbery victims often remember details of the assailant's gun, but do not remember much about his appearance. This "weapon focus" phenomenon accords with the Easterbrook hypothesis: attention is riveted to the most important aspect of the scene. Psychologists have studied this phenomenon in the laboratory. For example, Elizabeth Loftus and her colleagues had subjects view one of two slide sequences. In one sequence, a customer at a fast food restaurant hands a worker a check and receives money in return. In the other version, the customer pulls out a gun, and the worker hands over the money.

In one experiment the researchers tracked the subjects' eye movements during the slide sequence. Subjects who saw the robbery fixed their eyes on the gun more often and for longer periods than the other subjects fixed theirs on the check, and when questioned after the viewing were marginally less accurate in identifying the customer in a photo lineup. In a second experiment significantly fewer subjects who saw the gun than subjects who saw the check identified the customer (15 percent versus 35 percent). If weapon focus occurs in the laboratory, it may occur with even greater frequency in real-life robberies (Loftus, Loftus, and Messo 1987).

In another study, by Gary Wells and Michael Leippe (1981), eyewitnesses who correctly identified in a photolineup the person who stole a calculator in a staged theft remembered fewer peripheral details about the event than did those who identified an innocent person as the culprit. Apparently, attention to the thief precluded encoding of trivial background information. In a worrisome secondary finding, because the mistaken witnesses provided many peripheral details about the "crime," mock jurors regarded them as more credible than the witnesses who correctly encoded the thief's identity at the expense of peripheral details.

Encoding of central elements of an emotional episode does not invariably preclude encoding of other aspects. Sometimes peripheral details are remembered as well as central ones. Friderike Heuer and Daniel Reisberg (1990) had subjects view a narrated slide story about a boy and his mother visiting his father at work. The emotional version depicted the boy watching his father perform surgery, whereas the neutral version depicted him watching his father repair an automobile. Memory tests two weeks later indicated that subjects retained more peripheral as well as more central details from the emotional version than from the neutral one. Emotional arousal enhanced memory for central, plot-relevant details without impairing memory for peripheral, plot-irrelevant details.

A subsequent study by this research team, headed by Alafair Burke, had a different outcome. Subjects who witnessed the emotional sequence remembered more central, plot-relevant details, but *fewer* plot-irrelevant background details, than did subjects who witnessed the neutral sequence (Burke, Heuer, and Reisberg 1992).

Do subjects fail to remember background details of emotional events because they failed to encode them, or because memory tests fail to provide sufficient cues to prompt recall? Psychologists have investigated whether altering retrieval conditions improves recollection of these details. Several studies have addressed whether repeated attempts to recall details of simulated traumatic events aid memory—that is, produce hypermnesia. Ellen Scrivner and Martin Safer (1988) had 90 students view a two-minute police training video that depicted the shooting of three residents during a home invasion. Subjects attempted to recollect details of the event during four recall sessions spread over a 48-hour period. The number of recollected details increased significantly across the recall sessions: 88 percent of the subjects accurately recollected more details during the fourth session than during the first one. False recalls were rare, but they too significantly increased across repeated sessions. Scrivner and Safer concluded that repeated attempts to recall aspects of an event may cue retrieval of hitherto unrecalled details.

Five months after an experimental accomplice "vandalized" equipment during a classroom demonstration, Roy Malpass and Patricia Devine (1981) had students attempt to recall what they had witnessed. Half of the subjects were asked to visualize the simulated crime. More of these subjects than of those who were not asked to visualize the scene identified the vandal from a photographic lineup (60 percent versus 40 percent).

Flashbulb Memories

Does memory for trauma differ qualitatively from memory for ordinary events? Are special mechanisms needed to explain how people encode, store, and retrieve events having overwhelming emotional significance? Similar questions were answered affirmatively 25 years ago by Roger Brown and James Kulik (1977), who coined the term *flashbulb memory* to denote a vivid, detailed recollection of the circumstances when one first received news of an emotionally shocking event, such as the assassination of President John Kennedy. Flashbulb memories do not merely concern the event itself, but rather concern memory for the reception context—where one was, what one was doing, how one felt, and so forth—when one first heard the news. Possessing almost perceptual clarity, flashbulb memories seem unforgettably engraved on the mind and resistant to decay. To explain these features, Brown and Kulik postulated a special quasi-photographic neurophysiologic mechanism that imprints the sensory details of the reception context in memory. They found that all but one of 80 subjects retained a vivid, detailed flashbulb memory of hearing about the Kennedy assassination 13 years after it had happened.

Brown and Kulik's work inspired many subsequent studies on flashbulb memories.[12] Their work also replicated a long-forgotten study on memory for an earlier presidential murder. The nineteenth-century American psychologist F. W. Colegrove (1899) found that 71 percent of his subjects could remember where they had been when they heard the news of President Abraham Lincoln's assassination many years before.

Brown and Kulik emphasized that flashbulb memories are not produced solely by consequential public events. Private events of emotional significance, such as receiving news of a loved one's death, can produce vivid, lasting memories as well. Indeed, David Rubin and Marc Kozin (1984) found that only 3 percent of the flashbulb memories described by their subjects concerned events of national importance. Moreover, flashbulb memories are not confined to unexpected events. Eugene Winograd and William Killinger (1983) found that people also report flashbulb memories of momentous, anticipated events, such as Neil Armstrong's first steps on the moon. They also found that the quality of the flashbulb memory depends on one's age when the event happened. Only about 10 percent of those who were 4 years old when Kennedy was assassinated report a flashbulb memory for the event, whereas about 70 percent of those who were 7 years old at the time report one.

Brown and Kulik's quasi-photographic mechanism presumably ensured the accuracy of flashbulb memories by faithfully registering the reception context. Unfortunately, direct tests of accuracy are impossible because researchers can hardly arrange to be present when people receive shocking news of some important event. Accordingly, they have used consistency of reports over time as a proxy for accuracy. If flashbulb memories are as permanent as people believe them to be, the details provided in later reports should match those provided in the initial report.

Occasionally people do retain consistent flashbulb memories over time. David Pillemer (1984) assessed memories for the assassination attempt on President Ronald Reagan one and seven months after the shooting, and found that nearly all subjects at both assessments remembered the circumstances in which they heard the news (97.7 percent and 90.9 percent). Subjects' memories for where they were, what they were doing, and so forth were generally consistent across time: on average they scored 4.88 on a scale of consistency ranging from 0 to 6. Strong emotional reactions to the event were associated with detailed narratives, visual memories, and consistency of recollections over time.

Working in Belgium, Catrin Finkenauer's research team (1998) applied sophisticated mathematical methods to determine how certain variables combined to form flashbulb memories of the shocking, unexpected death of their country's beloved King Baudouin. They found that how surprising a person rated the event directly influenced whether the person had a flashbulb memory about hearing the news. Surprise, combined with perceived importance of the event and attitude toward the royal family, determined the intensity of emotional response. Emotion, in turn, increased rehearsal (how often the person thought about the event), which strengthens the memory for the original event, thereby contributing to the formation of a lasting, vivid, flashbulb memory.

Months and years after the flashbulb event, subjects can often provide—with great confidence—detailed accounts of where they were and what they were doing when they heard the momentous news. But confidence in a detailed memory does not guarantee its accuracy. Longitudinal studies have shown that vivid flashbulb memories often change over time, unbeknownst to the rememberer. One day after the *Challenger* explosion, Ulric Neisser and Nicole Harsch (1992) asked 106 college students to provide an account of how they had heard about the disaster, and to answer specific questions about key details (Where were you? What were you doing? Who told you?). Two and a half years later, they reassessed the flashbulb memories of 44 of these students. Subjects' second account was compared with their first account;

consistency across time was a proxy for accuracy. Although subjects expressed great confidence in the accuracy of their second account, their mean score was only 2.95 on an accuracy index that ranged from 0 to 7. Only three subjects received a score of 7 by providing the same account on both occasions, and 25 percent were wrong about every key detail. Half of the subjects got one key detail right (for example, who told them), while getting the others wrong (where they were, what they were doing).

Soon after the testing, Neisser and Harsch interviewed 40 of these subjects. Using subjects' original accounts, they provided hints to see whether reminders might jog subjects' memories. Even these clues failed to reactivate the original, and presumably accurate, memory. Moreover, when confronted with their original accounts, the subjects were amazed that their current, confidently held memories about how they first heard about the disaster could be so inaccurate. Hence neither the vividness of a memory nor the confidence with which it is held guarantees its accuracy.

The longer the period between the original, baseline assessment and the second assessment, the more distortion creeps into flashbulb memory accounts. For example, H. Schmolck and his colleagues assessed memory for the announcement of the verdict in the O. J. Simpson murder trial three days after the event, and then again either 15 or 32 months later. At baseline assessment, 98.4 percent of the subjects' recollections qualified as flashbulb memories. For subjects reassessed at 15 months, 50 percent of the memories matched the original reports very closely; only 11 percent contained major discrepancies. For subjects reassessed at 32 months, only 29 percent of the memories matched the original account, and 40 percent contained major discrepancies. At 32 months most of the subjects still provided vivid, flashbulb-like accounts of their memories of hearing the verdict—but these accounts bore little resemblance to their original ones. For example, one subject originally reported hearing the verdict while watching television with fellow students in a college lounge. Thirty-two months later the same subject furnished an equally vivid memory of hearing the news at home while eating a meal with family members (Schmolck, Buffalo, and Squire 2000).

We now know that flashbulb memories are neither permanent nor immune to distortion. Hence few psychologists today believe that a special neurological mechanism like the one proposed by Brown and Kulik is needed to explain them. Instead, a combination of ordinary mechanisms can do the job, such as emotional arousal at encoding, distinctiveness of the event, rehearsal of the reception context, perceived personal relevance, and surprisingness.[13]

Research on flashbulb memories converges with laboratory research on memory for emotional events. In both cases, memory for the central gist is retained, whereas memory for details fades or changes. People do not forget that President Kennedy was murdered, or that the *Challenger* exploded, or that terrorists destroyed the World Trade Center. But they may forget where they were and what they were doing when they heard about these shocking events, despite a subjective sense of the memory's immutability.

Field Studies

Field studies provide further evidence that people retain vivid memories of shocking events they have directly witnessed or experienced. John Yuille and Judith Cutshall (1986) interviewed 13 witnesses to a fatal shooting 4–5 months after they had told their stories to the police. They compared the memory of each witness to a composite account based on police reports, forensic evidence, and consensus information distilled from the testimony of all witnesses. Memories of the shooting were detailed and strikingly accurate, and even those witnesses most distressed by the event had high accuracy scores on the police and research interviews (93 percent and 88 percent, respectively). The 5 most distressed witnesses were significantly more accurate than those who were less distressed; they had also been closest to the shooting. High stress may have enhanced their memory; it certainly did not impair it.

Employing these methods, Cutshall and Yuille (1989) studied memories for other witnessed crimes. Two years after a fatal shootout between police and an armed robber, they interviewed four witnesses. Using police records as the standard, they found that witnesses were 100 percent accurate in their immediate reports. During the research interview conducted two years after the shooting, their mean accuracy was still 92.3 percent. When Cutshall and Yuille interviewed six witnesses of another fatal police shootout, the witnesses got 92.1 percent of the details correct immediately after the crime, and 84.6 percent 13–18 months later.

Cutshall and Yuille located 17 witnesses to bank robberies. During the police interviews immediately after the robberies, witnesses got 90.2 percent of the details right; two years later they got 82 percent right. Witnesses were shown photo spread lineups that either did or did not contain mug shots of the robber. Of the 10 witnesses who saw a photo spread including the culprit, only 4 identified him; 5 chose one of the other photographs, and another claimed that the culprit's picture was not in the photo spread. Of 6 witnesses who saw a photo spread lacking the culprit, 3 chose the wrong person.

Other researchers have also observed that witnesses have trouble identifying the culprit. Sven-Åke Christianson and Birgitta Hübinette (1993) asked 58 witnesses to 22 robberies to complete memory questionnaires 4–15 months after the crime, and compared their recollections with police records. Tellers who had been threatened at gunpoint accurately recalled circumstantial details (date, time) as often as central details (action, weapon) of the crime, whereas other employees and customers exhibited better recall for central than for peripheral details.

Finally, Ulric Neisser and his colleagues (1996) obtained memory reports from Californians exposed to the 1989 Loma Prieta earthquake 2–9 days after the event and again 18 months later. Recollections at 18 months were nearly perfect, as judged by the striking consistency between the two sets of reports, and significantly more accurate than the memories of control subjects in Atlanta who merely learned about the earthquake via the media. Memory retention, however, was not related to self-rated levels of stress. The researchers suggested that for the Californians, repeatedly discussing their earthquake stories prevented memories of the event from fading over time.

Memory for a directly experienced shocking event is more stable than a flashbulb memory of hearing about the same event, as evinced by the stability of the Californians' earthquake memories in contrast to those of the Atlantans. Not surprisingly, directly experiencing an earthquake is more memorable than first hearing the news about it.

Children's Memory for Stressful Events

For obvious ethical reasons, researchers do not induce highly stressful events in children to see how they remember them. Instead, they have studied memory for naturally occurring stressors, usually dental or medical procedures.

Gail Goodman and her colleagues (1991) found that emotional stress enhanced memory for a medical procedure among children aged 3–7. Memory for this procedure—either getting a shot or having blood drawn—was compared to memory for a nonstressful one—application of a washable "tattoo." Only when children exhibited very high levels of emotional stress was memory for the medical procedure better than memory for the tattoo application.[14]

In later studies, Goodman's research group (1994) studied memory for a voiding cystourethrogram fluoroscopy (VCUG), a painful medical procedure for diagnosing urinary tract problems which requires insertion of a tube through the urethra and infusion of liquid into the bladder. They found that memory for the VCUG was more accurate and detailed for older children (5–10 years) than for younger ones (3–4 years). Understanding the procedure, not being embarrassed, having an emotionally supportive mother, and taking pride in one's courage all predicted enhanced memory for the experience. A subset of children had endured the procedure as many as six times, but repeated VCUGs neither enhanced nor impaired their memory performance.

Working in Goodman's laboratory, Jodi Quas studied the memories of children, aged 3–13 years, who had undergone a VCUG between the ages of 2 and 6. Children who had been at least 4 years old when they received the VCUG remembered it well, whereas younger children did not. Those who had been most stressed were less likely to fall prey to suggestive questions, and high levels of stress during the VCUG were linked with later reluctance to describe it in detail. The more often a child had experienced VCUGs, the more correct details the child provided for the most recent one. Hence repetition improved memory in free recall. The researchers concluded that "stressful and traumatic memories tend to be governed by similar, age-related mechanisms that dictate whether early childhood experiences will be remembered in the long term" (Quas et al. 1999: 258).

Edith Chen and her associates (2000) examined memory for lumbar puncture, a painful aspect of cancer treatment, in 55 leukemia patients aged 3–18. One week after the procedure, children of all ages exhibited accurate memory for the event, and accuracy increased with age. The youngest (3–4 years) had a mean accuracy score of 42.4 percent, whereas the oldest (11–18) had a mean of 86.5 percent. Initial analyses suggested that increased distress was associated with poorer memory, but this correlation was weakened when the influence of age was controlled (that is, younger children tend to have poorer recall overall and tend to be most distressed).

Carole Peterson and Michael Bell (1996) found that children aged 2–13 retain impressively detailed and accurate memories of emergency room treatment for lacerations and fractures six months later. Among the 90 children they studied, older children exhibited better memory than younger ones, and all retained central details of the experience better than peripheral ones.[15]

Will a preverbal child who endures a stressful event be able to describe it later? To investigate this question, Peterson and Regina Rideout (1998) studied young children who had sustained injuries requiring emergency room treatment. There were three groups of children: young toddlers (13–18 months), older toddlers (20–25 months), and narrators (children verbally capable of conveying their experiences to others; 26–34 months). If verbal, they were interviewed within days of the event and again after 6, 12, 18, and 24 months. Young toddlers exhibited scant long-term verbal recall of the event, whereas older toddlers could describe the event 18 months later despite having been incapable of doing so at the time of injury. Most children in the oldest group, who were verbal when injured, could describe the event two years later. The oldest children were the most accurate. Of 12 children who were 2 years old, and whose narrative skills were developed, at time of injury, 11 could recount the central details of their experience two years later. Whether these memories would survive into adulthood is uncertain. None of the 7 young toddlers, when interviewed two years later, was able to furnish a narrative account of the event. Two of them did provide good accounts at the one-year interview, but appeared to have forgotten their experiences by the two-year interview. Several older toddlers, who lacked narrative skills at the time of the injury, were capable of providing a narrative account of their experiences after 18 months. One striking finding was that children tended to recall more details of their experiences over the course of the follow-up interviews. One possible explanation is that apparently scanty recall in 2-year-olds may reflect the difficulties of interviewing such young subjects. Apparent improvement in "memory" over time may reflect the ease of interviewing children as they age from 2 to 4 years.

Some evidence suggests that children who lack narrative skills at time of injury may nevertheless exhibit conditioned emotional responses indicating retention of the episode. For example, one child in Peterson and Rideout's young toddler group fell and cut his forehead, requiring him to be wrapped to a papoose board to prevent his struggling during suturing of his head. The child was so terrified that his screaming burst blood vessels in his neck, back, and chest. One week later he exhibited terror when blankets were placed on him, and two years later he still refused to be wrapped in a barber's smock when getting his hair cut. His parents reported that his fears did wane throughout his preschool years.[16]

Further analyzing Peterson and Rideout's data, Howe, Courage, and Peterson (1995) compared the initial and 6-month memory reports of children who had been 30, 36, or 48 months old at the time of their emergency room treatment. They studied narrative intrusions—inserted details that were not true, and that might have arisen from other medical events. An intrusion was more likely to occur at 6 months than initially, but only for the youngest group. Interestingly, the occurrence of intrusions did not impair accurate report of the stressful event. Children still got the basic facts right despite intruding false details. In summary, long-term recall (at least until the age of 4) of highly stressful experiences is extremely unlikely unless the child could narrate what happened at the time of injury. Regardless of how distressed the child was at the time, an inability to narrate precludes subsequent verbal recollection of the trauma. Some observations suggest, however, that Pavlovian fear conditioning established to physical cues present during the trauma may provoke fear and avoidance reactions some months later despite the child's lacking any recollection of the original conditioning episode.

Finally, five years after Peterson and Bell's original study, Peterson and Nikki Whalen (2001) reassessed 81 of the original 90 participants. Although their memories had faded somewhat, these children (who were now 7–18 years old) exhibited remarkable levels of retention. For example, children who had been at least 3 years old when taken to the hospital correctly recalled over 80 percent of the central details of their injury. Even the former 2-year-olds recalled over 50 percent of these details five years later. Central (injury) details were retained better than peripheral (hospital) ones. The more stressed the child was at the time, the more details about the hospital procedure were remembered five years later. Although Peterson and Whalen noted that very few events in the lives of 2- and 3-year-olds are remembered five years later, certain events do seem to survive early childhood amnesia. Highly distinctive, unembarrassing, extremely stressful events, which the child understands at the time, and which are discussed later (as in the repeated assessment interviews) are those likely to be remembered during the school-age years and perhaps beyond.

Laboratory experiments, flashbulb memory studies, and field research all point to the same conclusion: emotional stress enhances memory for the central features of the stressful experience. Stress does not impair memory; it strengthens it. Granted, superior memory for central aspects of the experience may occur at the expense of peripheral details, as the Easterbrook hypothesis suggests. But stress does not abolish memory for the stressful event itself. The studies reviewed here provide no support for the notion that a Yerkes-Dodson inverted-U function describes the relation between stress and memory; memory for stressful experiences does not deteriorate at high levels of stress.

Although speculation about the evolutionary origins of human cognition is fraught with dangers, one can easily imagine that natural selection would have favored a capacity to remember trauma. Our ancestors who remembered life-threatening situations they had survived would have been more likely to avoid similar dangers in the future than those who failed to remember them. Indeed, what is difficult to imagine is how something as maladaptive as a mechanism for repressing, dissociating, or otherwise forgetting trauma could possibly have evolved throughout the course of natural history. To be sure, being haunted by memories of trauma is a singularly unpleasant experience. But natural selection does not care whether we are happy. The painful capacity for remembering trauma may be the price we pay for possessing memory mechanisms that allow us to remember dangers, survive, and reproduce.[17]

Brain, Emotion, and Memory

Scientists have sought to discover the brain mechanisms that mediate our ability to remember extremely emotional events so well. Pioneering animal research by the behavioral neuroscientist James McGaugh among others confirmed the role of the amygdala, a subcortical structure located deep in the brain, in emotional memory (for a review see McGaugh et al. 2000). An emotional stimulus activates the amygdala, which in turn enhances explicit memory for the experience by modulating activity in the hippocampus, a neighboring subcortical brain structure.

Research on human subjects confirms the role of the amygdala in emotional memory (for reviews see Cahill 2000; Hamann 2001). The amygdala and the hippocampus work closely together to ensure that emotional stimuli and emotional experiences are firmly established in conscious, explicit memory. As we saw in the case of the amnesic patient H.M., the hippocampus is essential for consolidating experiences into long-term memory, and activation of the amygdala amplifies this process. The activated amygdala interacts with stress hormones released during and following exposure to emotional events, and such activation modulates the storage of memory for the event elsewhere in the brain. Damage to the amygdala does not impair a person's ability to experience emotion or to express it, but it does reduce a person's ability to encode emotional stimuli.

Neuroimaging studies on normal human subjects also confirm the role of the amygdala. Using positron emission tomography, Larry Cahill and his colleagues (1996) found that increased activity in the right amygdala while male subjects watched film clips with content likely to arouse negative emotions (fear, disgust) predicted their ability to remember these film clips several weeks later. A follow-up study with female subjects yielded the same result, except that activity in the *left* amygdala predicted memory for negative emotional film clips (Cahill et al. 2001). Amygdala activity was related to memory for neutral film clips in neither study, and men and women expressed equivalent levels of emotion in response to the negative film clips. Apparently the brains of men and women encode negative emotional stimuli differently, but it is unclear why.

In a functional magnetic resonance imaging study, Turhan Canli's group (2000) found that amygdala activity in female subjects was greatest for those negative scenes rated as most emotionally intense. Activation in the left amygdala predicted subsequent memory for these scenes.

Amygdala activation is not confined to the encoding of negative emotional experiences; it enhances memory for any emotionally arousing experience. For example, Stephan Hamann and his colleagues (1999) found that bilateral amygdala activity predicted later recognition memory for positive as well as negative (but not neutral) pictures. Moreover, activity in the amygdala was correlated with activity in the hippocampus, consistent with the view that these two structures work together to establish vivid emotional memories. Likewise, R. J. Dolan's group (2000) found that the left amygdala became activated during successful intentional retrieval of memories of positive as well as negative pictures that had been encoded minutes earlier. On the other hand, as Larry Cahill (2000) has pointed out, the act of retrieving an emotional memory can itself be arousing (as when we remember a traumatic event). Accordingly, in Dolan's study, it is possible that amygdala activation occurred during retrieval because subjects were encoding the new emotional experience of retrieving an old emotional memory. In any event, these studies indicate that the amygdala becomes activated during encoding of positive as well as negative arousing experiences, and that it may figure in the retrieval of these experiences as well.

Studies on patients with amygdala damage provide further evidence of the amygdala's key role in emotional memory. Whereas normal subjects exhibit enhanced memory for the emotional elements in a story, no such enhancement occurs for patients with Urbach-Wiethe disease, a congenital condition characterized by damage to the amygdala (Cahill et al. 1995). Patients with damage to the left amygdala fail to show the expected memory enhancement for emotional pictures (Adolphs, Tranel, and Denburg 2000). In another study, subjects with damage to the right amygdala showed the normal memory enhancement for both emotional verbal and pictorial stimuli, whereas those with damage to the left amygdala failed to exhibit the enhancement effect, a deficit especially pronounced for emotional verbal stimuli (Buchanan et al. 2001). Impairment in emotional memory for the Kobe earthquake was related to extent of amygdala damage among patients with early Alzheimer's disease (Mori et al. 1999).

Laboratory studies done by Cahill's group (1994) on memory for emotional stories in normal subjects also implicate the amygdala. The researchers had subjects view a series of narrated slides that depicted either a stressful or a neutral story. The two versions of the story were identical, except that midway through the stressful version a boy was struck by a car. Before viewing one of the slide sequences, subjects received either propranolol hydrochloride or placebo. Propranolol blocks peripheral (throughout the body) and central (within the brain) beta-adrenergic receptors, thereby reducing heart rate and other measures of arousal. One week later, subjects who had received placebo exhibited better memory for the stressful story than did those who had received propranolol, whereas the groups did not differ in their memory for the neutral version. The beta-blocker, propranolol, selectively abolished the characteristic declarative memory advantage ordinarily associated with stressful material.

Subsequent research by Cahill's group has yielded conflicting results. In one experiment, they again found that propranolol selectively eliminated the memory advantage for stressful slides, whereas another beta-blocker, nadolol, did not (van Stegeren et al. 1998). Nadolol, however, blocks only peripheral beta-adrenergic receptors, whereas propranolol blocks central ones as well. Although these data suggest that a beta-blocker must have effects within the brain to diminish declarative memory for emotional material, another experiment revealed that propranolol, as well as nadolol, failed to attenuate memory for emotional slides (O'Carroll et al. 1999a). In yet another study, subjects received either metoprolol, yohimbine, or placebo before viewing a narrated slide show whose middle slides depicted a boy being injured in an accident and having his severed feet reattached by surgeons. Metoprolol reduces autonomic arousal by selectively blocking beta-1 receptors, which are mainly in cardiac tissue, whereas yohimbine increases arousal by blocking alpha-2 inhibitory autoreceptors in the brain. Surprisingly, all groups exhibited similarly excellent recognition memory for the stressful slides in the middle of the sequence regardless of the drug they received. Yohimbine did not enhance memory for emotional material, and metoprolol did not impair it, relative to placebo (O'Carroll et al. 1999b).

In an extension of this research, Roger Pitman and his colleagues (2002) tested whether propranolol might prevent the development of PTSD symptoms among accident survivors who began receiving the drug shortly after arriving in the emergency room. If this drug dampens emotional arousal, then perhaps, Pitman reasoned, it might prevent the establishment of emotionally intense traumatic memories. As it turned out, most survivors reported few stress symptoms at follow-up, regardless of whether they had received propranolol or placebo. However, propranolol-treated patients were significantly less physiologically reactive when listening to an audiotaped description of their accident than were those who had received placebo. This promising pilot study suggests that prompt administration of a drug that attenuates activity in the amygdala may diminish subsequent conditioned fear responses to reminders of the traumatic event. If further work along this line succeeds, then perhaps when people remember traumatic events they will do so with less painful emotion than might otherwise be the case.

False Memories

Just as the computer has provided an overall metaphor for information processing in the brain, other metaphors have guided thinking about how to gauge memory performance and how to conceptualize memory failures (see Koriat, Goldsmith, and Pansky 2000). The *storehouse metaphor* depicts memory as containing discrete, countable items of retrievable information. Memory performance is gauged by the quantity of items remembered, as exemplified by the classic work of the nineteenth-century psychologist Hermann Ebbinghaus (1885). Using himself as his only subject, Ebbinghaus memorized lists of nonsense syllables (such as *vup, pir*), and, after varying delays, tested how many he could recall. His memory failures were mainly those of omission: failing to recall items he had learned.

Stressing the reconstructive character of memory, the *correspondence metaphor* gauges performance by how closely what is remembered corresponds to what actually happened (see, e.g., Bartlett 1932). Accuracy, not quantity, is the paramount concern. Errors of commission as well as omission may occur. In the most dramatic errors of commission, people develop false memories of experiences that never happened.

The controversy concerning possible false memories of sexual abuse has sparked great interest in memory distortion among experimental cognitive psychologists.[18] These psychologists have done three types of relevant studies. The first began to appear before the current controversy, whereas the others emerged in response to it. The first type of study concerns how misinformation provided to subjects after they witness an event distorts their memory for the event. The second type concerns the production of false memories of having encountered certain words. The third type involves the implanting of false autobiographical memories.

Misinformation Studies

Survivors of combat, automobile accidents, sexual abuse, and other traumatic events are also eyewitnesses to the events. Accordingly, research on how people remember—or misremember—witnessed events bears directly on memory for trauma. Scientific interest in the accuracy of eyewitness testimony has waxed and waned since the early twentieth century (see, e.g., Whipple 1909). Contemporary interest was sparked by the landmark research of Elizabeth Loftus, whose experiments have shown that giving witnesses misleading information after an event can distort their memory reports of the event. The basic procedure consists of three phases. First, subjects view a videotape or a slide sequence depicting an event, such as an automobile accident or a theft. Second, they receive a questionnaire about the event or read a narrative summary of it. Some subjects receive questionnaires or summaries containing misleading information ("Did another car pass the red Datsun while it was stopped at the *yield* sign?"), whereas others receive accurate information ("Did another car pass the red Datsun while it was stopped at the *stop* sign?") or neutral information ("Did another car pass the red Datsun while it was stopped at the *intersection?*"). Third, subjects take recognition tests about the event. The *misinformation effect* occurs when subjects endorse having seen items that were misleadingly suggested (such as claiming to have seen a yield sign when a stop sign was depicted).[19]

Many experiments have shown that information provided to witnesses after an event affects how they later remember it, or at least how they report it. Even subtle differences in the wording of postevent questions exert an effect. In a classic early study, Loftus and John Palmer (1974) had subjects view a filmed traffic accident and estimate the speed of the moving car. Subjects who were asked how fast the car was moving when it "smashed" into the other car provided faster speed estimates than those who were asked how fast it was moving when it "hit" the other car (40.8 versus 34 miles per hour). Subjects were asked one week later whether they had seen any glass. Although no broken glass was depicted in the film, 32 percent of subjects who had received the "smashed" wording, but only 14 percent of those who had received the "hit" wording, said they had seen glass. In a similar study, subjects who were asked whether they saw "the" broken light on the car were more likely to affirm, incorrectly, that they had seen it than were those who were asked whether they saw "a" broken light (Loftus and Zanni 1975). Subjects who were asked to estimate the car's speed when it passed a barn were more likely to report having seen a barn in the film than were those who were asked to estimate the car's speed as it went down the road (17.3 percent versus 2.7 percent), even though no barn appeared in the film (Loftus 1975).

Subtly misleading questions can produce more memory distortion than blatant, directly misleading ones. Subjects were queried about a film depicting an accident. Some subjects received a subtle misleading question about a (nonexistent) bus ("Did you see the children getting on the bus?"); others received a direct question ("Did you see the school bus in the film?"). When tested one week later, 29.2 percent of those who had received the subtle wording incorrectly affirmed having seen a bus, whereas only 15.6 percent of those who had received the directly misleading question did so (Loftus 1975). Another study showed that memory distortion was greatest when misleading information was provided one week after subjects witnessed slides depicting an accident and immediately before their memory for the slides was tested (Loftus, Miller, and Burns 1978). These data suggest that subjects' memories may be especially vulnerable to distortion if a delay separates the event from the delivery of the misleading information.

Subsequent studies have further elucidated the misinformation effect. Subjects who fall prey to misleading information consciously *remember* witnessing things that they have not seen, and they hold these false memories with great confidence. The false memory effect occurs even when subjects are warned that postevent information contained inaccuracies. Repeated exposure to suggestive, misleading questions increases the likelihood of false memories developing, apparently because repeated attempts to visualize the witnessed event alter the original memory trace. Questions that falsely presuppose the presence of an object in the witnessed scene ("Was the umbrella stand in the corridor made of brass?") are more likely to produce false recollection of the object than questions that do not ("Was the umbrella stand in the corridor?"), perhaps because presuppositional misleading questions are especially likely to prompt visual imagery about the nonexistent object. False memories are increased when a delay separates the delivery of the postevent misinformation from the memory testing (for example, 1 week versus 15 minutes).[20]

The postevent misinformation effect occurs in the "real world" as well as in the laboratory. Ten months after an airplane crashed into an apartment building near Amsterdam, Hans Crombag and his colleagues asked 193 subjects whether they had seen television footage of the plane striking the building. In reality, the crash had not been captured on film. Nevertheless, 55 percent claimed to have seen it on television. In a second study, two-thirds of a group of law students claimed to have seen this crash footage, and some even provided details about what they had "seen." Crombag and his colleagues suggested that widely publicized disasters prompt visual imagery of the events that can be mistaken for witnessing the event on film (Crombag, Wagenaar, and van Koppen 1996). Likewise, in Britain James Ost and his associates

(2002) found that 44 percent of their subjects claimed to have seen a (non-existent) film of the crash that took the life of Princess Diana and were capable of providing details about their false memory.

The misinformation effect has several causes, as Elizabeth Loftus and others have long agreed. One possibility is that postevent misinformation may alter, overwrite, or replace the original memory of the witnessed event. If so, then the original memory would be gone for good, replaced by the inaccurate one. Another possibility is that subjects may encode the original element (such as seeing a jar of Maxwell House coffee in a scene), and encode the postevent (mis)information (about Folger's coffee), but forget the source of each memory. They may remember something about Maxwell House and Folger's, but forget when they heard something about each of them. Finally, they may simply fail to notice the relevant detail in the original scene (the jar of Maxwell House), and thereby affirm, by default, having seen Folger's because Folger's was mentioned during the postevent misinformation. Regardless of which of these mechanisms is operative in any particular case, the misinformation effect is robust and replicable. Suggestive, misleading information provided after an event routinely distorts witnesses' memory reports of the event.[21]

Producing False Memories in the Laboratory

Cognitive psychologists have published accounts of dozens of experiments designed to illuminate how people develop false memories in the laboratory. Most of these experiments were directly inspired by an article by Henry Roediger and Kathleen McDermott (1995). Resurrecting a task introduced by James Deese (1959), Roediger and McDermott conducted two experiments that involved what has come to be known as the Deese-Roediger-McDermott, or DRM, paradigm. Both experiments showed that it was startlingly easy to foster false memories among college students in the laboratory.

In Roediger and McDermott's first experiment, subjects heard 6 study lists, each comprising 12 words sharing a common theme. For example, one list contained words related to the theme of sleep, such as *bed, rest, awake, tired,* and *dream*. However, the word *sleep* was not mentioned. Roediger and McDermott tested whether subjects would "remember" having heard words that had been merely suggested, not presented (these are called critical lures), like *sleep*. Not only did subjects correctly recall 65 percent of the words that had appeared on the study list, they also "recalled" 40 percent of the critical lures that had not, in fact, been presented. Moreover, not only did subjects correctly recognize 86 percent of the study words, they "recognized" 84 percent of the critical lures as well.

In Roediger and McDermott's second experiment, rates of false recall (55 percent) and recognition (76 percent) were strikingly similar to rates of correct recall (62 percent) and recognition (72 percent). Also, in this experiment, they had subjects provide *remember* versus *know* judgments for each word they claimed to have recognized. Remember judgments were appropriate when subjects had a vivid, specific memory of the word's presentation, such as recollecting what they were thinking when they heard the word or the sound of the experimenter's voice pronouncing it. Know judgments were appropriate when subjects were confident that the word had appeared on a study list despite failing to recollect any details about its presentation. Subjects provided remember judgments for 49 percent of the study words they correctly recognized. That is, for about half of the words they correctly recognized as having appeared on the study list, they had a recollective experience of the word's presentation (such as remembering the experimenter's voice saying the word). Strikingly, the same thing happened for the critical lures that had not been presented. Subjects provided remember judgments for 48 percent of the critical lures they had falsely "recognized." Roediger and McDermott concluded that "the illusion of remembering events that never happened can occur quite readily" (1995: 812).

Subsequent DRM studies have shown how easily false memories develop in the laboratory and how long-lasting they can be. Not only can rates of false recall and recognition match those of true recall and recognition, but false recall persists, or even increases, over time, whereas true recall declines. The false memory effect is not confined to word lists. Subjects who view a series of colored pictures sharing a common theme (e.g., boats or cats) are prone to "recognize" critical lure pictures that were not presented during the study phase. Subjects who view pictures of stereotypical scenes, such as a schoolteacher standing before a classroom, subsequently "recognize" objects that were not in the picture (e.g., a blackboard). False recognition of pictorial critical lures, however, appears to occur at a lower rate than false recognition for verbal critical lures.[22]

In some DRM experiments, subjects have provided *remember* responses for critical lures as often as for studied words, but in others they have not. Also, false memories are sometimes associated with less detail and endorsed with less confidence than are true memories.[23] Nevertheless, they are falsely recognized and recalled at very high rates. Using positron emission tomography methods, Daniel Schacter, Eric Reiman, and their colleagues (1996) detected greater activation in the left temporoparietal region of the brain, a region that processes auditory input, when subjects correctly recognized study words than when they falsely recognized critical lures. Measuring electrical activity of the brain, Monica Fabiani and her colleagues detected different brain responses when subjects falsely remembered critical lures than when they correctly remembered words that had appeared on the study list. The brains of the subjects could tell the difference, so to speak, between words that had been presented and those that had not, even though the subjects themselves could not distinguish between presented words and critical lures (Fabiani, Stadler, and Wessels 2000).

Cognitive psychologists have identified variables that either increase or decrease false memory effects in the DRM paradigm. False memories are increased by repeated retrieval attempts, by increases in the number of associated words on study lists, by increased emotional stress, and when study words are grouped by theme rather than intermixed with unrelated words. False memories are attenuated when subjects are unaware of the forthcoming memory test, when they are forewarned about the false memory phenomenon, when they see words rather than hear them during the study phase, and when each aurally presented study word is accompanied by a line drawing corresponding to its meaning. But the false memory effect is very robust; variables that attenuate it seldom abolish it.[24]

Psychologists have proposed several hypotheses to explain how false memories develop in the DRM paradigm. One possibility is that subjects may generate an implicit associative response while studying words that converge on a common theme (Underwood 1965). Someone who hears words like *bed*, *rest*, and *pillow* may think "sleep" while listening to these words, and therefore may misremember *sleep* as having appeared on the list itself.

Another possibility is that subjects may form a verbatim memory trace for each word and a generic memory trace for the gist of the study list (Brainerd and Reyna 1998). If, during the subsequent memory test, they rely on their generic memory trace, they are likely to misremember having encountered words that merely share the same theme as the words on the study list.

Yet another possibility is that subjects may fail to notice distinctive features of items on the study list (Schacter, Israel, and Racine 1999). Anything that renders individual study items especially distinctive will enhance their memorability, thereby reducing false memory effects by making the actual study list items very memorable. Conversely, anything that emphasizes shared gist among study items at the expense of their distinctiveness is likely to foster gist-based memory, thereby increasing false memory for critical lures. So, for example, pairing words with distinctive pictures reduces the false memory effect, and grouping many related words together during the study phase underscores shared gist, thereby increasing the false memory effect.

There is little doubt that interest in the formation of false memories in the laboratory has been heightened by the debates regarding false memories of childhood sexual abuse arising in the clinic (Bruce and Winograd 1998). Although cognitive psychologists have demonstrated how easily people develop false memories, it is important to emphasize that most studies have concerned false memories of having encountered a word during an earlier phase of the experiment. Accordingly, the psychologists Jennifer Freyd and David Gleaves (1996) have warned that this easy development of false memories of neutral critical lure words in laboratory experiments does not mean that people so readily develop entirely false autobiographical memories, especially for stressful experiences. Indeed, they have emphasized that we should be very cautious about extrapolating from false memory effects for words in the DRM paradigm to alleged false memories of sexual abuse.[25]

Creating False Autobiographical Memories

Misinformation effects found in experiments have often concerned minor details of witnessed scenes, exemplified by subjects' misremembering a jar of Maxwell House coffee as a jar of Folger's. Implanting a false detail about the brand of coffee seems a far cry from implanting an entirely false memory of an emotional episode in a subject's past. But research has shown that investigators can create false memories of whole episodes in unwitting subjects.

In fulfillment of an extra credit assignment in Loftus's cognitive psychology class, James Coan managed to implant such a memory of having been lost in a shopping mall in his 14-year-old brother, Chris. Although their mother confirmed that no such thing had ever happened to Chris, Chris "remembered" many details of his supposed experience.[26]

Following these informal observations, Loftus and Jacqueline Pickrell

(1995) sent 24 adult subjects a booklet describing four events that older relatives supposedly said had happened to the subjects in childhood. Three events had really happened, but the fourth (getting lost when 5 years old) had not. After returning their booklets, the subjects attempted to recall further details of the events during two interviews. Overall, they recalled 68 percent of the true events, and 6 subjects recalled the false event.

Ira Hyman and his colleagues extended this line of research, implanting false memories of stressful events in adult subjects (Hyman, Husband, and Billings 1995). In their first experiment, they asked 20 undergraduates to recall several experiences from childhood, including genuine ones whose descriptions were provided by parents and a false one (either being hospitalized overnight with a high fever and an apparent ear infection or having a clown attend their fifth birthday party). The interviewer provided a brief cue (such as "an eventful birthday party at age 5"), and the subject attempted to recall and describe the event. No subject recalled any false events during the first interview, but, after being instructed to think about the events during the intervening days, 4 of them recalled a false event during the second interview.

In their second experiment, Hyman's group had 51 college students attempt to recall several actual events, provided by their parents, and one false event (such as spilling a punchbowl during a wedding reception). The interviewer informed subjects that the goal was to make every effort to recollect details from these events during three subsequent interviews. The false events were said to have occurred at either age 2, 6, or 10. No subject recalled the false event during the first interview, but 9 did so during the second interview and 13 during the third.[27]

Some psychotherapists have used guided imagery to help patients recover presumably repressed memories of sexual abuse. Critics of this approach claim that imagery may foster false memories. This controversy inspired Hyman and Joel Pentland (1996) to test whether having subjects imagine events they could not recall would produce higher rates of false recollection than having them merely think about each unremembered event for one minute. Subjects in both groups recalled about 75 percent of the true events during the first interview, and their recall improved across the remaining two interviews; guided imagery did not enhance recall of true memories. The number of false memories also increased over the course of the interviews, especially in the group that used guided imagery. By the end of the third interview, 37.5 percent of the subjects who had imagined the events and only 12.1 percent of the control subjects had created a false memory of spilling a punchbowl. These subjects were just as confident about their false memories as they were about their true memories. Hyman and Pentland concluded that guided imagery may foster false memories.

Hyman and James Billings (1998) asked college students to recall and describe 2–5 parent-provided events from their childhood, plus the false punchbowl event, in two interviews. Only 2 of the 66 subjects falsely recalled the punchbowl incident during the first interview, but 18 of them did so during the second interview. Hyman and Billings obtained data on individual differences for 48 of the 66 students. A questionnaire measuring dissociative symptoms significantly predicted scores on a scale indicating the clarity and completeness of the false memories ($r = .48$), but it did not predict the number of true events recalled ($r = .04$). A measure of hypnotizability also predicted false memory formation ($r = .36$) but not the number of true events recalled ($r = .05$).[28]

Kathy Pezdek and her associates tested whether false memory implantation varies as a function of the plausibility of the false events and subjects' background knowledge (Pezdek, Finger, and Hodge 1997). In their first experiment, they asked 29 Catholic and 22 Jewish high school girls to read accounts of five events (two of them false) that supposedly had happened to them when they were eight years old, and to recall and describe further details of each remembered event. One false event concerned a Jewish ritual (Shabbot) and the other concerned a Catholic one (Communion). Three of 22 Jews remembered the false Shabbot event, whereas none falsely remembered the Communion event. Ten of 29 Catholics remembered false events (seven Communion, one Shabbot, two both). Thus 34.5 percent of the Catholics and 13.6 percent of the Jews recalled at least one false memory. When subjects remembered a false specific event, it was overwhelmingly one for which they had preexisting general background knowledge.

In a second experiment, they had confederates read descriptions of three events to a younger adolescent sibling or close relative. Each concerned an event that happened when the subject was 5–6 years old. One event was true, whereas two were false (getting lost in a shopping mall; receiving an enema). Confederates read the events to the 20 subjects on two occasions separated by one week, asking whether they remembered each event, and, if so, to describe it. Two subjects falsely recalled being lost in a shopping mall during the first session, and another did so during the second session, but no subject falsely recalled receiving an enema. Taken together, these two studies indicate that false memory implantation is more likely to occur for plausible events for which individuals have a preexisting script.

But as Giuliana Mazzoni and her colleagues (2001) have shown in a series of experiments, suggestive procedures can increase an event's perceived plausibility. In one experiment, they asked Italian college students whether they had ever seen anyone become "possessed." Then they gave the students apparently authoritative written material stating that possession is more common than most people think. When queried again, 18 percent of the subjects who had initially denied ever witnessing someone become possessed claimed that they had seen such a phenomenon.

In another study, Mazzoni and her colleagues (1999) found that having a clinician interpret a research subject's dreams as indicative of a frightening early childhood experience (such as getting lost at age 3) increased the subject's confidence that such an event had actually happened. Spanos and his group (1999) gave college students supposedly authoritative information about how hypnosis enables people to recall even their earliest memories, then administered hypnotic age-regression procedures. Strikingly, 87 percent of these age-regressed subjects recovered memories from the day after their birth (such as vividly recalling a mobile hanging above their crib), and 49 percent of those "remembering" infancy considered their experiences to be memories, not fantasies. Subjects who scored low on hypnotizability were just as prone to false memory formation as were the highly hypnotizable subjects. That is, being given an authoritative rationale for why people are able to recall memories from infancy rendered even those with low hypnotic ability vulnerable to developing false memories of the day after birth.

Results like these led Mazzoni and her colleagues to suggest that people can develop false memories of unusual experiences if three steps occur. First, they are exposed to information that increases the perceived likelihood of the unusual event. Second, they acquire the suspicion that it happened to them. Third, they encounter a therapist or other authority figure who interprets their thoughts, dreams, and fantasies as memories of having experienced the implausible event (Mazzoni, Loftus, and Kirsch 2001).

The aforementioned studies show that an authority figure who provides convincing information about possession or recollection of memories of infancy can foster false memories of these unusual events. The authors of these studies suggested that their findings are relevant to claims about therapists unwittingly generating false memories of trauma in their patients. Some psychologists have questioned whether implanting false memories of getting lost as a child has any relevance for allegations that some therapists have unwittingly implanted false memories of abuse in their patients. Getting lost, spilling punchbowls, and the like are a far cry from being repeatedly molested as a youngster.

Ethical principles, of course, prohibit experimental implantation of traumatic memories. Researchers have, however, been able to implant false memories of unusual, emotionally intense events. Over the course of three sessions, Stephen Porter and his colleagues had college students use guided imagery and repeated retrieval attempts to recall a memory of a childhood event that Porter knew they had not experienced. Eventually 25 percent of subjects recalled a complete memory of the event, and an additional 30 percent recalled a partial memory of it. Rates of false memory implantation were 16.7 percent for getting lost, 31.2 percent for being seriously harmed by another child, 25 percent for a serious medical procedure, 36.8 percent for a serious animal attack, and 33.3 percent for a serious outdoor accident. (Immediately after the experiment, the researchers informed the subjects that the memories were false and that such false memories occur to many people. No subject was distressed by the experiment, and most found it interesting.) These data indicate that false memories of unusual, emotionally negative events can be implanted in a nontrivial minority of presumably mentally healthy subjects (Porter, Yuille, and Lehman 1999).

Psychologists have conclusively demonstrated that our memories are fallible records of what we experience. To what extent are these conclusions relevant to the question of whether people develop false memories of sexual abuse or other traumatic events? Objections to laboratory demonstrations of the misinformation effect as irrelevant to the real world of psychotherapy have much less force today than they originally did. Scientists have responded to these objections by demonstrating that it is possible to implant false memories of diverse experiences ranging from getting lost as a small child to witnessing someone being possessed by spirits. Some psychotherapists continue to question the relevance of these studies, claiming that implanting false memories of getting lost as a child is a far cry from inculcating false memories of, say, satanic ritual abuse. In response to this objection, psychologists have shown that it is possible to implant false memories of frightening events such as being bitten by a dog. However, there are obvious ethical limits to what researchers can do to test the kinds of false memories one can implant. Ironically, the most impressive demonstrations of the creation of false memories have arisen in clinical settings (see Chapter 8), not in the laboratory.

This brief survey of research on memory provides a backdrop against which claims about the special status of traumatic memories can be evaluated. Several points warrant emphasis. First, memory can be expressed in behavior as well as in thought. Although recalling facts about the world and experiences from one's life remains the core of memory, skilled behavior, conditioned emotional responses, and other effects of experience also fall under the rubric of memory. Second, autobiographical memory is reconstructive; it does not operate like a video recorder. Recollection entails reassembly of encoded elements of experience that are distributed throughout the brain. Third, developmental changes in childhood make it very difficult to remember most of our earliest experiences. The inability to remember much that happened before we were 3 or 4 years old is normal, not indicative of trauma or repression. Fourth, intense emotion enhances memory for the central aspects of stressful experiences, sometimes at the expense of peripheral details. Activation of the amygdala enhances the ability of the hippocampus to establish long- lasting memories of emotionally arousing positive as well as negative experiences. From an evolutionary perspective, this makes perfect sense. Conversely, it is difficult to imagine how a repression mechanism that undermines memory for significant events could have evolved. Finally, a significant minority of people can unwittingly come to believe they experienced stressful events that never happened.

3

WHAT IS PSYCHOLOGICAL TRAUMA?

WHAT MAKES A STRESSOR "traumatic"? How are traumatic stressors different from ordinary ones? Any attempt to understand how people remember "trauma" presupposes at least provisional answers to these questions and a working definition of what counts as a traumatic experience. As the psychologist Bonnie Green (1990) has pointed out, three variables may figure in how one defines trauma: an objectively defined event, the person's subjective interpretation of its meaning, and the person's emotional reaction to it. The definitional process is fraught with complexities.

During the Vietnam war, several hundred Americans, mostly pilots, were captured by the North Vietnamese. Despite rumors of maltreatment, Hanoi insisted that the prisoners of war (POWs) were being treated humanely in accordance with international law. Many American opponents of the war believed Hanoi, and suspected that the rumors had been manufactured by the U.S. government to mobilize support for continued military intervention. As it turned out, the rumors were true after all. When the POWs were released in April 1973, the public was horrified at their condition. They had been subjected to years of starvation, torture, and sometimes solitary confinement, and their diseases and injuries had been left untreated (Lewy 1978: 332–342). Physicians documented the injuries caused by torture designed to coerce the prisoners into signing antiwar statements. By any objective criteria, these events qualified as "traumatic." Yet few of these men suffered from posttraumatic stress disorder (Nice et al. 1996).

Some psychologists have emphasized the subjective interpretation of events as the key to explaining a person's emotional reaction to them.

Claudia Avina and William O'Donohue (2002) have argued that certain forms of sexual harassment in the workplace may qualify as traumatic stressors capable of producing PTSD. For example, they argue that a woman who frequently overhears sexual jokes at work may become so distressed that her job performance suffers, placing her at risk for being fired. Although Avina and O'Donohue acknowledge that losing one's job is not life-threatening, they maintain that it nevertheless may present a threat to the person's physical integrity, thereby counting as a traumatic stressor. Recognizing diverse forms of sexual harassment as PTSD-inducing stressors would make it possible for plaintiffs to sue their employers and win monetary compensation for their psychological injuries.

Given that psychologists have classified events ranging from years of starvation and torture to years of overhearing sexual jokes as stressors capable of producing PTSD, it is little wonder that controversy abides in this field. On the one hand, we might define as *traumatic* only those stressors associated with serious injury or threat to life. On the other hand, we might allow any stressor to count as traumatic if it terrifies the person or produces certain symptoms. Accordingly, *trauma* might be defined by the objective attributes of the stressor, by the subjective response of the victim, or by both. Combining the objective and subjective approaches, DSM-IV defines traumatic stressors as events involving "actual or threatened death or serious injury, or a threat to the physical integrity of self and others" that produce "intense fear, helplessness, or horror" (APA 1994: 427, 428). Unless a person has been exposed to a stressor meeting these criteria, a diagnosis of posttraumatic stress disorder (PTSD) cannot be made, regardless of how distressed the person happens to be. Therefore, someone suffering from nightmares, disturbing thoughts, and other PTSD-like symptoms cannot be diagnosed with the disorder unless these symptoms were triggered by an identifiable traumatic stressor. We cannot assume that symptoms in someone denying a history of trauma are attributable to traumatic experiences that have been dissociated from awareness, repressed, or otherwise forgotten.

THE DOSE-RESPONSE MODEL

It is not unreasonable to assume that the more traumatic a stressor is, the worse a victim's psychiatric symptoms will be. This idea is embodied in the *dose-response model* of trauma, which holds that symptoms worsen as the severity of the stressor increases. Many scientists interpret this model in terms of Pavlovian conditioning. They liken traumatic stressors to unconditioned stimuli that elicit the unconditioned response of fear and that establish neutral cues as conditioned stimuli that elicit the conditioned response of fear. For example, originally neutral stimuli associated with driving a car might become established as conditioned elicitors of fear for someone who has just survived a nearly fatal automobile accident. Accordingly, these scientists believe that a laboratory rat's response to inescapable electric shock illuminates the human response to overwhelming trauma. Just as increasing severity of shock worsens a laboratory rat's conditioned fear, so should increasing severity of trauma worsen a victim's PTSD symptoms.[1]

In fact, some studies do show that increasing doses of trauma predict greater severity of PTSD. World War II combat veterans who were tortured by the Japanese as POWs are far more likely to suffer from PTSD than their fellow veterans who were never captured and tortured. Combat veterans wounded in Vietnam are two to three times more likely to have PTSD than are those who returned unscathed. Proximity to the epicenter of the 1988 Armenian earthquake predicted severity of PTSD; extent of personal property damage predicted PTSD among those exposed to the Mount St. Helens volcanic eruption; and extent of injuries predicted PTSD among survivors of the Oklahoma City terrorist bombing.[2]

But as Marilyn Bowman's (1997, 1999) comprehensive reviews of the literature indicate, many studies refute the dose-response model. For example, the number of torture episodes suffered by imprisoned political activists in Turkey failed to predict the severity of their PTSD symptoms (Başoğlu et al. 1994), and seriousness of injury failed to predict PTSD symptom severity among accident survivors (Schnyder et al. 2001). There is no straightforward relationship between the severity of the trauma and the severity of PTSD.

Of course, these studies might indicate that the dose-response function is nonlinear (see Harvey and Yehuda 1999). If PTSD symptoms reached maximum severity after a certain "dosage" of exposure, further exposure to trauma would have no apparent additional impact on PTSD symptoms. Although a person tortured twice would be likely to have more symptoms than someone who had never been tortured, the person who had endured two torture episodes might be just as symptomatic as someone who had been tortured five, six, or seven times. Unfortunately, it would be difficult to disprove such a model because any pattern would be consistent with it (except, of course, a linear one).

Data inconsistent with a linear relationship between dose and response are not the only source of difficulty for the model; methodological and conceptual difficulties abound. For example, calibrating the magnitude of stressors is more complicated in trauma research than in animal conditioning experiments. Laboratory stressors are measured in purely physical terms (for example, shock amperage) entirely independent of the rat's behavior. But objective metrics for calibrating traumatic stressors are seldom available, and estimates of severity often depend on the retrospective reports of the victims themselves. That is, although the duration of exposure to trauma and the frequency of traumatic events qualify as objective metrics, their measurement usually rests on having victims try to remember, often many years later, how long a traumatic event lasted or how frequently such events occurred.

In a study exemplifying this problem, Vietnam veterans seeking treatment for PTSD completed a questionnaire asking them to indicate, on scales ranging from 1 ("never") to 5 ("very often"), how often they had been exposed to 20 kinds of combat experience. Not only did they have to estimate the frequency of long-ago events, they had to guess the meaning of ambiguous phrases on the questionnaire (such as "very often"). Seemingly confirming the dose-response model, the amount of self-reported exposure to combat predicted the severity of self-reported PTSD symptoms ($r = .50$; Friedman et al. 1986).

Yet the validity of this study, and many others like it, rests on the dubious practice of basing estimates of stressor severity solely on the retrospective reports of the victims. This approach presupposes that people can accurately and objectively recall their stressful experiences, unclouded by any psychiatric illness (such as depression or PTSD). Unfortunately, self-reports are often unreliable, especially when the traumatic events happened long ago.

The severity of current PTSD symptoms strongly affects the way survivors remember their traumatic experiences. The worse their current symptoms, the more severe they remember the trauma to have been. Six months after a fatal shooting at an elementary school in suburban Chicago, Eitan Schwarz, Jan Kowalski, and I asked school personnel to complete a questionnaire assessing their memory for this traumatic experience. We asked them to fill out the identical questionnaire again 18 months after the shooting. Strikingly, each subject remembered the event differently at 18 months than at 6 months. Severity of PTSD symptoms at 18 months predicted subjects' remembering the event as worse than they remembered it at 6 months. Those whose symptoms remained severe recalled the event as worse than they had before, whereas those who were doing much better at follow-up tended to remember the event as less harrowing than they had earlier (Schwarz, Kowalski, and McNally 1993).

Other investigators have replicated these findings. Liz Roemer and her colleagues (1998) asked 460 former peacekeepers who had just returned from Somalia to estimate how often they had received hostile fire, gone on dangerous missions, and so forth. When questioned again one to three years later, this group of veterans reported having experienced more trauma than they had originally reported. Severity of PTSD symptoms at follow-up predicted the magnitude of this memory inflation effect, implying that current clinical state distorts memory for stressors.

Steven Southwick and his colleagues asked veterans of the Gulf War to complete questionnaires concerning their exposure to war-related stressors one month and again two years after their return to the United States. Memory for traumatic events changed from first to second assessment for 88 percent of the veterans: 70 percent recalled a traumatic event at two years which they had not mentioned one month after the war; 46 percent mentioned a traumatic event at one month which they failed to mention at the two-year follow-up. Severity of PTSD symptoms at two years significantly predicted the number of traumatic events reported at two years that were not reported at one month. That is, veterans with the most PTSD symptoms, as Southwick and his colleagues observed, "tend to amplify their memory for traumatic events over time" (Southwick, Morgan, et al. 1997: 176). It is unlikely that the veterans were even aware of how their memories of trauma had changed.

Studying 2,942 Gulf War veterans, Daniel King and his colleagues (2000) also found that severity of PTSD symptoms predicted how subjects remembered their traumatic experiences. They assessed subjects within 5 days of their return from the Gulf and again 18 and 24 months later. An increase in recollected exposure to trauma from the first to the second recall was predicted by current severity of PTSD symptoms ($r = .26$).

Allison Harvey and Richard Bryant (2000) interviewed 56 accident survivors about their acute stress disorder symptoms one month and two years after the accident. During the second interview they asked whether subjects had experienced certain symptoms, and, if so, when the symptoms had emerged. These questions enabled them to test how well subjects remembered their symptoms, as originally reported. In the two-year follow-up interviews, only 25 percent accurately recalled the symptoms they had experienced one month after the accident. The subjects' clinical state strongly predicted the degree and direction of memory distortion. The more severe their PTSD at two-year follow-up, the more likely they were to "remember" symptoms that they had not reported during the interview one month after the accident ($r = .43$). Psychiatrically healthy survivors, in contrast, often forgot to mention symptoms that they had reported one month after the accident.

Studying memory for trauma among Dutch peacekeepers three and four years after their return from Cambodia, Inge Bramsen and her colleagues (2001) found that inconsistencies between the first and second assessments were not significantly related to PTSD symptoms at the second assessment. Although the authors interpreted these findings as a possible "reason for optimism" about the stability and validity of retrospective self-reports of trauma, this sanguine conclusion is unwarranted. The magnitude of the relation between PTSD symptoms and increase in remembered trauma from first to second assessment was very similar to that in Roemer's study. Because Roemer had more subjects than Bramsen, she had greater statistical power to detect significant effects.

Taken together, these studies raise a red flag about the validity of retrospective self-reports of traumatic events, at least as assessed by checklists and questionnaires. As the traumatic events recede in time, memory for them may be increasingly subject to distortion. People with chronic PTSD, seeking to make sense of their continued distress, may be especially prone to misremember traumatic events as having been worse than they originally experienced them to be. Conversely, people without the disorder may retrospectively minimize their traumatic experiences.

Animal conditioning models of PTSD require direct exposure to traumatizing stimuli. These models affirm a functional similarity between laboratory rats exposed to inescapable electric shocks and people exposed to life-threatening events. But as DSM-IV acknowledges, people do not have to be direct recipients of harm to develop PTSD. Unlike laboratory rats, they can develop PTSD vicariously by witnessing the traumatic misfortunes of others. In fact, in an epidemiologic survey conducted in the Detroit area, Naomi Breslau and her colleagues (1991) found that people who reported seeing someone else get killed or seriously injured were twice as likely to develop PTSD than those who were themselves in an accident or suddenly injured.

Other studies indicate that people do not have to witness the trauma suffered by others to develop PTSD. Studying veterans of the Gulf War, Patricia Sutker's research team (1994) discovered that 65 percent of the soldiers assigned to grave registration duty developed PTSD. These veterans were not directly exposed to danger; nor did they witness the deaths of others. But performing the gruesome task of collecting, tagging, and burying the scattered body parts of the dead was enough to trigger the disorder in these soldiers.

Merely hearing stories about trauma seems to precipitate PTSD in some people. In war-torn Lebanon in the 1980s, Philip Saigh (1991) diagnosed 230 children with PTSD and found that 13 of them had developed the disorder after learning that their friends and relatives had been tortured or killed.

The relation between dose of exposure and symptoms is far from straightforward. All things being equal, severe stressors are more likely than less severe ones to produce PTSD symptoms. But all things are rarely equal, and many studies have not confirmed the dose-response model of trauma. People who are already psychologically vulnerable may react more intensely than others to the "same" dose of trauma. Moreover, memories of traumatic events can be affected by the victim's current clinical state. Retrospective self-reports of trauma may inadvertently inflate the correlation between severity of stressors and current PTSD symptoms. If psychiatrically ill survivors remember stressors as worse than they were originally reported to be, this will exaggerate the strength of the dose-response relationship.

Guilt, Shame, and Trauma

The animal conditioning perspective that provides the theoretical basis for the dose-response model cannot easily accommodate cases of PTSD due to someone witnessing another person's trauma, let alone hearing about another person's trauma. Procrustean attempts to reinterpret these pathways as functional equivalents of inescapable shock strain credibility. But even if we broaden our definition of what counts as a conditioning event to include

DSM-IV stressors such as hearing about the murder of a loved one, another problem arises. The conditioning model implies that traumatic stressors precipitate PTSD by producing toxic levels of fear. Like the rat exposed to inescapable shock, the person is helplessly terror-stricken by an uncontrollable stressor. This picture is accurate, but incomplete. Terror is not the only toxic emotion triggering PTSD. Stressors can traumatize by inciting guilt and shame, not just fear.

Early reports on Vietnam veterans indicated that perpetrators of atrocities—deliberate harming and killing of noncombatants—can suffer posttraumatic symptoms, haunted by the memories of their misdeeds. Epidemiologic data from the National Vietnam Veterans Readjustment Study confirmed that involvement in atrocities strongly predicts PTSD (King et al. 1995). Even among veterans qualifying for a PTSD diagnosis, commission of atrocities (or at least having witnessed them) predicts severity of PTSD symptoms beyond that predicted by extent of combat exposure. Hence those who traumatize others can themselves fall prey to PTSD as a consequence of their actions. (Historians, however, have questioned the authenticity of some of these atrocity reports).[3]

Even socially approved killing of the enemy seldom comes easily to most combatants. Nearly 90 percent of the muskets retrieved from the Gettysburg battlefield had never been fired, and nearly half had been loaded twice, indicating that many soldiers had merely been pretending to fire at the enemy (Grossman 1995: 21–22).

The role of guilt and shame in PTSD is not confined to war. Imprisoned Turkish political activists forced to torture fellow prisoners have said that torturing others is worse than being tortured oneself. Even convicted murderers sometimes develop PTSD after killing a loved one. Also, shame predicts emergence of PTSD symptoms among survivors of attempted or completed sexual or physical assault.[4]

That guilt about having harmed others can produce PTSD underscores the moral complexity of trauma and the limitations of animal models of PTSD. Some scholars, such as the psychiatrist John March (1993), have attempted to accommodate these facts by interpreting the commission of atrocities as a high-magnitude stressor *for the perpetrator*. But this gambit reverses the roles of victim and perpetrator, obscuring important issues. For example, it obscures the fact that the Pavlovian conditioning model cannot explain PTSD developing in agents of trauma; it can only explain PTSD developing in recipients of trauma. Indeed, Roger Pitman, Bruce Altman, and their colleagues (1991) found that combat veterans, haunted by atrocities they had committed in Vietnam, responded poorly to a behavior therapy treatment (imaginal exposure) whose rationale is the reduction of conditioned fear.

Unlike fear, which can be experienced by rats, guilt and shame are complex emotions emergent only in animals possessing a sense of self. As Jerome Kagan (1998) has observed, it is impossible to "model" guilt in the animal conditioning laboratory without distorting the meaning of the concept beyond recognition. Only human beings, who can conceptualize themselves as objects worthy of praise or censure, can experience these emotions. In humans, moral threats often loom larger than mortal ones. Fear of letting one's fellow soldiers down by cowardly behavior during combat can overshadow fear of death (Grossman 1995: 52–53, 90). Soldiers have murdered civilians and POWs, fearing charges of cowardice should they fail to do so (Bourke 1999: 187). Pavlovian animal conditioning models promise to "reduce" trauma to its biological basis, but they risk obscuring the moral, uniquely human, dimension of trauma.

Committing atrocities can produce PTSD symptoms by inducing toxic levels of guilt and shame. Consider so-called judicial torture. During the Algerian war of independence in the 1950s, France authorized its colonial police and military to use torture to extract information from captured rebels. According to the historian Michael Ignatieff (2002), torture was first authorized only to compel Algerians to disclose plans for terrorist attacks against French settlers. But once the authorities stepped onto this slippery slope, torture became routine and widespread, brutalizing not only its obvious victims but also the perpetrators themselves. One spokesman for the Algerian cause, the French-trained Afro-Caribbean psychiatrist Frantz Fanon, provides a graphic example of how torture can destroy the torturer. Practicing in Algeria during the war, Fanon treated many victims of torture, but he also encountered torturers among his patients. One colonial police officer sought Fanon's psychiatric expertise to enable him to cope with his job—torturing Algerian suspects for up to 10 hours each day. The policeman suffered from nightmares, extreme irritability, and intolerance for noise. As Fanon said, "he asked me without beating about the bush to help him to go on torturing Algerian patriots without any prickings of conscience, without any behavior problems, and with complete equanimity" (1961: 269–270). Try as he might, this officer could never quite get used to inflicting extreme pain on his fellow human beings day after day.

However, acts of violence that are not interpreted as violating one's moral code will not produce PTSD regardless of how horrific they may seem to others. For example, the Greek psychologist Mika Haritos-Fatouros (1988) studied former torturers who served in elite military police units during the years of her country's military dictatorship (1967–1974). They had recently been released from prison after having been convicted of torturing suspected Communists during the military regime. None of these men felt any guilt about what they had done, but neither were any of them sadists—individuals who experience pleasure by inflicting pain. Instead, as Haritos-Fatouros discovered, each had volunteered for special training in these elite units. All of them had been tortured themselves as part of their police training, and all were ideologically committed to do whatever was necessary to extirpate Communism in their nation. In their view, torturing others was a noble, patriotic duty, not an atrocity.

A videotape that was discovered in Afghanistan among the belongings left behind by the fleeing Taliban provides another chilling example. The tape showed a dinner party hosted by a visiting Saudi cleric in honor of Osama bin Laden and Azman al-Zawahiri. At this gathering, bin Laden described, with great pride and pleasure, how he had masterminded the attacks on the World Trade Center that killed nearly 3,000 civilians. Although these atrocities have been widely condemned as nothing less than premeditated mass murder, bin Laden interprets them as entirely consistent with his moral code and religious beliefs. He is therefore unlikely to suffer from PTSD.

DOES TRAUMA CAUSE PTSD?

Traumatic stressors were once viewed as rare events likely to produce marked distress in almost anyone (APA 1987: 250). Destigmatizing victims, this view implied that PTSD might be a normal response to an abnormal stressor.[5] This assumption is no longer tenable. Epidemiologic studies indicate that large numbers of Americans have been exposed to stressors classified as traumatic in the DSM, such as physical assault, accident, or rape, but only a minority of them have developed PTSD. In the National Comorbidity Survey, Ronald Kessler and his colleagues (1995) found that 60.7 percent of a random sample of American adults reported exposure to DSM traumatic stressors. But among those trauma-exposed respondents, only 8.2 percent of the men and 20.4 percent of the women had ever developed PTSD. Naomi Breslau's research team found that 89.6 percent of Detroit-area adults had been exposed to traumatic stressors, but among these trauma-exposed individuals, only 6.2 percent of the men and 13 percent of the women had developed PTSD (Breslau et al. 1998). In contrast, Carol North and her colleagues (1999) reported that 34.3 percent of the survivors of the Oklahoma City terrorist bombing developed PTSD. The blast killed 46 percent of those in the building and injured 93 percent of the survivors. Only 7 percent of the blast survivors had no PTSD symptoms at all.

Reviewing recent epidemiologic studies, Rachel Yehuda (2002) emphasized that interpersonal violence tends to produce PTSD at higher rates than does other trauma. For example, PTSD developed in 55 percent of rape victims but in only 7.5 percent of accident victims and 2 percent of those who had learned about a trauma. The most frequent traumatic event was learning about the sudden, unexpected death of a loved one, which accounted for 27 percent of all cases of PTSD in women and 39 percent of all cases of PTSD in men. In a recent community study, Breslau and her colleagues found that men are more likely to be exposed to trauma than women, but that trauma-exposed women develop PTSD twice as often as do trauma-exposed men, mainly because exposure to assaultive violence produces PTSD in women at a much higher rate than it does in men (35.7 percent versus 6 percent; Breslau, Chilcoat, Kessler, Peterson, and Lucia 1999).

How did the terrorist attacks of September 11, 2001, affect the residents of New York City? Interviewing a random sample of Manhattan adults living south of 110th Street 5–8 weeks after the attacks, Sandro Galea and his colleagues (2002) found that 7.5 percent had developed PTSD in response to these events. Of those living south of Canal Street near the former site of the World Trade Center, 20 percent had PTSD. Therefore, Galea estimated, the attacks triggered approximately 67,000 new cases of PTSD south of 110th Street. However, in a follow-up survey completed in February 2002, Galea's group found that only 1.7 percent of New Yorkers still suffered from PTSD caused by the attacks (Galea et al., in press). The original rate of 7.5 percent occurring within weeks of September 11 may have reflected temporary distress rather than lasting disorder.

Moreover, when PTSD does develop in the wake of trauma, it is seldom the only disorder to emerge. High rates of *comorbidity*—multiple psychiatric disorders in the same person—are common (Yehuda and McFarlane 1995). For example, the National Vietnam Veterans Readjustment Study revealed that 98.9 percent of men who met criteria for PTSD also met criteria for at least one other psychiatric disorder during their lives, often depression and alcoholism (Kulka et al. 1990: 130). Moreover, historical sources link additional disorders to participation in combat. During the American Civil War, not only did traumatized soldiers suffer from PTSD-like symptoms, some also developed chronic psychosis. One of the most common psychiatric illnesses was called *nostalgia*, a kind of pathological homesickness. Soldiers diagnosed with nostalgia experienced loss of appetite, sadness, and an unremitting longing for home (Dean 1997: 115–160). Throughout history, traumatic stressors have not invariably produced syndromes similar to today's PTSD.

Traumatic stressors produce PTSD in only a minority of victims. This fact has prompted research designed to identify risk factors that may render some trauma-exposed people more vulnerable to the disorder than others.[6] Research on risk factors offends people who believe it entails blaming victims for their plight. This is especially true for certain findings, such as the finding that lower intelligence predicts PTSD symptoms among those exposed to trauma. Yet science cannot guarantee that the data will always conform to our wishes, politics, or ideological preferences. Sometimes it will, and sometimes it will not. Discovering risk factors is essential for understanding PTSD just as it is for understanding heart disease. The alternative is ignorance, and ignorance is an unreliable basis for treatment and prevention of any disorder, including PTSD.

Risk factors predict increased likelihood of developing a disorder. Some play a direct causal role, whereas others may merely be correlated with the true causes (McNally 2001b). When certain features are especially common among people with PTSD, one seldom can tell whether the feature preceded the emergence of the disorder—and thus may be a risk factor—or whether it is merely a consequence of having the disorder. Features correlated with a disorder need not be causes or risk factors for the disorder. Ideally, one would identify certain candidate risk factors prior to a person's exposure to traumatic stress, but studies meeting this criterion are scarce.

Risk Factors for Exposure to Trauma

The diagnosis of PTSD requires exposure to traumatic stressors. Accordingly, risk factors for exposure are indirectly risk factors for PTSD itself. Although some traumatic stressors, such as earthquakes, strike people at random, many others do not. For example, drunk drivers are at heightened risk for exposure to traumatic automobile accidents. Depending on the kind of stressor, some people are more likely than others to be traumatized. Conducting a prospective epidemiologic study in the Detroit area, Naomi Breslau's research team found that extroversion and neuroticism predicted later exposure to traumatic events (Breslau, Davis, and Andreski 1995). That is, outgoing, stress-prone people were exposed to trauma more often than retiring, calm people. They also found that black subjects were at greater risk for exposure to traumatic events than white subjects, and male subjects and those having less than a college education were at greater risk than female subjects and college graduates. In an earlier, retrospective study, Breslau's group found that people with a family history of psychiatric illness and a personal history of childhood conduct problems were those most likely to be exposed to trauma as adults (Breslau et al. 1991). Thus growing up with mentally ill family members and having been a juvenile delinquent are variables that increase the likelihood of getting in harm's way as an adult.

Cross-Sectional Studies

Researchers have often claimed to have identified risk factors for PTSD among people exposed to trauma. Unfortunately, most of their studies have been done on individuals who already have the disorder. This raises a serious interpretive problem: If a certain feature is present more often among those with PTSD than among trauma-exposed people without PTSD, how can we tell whether the feature is a genuine risk factor for the disorder or a consequence of the disorder? For example, combat veterans with PTSD report lower levels of social support than do those without the disorder.[7] It is impossible to interpret these results. Does a lack of social support impede recovery from the acute symptoms of traumatic stress? Or do these symptoms alienate friends and family, thereby cutting off sources of social support? Or are both processes operative?

But some features associated with PTSD are unlikely to be consequences of the illness, and therefore may well constitute risk factors for PTSD. Among these are lower intelligence, neuroticism, and neurological soft signs.[8] Neurological soft signs reflect subtle abnormalities in the central nervous system. These defects in language, perception, and motor coordination are nonspecific—it is impossible to locate precisely where in the nervous system they originate. Other features, although gleaned from patients' own retrospective reports, may have preceded the disorder and therefore may have been risk factors for PTSD. Among these are living in an unstable family during childhood, preexisting anxiety or mood disorder, and a history of anxiety or mood disorder in family members. Patients with PTSD related to trauma in adulthood have often mentioned having been sexually or physically abused during childhood.[9]

Prospective Studies

What is the best way to identify risk factors for PTSD? Ideally, researchers would obtain measurements on a large number of potential risk factors in individuals at risk for exposure to trauma (such as firefighters and soldiers). They would then follow these individuals over time to see what variables predicted the emergence of PTSD among those who were exposed to trauma. Unfortunately, such expensive prospective studies are seldom feasible. Instead, researchers have used two related approaches. In one approach, they have obtained archival data on people who have developed PTSD to see whether any preexisting variables predicted the disorder. In the other, they have investigated whether individuals' immediate reactions to a traumatic event predict their risk for developing PTSD.

Using the first approach, Roger Pitman's research team (Pitman, Orr et al. 1991) consulted predeployment military records and found that lower arithmetic aptitude, self-reported school problems, and lower heart rate distinguished Vietnam veterans who later developed combat-related PTSD from those who did not. Similarly, researchers have examined whether personality variables, measured prior to trauma exposure, predict subsequent PTSD symptoms. Paula Schnurr and her colleagues obtained collegiate Minnesota Multiphasic Personality Inventory (MMPI) scores of Dartmouth College graduates who later fought in Vietnam (Schnurr, Friedman, and Rosenberg 1993). After controlling for amount of combat exposure, they found that elevations on the scales measuring femininity, paranoia, hypochondriasis, and psychopathic deviance predicted PTSD symptoms. Inge Bramsen and her associates found that negativistic personality traits, measured predeployment, predicted PTSD symptoms among Dutch peacekeepers who served in the former Yugoslavia (Bramsen, Dirkzwager, and van der Ploeg 2000).

My colleagues and I, in a study headed by Michael Macklin (1998), used military archival data to obtain precombat intelligence test scores for men who had fought in Vietnam. The mean precombat IQ for those who later developed PTSD fell within the normal range (M = 106.3), whereas the mean precombat IQ for those who did not develop PTSD was clearly above average (M = 119.0). Lower precombat intelligence predicted current severity of PTSD symptoms, even after we controlled statistically for amount of combat exposure. Severity of PTSD was unrelated to differences between precombat and current intelligence, thereby indicating that lower precombat intelligence increases risk for PTSD, rather than PTSD lowering IQ scores. Above-average cognitive ability may increase a person's ability to cope with stressors, thereby reducing the likelihood of PTSD.

Others have reported similar findings. Raul Silva's research group (2000) found that IQ was the best predictor of resilience against PTSD among inner-city trauma-exposed children and adolescents. Among those with above-average intelligence, 67 percent had neither PTSD nor subthreshold PTSD, whereas among those with below-average intelligence only 20 percent were free of PTSD or PTSD symptoms.

Testing 901 young men prior to their induction into the Israeli military, Zeev Kaplan's group (2002) was able to study prospectively several risk factors for later PTSD resulting from either combat or accidents. Below-average intelligence, above-average social functioning, and low motivation to serve in the armed forces all predicted later PTSD. The strongest predictor was a culture-free measure of cognitive ability: the lower the score on this test, the more likely the soldier was to develop PTSD. When Kaplan controlled statistically for scores on the motivation-to-serve measure, the predictive power of lower intelligence disappeared. This statistical adjustment, however, is inappropriate. Because lower motivation to serve and lower intelligence were strongly correlated, statistically controlling for either variable "controls away" a real effect. This would be like someone statistically "controlling" for body weight and then claiming that percentage of body fat no longer predicts risk for heart disease.

If general intelligence reflects problem-solving ability, then it is little surprise that higher intelligence is related to diminished risk for PTSD. Certainly coping with the emotional aftermath of exposure to horrific events is a "problem to be solved."

The second approach, investigating whether immediate reactions to a traumatic event predict risk for developing PTSD, is not truly prospective because measures are taken after people have been exposed to traumatic events. However, such studies are prospective in the sense that measures are taken prior to the emergence of PTSD. Some studies have suggested that *peritraumatic dissociation*—dissociative responses occurring during the trauma itself, assessed by self-report immediately thereafter—predicts subsequent PTSD. For example, during the traumatic event a person might experience the sense of time slowing down or the feeling that everything is unreal. Peritraumatic time distortion and derealization predicted who developed PTSD among Israeli citizens exposed to traumatic accidents, and peritraumatic time distortion and a sense of bodily distortion predicted PTSD among French citizens exposed to violent crimes. Peritraumatic emotional numbing, depersonalization, motor restlessness, and a sense of reliving the trauma reported shortly after the event predicted subsequent PTSD among survivors of automobile accidents in Australia. The occurrence of peritraumatic dissociative symptoms—a sense of time slowing down or speeding up being the most common—increased the risk of PTSD by nearly a factor of five among American survivors of motor vehicle accidents.[10]

Shalev and his colleagues (1998) reported that elevated heart rate among civilian trauma survivors assessed in the emergency room was associated with the subsequent development of PTSD. Interpreting this finding within a Pavlovian conditioning model, they suggested that the intensity of the unconditioned (emotional) response to the event, not the unconditioned stimulus (objective severity of the event), might best predict later PTSD. Yet Edward Blanchard and his colleagues obtained precisely the opposite results. They found that survivors of motor vehicle accidents with lower emergency room heart rates were more likely to develop PTSD than those whose heart rates were higher (Blanchard, Hickling, Galovski, and Veazey, 2002). Clearly, this issue warrants further research.

Genetics

Differences among people on measures of psychopathology are often attributed to differences among their environments, especially their childhood ones. If a battered child, reared by impulsive, violent, and alcoholic parents, develops psychiatric problems, social scientists often assume he has developed these problems because of the way he was treated by his parents.

But this assumption may be unwarranted. Psychological problems exhibited by a child reared by disturbed parents may be attributable to genes shared by the child and his parents, not to adverse social environmental influences such as abusive parenting. Under ordinary circumstances it is difficult to disentangle shared genetic influences from environmental ones. For example, physically abused children sometimes grow up to be abusers themselves, but one cannot unambiguously attribute their violent behavior as adults to the violence they suffered as children. Inheritance of genes predisposing toward violence may be the key to explaining the transgenerational transmission of violent tendencies. In contrast, if foster children reared by violent parents become abusers, a genetic explanation does not apply because the children have not inherited any genes from their foster parents.[11]

Almost all research on risk factors for PTSD fails to disentangle genes from environment. For example, Michael Nash and his colleagues (1993) found that the connection between a history of childhood sexual abuse and adult psychopathology disappeared once they controlled statistically for perceived family environment. They warned psychologists not to attribute causal influence solely to sexual abuse when other aberrant family processes may explain the connection to adult problems. Unfortunately, Nash was unable to rule out the alternative genetic hypothesis: the connection between perceived family environment and adult pathology may have been mediated entirely by genes shared by his subjects and their parents. It may have nothing directly to do with aberrant interactions among family members.

Two research groups, however, have clarified the relative influence of genetic and environmental factors on the emergence of psychopathology among people exposed to trauma. Kenneth Kendler and his associates (2000) conducted an epidemiologic study of female twins to determine genetic and nongenetic influences on whether women exposed to childhood sexual abuse develop psychopathology. Among more than 1,400 adult twins assessed, 30.4 percent reported some form of childhood sexual abuse, ranging from being invited to engage in sexual activity or being hugged in a sexual way to being forced to have intercourse. Forced sexual intercourse was reported by 8.4 percent of the subjects.

Risk for psychiatric disorders increased as a function of severity of abuse; forced sexual intercourse was the strongest predictor of a range of subsequent disorders including major depression, bulimia, panic disorder, drug dependence, alcohol dependence, and generalized anxiety disorder. PTSD and dissociative disorders were not assessed. Shared family environment, often chaotic, was an implausible explanation for the connection between abuse and psychopathology: the risk for psychopathology was much greater in the twin who had been sexually abused than in the twin who had not been sexually abused, even though both had been reared in the same family. Hence growing up in a chaotic environment did not increase risk for subsequent psychopathology as much as having been sexually abused. Moreover, the abuse-psychopathology connection diminished only slightly when Kendler controlled statistically for psychopathology in the parents. This implies that genetic factors shared by parents and children could not explain the harmful effects of childhood sexual abuse. Finally, abuse was associated with increased risk for a wide range of disorders. The twins of the abused subjects often confirmed that the abuse had occurred.[12]

As Kendler and his colleagues observed, their findings were inconsistent with some previous studies, such as those meta-analyzed by Bruce Rind and his associates (Rind, Tromovitch, and Bauserman 1998). Kendler studied the connection between sexual abuse and *lifetime* prevalence of psychiatric disorders, whereas other researchers have often studied the connection between sexual abuse and *current* levels of distress. Sexually abused people may experience psychiatric disorders but then recover from them by the time they participate in research studies. If so, then a sole focus on current symptoms will underestimate the harmful effects of abuse.

Researchers have estimated the relative impact of genes and environment on PTSD symptoms by studying monozygotic (MZ) and dizygotic (DZ) twin pairs who were in the military during the Vietnam war era. MZ (identical) twins share 100 percent of their genes, whereas DZ (fraternal) twins share 50 percent of their genes, on average. By studying twins, researchers can arrive at estimates about the relative impact of genetic variance and environmental variance on differences among veterans in their severity of PTSD symptoms. Although the estimates are based on twins, it is usually safe to generalize the results to others.

Genetic variance refers to differences among people in their genetic make-up. Environmental variance refers to differences among people in their environments. Some sources of environmental variance are shared by children reared in the same family, such as family income, neighborhood, and parental rearing practices. Other sources of environmental variance are not shared by family members. For example, one child may have been severely injured in a car accident, whereas his siblings were not.

Researchers have found that 47 percent of the variation in exposure to combat is associated with genetic variance. Genetic differences in certain personality traits, such as sensation-seeking, may increase the likelihood that certain individuals will volunteer for dangerous duty. Therefore, genetic differences among veterans may indirectly affect differences in the kinds of environments to which they are exposed. Genetic differences among people may influence their relative likelihood of getting in harm's way.

After controlling statistically for differences in combat exposure, William True and Michael Lyons (1999) found that genes accounted for 13–30 percent of the variation in reexperiencing symptoms, 30–34 percent of the variation in avoidance symptoms, and 28–32 percent of the variation in arousal symptoms. They found no evidence that shared environment influenced variation in PTSD symptoms. That is, differences in socioeconomic class, schooling, and so forth did not contribute to differences in risk for PTSD: most of the variation in PTSD symptoms was attributable neither to shared childhood rearing conditions nor to genes, but rather to other environmental factors, such as combat in Vietnam. Thus genetic factors influence whether a person is exposed to traumatic stressors, and they also influence, to a modest extent, whether someone will develop PTSD symptoms following exposure.

Subjective Interpretation

Research on risk factors has provided clues as to why people react so differently to similar stressors. The final proximal cause of PTSD may be the way the person interprets the meaning of the stressor. Ultimately, the psychological interpretation of the event may be the crucial determinant of whether it produces PTSD.

Psychologists have long debated about how to define "stress." According to one view, expressed by Bruce Dohrenwend and Patrick Shrout, researchers should "measure pure environmental events, uncontaminated by perceptions, appraisals, and reactions" (1985: 782). That is, the event itself should be defined and measured independently of the person's reaction or interpretation of it. According to the other view, expressed by Richard Lazarus and his associates (1985), it is impossible to isolate "pure" psychological stressors; interpretation invariably mediates the impact of environmental events. As applied to PTSD, this view implies that traumatic stressors cannot be identified solely by their objective, physical properties. Indeed, subjective measures of distress or perceived threat predict PTSD symptoms better than do objective measures of danger among combat veterans, torture survivors, burn victims, and accident survivors.[13]

Some people develop PTSD following exposure to noncatastrophic, non-life-threatening stressors, underscoring the importance of subjective appraisal of threat. People have developed the disorder after experiencing panic attacks, discovering spousal infidelity, getting divorced, having a miscarriage, and giving birth. Others have developed PTSD symptoms after seeing the movie *The Exorcist*, and after accidentally killing a group of frogs with a lawnmower.[14]

The emergence of PTSD after exposure to such stressful but noncatastrophic events poses theoretical problems. Subsuming noncatastrophic events under the traumatic stressor rubric produces a kind of conceptual bracket creep whereby increasingly trivial events are awarded causal significance as triggering PTSD. If full-blown PTSD does emerge in the wake of these stressors, then this seems to point to personal vulnerability factors as the causal culprit, not to the event itself. In fact, some theorists believe that the less severe the event, the more important the role of personal vulnerability or risk factors among those who develop PTSD. Conversely, if the trauma is truly catastrophic, then most people will become symptomatic irrespective of personal risk or protective factors. For example, World War II data indicated that 60 days of continuous combat caused psychiatric breakdown in 98 percent of fighting men (Grossman 1995: 43–45). Doctors concluded that every soldier had his breaking point, and that relentless exposure to extreme danger eventually overwhelmed nearly everyone, regardless of personal qualities.

Conceptual bracket creep may partly explain why rates of PTSD have been so low in epidemiologic studies that have reported extremely high rates of traumatic stressors in the population. If what counts as a traumatic stressor is broadened, it is little surprise that rates of PTSD are low relative to rates of trauma exposure. To rectify these matters, the psychiatric epidemiologist Bruce Dohrenwend (2000) has advised that truly traumatic stressors must be distinguished from ordinary stressors if we wish to detect connections between stress and psychopathology. According to Dohrenwend, negative life events are traumatic when they are unpredictable, uncontrollable, life-threatening, physically exhausting, extremely disruptive of the person's usual activities, and extremely disruptive to central life goals. (He has also argued that personal vulnerability becomes increasingly implicated as the objective magnitude of the stressors lessens.)

The aforementioned cases—panic attacks, *The Exorcist*, and so on—are surprising because people developed PTSD following relatively ordinary stressors. Other cases are surprising because PTSD does *not* develop despite exposure to extraordinary trauma. Seemingly confirming Friedrich Nietzsche's maxim (1888: 467)—"*Out of life's school of war:* What does not destroy me, makes me stronger"—some survivors are strengthened by their ordeals. Veterans have emphasized the psychological benefits of mastering stressors in Vietnam (Schnurr, Rosenberg, and Friedman 1993). Among air force pilots shot down, captured, and tortured for years by the North Vietnamese, 61.1 percent said they had benefited from their brutal experiences. They stressed that captivity had produced favorable changes in their personalities, bolstering their self-confidence and teaching them to value what is important in life. Moreover, the subjective sense of personal growth was correlated with severity of their treatment by the North Vietnamese (Sledge, Boydstun, and Rabe 1980).

Stephen Nice and his colleagues (1996) conducted annual psychiatric and general medical assessments of former U.S. Navy aviators who were tortured as POWs by the North Vietnamese. Only 3 of the 70 former POWs had ever developed PTSD. Nice suggested that the extremely low rate of PTSD might be attributable to the POWs' older ages at enlistment, their higher educational levels, and the special training they had received to prepare them for possible capture.

These findings have been replicated by Metin Başoğlu and his colleagues (1997), who found that left-wing political activists tortured during Turkey's military regime had lower rates of PTSD than tortured nonactivists who had been mistaken for activists or who had been charged with nonpolitical crimes. The activists scored higher than the nonactivists on a scale of psychological preparedness for arrest and torture, leading Başoğlu to conclude that ideological commitment to political struggle and psychological stoicism buffered the activists against the pathogenic effects of torture.

Extensive military training, patriotism, and ideological commitment are not the only buffering factors that reduce the traumatic impact of torture. Religion seems to help, too. Assessing Bhutanese torture survivors in refugee camps in Nepal, Nirakar Shrestha's research team (1998) found that only 14 percent of them developed PTSD. These predominantly Hindu individuals interpreted their misfortunes as resulting from bad Karma accumulated by misdeeds they assumed they must have performed in previous lives. They coped by engaging in religious rituals to appease the gods.

According to DSM-IV, witnessing another person being killed qualifies as a traumatic stressor. Yet throughout history attendance at executions has often been a form of family entertainment, and legal efforts are under way to permit family members of murder victims to witness the convicted murderer's execution, supposedly to gain "psychological closure" (Domino and Boccaccini 2000). Some police officers who had identified dead bodies following a disaster reported positive benefits from this gruesome work (such as pride in doing their duty well; Alexander and Wells 1991). Taken together, these findings highlight the importance of a person's subjective appraisal of an event for determining whether the event will function as a traumatic stressor.

The most controversial case of appraisal determining a stressor's impact is that of female genital surgeries in Africa. Approximately 80–200 million African women have undergone traditional coming-of-age ceremonies involving surgical alteration of their genitalia. Procedures range from slicing the prepuce covering the clitoris to amputating all visible parts of the clitoris and the labia. Done "naturally" without anesthesia, the procedure is very painful. Nothing, it may seem, would constitute a better example of physical and sexual abuse of girls than the socially approved carving up of their genitalia (Shweder 2000).

The practice has incited widespread protest among feminists and human rights activists throughout the West who view it as a form of institutionalized child abuse. Patricia Schroeder wrote while she was a member of the U.S. Congress, "Female genital mutilation is an action that always endangers the child. Genital mutilation irreparably cripples a girl's sexuality and produces long-term health risks" (1994: 740).

But as Carla Obermeyer's (1999) comprehensive epidemiologic review has shown, genital surgeries do not impair sexual pleasure and rarely result in medical complications. Moreover, anthropological studies have revealed that the practice is conducted and supported entirely by women themselves. Girls eagerly anticipate this coming-of-age ceremony as a test of their courage and as confirmation of their entrance into womanhood. And as the anthropologist Richard Shweder observed, they believe that "genital alterations improve their bodies and make them more beautiful, more feminine, more civilized, more honorable." Unsurprisingly, he noted, they regard "unmodified genitals as ugly, unrefined, and undignified, and hence not fully human," often expressing pity for female anthropologists who have not undergone the procedure (2000: 218, 219). Hence an event that would unquestionably qualify as a serious traumatic stressor in the Western world is valued as a personal milestone in the lives of female adolescents. Needless to say, its African advocates regard criticism of the practice as another instance of Western cultural imperialism.

Just as genital surgeries incite horror among Westerners, activities valued by Westerners can be traumatic for non-Westerners. For example, one common method of torture in Bhutan is to force Hindu captives to eat beef or pork. Eating pork is taboo for Hindus, especially those of high caste, and therefore is traumatic (Shrestha et al. 1998).

Finally, not only does interpretation of the stressor itself influence its impact, interpretation of the meaning of the stressor-produced symptoms may affect whether someone subsequently develops PTSD. As Anke Ehlers, David Clark, and their associates have found, if trauma survivors interpret nightmares or other common stress reactions as signs of personal weakness, impending psychosis, and so forth, they may be at greater risk for developing PTSD. For example, consider a survivor who mistakenly believes that intrusive thoughts are a sign of impending psychosis. This person may attempt to suppress such thoughts. But attempts to suppress unwanted thoughts often backfire, producing an increase in the frequency of their occurrence. An increase in frequency will increase fears of impending psychosis even more, in a vicious circle.[15]

INFERRING TRAUMA FROM SIGNS AND SYMPTOMS

Some people do not develop PTSD even after being exposed to the most horrific stressors. Others develop these symptoms following exposure to seemingly minor stressors. Still others report PTSD-like symptoms but deny ever having been exposed to traumatic stressors. This third category of patient has been the source of much controversy. As John Briere and Jon Conte observed, many clinicians have encountered patients "whose clinical presentations are highly suggestive of a sexual abuse history, but who do not recall having been molested." Accordingly, they concluded, "it is likely that some significant proportion of psychotherapy clients who deny a history of childhood sexual victimization are, nevertheless, suffering from sexual abuse trauma" (1993: 22, 26).

To aid identification of patients suffering the effects of dissociated, repressed, or denied memories of abuse, therapists have drawn up lists of possible indicators of an abuse history. As possible indicators of repressed memories of incest, E. Sue Blume (1990: xviii–xxi) lists psychiatric syndromes (for example, eating disorders, phobias, substance abuse, depression, multiple personality, obsessive-compulsive behavior), emotions (guilt, shame, constant anger), and miscellaneous features (wearing baggy clothes, avoidance of mirrors, nightmares, inability to remember periods of one's childhood, humorlessness or extreme solemnity, feeling different, stealing, instinctively knowing the needs of others, being very appreciative of small favors). Listed as additional consequences of incest are either avoidance of sex or sexual promiscuity, trusting others too much or trusting others too little, risk taking or inability to take risks. Finally, denial of having been sexually abused is itself listed as an aftereffect of incest, as is repression of one's traumatic memories.

Catherine Gould (1992), a specialist in treating children for the effects of ritualistic abuse, listed no fewer than 106 possible symptomatic indicators of this kind of trauma. For example: fear of doctors; excessive fear of receiving injections; poor attention span; tantrums; acting fearful, clingy, and withdrawn; becoming excessively upset when told what to do by parents; speaking to an imaginary friend whom the child will not discuss; and frequent somatic complaints (such as stomachaches). The psychologist R. W. London compiled a list of more than 900 symptoms that trauma therapists had claimed indicate a history of abuse. He had culled these alleged indicators from books and advertisements for clinical services (London cited in Freyd 1999).

Many trauma specialists have reported a link between dissociative symptoms and a history of trauma.[16] Bessel van der Kolk and William Kadish even went so far as to say that "except when related to brain injury, dissociation always seems to be a response to traumatic life events" (1987: 185). But as the clinical and cognitive psychologist John Kihlstrom (1997b) has pointed out, these inferences are unwarranted because van der Kolk and others have failed to appreciate that a 2 × 2 matrix (trauma-exposed versus not exposed, and dissociative symptoms present versus dissociative symptoms absent) is vital for understanding the link between exposure to trauma and dissociative symptoms. We cannot assume that trauma causes dissociation without examining how often trauma exposure occurs in the absence of dissociative symptoms, and how often a history of trauma is absent among those reporting dissociative symptoms.

The child abuse experts Jan Bays and David Chadwick (1993), however, noted that there are several circumstances in which one can conclude that a child or adolescent has been victimized (for example, pregnancy, HIV infection not acquired perinatally, fresh genital or anal injuries in the absence of plausible accidental explanation, positive culture test for syphilis or gonorrhea that has not been perinatally acquired). They cited other physical findings potentially consistent with a history of sexual abuse. And they emphasized the risk of false negatives: many, perhaps most, instances of abuse are not accompanied by medical signs of molestation, especially when time has elapsed since the abuse. Likewise, the clinical psychologist Kenneth Pope (1998) suggested that there are certain circumstances in which one is justified in suspecting an unreported history of abuse, such as detection of a sexually transmissible pathogen in a young child. Would not this permit one to reason backward from the indicator to a history of abuse?

At first glance, the answer would seem to be yes. But even here the issues are more complex than they first appear to be (Alexander 1988). Routine laboratory tests for venereal disease, such as antigen detection procedures, present a serious risk of false positives when the base rate in the relevant population is less than 10 percent, as it is among young children (Hammerschlag, Rettig, and Shields 1988). Although the reliability and validity of these tests are satisfactory in a sexually active adult population, this does not hold for tests on children. For example, allegations of sexual abuse arose when laboratory tests indicated the presence of *Chlamydia trachomatis* in one group of 5 children and *Neisseria gonorrhoeae* in another group of 14 children.[17] Tests done on culture, however, revealed each of these cases as false positives. Accordingly, medical scientists recommend that multiple independent tests, including assessment of culture, are necessary to distinguish sexually transmitted diseases from similar bacterial strains that commonly inhabit the bodies of children.

When considering whether a symptom indicates a history of abuse, one must not only be concerned with how accurately the symptom indicates such a history. One must also take into consideration the frequency of abuse in the general population (its base rate). A test can be very accurate yet produce many incorrect results, as illustrated by HIV tests. The screening test for HIV is extraordinarily accurate; its *sensitivity* is 98.0 percent and its *specificity* is 99.8 percent. That is, 98.0 percent of HIV-infected individuals will test positive for HIV, and 99.8 percent of those without HIV infection will test negative for HIV. However, a person drawn at random from the general population who tests positive for HIV is very unlikely to be infected, despite the impressive accuracy of the test. The reason lies in the low base rate of HIV infection in the general population: 0.035 percent. That is, despite the impressive accuracy of the test, the low base rate of HIV infection in the general population means that a positive HIV test will almost always be wrong. The value of any proposed indicator of HIV, hidden abuse, and so forth relies on its sensitivity, its specificity, *and* the prevalence of the condition in the relevant population.[18]

Throughout the 1980s and 1990s many psychotherapists believed that "laundry lists" of diverse symptoms indicated possible hidden memories of childhood sexual abuse. As the flaw in this line of reasoning has become increasingly publicized, some prominent clinicians have revised their views. For example, in a talk delivered at the Twelfth International Congress on Child Abuse and Neglect, John Briere stressed that if patients "say they weren't abused, then they probably weren't" (quoted in Russell 1999: xxxiii). Briere's current view explicitly repudiates Ellen Bass and Laura Davis's well-known maxim: "If you think you were abused and your life shows the symptoms, then you were" (1988: 22). A recent president of the International Society for Traumatic Stress Studies, Briere is among the world's most influential clinical experts on trauma. When psychotherapists like Briere issue warnings about the fallacies of inferring abuse histories in those without memories of abuse, there is reason to hope that many therapists will listen and alter their views and practices accordingly.

Clinical research on what constitutes trauma suggests several conclusions. There is no simple relationship between the "dose" of trauma and resultant symptoms, and measuring the dose of trauma is fraught with difficulties. Most researchers have relied on the retrospective self-reports of patients themselves to provide a basis for calibrating trauma exposure. But retrospective appraisal of exposure to stressors appears to be distorted by the person's current clinical state. The vast majority of people exposed to serious traumatic events do not develop PTSD. Risk factors strongly affect whether the almost universal acute stress symptoms subside or whether they develop into chronic PTSD. Attempts to ground a definition of psychic trauma in animal conditioning models capture the fear aspect of trauma, but fail to capture its moral complexity as exemplified by the traumatic potential of shame and guilt.

4

MEMORY FOR TRAUMA

FOR PEOPLE WITH posttraumatic stress disorder, remembering trauma feels like reliving it. Traumatic events from the past are recalled with such vividness and emotional intensity that it seems as if the trauma were happening all over again. Most people are troubled by disturbing memories in the days and weeks following a terrible trauma. These problems do not suggest possible psychopathology unless they persist for more than one month.

Clinicians who study posttraumatic stress disorder (PTSD) have identified several ways that people reexperience trauma in memory: intrusive recollections, nightmares, flashbacks, and psychophysiologic reactivity to reminders of the event. *Intrusive recollections* are disturbing thoughts and images of the event that come to mind even when the person does not want to think about it. These recollections can be very disruptive in everyday life. Children who had resettled in the United States after surviving the horrors of Pol Pot's regime in Cambodia often had difficulty paying attention in school. While trying to listen to the teacher, they were disturbed by images suddenly coming to mind of the killings they witnessed in their homeland. Likewise, New York City firefighters have mentioned being haunted by vivid, horrific images of people leaping from the burning twin towers of the World Trade Center following the terrorist attacks.

Memories of trauma can recur in *nightmares*, plaguing survivors while they sleep. One Vietnam veteran, who had survived the siege of Khe Sanh, described repetitive dreams of emerging from his bunker and seeing the rotting corpses of the enemy scattered everywhere. In a gruesome departure from what had actually happened, the bodies of the enemy came to life and began to stalk him. At this point he would awaken. Similarly a young girl who had been raped described repetitive nightmares of a dark figure coming upstairs to her bedroom.

Sometimes intrusive recollections are so vivid that it seems as if the trauma is actually happening again. In these *flashbacks*, the person may see, hear, smell, or feel the original sensations while remembering the trauma. One survivor of the August 1999 Turkish earthquake described smelling decaying corpses even though the bodies had been retrieved from the rubble and buried. She knew there were no dead people present, but physical reminders of the devastation provoked this sensory memory. For another survivor, large trucks rumbling down the street provoked sensory memories of how the earth had shaken during the earthquake.

Psychophysiologic reactivity refers to the fact that survivors often react physically as well as psychologically when confronted with reminders of the trauma. That is, while feeling fear, they may sweat, tremble, and experience their heart pounding. One former Marine, who had nearly been sliced in half by enemy machine-gun fire in Vietnam, reported that the sound of a car backfiring always sent him ducking for cover. Not only did the backfire incite intense fear, but it made his heart pound violently and his body shake all over. Like many other Turkish earthquake survivors, a man who was buried alive when his apartment building collapsed still prefers to sleep outside in a tent; being indoors at night provokes too much fear to allow him to sleep.

Almost everything known about these reexperiencing symptoms is based on retrospective reports of trauma survivors. Seldom have researchers studied the phenomena prospectively, such as by asking survivors to record traumatic nightmares in dream diaries upon awakening. This is unfortunate. Asking people to estimate the frequency and the severity of symptoms occurring over the past several weeks, months, or years may require much guessing. By relying on memory, some survivors may underestimate the frequency and intensity of their symptoms, whereas others may overestimate them. With this constraint in mind, I turn to what has been learned about how people remember traumatic events.

INTRUSIVE RECOLLECTIONS

Intrusive, distressing recollection—involuntary thoughts about the trauma—is the most common reexperiencing symptom. Interview studies have revealed high rates among survivors of World War II Japanese POW camps (83 percent), combat veterans of the Pacific Theater in World War II (66 percent), tortured political activists in Turkey (40 percent), Cambodian survivors of Pol Pot's regime (75 percent), and assault victims (61 percent).[1] To study the course of intrusive recollection over time, researchers have merely interviewed survivors on more than one occasion; they have not had them track and record intrusive thoughts soon after they occur. In fact, the cognitive psychologist Dorthe Berntsen (1996, 1998) is the only person to have collected prospective data concerning this topic. She asked college students to record involuntary memories in structured diaries. Strikingly, she found that the students' involuntary memories usually concern recent, emotionally positive events, such as the start of a new love affair. Hence there is no special relationship between the intrusive or involuntary character of an autobiographical memory and its relevance to trauma. Involuntary traumatic memories may constitute only a small subset of the memories that intrude into consciousness in everyday life.

In her most recent research, Berntsen had 12 Danish college students, all of whom qualified for a diagnosis of PTSD, record their first involuntary memories each day until a total of 50 involuntary memories had been logged. Of the 600 total memories recorded prospectively by these students, only 31 (5.2 percent) directly concerned the traumatic event, and 11 of these qualified as flashbacks because of their extreme vividness, their effect on the subject's mood, and the physical reactions that accompanied them. Memories of traumatic events that had occurred more than five years ago were just as vivid as those occurring within the past year. Whereas only 5.2 percent of the involuntary memories directly concerned the trauma, 61 percent of them concerned either positive or neutral events; the others were thematically linked to the trauma. Strikingly, 61 of the students' flashbacks were nontraumatic, often of an intensely positive experience. As Berntsen said, "In short, flashback is not a trauma effect" (2001: S145). So even in people with PTSD, most involuntary memories are not recollections of the traumatic event and most flashbacks are not replays of the trauma.

If research on panic disorder provides any guide, retrospective reports probably inflate the frequency and severity of reexperiencing symptoms, thereby distorting our understanding of how people remember trauma. Prospective recording of panic attacks in structured diaries reveals that panics are often less severe than patients retrospectively remember them to be

(McNally 1994: 20–23). Similar self-monitoring studies on intrusive recollection are long overdue.

NIGHTMARES

Many people have terrifying dreams following stressful events, but their frequency fades with time. Persistent nightmares about trauma, however, are specific to PTSD. For example, the proportion of Vietnam veterans experiencing frequent nightmares is far higher in those with PTSD (52.4 percent) than in those without PTSD (4.8 percent), veterans who served during the Vietnam era but not in Vietnam (5.7 percent), or civilians (3.4 percent) (Neylan et al. 1998).[2]

Most dreams occur during a stage of sleep characterized by intermittent rapid eye movements (REM), large muscle paralysis, and brain wave activity similar to that of wakefulness. REM dreams are often vivid, emotional, and bizarre, whereas non-REM dreams are vague, fragmented, and more conceptual than visual (Ross et al. 1989; Foulkes 1962). Although most people have their nightmares during REM sleep, trauma survivors have them during non-REM sleep as well. Because the muscles are not paralyzed during non-REM sleep, non-REM nightmares can be accompanied by violent thrashing and attacks against bed partners.[3]

Despite their complaints about frequent nightmares, trauma survivors have seldom experienced them in sleep laboratory studies. Either the laboratory environment somehow suppresses their occurrence, or they are less common than the survivors believe.[4] In fact, as the sleep researcher Peretz Lavie (2001) has observed, PTSD patients seem to dream less than other people. Control subjects report dreams on 60–90 percent of the occasions when researchers awaken them during REM sleep, whereas PTSD patients report dreams on only 20–60 percent of the REM awakenings. Dreams are especially rare among Holocaust survivors, especially those who are well adjusted (Kaminer and Lavie 1991). In general, as Lavie has emphasized, objective findings have seldom corroborated complaints of lack of deep sleep, insomnia, and frequent nightmares in PTSD patients. Most patients are sleeping much better than they think they are.

Ordinary nightmares do not replicate the stressful events of everyday life. Yet many survivors claim that their nightmares are often exact replicas— "instant replays"—of actual traumatic experiences. Many trauma survivors, from war veterans to kidnapped children, mention this striking phenomenon. These claims imply that traumatic nightmares are a form of autobiographical memory.[5]

An influential study by the psychiatrist Bessel van der Kolk and his colleagues (1984) popularized the notion that traumatic nightmares replicate genuine events. They interviewed 15 Vietnam veterans with PTSD and 10 Vietnam veterans who had not seen combat but who suffered from lifelong nightmares. All of the PTSD veterans reported repetitive nightmares, and 11 of them said these dreams were usually exact replicas of actual combat events. The noncombat veterans had typical REM anxiety dreams that varied in content. Replicating van der Kolk's findings, a Dutch research team reported that 42 percent of 102 survivors of World War II claimed that their repetitive nightmares replicated traumatic experiences. Another 35 percent described them as depicting distorted versions of these events (Schreuder, Kleijn, and Rooijmans 2000).

Criticizing this work, the psychoanalytic psychologist Brooks Brenneis pointed out that van der Kolk and his colleagues "based their 'exact replica' conclusion on the dreamers' statements of equivalence without collecting any dreams" (1994: 432). Rather than having patients prospectively record their dreams, they simply asked them whether their nightmares matched actual combat events. Nor did they obtain (and verify) narratives of the events supposedly replicated during sleep.

The methodological quality of studies on this topic has improved. Karin Esposito and her colleagues (1999) had 18 Vietnam veterans with combat-related PTSD record their dreams in a structured diary for a week. Nearly half of the dreams concerned war, but only 21 percent reportedly replicated an actual combat event.

The psychiatrist Bas Schreuder and his associates (1998) had 39 Dutch survivors (33 of whom met criteria for PTSD) of World War II record their dreams upon awakening for 28 days. Although most dreams were war-related, only 39 percent of the combat veterans and 14 percent of the civilians claimed that their nightmares replicated actual traumatic experiences.

The psychiatrist Thomas Mellman's research group (2001) had 60 people who had been injured in life-threatening accidents or assaults record their dreams each morning during their initial hospitalization. Eighteen patients produced a total of 21 dream reports, 10 of them trauma-related. Only 6 trauma dreams were experienced as exact replications of what had happened;

the other 4 contained distortions. The authors speculated that replicative nightmares might be most common immediately after the trauma, waning in frequency thereafter.

In short, prospective studies indicate that a minority of survivors do, indeed, experience some nightmares as if they were replays of actual traumatic events. Upon reflection, though, one can see why this cannot literally be the case. Literal replication would require a quasi-photographic mechanism that faithfully preserves the sensory details of the trauma on a mental videotape that gets replayed during sleep. But psychologists have long known that autobiographical memory does not operate like a video recorder. If recollection during waking hours is not literally a replaying of a mental videotape, why should "recollection" during sleep be any different? Why should traumatic nightmares be immune from the reconstructive processes that characterize all autobiographical recollection, including recall of traumatic events?

Moreover, there is a paradox embedded in the claim that nightmares replay actual events. A dreamer who makes this claim must compare the nightmare with the event as recalled during waking hours. However, the standard against which the nightmare is compared—the event as recalled by the dreamer when awake—is itself a reconstruction of what happened. If the standard of comparison is itself a fallible reconstruction of the original experience, how can anyone be certain that the dream replicates what actually happened? In any event, even if replicative nightmares are nothing more than compelling memory illusions, that dreams can *seem* to replay the event is an important fact about how people remember trauma. Only trauma survivors appear to report the memory illusion of having their traumatic experiences replayed with frightening regularity while they sleep.

Although many therapists view traumatic nightmares as (relatively) unmodified memories of actual events, those trained in the psychoanalytic tradition believe that trauma can also surface in disguised form during dreams. For example, the child psychiatrist Lenore Terr (1979) related a dream experienced by a girl who had been kidnapped. It concerned a caged monkey "bossed" by an animal trainer. The monkey was eventually released, and the trainer punished. Terr interpreted the caged monkey as symbolizing the kidnapped girl, and the trainer as symbolizing the kidnappers. Unfortunately, it is impossible to tell whether Terr was right. Had Terr not known the girl's history, would she have been able to decode a history of kidnapping by analyzing this dream? Or, conversely, knowing the girl's history, would Terr have been able to predict the content of her disguised dreams?

If interpreting dreams as disguised symbols of *known* traumatic events is a questionable practice, interpreting them as disguised versions of *unknown* trauma is downright hazardous. Freud popularized this practice, as in his celebrated case of the "Wolf Man." His patient recalled an early childhood dream in which he saw several white dogs perched motionless in a tree outside his bedroom window. Freud (1918) decoded this dream as evidence that the patient had been traumatized by witnessing his parents having sexual intercourse (the "primal scene"). Ethan Watters and Richard Ofshe summarized Freud's reasoning: "The six dogs were actually the two parents; their whiteness indicated the color of bedsheets; their *lack* of motion means the opposite—grinding sexual movement; that they are dogs means that the parents were engaged in sex dog-like, from behind; and finally, the dogs' big tails indicated the baby-Wolfman's assumption that his mother's genitals had been 'castrated'" (1999: 60).[6] Once convinced that his patient harbored repressed memories of having witnessed the "primal scene," Freud proceeded to interpret everything as consistent with this preordained conclusion. Thanks to Freud's unconstrained, freewheeling interpretive method, nothing the patient could have said would have counted as evidence against Freud's hypothesis.

Following Freud, some contemporary psychoanalytic therapists interpret dreams as symbolizing repressed memories of sexual abuse in childhood. They diagnose histories of abuse even among patients who have no memories of such trauma. Psychoanalyzing a young man who had recurring dreams about anal rape, Miriam Williams concluded that his dreams "had preserved experiences and impressions of an indelible nature" (1987: 152). The patient, however, denied having been assaulted. Apparently Williams believed that such experiences can make indelible impressions on dreams without leaving a trace in ordinary autobiographical memory.

Others have likewise published case studies showing how therapists can identify hidden trauma histories among patients who complain of nightmares and other problems. For example, the psychoanalytic psychologist Judith Alpert described her method for recovering repressed memories of sexual abuse in her case report of "Mary." Mary was an angry young woman who entered psychotherapy convinced that she was an incest victim. She had no memories of abuse, other than recalling that her father once attempted to give her a lingering kiss when she was 17 years old. For the first eight months of therapy, Alpert's goal was "recovering, reconstructing, and reintegrating traumatic memories with their associated affects" (1994: 218). Mary eventually recalled having been repeatedly molested, between the ages of 3 and 7, by her father, and having sexually molested her younger brother. According to Alpert, because the abuse was so severe, all of Mary's memories of incest had been subjected to "massive repression" (222). By interpreting Mary's dreams as fragments of incest memories, and by interpreting other clues as further evidence of abuse, Alpert assembled a trauma narrative to explain Mary's chronic anger. Her conviction that Mary was an incest survivor was based on "the content and manner of [Mary's] defenses, the reoccurrence in nightmare after nightmare of the traumatic events, the fragments of memory, the repetition of the abuse in her life patterns [behavior supposedly symbolizing abuse], and the transference that took place. All of these indicated the reality of some experience that was being worked on in the unconscious, and all of these repetitive representations and fragments of memory pointed to the accuracy of the narrative, as it unfolded" (233–234).

Interpreting nightmares as symbolic evidence of repressed memories of abuse is a seriously flawed enterprise. It is based on the notion that some survivors reexperience the trauma (in disguised form, no less) only during sleep, while being entirely incapable of remembering it during the day. This flies in the face of everything known about how people remember trauma—or anything else, for that matter. Daytime intrusive recollection is the most common reexperiencing symptom, and anyone having traumatic dreams will surely remember the trauma all too easily while awake.

Moreover, nightmares are common in the general population, and need not signify a history of trauma or even a high level of anxiety. For example, the clinical psychologists James Wood and Richard Bootzin (1990) had college students prospectively record frightening dreams for several weeks. Using these data to compute an annual rate, Wood and Bootzin discovered that the average college student has 23.6 nightmares per year, and that frequency of nightmares is unrelated to measures of anxiety. Certainly the number of people who have frequent nightmares must exceed the number of people who harbor repressed memories of trauma. Kathryn Belicki (1992) extended these results by showing that nightmare frequency is unrelated to other measures of psychopathology as well.

Even some psychoanalytic practitioners have questioned the wisdom of inferring repressed trauma from dreams. As Brooks Brenneis (1997a) has pointed out, if it were possible to divine hidden trauma from dreams, then therapists should be able to sort victims from nonvictims solely on the basis of their dream reports. There is no evidence that this can be done. Furthermore, even when "memories" are recovered in therapy, it is difficult to rule out inadvertent suggestive effects. In Alpert's case, both the patient and the therapist focused on dreams as a means of uncovering memories of incest. It is little wonder that a patient preoccupied with discovering memories of incest would sooner or later start having dreams about sexual abuse (see Brenneis 1994). The occurrence of these dreams tells us more about the therapy than about the history of the patient.

Finally, the entire Freudian enterprise of interpreting dreams rests on the dubious assumption that dreams are a kind of language. Treating dreams as symbolic messages hiding deeper meanings, psychoanalysts have endeavored to decode dream imagery and to translate it into ordinary speech. But dreams are not like language. Although one might translate dream imagery into narrative, one cannot translate narrative into dream imagery. We can translate Spanish into English, and English into Spanish, but we cannot do this for dream imagery. No back translation is possible for dreams (Wittgenstein 1966: 48).

Even the one-way translation from dreams to ordinary speech is uncertain. How do we know whether our translation (interpretation) is correct? There is no universal dictionary enabling us to decode the symbols of dreams. A psychoanalyst might reply that symbols are idiosyncratic, and that one must first know the patient thoroughly if one is to interpret what the dream symbols mean. But if such extensive prior knowledge is essential for correct interpretation, what possible new information could dreams possibly add to what is already known about the patient? By the time we get to know the patient well enough to interpret his dreams, any further insights from his dreams will surely be redundant with what we already know about him.

FLASHBACKS

Flashbacks are sudden, unbidden, emotionally intense sensory experiences (such as visual images or smells) that seemingly reinstate the sensory impressions that occurred during the trauma. The vividness of the imagery produces a disturbing sense of reliving the experience. DSM-IV distinguishes between intrusive recollections and flashbacks. However, it is unclear whether flashbacks are supposed to be a distinct form of traumatic memory or merely an especially vivid kind of intrusive recollection. Furthermore, as Berntsen discovered, involuntary, vivid recollections accompanied by physical reactions need not be related to trauma. Many flashbacks concern intensely positive experiences.

The term *flashback* originated in the motion picture industry. Psychiatrists first used it in the 1960s to denote perceptual disturbances in former users of hallucinogenic drugs, only later applying it to the especially vivid recollections of trauma in Vietnam combat veterans (Frankel 1994). Studies based on the retrospective self-reports of trauma survivors indicate that flashbacks involve intense visual imagery, last about one minute, are accompanied by panic attack symptoms, are associated with dream disturbances, and occur most often in PTSD patients who score high on a measure of general imagery ability.[7]

Researchers have endeavored to study flashbacks in the laboratory. On the face of it, this seems paradoxical. How can scientists induce something in the laboratory that is, by definition, involuntary and unpredictable? The approach they have taken is based on the observation that flashbacks are often accompanied by panic attack symptoms. Accordingly, scientists have exposed PTSD patients and control subjects to safe pharmacologic substances that trigger panic attacks in people with panic disorder, to see whether these substances trigger flashbacks in people with PTSD. These experiments are conducted only after the hospital or university human subjects committee reviews the procedure, weighs the risks and benefits, and ensures that volunteer participants are fully informed about the possibility that they might experience a frightening (but harmless) panic attack or flashback symptoms. These patients, of course, experience panic and flashbacks in everyday life. The procedure simply reproduces them in the laboratory so that clinical scientists can gain a better understanding of the causes of panic attacks and flashbacks in the lives of their patients (for reviews see McNally 1994: 52–70; 1999b).

Several studies have shown that certain pharmacologic agents trigger flashbacks and panic attacks in Vietnam veterans with PTSD. In their first experiment, the biological psychiatrist Steven Southwick and his colleagues found that 8 of 20 PTSD patients reported a flashback after receiving yohimbine, and that 14 of them panicked as well. One patient also had a flashback during infusion of saline, a pharmacologically inert placebo. None of the nonveteran control subjects had flashbacks or panic attacks in response to yohimbine (Southwick et al. 1993). In their second experiment, this group found that 3 of 10 PTSD patients reported a flashback after receiving yohimbine, and that 6 of them panicked as well. None of the nonveteran control subjects had flashbacks or panic attacks (Bremner, Innis, et al. 1997). In their third experiment, they used two pharmacological agents: yohimbine and meta-chlorophenylipiperazine (m-CPP). Among the 26 PTSD patients, 8 reported flashbacks and 11 reported panic attacks in response to yohimbine, whereas 7 reported flashbacks and 8 reported panic attacks in response to m-CPP. Two patients experienced flashbacks during the saline placebo infusion. One of the 14 control subjects panicked in response to yohimbine, but otherwise this group was nonreactive (Southwick, Krystal, et al. 1997).

Liberzon and colleagues (1996/1997) described a Vietnam veteran with combat-related PTSD who reported experiencing a flashback during an experiment in which his regional cerebral blood flow (rCBF) was being measured via single photon emission computerized tomography (SPECT). When they presented him with audiotaped combat sounds, he reportedly saw the enemy's black uniform in the laboratory. In this man's brain, unlike those of other PTSD patients in the experiment who did not report flashbacks, relative activity increased in the thalamus and decreased in the cortex.

Southwick and his colleagues classified a reaction as a flashback if the patient reported a vivid recollection of a traumatic event accompanied by at least one sensory impression. They did not directly evaluate how closely the flashback mirrored the event. In fact, this issue was addressed in only one study, conducted by John Rainey and his colleagues (1987). They tested Vietnam combat veterans, six with PTSD and one with past PTSD. Sodium lactate triggered flashbacks in all seven subjects, and isoproterenol triggered flashbacks in two subjects. One subject reported a flashback during a dextrose/water placebo infusion. Eight of the 10 flashbacks were accompanied by panic attacks. In all but one case, the flashback preceded panic. Contrary to clinical lore, the flashbacks did not occur suddenly; they began gradually, increasing in severity and intensity over several minutes. Further contrary to clinical lore, they seldom replicated actual traumatic experiences. One veteran saw himself killing a Vietnamese woman, who promptly rose from the dead. Another saw himself, from the perspective of an observer, undergoing surgery following a combat wound. Although such images were clearly related to the war, they could not have been reinstatements of what the patients had seen in Vietnam.

Other reports confirm Rainey's observation that flashbacks contain distortions of what actually happened during the trauma. For example, one veteran experienced flashbacks of receiving a serious leg wound in Vietnam that differed markedly from how he had been wounded. A study of victims of serious hand injuries revealed that about two-thirds of their flashbacks involved distortions, usually imagery of even more serious injuries. A study of college students who had suffered serious trauma revealed that the more flashback-like their intrusive images were, the more likely the imagery exaggerated the severity of what had actually happened.[8]

Strikingly, flashbacks occur even among people who did not actually witness the traumatic event. One study revealed that 17 out of 18 individuals whose loved ones had been murdered experienced repetitive nightmares and flashbacks about the murders even though only one of them had witnessed the crime. A man experienced intrusive visual images of his son's scalding, even though he had not been present when the accident occurred. A woman experienced intrusive visual images of her murdered father's mutilated body, even though she had not been at the crime scene.[9]

Finally, distressing, intrusive images have been mistaken for flashbacks of repressed traumatic events. In these cases, reported by the psychiatrists Joseph Lipinski and Harrison Pope (1994), the patients were suffering from obsessive-compulsive disorder that remitted with medication. Each patient, however, had been misdiagnosed by other therapists as suffering from flashbacks linked to repressed memories of childhood trauma. One patient experienced an intrusive image of her father about to stab her, and of herself, as a child, sitting in a pool of blood. Another patient had intrusive images of bloody corpses and dead animals. A third patient suffered intrusive images of a severed head and of a mutilated woman's corpse under a tarpaulin on a woodpile. None of these patients had ever recalled events that corresponded to the content of the intrusive images, and all of them had other clear-cut signs of obsessive-compulsive disorder, such as compulsive handwashing. Unfortunately, their original therapists completely missed the obvious obsessive-compulsive diagnosis and misinterpreted the obsessional imagery as flashbacks arising from repressed memories of trauma. Clinicians cannot assume that a recurrent, intrusive image reflects a traumatic memory, let alone a repressed one.

As we have seen, flashbacks are vivid, emotionally intense experiences that produce the illusion of reliving the trauma. But they are not literally the reactivation of sensory impressions engraved indelibly on the mind. Like autobiographical memories in general, including "flashbulb" ones (see Sierra and Berrios 1999), flashbacks inevitably entail reconstruction and distortion.

"Behavioral Memories"

Lenore Terr popularized the idea that traumatic memory can be expressed unconsciously in behavior, especially among preverbal children. Even children traumatized as young as six months of age, she believes, will exhibit behavioral memories, despite being incapable of describing the trauma. Older children, she holds, will express their memories in language as well as in behavior. Terr coined the term "posttraumatic play" to capture a common form of behavioral memory. For example, she observed young kidnapping survivors who reenacted their abduction during play or who dressed up as kidnappers for Halloween.[10]

Some of Terr's examples are convincing, whereas others are ambiguous. She described an adolescent girl who made a point of sobering up drunken friends at parties (Terr 1981). Noting that this girl had once watched helplessly as her grandfather suffered a stroke, Terr interpreted her aiding drunks as reflecting behavioral memory of her grandfather's stroke. But in what sense does helping her friends "reflect" memory of her grandfather's stroke? Perhaps she would have helped them even if her grandfather had never fallen ill. In another ambiguous case, a young boy acquired a fear of the dark after being trapped in an elevator (Terr 1988). Although he insisted that the lights had never gone out in the elevator, and although fears of the dark are common among young children, Terr interpreted the boy's fear of darkness as a behavioral memory of his confinement in the elevator. If anything, one would have expected him to develop claustrophobia, or at least a specific fear of elevators.[11]

Terr knew the histories of these children. Her knowledge may have biased her to see behavioral memories of trauma where none existed. One can seldom infer a trauma history from behavior alone. Although it is tempting to assume that people with animal phobias must have been bitten or otherwise traumatized by their feared animal, the evidence does not bear this out. Gail Steketee and I found that patients with extreme phobias of dogs, snakes, and so forth had never been attacked, and two-thirds of them said they had been phobic for as long as they could remember (McNally and Steketee 1985). Others have likewise observed that phobias seldom originate in traumatic conditioning episodes (see Menzies and Clarke 1995). These studies underscore the hazards of inferring a history of trauma from behavior alone.

PSYCHOPHYSIOLOGIC REACTIONS TO REMINDERS OF TRAUMA

Just like people with other anxiety disorders, those with PTSD react physiologically to distressing stimuli. When people with PTSD encounter situations, stimuli, or other reminders of traumatic experiences, they experience the bodily accompaniments of fear as well as the subjective sense of distress—hence a "psychophysiologic" reaction. Physical reactions include trembling, pounding heart, and sweating. One difference, however, is that physiologic responses in PTSD are triggered by reminders of past threats, whereas those in phobic and other anxiety disorders are triggered by future, impending threats. A combat veteran with PTSD may experience a sharp increase in heart rate while watching a war movie reminiscent of his tour in Vietnam, whereas a dog phobic may have the same reaction when encountering an unleashed dog in a park.

Researchers have studied psychophysiologic reactivity to reminders of trauma in two ways in the laboratory (for a review see Blanchard and Buckley 1999). In one type of study, they expose PTSD subjects and control subjects to audiovisual presentations relevant to their traumatic experience. Combat veterans with PTSD might view a series of slides of war scenes accompanied by a soundtrack containing gunfire, screaming, and so forth. Control subjects would typically be psychiatrically healthy combat veterans. Edward Blanchard and others have shown that Vietnam veterans with PTSD exhibit greater heart rate increases to these kinds of stimuli than do healthy combat veterans. PTSD and control groups seldom respond differently to neutral stimuli. Hence enhanced reactivity in the PTSD group is specific to reminders of the trauma.[12]

In the second type of study, PTSD patients and control subjects listen to brief audiotaped scripts that relate events from their own lives. Some scripts describe traumatic events experienced by the subject, whereas others describe neutral, positive, and stressful but not traumatic experiences. Subjects are asked to imagine the events as if they were happening again, and researchers measure the subjects' psychophysiologic responses during this script-driven imagery.

In studies on combat veterans from World War II, the Korean war, and Vietnam, Roger Pitman, Scott Orr, and their colleagues have shown that autobiographical trauma scripts provoke greater psychophysiologic reactions in veterans with PTSD than in those without PTSD. These scripts do not provoke heightened psychophysiologic reactions in combat veterans who have anxiety disorders other than PTSD. Female military nurses who developed PTSD in Vietnam exhibit enhanced psychophysiologic reactivity, but only to trauma scripts. Psychiatrically healthy nurses do not respond this way when they hear audiotaped descriptions of their own traumatic experiences.[13]

Psychophysiologic reactivity during trauma imagery is not confined to individuals whose PTSD arose from war. Civilians who have developed the disorder following motor vehicle and other accidents are more reactive than accident survivors without PTSD.[14] Scott Orr and his colleagues (1998) used the script-driven imagery paradigm to study traumatic memories in female survivors of childhood sexual abuse. Those with PTSD had higher heart rate and greater corrugator electromyographic (EMG) activity (facial muscle tension) during imagery of personal trauma scripts than did those who had never developed PTSD. The heart rate responses of abuse survivors who had had PTSD in the past fell midway between the current PTSD and always-healthy groups. Seventeen subjects who reported having recovered memories of long-forgotten abuse exhibited significantly greater corrugator EMG and trends toward greater frontalis EMG (facial muscle tension) and heart rate than did the 54 subjects who reported always having remembered their abuse.

Replicating the basic findings of Orr's group, Annmarie McDonagh-Coyle and her colleagues (2001) found that women with histories of childhood sexual abuse were more physiologically reactive to scripts related to their abuse than to a consensual sex script or a neutral one. Correlational analyses revealed that severity of PTSD symptoms was strongly related to heart rate increases provoked by the trauma scripts.

In the largest psychophysiologic study ever done in the trauma field, Terence Keane and his colleagues (1998) recruited Vietnam combat veterans from hospitals around the country. Keane's group tested 778 veterans with current PTSD, 181 with past PTSD, and 369 with no history of PTSD. During both autobiographical combat scripts and standardized audiovisual combat presentations, those with current PTSD had greater heart rate, skin conductance, EMG, and diastolic blood pressure than those with no history of the disorder. Subjects with past PTSD tended to fall midway between the other groups in terms of physiologic reactivity.

Interestingly, about one-third of the subjects with current PTSD did not qualify as "physiologic responders" to combat stimuli in the laboratory. That is, although their self-reports indicated PTSD, the objective, biological data indicated otherwise. The reason for this is unclear. Nonresponders may have exaggerated the severity of their symptoms to clinical interviewers (Frueh et al. 2000). In another study, PTSD subjects who scored high on a measure of image control were nonreactive to traumatic imagery scripts (Laor et al. 1998). Therefore, perhaps enhanced ability to control their mental imagery enables some PTSD patients to suppress their emotional responses while listening to trauma scripts.[15]

Reexperiencing Trauma without Remembering It?

Freud (1893) believed that severe threats to life produce traumatic neuroses only if the person remains conscious during the experience. People who are knocked unconscious by a blow to the head, as in a severe automobile accident, should fail to encode the experience. Failure to encode it would seemingly prevent the emergence of intrusive memories. Traumatic recollection implies prior encoding, which, in turn, requires conscious registration of the experience. Consistent with Freud's intuition, some studies suggest that survivors of auto accidents whose head injuries produce amnesia report few, if any, PTSD symptoms (Bryant and Harvey 1995a; Sbordone and Liter 1995). Likewise, loss of consciousness apparently attenuated posttraumatic reactions among many survivors of the catastrophic fire at Boston's Cocoanut Grove nightclub (Adler 1943).

But mild traumatic brain injury that produces unconsciousness and posttraumatic (anterograde) amnesia for less than 24 hours does not preclude the development of PTSD (Bryant 2001). Sometimes brief periods of consciousness during the accident are sufficient to establish PTSD (McMillan 1996). In a study of 309 survivors of traffic accidents whose medical records documented loss of consciousness of not more than 15 minutes, Richard

Mayou and his colleagues found that PTSD three months after the accident was *more* common among those who had lost consciousness (48 percent) than among those who had not (23 percent). Their intrusive recollections concerned events occurring just before and just after the accident (for example, being rescued, receiving emergency first aid). Among 23 patients who were excluded from the main analyses because they had sustained major brain injury, as marked by *prolonged* unconsciousness, none developed PTSD (Mayou, Black, and Bryant 2000).[16]

However, Richard Bryant and his colleagues (2000) found that 26 of 96 patients who had suffered severe traumatic brain injury qualified for PTSD even though none of them had any conscious recollection of the accident. On the face of it, this seems impossible. If a person's head injury is so severe that he cannot remember anything about the accident, how can he possibly develop PTSD? After all, the diagnosis of PTSD requires the presence of reexperiencing symptoms. Clearly, if survivors cannot remember the accident, they cannot recollect it in intrusive recollections, flashbacks, or nightmares. Alternatively, it is conceivable that survivors might react physiologically to stimuli associated with the accident without being aware of why these cues trigger heart rate increases and so forth. In fact, this is precisely what Bryant hypothesized: physiologic reactivity to trauma cues might reflect implicit memory for the accident, established via Pavlovian conditioning.[17]

Allison Harvey and Richard Bryant (2001) studied 79 motor vehicle accident victims who had suffered mild traumatic brain injuries resulting in marked or total amnesia for the accident. Two years later, when they reassessed 50 of these subjects, 40 percent of them said they now remembered the accident. This reported ability to remember the event after two years was associated with a shorter duration of posttraumatic amnesia and with emotional numbing during the hours following the trauma.

If victims are unconscious during the trauma and do not encode the event, how is it possible for them to reexperience it later? One possibility, as Bryant suggested, is that they acquire a Pavlovian conditioned response, established without their awareness. Such an implicit, conditioned fear might provide the basis for later symptoms. The possibility that declarative, explicit memory is undermined by lack of consciousness, but that nondeclarative, implicit memory is left intact (Bryant et al. 2000), accords with Chris Brewin's dual representation theory of PTSD. Dual representation theory posits two memory systems: a *verbally accessible memory* (VAM) system and a *situationally accessible memory* (SAM) system. Information stored in the VAM system was first consciously processed in working memory prior to transfer to long-term memory. VAM memories require conscious attention and encoding, and they can later be retrieved deliberately. They can also come to mind involuntarily, and can be expressed in language. In contrast, SAM memories contain sensory information (autonomic, kinesthetic, visual) that received extensive perceptual, but scant conscious, processing at the time of the trauma. SAM memories are not accessible via effortful search; they are triggered only by cues that match those present during the trauma. The SAM system is said to underlie flashbacks, nightmares, and physiologic reactivity to stimuli associated with the traumatic event.[18]

Brewin's theory requires that Pavlovian fear conditioning occur in the absence of awareness or declarative knowledge. But research on people with organic amnesia indicates that conditioned emotional responses can be established only under highly restrictive conditions (Clark and Squire 1998). If even half a second elapses between the conditioned stimulus (CS), such as a light, and the unconditioned stimulus (US), such as a loud noise, a conditioned emotional response will not develop in people with organic amnesia. However, Lovibond and Shanks have identified methodological problems in nearly all the experiments adduced in support of the claim that people can acquire Pavlovian conditioned responses in the absence of awareness of the CS-US relationship.[19]

Then again, a car crash in the real world is a far more severe US than a loud noise in the laboratory: perhaps in a car crash a person might develop conditioned emotional responses while unconscious despite departures from laboratory-like conditions. For example, one case report that supports Brewin's theory described a man who apparently developed conditioned fear responses despite having lost consciousness while buried alive in a work accident (Krikorian and Layton 1998). In another case, a pedestrian was knocked unconscious when a truck swerved onto the sidewalk. He had no memory of the accident, but he developed conditioned fear reactions to trucks of the same size and color as the one that had nearly killed him (King 2001).

But there is another possible explanation for these findings, and perhaps a more plausible one than conditioning without awareness. It may be that some victims who lose consciousness during an accident later hear or read the details of the event, and this knowledge prompts their intrusive thoughts, nightmares, and psychophysiologic reactivity. Even though they cannot literally *remember* their trauma, they *know* what happened. They suffer from a "false" memory of trauma that corresponds to a genuine event. For example, one accident survivor saw photographs of his demolished car, and another learned how his passenger had been killed. This knowledge furnished the content of their terrifying intrusive "memories" (Bryant 1996).

PTSD patients who vividly recall their accidents experience intrusive imagery whose content is corroborated by others who witnessed the accident, whereas PTSD patients who are amnesic for the accident experience intrusive images inconsistent with what actually happened. The genuine intrusive memories of the first group and the pseudomemories of the second group are both experienced as involuntary, vivid, and emotionally evocative (Bryant and Harvey 1998). That is, genuine memories and pseudomemories of trauma *feel* the same, but one is historically accurate and the other is not.

There is no obvious ethical way to test whether Brewin's implicit conditioning explanation or the reconstruction one better accounts for PTSD in amnesic accident survivors. To test this, one would have to tell a group of amnesic mugging victims, for example, that they had survived a car accident, and tell a group of amnesic victims of auto accidents that they had been mugged. Brewin's theory would predict that survivors would be psychophysiologically reactive only to cues that had actually been present during the trauma (such as driving cues in the car accident victims) regardless of what they had been told about their traumatic experience. The reconstruction hypothesis would predict that the content of intrusive symptoms and the cues to which patients react would accord with the verbal accounts of their trauma whether accurate or bogus. But this clearly unethical experiment can never be performed.

According to the standard view, embodied in DSM-IV, memory for traumatic events—at least among those suffering from PTSD—is expressed in intrusive thoughts, nightmares, flashbacks, and psychophysiologic reactivity to cues reminiscent of the trauma. Most of what we know about how people remember trauma has been gleaned from the self-reports of survivors. This rich clinical database has provided the essential foundation for further inquiry, including prospective self-monitoring studies of traumatic nightmares and laboratory studies designed to provoke flashbacks and psychophysiologic reactivity. Systematic research has supported some aspects of clinical lore while modifying others. We now know that nightmares and flashbacks are not like videotaped replays of traumatic events. Nevertheless, with dreams, a significant minority of PTSD patients do report the compelling illusion that they are reliving their trauma during sleep. As for flashbacks, many depart significantly from what actually happened during the trauma, and some people experience intrusive emotional images for events that never happened at all. The most intriguing recent finding concerns individuals who lost consciousness during the trauma, but who developed reexperiencing symptoms for events they had never consciously experienced. Whether these emotional reactions in the absence of autobiographical memory for trauma reflect conditioning without awareness or the acquisition of frightening knowledge about the traumatic event remains to be seen.

5

MECHANISMS OF TRAUMATIC MEMORY

People with ptsd remember trauma all too well. In addition to suffering from excellent memory for their terrible experiences, survivors often complain of general forgetfulness. For example, a Cambodian refugee who was haunted by her vivid memories of Pol Pot's genocidal regime also mentioned her frustration about forgetting things in everyday life, such as leaving something to burn to a crisp in the oven. What do we know about how trauma affects general memory functioning? Furthermore, what are the mechanisms of traumatic memory?

General Memory Impairment

Many people complain of having a "bad memory." Trauma survivors, especially those with PTSD, are no exception. But subjective complaints about memory dysfunction are not always accurate. Psychologically distressed people may have a negatively biased view of their ability to think and to remember. Consider Bradley Axelrod and Boaz Milner's (1997) study of Persian Gulf War veterans. One group of veterans worried that the war had damaged their ability to think; a control group of veterans expressed no such worries. But objective neuropsychological tests of attention and memory uncovered no deficits in either group. Although veterans in the first group worried about their cognitive functioning, the evidence revealed no basis for these fears.[1]

Other studies have likewise uncovered few, if any, objective memory deficits in trauma survivors. Murray Stein and his colleagues (1999) found that women reporting a history of childhood sexual abuse, most of whom had PTSD, performed no worse than nonabused women on tests of verbal memory and visual memory. Their performance on the memory tests was unre-lated to either the severity of their PTSD symptoms or their reported extent of previous amnesia for abuse. Melissa Jenkins and her associates (1998) re-ported that rape victims with PTSD recalled fewer words than did rape vic-tims without PTSD. But the difference between the groups was minuscule and it vanished on a recognition memory test.[2]

Psychologists have, at times, detected genuine memory impairment in trauma survivors. Studying veterans of the Gulf War, Jennifer Vasterling and her colleagues (1998) found that those with PTSD performed worse than healthy veterans on tests of sustained attention, working memory, initial learning, and retroactive interference (that is, when learning new items in-terferes with remembering previously learned ones). She also found that problems in ignoring distracting information were correlated with severity of intrusive reexperiencing symptoms.

Two studies have revealed verbal memory deficits in Vietnam combat vet-erans with PTSD, and another revealed similar deficits in adult survivors of childhood sexual abuse with PTSD. Moreover, severity of reported sexual abuse predicted severity of short-term verbal memory deficits. Another study failed to detect any memory impairments in maltreated children with PTSD.[3]

Unfortunately, these studies involved comparisons between subjects with PTSD and control subjects who had never been exposed to trauma. Accord-ingly, it is impossible to tell whether these deficits result from being exposed to trauma (regardless of whether PTSD develops) or whether they emerge only in those trauma-exposed people who develop PTSD. A third possibility is that these deficits might precede exposure to trauma, and perhaps consti-tute a risk factor for developing PTSD.

When memory problems do occur, they may have nothing to do with trauma or PTSD as such. They may be linked with any psychiatric illness, not just PTSD. Tzvi Gil's research team (1990) found that verbal and visual memory deficits occurred just as often in patients with other psychiatric dis-orders as in those with PTSD. They found no special connection between memory problems and PTSD. Both groups performed worse than a healthy control group.

Drue Barrett's research group (1996) obtained similar findings in Vietnam veterans selected from among participants in a large epidemiologic study conducted by the Centers for Disease Control. Barrett found that 236 veterans who had had PTSD at some point in their lives, but who had no other psychiatric disorder, performed just as well on verbal and visual memory tests as did a control group of 1,835 psychiatrically healthy veterans. Memory deficits did occur in another group of 128 PTSD veterans, but these men also had at least one other mental disorder (such as depression, generalized anxiety disorder, substance abuse or dependence). Therefore, the presence of PTSD *alone* was not associated with memory problems.[4]

Psychologists have found memory deficits in former POWs, especially those who were starved during captivity. Unlike purely psychic forms of trauma, starvation is likely to have adverse physical effects on the brain. Patricia Sutker and her colleagues (1990, 1995) reported that the amount of body weight lost during internment predicted severity of memory problems many years later among POWs from World War II and the Korean war. In another study on Korean war veterans, Sutker's group (1991) found that 86 percent of former POWs had PTSD, and 86 percent of them also fell into the clinically impaired range on an immediate memory task. Only 9 percent of the non-POW combat veterans had PTSD, but 41 percent fell into the clinically impaired range on this memory test.[5]

When studying memory in people with PTSD, researchers need to compare their performance with that of trauma-exposed people without the disorder. It is also useful to compare their performance with population norms, as Mark Gilbertson and his colleagues (2001) discovered. They found that 19 Vietnam combat veterans with PTSD performed worse on attentional and memory tests than did 13 psychiatrically healthy combat veterans. But comparison of their performance with population norms revealed that PTSD patients did not do worse than average. Rather, combat veterans who had never developed PTSD did *better* than average. Gilbertson concluded that better-than-average cognitive functioning may have protected these men from developing PTSD.

The largest study ever done on this topic revealed no evidence of general memory impairment in individuals with PTSD. Randomly selecting Vietnam veterans from among participants in the Centers for Disease Control epidemiologic study, Christine Zalewski and her colleagues tested 241 veterans with PTSD, 241 veterans with generalized anxiety disorder, and 241 veterans with no history of psychiatric disorder. The groups did not differ on verbal or visual memory tests, and their performance fell within normal limits (Zalewski, Thompson, and Gottesman 1994).[6]

In short, although people with PTSD often complain about having a poor memory, their memories are rarely worse than anyone else's, unless they have other disorders as well or were once a starving POW.

Memory and Multiple Personality Disorder

Multiple personality disorder (MPD) is the most controversial syndrome in psychiatry (see Acocella 1999). Some specialists believe that MPD is a genuine disorder caused by years of horrific physical and sexual abuse suffered during childhood—an especially severe form of posttraumatic stress disorder (Gleaves 1996). Others question the link between childhood trauma and MPD, arguing instead that psychiatrically disturbed people adopt the media-influenced, socially scripted role of MPD patient as a means of expressing distress, unwittingly aided by therapists who hypnotize them in search of repressed memories of trauma harbored by alternate personalities or "alters" (Lilienfeld et al. 1999). Everyone agrees, however, that people qualifying for this diagnosis report spectacular memory deficits. Information encoded by one "personality" is often said to be inaccessible to other "personalities."

Psychologists have attempted to test this clinical observation experimentally. Unfortunately, most memory experiments on MPD have involved only a few patients or a single patient studied intensively (for a review see Dorahy 2001). Consistent with clinical observations, early studies indicated that neutral material encoded by one personality was, in fact, difficult for other personalities to retrieve. Words learned by one personality were seldom recalled or recognized by other personalities. This also held for implicit memory tests that required patients to process the meaning of the words (such as stem-completion tasks). But memory transfer did occur across personalities on perceptual implicit memory tests that did not require subjects to process the meanings of words (such as word fragment completion tests). So, for example, if patients studied the word *lullaby*, they would exhibit priming effects by successfully completing the word fragment *l_l_a_y* with its only possible completion (*lullaby*) even if one personality was operative during the study phase and another was operative during the test phase. But if one personality studied a list of words (such as *apple*) and another completed word stems (such as APP) with the first word that came to mind, the second personality was no more likely to complete the stem with APPLE than with APPLY.

Therefore, if a task requires the subject to pay attention to the meaning of the word, information encoded by one personality is likely to seem inaccessible to other personalities. However, it is impossible to tell whether these other personalities are generally *unable* to remember the information or whether they are merely *unwilling* to report. Part of the role of MPD patient is failure to remember things encoded by one's other personalities. Therefore, a patient might remember an item encoded by another personality but decline to disclose it on a memory test.[7]

In recent methodologically sophisticated studies, Rafaële Huntjens and her associates have greatly clarified our understanding of memory in MPD. In contrast to previous research, their studies have included many more subjects and have included two control groups, one of which is trained to simulate MPD. The simulators are shown a documentary film about an MPD patient, and are taught how to role-play the disorder—how to pretend to have alternate personalities and how to switch from one personality to another. Both MPD subjects and simulators are in one personality while encoding emotionally neutral words, but then switch to another personality when their memory for these words is tested.

In their first study, Huntjens and her colleagues found that MPD patients exhibited priming effects across different personalities on conceptual as well as perceptual implicit memory tests. Even though they claimed amnesia for material encoded by the first personality, the data indicated that exposure to material during encoding affected their performance during testing. That is, they exhibited normal implicit memory effects across personalities (Huntjens, Postma, Peters, Hamaker, et al. in press).

In their second study, Huntjens's team (in press) had subjects learn words from List A, comprising names of vegetables, animals, and flowers. MPD subjects and simulators then switched to another personality prior to learning List B, which comprised names of other vegetables, other animals, and furniture. Before the second personality learned List B, the researchers asked her whether she knew anything about List A. Most MPD subjects denied any knowledge of List A. However, when asked to recall words they had learned, both MPD subjects and other subjects recalled words from List A as well as from List B. Had MPD subjects been genuinely amnesic for List A, they would not have recalled words from this list. One week later, subjects were given recognition tests. Again, MPD subjects (while in the second personality) recognized words from List A as well as from List B. Indeed, the second personality recognized 50 percent of the words learned by the first personality despite the second personality's claim to have amnesia for List A.

Huntjens and her associates have shown that MPD patients do not exhibit between-personality amnesia for neutral material on objective tests of explicit memory. Two interpretations are possible. First, MPD patients might simply be lying about their amnesia. Despite recollecting material encoded by another personality, they might deny remembering it. Second, MPD patients might genuinely believe they cannot remember material which objective tests show they can, indeed, remember. That is, MPD might be characterized by a disconnection between subjective experience of remembering and objective memory performance.

Two case studies of MPD patients addressed the question of whether one personality can recall everyday events experienced by other personalities. Daniel Schacter and his colleagues (1989) asked a patient to recall personal memories in response to cue words. They compared her performance to that of a control group of nonclinical subjects. She could not retrieve any memories from before the age of 10. Her earliest memory of her sexually abusive father dated from the age of 16. Whereas control subjects retrieved childhood memories in response to 86.2 percent of the cue words, the patient could do so for only 20.8 percent.

Using similar methods, Richard Bryant (1995) asked a patient to retrieve autobiographical memories in response to cue words both before and after she received a diagnosis of MPD. Before she was formally diagnosed as a multiple personality, she retrieved mainly recent memories. But after her diagnosis, she switched to a childhood "alter" and began retrieving many memories from childhood. Her "host" personality tended to retrieve recent, generally positive memories, whereas her child alter retrieved childhood memories that were often negative in emotional tone.

Memory research on people with multiple personality disorder remains in its infancy. It will be important to determine whether apparent memory deficits across personalities reflect genuine retrieval problems or whether patients are merely simulating their apparent inability to remember things encoded by their other "personalities."

Overgeneral Autobiographical Memory

While investigating how mood affects memory, Mark Williams and his associates discovered that depressed and suicidal patients had great difficulty recalling specific personal memories in response to cue words (Williams and Broadbent 1986; Williams and Scott 1988). When Williams asked nondepressed subjects to think of a specific personal memory in response to words like *happy*, they had no problem doing so. They easily remembered specific events, such as "*Happy* reminds me of the day last summer when we went to Disney World." Depressed subjects, in contrast, provided *overgeneral* memories that made no reference to any specific episode. They would say things like "*Happy* reminds me of when I'm playing squash" or "*Happy* reminds me of when I was in elementary school."

Williams also discovered that this phenomenon of overgeneral memory has considerable clinical implications. The relative inability to retrieve specific memories from one's past is associated with impaired problem-solving skills (Evans et al. 1992) and with difficulty recovering from depression (Brittlebank et al. 1993). Apparently, difficulty retrieving specific autobiographical memories makes it harder to solve personal problems in the present, and this, in turn, makes it harder to overcome depression. That is, to cope with depressing problems today, it helps to be able to remember which solutions worked and which did not when one encountered similar problems in the past.

My colleagues and I investigated overgeneral memory in Vietnam veterans with PTSD—a group more chronically impaired than most people with serious depression. In our first experiment, we found that veterans with PTSD had difficulty recalling specific personal memories in response to cue words having either neutral (such as *appearance*), positive (*kindness*), or negative (*panic*) meaning (McNally et al. 1994). Healthy Vietnam combat veterans did not have this problem. We also wondered whether this memory difficulty might be temporarily worsened if PTSD veterans were reminded of their war experiences. That is, would experimental induction of intrusive thoughts make it tougher to retrieve specific memories from their past?

To test this, we showed subjects either a combat videotape or a neutral one depicting furniture. Watching the combat tape exacerbated the overgeneral memory effect to neutral words among PTSD patients, but not among healthy veterans. A second control group, comprising Vietnam combat veterans with other psychiatric disorders (mainly depression and alcohol dependence) resembled the PTSD group in its pattern of overgeneral recall. In another experiment done by our research group, patients with obsessive-compulsive disorder did not exhibit overgeneral memory unless they were also currently depressed (Wilhelm et al. 1997). Although both PTSD and obsessive-compulsive disorder are associated with unwanted thoughts, overgeneral memory seems linked to PTSD and depression.

In a subsequent study, we asked Vietnam combat veterans with and without PTSD to recall specific personal memories of times when they had demonstrated traits denoted by positive and negative cue words. If PTSD is associated with self-reproach, then veterans with the disorder should find it especially tough to recall specific memories in response to words like *kind* relative to ones like *guilty*. Once again, healthy combat veterans had little difficulty retrieving specific memories, especially in response to positive trait words. But those with PTSD had trouble retrieving specific memories to both positive and negative trait words, and this deficit was especially apparent in those PTSD subjects who arrived at the laboratory wearing Vietnam war regalia. These men came dressed in combat fatigues, wore patches from their units, and displayed POW/MIA buttons. One even arrived at the laboratory carrying a loaded gun. The regalia-wearing PTSD subjects disproportionately retrieved memories from the war—overgeneral as well as occasionally specific. The other subjects typically recalled specific memories from the past month. Wearing military regalia in everyday life not only reveals a fixation to a war fought three decades ago, but also is a marker for problems with autobiographical memory. The more a veteran was stuck in the past, the greater was his autobiographical memory disturbance (McNally et al. 1995).[8]

Allison Harvey and her colleagues found that difficulty recalling specific memories in response to positive cue words predicted PTSD symptoms six months later among survivors of motor vehicle accidents. She asked them to try to remember a specific memory from within 24 hours of the accident, and their difficulty doing so was an ominous predictor of emerging, persistent PTSD. They had no difficulty recalling specific memories in response to negative cue words. Those subjects who met criteria for acute stress disorder shortly after the accident recalled fewer specific memories in response to positive cue words than did those who did not meet these criteria; they also recalled overgeneral memories when they attempted to retrieve specific memories from any period in their lives (Harvey, Bryant, and Dang 1998). Like people with chronic PTSD related to the Vietnam war, those with acute stress disorder have trouble retrieving specific memories from their past.[9]

Some psychotherapists have observed that adult survivors of childhood sexual abuse often remember few details from their childhood. Perhaps abuse motivates children to encode as little as possible, thereby fostering an overgeneral retrieval style. Some research suggests that this may be the case. Evan Parks and Richard Balon (1995) asked three groups of adults to recall specific memories from before the age of 16 in response to emotion, object, and activity cue words. One group comprised patients who reported childhood histories of abuse (defined as sexual abuse, physical abuse, neglect, or having had substance-abusing parents), a second group comprised psychiatric patients without trauma histories, and the third group comprised healthy control subjects. The trauma group more often failed to retrieve any memory in response to emotion cue words than did the other groups. The trauma group also took longer to retrieve memories, and the earliest memory they retrieved on average was from an older age than those of the other groups. The healthy control group averaged the earliest memories, whereas the psychiatric control group fell midway between the other groups. Relative to healthy control subjects, trauma subjects tended to recall fewer memories from their earlier than later childhood years. Notably, the greater number of retrieval failures occurring in the trauma group was confined solely to their attempts to retrieve memories in response to emotion cue words.

Since Parks and Balon's study, evidence has continued to accumulate linking childhood adversity to overgeneral memory problems in adulthood. College women with histories of sexual abuse retrieved fewer specific memories than did those who had never been sexually abused (Henderson et al. 2002). Adolescent psychiatric inpatients with histories of sexual abuse, physical abuse, or neglect recalled fewer autobiographical facts (such as the color of the wallpaper in their bedroom at age 12) than did their fellow inpatients (Meesters et al. 2000). Unlike healthy control subjects, patients with borderline personality disorder had difficulty retrieving specific personal memories to positive, neutral, and (especially) negative cue words (Jones et al. 1999).

(People with borderline personalities cannot regulate their emotions very well, have stormy interpersonal relationships, and frequently report histories of childhood abuse.)

Yet another study revealed no evidence of overgeneral memory in borderline personality disorder patients, and no relation between childhood trauma and overgeneral memory (Arntz, Meeren, and Wessel 2002). Depressed women with histories of sexual abuse had problems retrieving specific personal memories in response to both positive and negative cue words, whereas depressed women without such histories did not (Kuyken and Brewin 1995). Overgeneral memories were especially common in women who said they tried hard to avoid thinking about their disturbing pasts in everyday life (Brewin et al. 1998). In contrast, a recent study found that overgeneral memory problems among psychiatric outpatients were associated with current clinical depression, but not with a history of childhood trauma (Wessel et al. 2001). However, no patient in the study had PTSD and the degree of trauma was only mild to moderate.[10] Psychiatric patients, most with PTSD, who had been brutalized by the Japanese during World War II as children retrieved more overgeneral memories than did healthy control subjects who had been similarly traumatized during the war (Wessel, Merckelbach, and Dekkers 2002). Therefore, it seems that psychiatric illness associated with childhood trauma—rather than childhood trauma per se—may give rise to overgeneral memory problems.

Trauma survivors seldom have trouble remembering neutral material in standardized tests of verbal or visual memory. But the picture changes when it comes to autobiographical memory. Most studies indicate that trauma survivors, especially those with PTSD, have a hard time recalling specific episodes from their personal lives. But the problem of overgeneral memory does not imply that patients are unable to remember their terrible experiences. Typically, patients remember their trauma all too well, but have difficulty remembering other parts of their past in detail. It is unclear whether this overgeneral style of remembering predates or results from PTSD. It may develop as a means of avoiding thinking about one's painful past. Finally, as noted in DSM-IV, some people with PTSD express a sense of foreshortened future. That is, after experiencing horrific events, they find it difficult to envision what their life will be like in the years to come. Perhaps difficulties recalling the past, exemplified by overgeneral memory problems, underlie difficulties envisioning the future.

NARRATIVE MEMORY FOR TRAUMA

The psychiatrist Bessel van der Kolk believes that the emotional intensity of trauma often makes it hard for survivors to piece together a coherent narrative of what happened (van der Kolk and Fisler 1995). Pursuing this issue empirically, several research groups have studied narrative fragmentation and coherence in PTSD patients. The clinical psychologist Edna Foa and her colleagues evaluated rape narratives in 14 female survivors of sexual assault at the beginning and the end of cognitive-behavioral treatment. Therapy required patients to describe in detail what had happened during the assault, and to do so repeatedly until their distress subsided. Foa's group defined narrative fragmentation as repeated phrases, speech fillers, and unfinished thoughts that disrupted the smooth flow of the story. Decreases in fragmentation over the course of therapy predicted improvement in PTSD symptoms (Foa, Molnar, and Cashman 1995).

In a subsequent study by Foa's group, Nader Amir and others (1998) investigated the complexity of sexual assault narratives and its relation to subsequent PTSD. They measured narrative complexity by using a computer program that counts the number of syllables per word and the number of words per sentence. The program calculates a "reading level" index for any text. Using this index as a measure of narrative complexity, they found that less complex narratives were associated with worse PTSD symptoms three months later ($r = -.63$). However, in a replication of this study, Matt Gray and Thomas Lombardo (2001) found that this inverse relation between narrative complexity and PTSD symptoms disappeared once they controlled statistically for the effects of verbal intelligence. That is, trauma survivors who have higher levels of verbal intelligence are more likely to provide complex, articulate trauma narratives and to have greater cognitive resources to enable them to overcome the effects of trauma.

Moreover, researchers have not compared the complexity of trauma narratives with the complexity of other kinds of narratives. Survivors who provide relatively inarticulate narratives of trauma might be just as inarticulate about neutral and positive experiences. There may be no direct connection between narrative complexity or coherence and trauma.

Mary Koss's research group has compared the structure of rape memories and other memories. In a mail survey of several thousand women (to which over 3,000 women responded), they asked whether the women had ever been raped. Approximately 30 percent of the respondents had been raped. Rape survivors answered questions about their memory for this event, whereas those who had not been raped answered questions about another emotionally intense experience that was either positive or negative. Relative to other unpleasant memories, rape memories were less vivid and clear, less visually detailed, less likely to be described in a meaningful order, less frequently recalled, less discussed with others, and less well remembered. Moreover, memories of rape contained fewer sensory components such as taste, sound, touch, and smell (Koss et al. 1996; Tromp et al. 1995).

Trauma survivors can furnish narratives of their experiences, albeit with varying degrees of coherence. Although initial narrative coherence is related to recovery from PTSD, both narrative coherence and recovery may be results of a third variable such as cognitive ability.

Does Traumatic Stress Damage the Brain?

Not only do stressors cause feelings of fear, they also prepare the body to fight or flee. Honed throughout evolutionary history, this fight-or-flight response to stress energizes the person to defend against danger. It is clearly adaptive, at least in the short run.

But the pioneering research of the biologist Robert Sapolsky uncovered a dark side to the fight-or-flight response. He found that prolonged activation of the stress response can actually damage the hippocampus, at least in rats and monkeys. Needless to say, these findings alarmed psychotherapists and researchers working in the field of traumatic stress. Could it be that traumatic stress damages the brains of survivors? Alternatively, might the chronic stress of having PTSD continue to harm the brain long after the stressor itself has passed? Answering these questions requires, first, a brief review of the biology of the stress response (see Sapolsky 1998).

In response to a stressor, the sympathetic branch of the autonomic nervous system becomes activated and the parasympathetic branch becomes suppressed. The two branches affect many of the same organs, but in opposite directions. When neurons in the sympathetic branch are activated, they release a substance called norepinephrine throughout the body, including sweat glands and blood vessels. This results in more blood flowing to the muscles and an increase in heart rate and blood pressure. In a matter of seconds, the body has fully mobilized for fight or flight. The hormone epinephrine is secreted by the adrenal glands on top of the kidneys, further activating the body. Meanwhile, the brain's hypothalamus secretes corticotropin releasing factor (CRF) and other "stress" hormones into the private circulatory system shared by the hypothalamus and the anterior pituitary gland. Within approximately 15 seconds, CRF causes the pituitary gland to secrete adrenocorticotropic hormone (ACTH) into the general circulatory system. Traveling through the bloodstream, ACTH reaches the adrenal glands on the kidneys. Within several minutes, it triggers the adrenal glands to release glucocorticoid (GC) into the bloodstream. GCs are stress-responsive hormones that act over the course of minutes and hours. The primary GC secreted in monkeys and man is cortisol, whereas the primary GC secreted by mice and rats is corticosterone. The pancreas releases glucagon, a hormone which, in conjunction with GCs and the sympathetic nervous system, raises levels of the sugar glucose in the bloodstream, thereby increasing available energy for action. The brain and pituitary gland secrete endorphins and enkephalins, substances that diminish perception of pain.[11]

The defensive response to threat is adaptive in the short run, but bodily damage can result from chronic, continual activation of this response. That is, GCs mobilize the body to defend against *immediate* threat, but prolonged GC secretion may be harmful. Because it contains so many GC receptors, the hippocampus is especially vulnerable to excessive GC exposure.

Animal research has shown that excessive exposure to GC can damage the hippocampus. Scientists elevate levels by injecting GCs into rats and monkeys. Chronically elevated GC levels render the hippocampus vulnerable to neurologic insults such as oxygen deficiency, hypoglycemia, and toxins. After administering excessive GCs to rodents for several days, researchers noted that the ability of hippocampal neurons to survive injury caused by insufficient blood flow had been compromised (Sapolsky and Pulsinelli 1985). When GC exposure continued for several weeks, hippocampal dendrites began to atrophy, even without any neurologic insult (Woolley, Gould, and McEwen 1990). (Dendrites are thin "tubes" that branch out from a neuron, enabling it to receive signals from other neurons.) Other studies have shown that cortisol-secreting pellets, implanted in the hippocampi of vervet monkeys for one year, caused neuronal atrophy (Sapolsky et al. 1990); that a single dose of dexamethasone, a synthetic GC, given to pregnant rhesus monkeys, damaged hippocampal neurons in their near-term fetuses (Uno et al. 1990); and that rats receiving three months of daily injections of corticosterone that kept GCs circulating at high physiologic levels actually experienced a loss of hippocampal neurons (Sapolsky, Krey, and McEwen 1985).

Social stressors that trigger high GC release in nonhuman primates can also damage the hippocampus. When a marmoset monkey is placed into the home cage of an unfamiliar adult male marmoset monkey, the "intruder" experiences great stress. This social stress generates GC release and inhibits the formation of new neurons in the hippocampus of the intruder monkey (Gould et al. 1998). The brains of eight socially subordinate vervet monkeys that had died in captivity exhibited extensive evidence of GC-related hippocampal damage. Scars and other circumstantial evidence strongly indicated that these monkeys must have been often attacked by other monkeys (Uno et al. 1989). Monkeys occupying the lowest rung of the social hierarchy are exposed to chronic, repeated social stressors that maintain GCs at high levels.

Research on human subjects indicates that elevated GCs can impair performance on explicit memory tasks requiring the hippocampus (for a review see Lupien and McEwen 1997). Testing healthy volunteers, John Newcomer's research group (1999) found that several days of exposure to oral doses of cortisol, similar to levels produced by major stress (such as cardiac surgery), lowered performance on a verbal recall task. Memory performance returned to normal once levels of cortisol returned to normal. C. Kirschbaum's research team (1996) exposed subjects to a social stressor (giving a speech followed by solving arithmetic problems out loud) before having them learn and recall a list of words. The higher the cortisol levels induced by the social stressor, the fewer words the subjects recalled. In Kirschbaum's second experiment, subjects who had received a dose of cortisol performed less well on a declarative memory test than those who had received placebo. No differences emerged between the groups on a procedural memory test that did not require hippocampal involvement. Dominique de Quervain and his colleagues (2000) administered cortisone to healthy volunteers either one hour before learning a word list, one hour after learning it, or one hour before a recall test administered 24 hours later. (Cortisone is rapidly absorbed and transformed into cortisol.) Cortisone reduced recall only in the third group of subjects. That is, cortisone made it harder to recall words that had already been learned, but it did not impair learning them in the first place. It did not lower performance on a recognition test for any of the groups. Hence, for students, stress-related increases in cortisol during final exams may be more likely to impair performance on an essay exam than on a multiple-choice test requiring only recognition of the correct answer.

Some studies suggest that chronically elevated cortisol may actually shrink the human hippocampus. Studying elderly subjects, Sonia Lupien and her colleagues (1998) found that cortisol levels were correlated with smaller hippocampi and with poor recall of line drawing and poor performance on a maze task. Monica Starkman and her colleagues (1992) found that patients with Cushing's Syndrome, a condition characterized by chronically elevated cortisol stemming from an adrenal tumor, had reduced hippocampal volume and verbal (but not visual) learning and memory deficits. Moreover, the higher their plasma cortisol level, the smaller their hippocampi, and the smaller their hippocampi, the worse their verbal memory deficits. Taken together, these data led Robert Sapolsky (1996) to conclude that "stress is bad for your brain."

Aware of the toxic effects of excessive GC exposure in animals, the biological psychiatrist Douglas Bremner and his colleagues wondered whether stress might have damaged the brains of their PTSD patients. In particular, given the density of GC receptors in the hippocampus—and the vital role of this subcortical temporal lobe structure in memory—they hypothesized that the hippocampi of PTSD patients might show signs of atrophy relative to the hippocampi of control subjects. To test this hypothesis, they used magnetic resonance imaging (MRI) methods. This scanning technique produces images of the brain that enable scientists to measure the volume of various structures. They found that a group of 26 Vietnam combat veterans with PTSD had significantly smaller right hippocampi (by 8 percent) and nonsignificantly smaller left hippocampi (by 3.8 percent) than did a control group of nonveterans. Moreover, the smaller a veteran's right hippocampus, the worse was his score on a verbal memory test. These findings were consistent with the hypothesis that stress had actually shrunk the right hippocampus of the PTSD veterans (Bremner, Randall, Scott, Bronen, et al. 1995).[12]

The connection between trauma and smaller hippocampi is not confined to Vietnam veterans. Bremner's group found that patients whose PTSD was associated with childhood physical or sexual abuse had significantly smaller left hippocampal volume (by 12 percent) and nonsignificantly smaller right hippocampal volume (by 5 percent) than did nonabused control subjects.

This time, however, smaller (left) hippocampal volumes were unrelated to verbal memory deficits (Bremner, Randall, Vermetten, et al. 1997).[13]

Nor was Bremner's group the only one to report smaller hippocampi in trauma survivors. The biological psychiatrist Murray Stein and his associates (1997) found that 21 women who reported histories of childhood sexual abuse had significantly smaller left hippocampi (by 4.9 percent) and nonsignificantly smaller right hippocampi (by 2.9 percent) than did 21 psychiatrically healthy women who denied a trauma history. Fifteen abused women qualified for PTSD and 15 also qualified for a dissociative disorder. Although no subject had ever been amnesic for her abuse, smaller left hippocampal volume was strongly related to dissociative symptoms in the abused group ($r = -.73$). Hippocampal volume was unrelated to history of alcohol problems, severity of abuse, or a measure of explicit memory functioning. Finally, abused subjects with PTSD did not differ from abused subjects without PTSD in terms of hippocampal volume (Sapolsky 2000).[14]

The most dramatic evidence of possible atrophy was published by Tamara Gurvits and her colleagues (1996). They studied seven Vietnam combat veterans with PTSD, seven Vietnam combat veterans without PTSD, and eight healthy nonveteran control subjects. Finding no differences in hippocampal volume between the two non-PTSD control groups, Gurvits combined them and compared them with the PTSD group. PTSD subjects had significantly smaller left (by 26 percent) and right (by 22 percent) hippocampi than did control subjects. When the authors statistically adjusted for age and whole brain volume, the effects diminished but remained significant for the left hippocampus. However, hippocampal volume was unrelated to memory functioning. Gurvits and her colleagues detected twice as many neurological soft signs in the PTSD group as in the combat veteran control group. (Neurological soft signs are nonspecific indications of abnormality that cannot be localized in the nervous system. Examples include a history of childhood bedwetting, attention deficit problems, and delays in learning to walk and talk.)[15]

Other scientists have investigated possible hippocampal atrophy in trauma survivors who have other primary diagnoses. For example, Martin Driessen and his colleagues (2000) conducted an MRI study on 21 women with borderline personality disorder and 21 women without psychiatric illness. The borderline group had significantly smaller left (15.7 percent) and right (15.8 percent) hippocampal volumes than did the control group. This pattern was not confined to the 12 patients who also qualified for PTSD; the 9 patients who did not have PTSD also had significantly smaller hippocampi than did the control subjects. The borderline and control groups did not differ on any measure of verbal or visual memory, nor were hippocampal volumes related to memory function. However, when Driessen combined the two groups, he found that hippocampal volume was significantly related to extent of reported childhood physical, emotional, and sexual abuse (the more abuse, the smaller the hippocampi; $r = -0.49$).[16]

Ingrid Agartz's research team (1999) found that alcoholic women and men had significantly smaller right hippocampi than did healthy control subjects, whereas the left hippocampal volume was smaller in female alcoholic subjects only. Twelve of the 26 alcoholic women had PTSD, but their hippocampal volumes did not differ from those of alcoholic women without PTSD. Therefore, alcoholism was more strongly associated with small hippocampi than was PTSD.

The aforementioned studies have led some scientists, such as Sapolsky (1996, 2000) and Bremner (1999, 2001), to suggest that traumatic stressors may elevate cortisol levels so high that hippocampal damage occurs. Another possibility is that the stress of having chronic PTSD may maintain cortisol at a dangerously high level, thereby wearing away at the hippocampus. That is, even if cortisol released during the trauma did not damage the hippocampus, the persistent stress of PTSD might do so.

Some specialists in traumatic stress have wondered whether stress-damaged, smaller hippocampi might make survivors vulnerable to forgetting traumatic experiences. After all, the hippocampus is vital for transferring autobiographical episodes into long-term memory, and any damage to this structure might foster amnesia for traumatic episodes. But as John Kihlstrom and Daniel Schacter (2000) have pointed out, this cannot be the case. Even if stress did damage the hippocampus, such harm could not explain amnesia for the traumatic events themselves. As the studies on H.M. illustrate, damage to the hippocampus prevents encoding of *new* experiences. It does not prevent people from recalling old experiences encoded before the damage occurred. Even if childhood trauma were to damage the hippocampi of abuse survivors, they would still be able to remember their trauma.

So, does stress damage the brains of trauma survivors? Probably not. The findings of these studies are better understood in another way.[17] For example, Omer Bonne and his colleagues (2001) used MRI to scan 37 trauma survivors one week after they had been admitted to a hospital emergency room. Unlike previous researchers, Bonne measured their hippocampi a second time, six months later. By this second assessment, 10 of the 37 trauma survivors had developed PTSD. If stress damages the brain, one would expect the hippocampi of the PTSD subjects to have gotten smaller over the course of the six months. This had not happened. The hippocampal volumes in the PTSD group had not changed over the course of six months. In fact, there was no difference in hippocampal volume between the PTSD and non-PTSD group, nor were PTSD symptoms correlated with hippocampal volume at either MRI scan. Neither exposure to a traumatic event nor having PTSD—for six months, at least—was sufficient to produce hippocampal atrophy.

Another serious problem for the atrophy hypothesis is that cortisol levels in PTSD patients are rarely high, as Rachel Yehuda and her colleagues have repeatedly shown. In one study, combat veterans with PTSD had *lower* average 24-hour urinary cortisol levels than did healthy control subjects or patients with major depressive disorder (Yehuda et al. 1990; Mason et al. 1986). In another study, both male and female Holocaust survivors with PTSD had lower urinary cortisol levels than did those without PTSD, Holocaust survivors with past PTSD, or control subjects who had not been exposed to trauma (Yehuda, Kahana, et al. 1995). Average values among PTSD patients usually fall in the 30–40 μg/day range, whereas non-PTSD subjects usually fall in the 50–60 μg/day range (Yehuda 1997). Only if someone's values fell outside the normal range (20–90 μg/day) would we suspect an endocrine disorder. Studies measuring plasma cortisol have likewise shown lower levels in veterans with PTSD than in psychiatrically healthy veterans (Yehuda et al. 1996; Boscarino 1996).[18]

De Bellis and his colleagues did report higher urinary cortisol levels in maltreated prepubertal children with PTSD than in healthy, nonabused children (De Bellis, Baum, et al. 1999). However, cortisol levels were just as elevated in a group of nonabused children diagnosed with overanxious disorder. So even when cortisol is elevated in PTSD subjects, it may have nothing to do with trauma as such. In any event, De Bellis's research group found that the hippocampi of maltreated children and adolescents with PTSD were no smaller than those of nonabused, healthy control children (De Bellis, Keshavan, et al. 1999).

Finally, in a large study of Vietnam veterans with PTSD, John Mason and his colleagues (2001) found cortisol levels to be entirely normal. Indeed, Mason's group reported an average cortisol value in veterans with PTSD (61.3 μg/day) nearly identical to that of the healthy control subjects in their early research (62.8 μg/day) (Yehuda et al. 1990). Cortisol is unlikely to bear any simple relationship to PTSD.

Most studies do not show elevated cortisol in PTSD patients. But perhaps the initial burst of cortisol is so extreme that damage to the hippocampus occurs almost immediately? Would this explain why the hippocampi of PTSD patients are so often small, despite the absence of chronically elevated cortisol (Bremner 2001)? This scenario seems unlikely. A massive burst of cortisol is an adaptive component of the fight-or-flight response. As Sapolsky's work shows, it takes weeks or months of exposure to extremely high GC levels to produce any hippocampal atrophy in animals. A brief, single burst, however massive, will not do any lasting damage.

Several researchers, cited above, have shown that administration of cortisol can reduce recall of emotionally neutral words in healthy subjects. Does this imply that cortisol, released during trauma, might impair later recollection of the traumatic event? This seems extremely unlikely. In fact, as Tony Buchanan and William Lovallo (2000) have shown, cortisol *enhances* memory in healthy subjects when the material encoded is itself emotionally arousing. Subjects were given either cortisol or placebo prior to viewing a series of pictures with positive emotional valence (such as attractive people), negative emotional valence (such as mutilated people), or neutral valence (such as household objects). One week later, subjects who had received cortisol exhibited better recall of both kinds of emotional pictures than of neutral pictures. Other studies showing that cortisol adversely affects recall have been confined to memory for emotionally neutral material. When what is encoded is itself arousing (as in trauma), cortisol enhances encoding and later recall. Indeed, the memory-enhancing effects of cortisol, acting in concert with other stress hormones (epinephrine), are consistent with research cited in Chapter 4 on memory for emotional events.

In fact, measurement of urinary cortisol during exposure to trauma confirms that it bears no straightforward relationship to trauma. John Howard and his colleagues (1955) measured urinary GCs while soldiers were undergoing artillery bombardment during the Korean war. Levels increased dramatically during the first day of shelling, diminished during the second day of shelling, and normalized once the bombardment ceased. Other data reported by this group indicated that on days without combat GC levels quickly returned to normal, and even on days when fatal ambushes occurred levels did not get as high as they did during artillery bombardment. Field studies during the Vietnam war also failed to show GC increases in combat situations, perhaps because these soldiers were highly trained, disciplined members of Special Forces units notable for their sense of mastery and control in threatening environments (Bourne, Rose, and Mason 1967, 1968).[19]

Research on Cushing's Syndrome provides strong evidence against the hypothesis that severe stress damages the hippocampi of trauma survivors. Ironically, this research also provides the strongest evidence that cortisol can shrink the hippocampus and produce explicit, declarative memory deficits. This apparent paradox is resolved by a few facts. Cushing's patients typically experience years of exposure to extremely high levels of cortisol caused by a tumor on the adrenal cortex. Cortisol levels are vastly higher than anything occurring in PTSD patients. For example, Monica Starkman and her colleagues reported an average cortisol level of 508 μg/day in their Cushing's patients. This value is far above the normal range (20–90 μg/day), and much higher than anything reported in the PTSD literature. Most important, after surgical treatment of the tumor, cortisol levels quickly normalize, memory deficits disappear, and the hippocampus returns to its normal size (Starkman et al. 1992, 1999, 2001).

A landmark MRI study by Mark Gilbertson and his colleagues (2002) has also refuted the hippocampal atrophy hypothesis. Gilbertson assessed hippocampal volume in a series of monozygotic (identical) twin pairs: 17 pairs in which one twin developed combat-related PTSD and the other twin had not seen combat and had no psychopathology, and 23 pairs in which the combat-exposed brothers had never developed PTSD and their twins had not seen combat and had no psychopathology. If chronic PTSD resulted in small hippocampi, then the hippocampi of the twins with PTSD should have been smaller than those of their brothers. Although Gilbertson and his colleagues replicated previous reports of smaller hippocampi in subjects with severe PTSD, they found that the hippocampi of their identical twins were just as small. The severity of PTSD symptoms was correlated with total hippocampal volume in trauma-exposed subjects (the worse the PTSD, the smaller the hippocampus; $r = -.64$), but it was just as strongly correlated with the total hippocampal volume of their twin brothers ($r = -.70$).

The striking concordance in hippocampal volume between pairs of identical twins—irrespective of the presence of PTSD or trauma history—indicates a genetic influence on the size of this brain structure. Gilbertson concluded that small hippocampi may constitute a preexisting risk factor for developing PTSD among those who are exposed to trauma. This interpretation, moreover, accords with other studies showing that some trauma-exposed people with PTSD have a history of neurodevelopmental abnormalities (Gurvits et al. 1993, 2000). Compromised neurocognitive functioning may hamper an individual's ability to cope with stressful events, thereby increasing the likelihood of PTSD.[20]

Is it possible that an environmental factor, shared by twins, reduced the size of their hippocampi? Perhaps twins with small hippocampi were both exposed to high levels of sexual and physical abuse as children (and higher levels than subjects with normal hippocampi and no PTSD), and the stress of this chronic trauma damaged their brains? For two reasons, this nongenetic explanation is implausible. First, Gilbertson found no significant differences in self-reported childhood sexual and physical abuse among the groups. Second, De Bellis found that abused children have hippocampi of normal size.

Cognitive Mechanisms of Traumatic Memory

Much of what we know about how people remember trauma is based on what survivors tell us during clinical interviews: their narrative descriptions of flashbacks, intrusive thoughts, and nightmares. But self-report of inner experience does not reveal the underlying psychobiological mechanisms that give rise to these reexperiencing symptoms. Just as we would not expect the introspective accounts of kidney patients or heart patients to illuminate what has gone wrong with their kidneys or hearts, we should not expect the introspective accounts of trauma survivors to provide satisfactory explanations of how their brains give rise to intrusive memories of trauma (McNally 2001c).

Appreciation of the limitations of self-report has inspired the application of experimental cognitive psychology methods to the study of PTSD and other anxiety disorders (McNally 1996, 1998; Williams et al. 1997). These methods rely on reaction time and other measures as a basis for inferring how people process information. They complement the standard self-report methods of the traumatic stress field: questionnaires and interviews.

The most popular experimental method for studying intrusive cognition has been the emotional Stroop task. The original (nonemotional) version was devised by a graduate student, John Ridley Stroop, in the 1930s. To study how people focus their attention in the midst of distraction, Stroop (1935) had subjects name the colors of a long series of words, printed on sheets of paper, as quickly and as accurately as possible. The words were names of colors themselves. For example, a subject might see the words *red, blue, green,* and so forth. On some sheets of paper, the stimuli were color-congruent—*red* appeared in red letters, *blue* in blue letters, and so on. When the meaning of the word and its color matched, subjects sailed through the task, naming the colors with great speed and accuracy. But when stimuli were color-incongruent, such as when *red* appeared in blue letters, subjects were much slower to name the colors. The meanings of the words automatically captured the subjects' attention, despite their efforts to concentrate on the color. The automatic activation of word meaning, and its slowing of color-naming, has been dubbed the "Stroop interference effect."

Variations of Stroop's task have been used in many studies on attentional and lexical processing (for reviews see MacLeod 1991a; Williams, Mathews, and MacLeod 1996). Yet soon after publishing his landmark dissertation, Stroop lost interest in the field and resumed his passionate study of the Bible. A devout Baptist, Stroop published seven books on the Bible, and he was eventually appointed Professor of Biblical Studies at a small religious college (MacLeod 1991b). Although Stroop forgot about psychology, psychology has not forgotten about him. His work has had a profound impact on clinical as well as cognitive researchers.

The clinical researchers Andrew Mathews and Colin MacLeod (1985) adapted the Stroop task to study automatic processing of threat-related words in anxiety patients, and my graduate students and I adapted it for the study of intrusive cognition in PTSD. If, as trauma survivors report, traumatic memories come to mind all too easily in people with PTSD, then a variant of the Stroop task might provide an objective, quantitative measure of this intrusive cognitive process. We asked Vietnam combat veterans with PTSD and healthy Vietnam combat veterans to name the colors of trauma words (such as *firefight*), other negative words (such as *feces*), positive words (such as *friendship*), neutral words (such as *concrete*), and nonwords (such as *ooooo*). Each stimulus was printed in either blue, red, green, orange, or black letters, and all stimuli from a specific category appeared on a single large card. The time taken to name the colors of all words on a card was the dependent variable. The PTSD patients took longer to color-name trauma words than other words; evidently they found it harder to suppress the meanings of the trauma words than those of the other words. The healthy combat veterans had no such problem. Hence the delay in color-naming trauma words provided a quantitative measure of intrusiveness (McNally, Kaspi, et al. 1990).

After developing a computerized version, which enabled us to measure each color-naming response in milliseconds, my students and I found that rape survivors with PTSD responded very similarly to the veterans with PTSD (Cassiday, McNally, and Zeitlin 1992). Other studies have replicated the trauma-related Stroop interference effect in people whose PTSD is linked to combat, rape, childhood sexual abuse, motor vehicle accidents, and disasters at sea.[21] Stroop interference increases as congruence between the stimulus words and the personal concerns of the subjects increases. Words that are specifically associated with trauma tend to provoke more interference than words that are less closely associated with trauma. That is, the more the meaning of the words reflects the content of intrusive thought, the slower patients are to color-name the words (for example, *ambush* versus *jeep*; *rape* versus *crime*). Moreover, interference for trauma words is more strongly associated with intrusive symptoms than with avoidance and numbing symptoms.[22]

These data suggest that trauma-related Stroop interference may provide a quantitative, nonintrospective index of the degree to which traumatic memories are intrusive. It may also provide an objective measure of recovery from trauma. Edna Foa and her colleagues (1991) found that rape survivors whose PTSD had been successfully treated via cognitive-behavior therapy did not show the trauma-linked Stroop interference effect, whereas symptomatic rape survivors did.[23]

Intrusive reexperiencing phenomena in PTSD appear to reflect automatic cognitive processes. Intrusive thoughts and flashbacks occur involuntarily. As emotional Stroop studies have shown, PTSD patients cannot help attending to trauma-related material. Is the information-processing system in PTSD biased in favor of automatic processing of traumatic information in other ways? Will patients with PTSD automatically process threat cues of which they are not consciously aware?

Studies on automatic, unconscious processing of traumatic material in PTSD have yielded conflicting findings. Researchers have used subliminal Stroop paradigms, in which each colored word appears on a computer screen too briefly to permit conscious registration of its meaning (for example, a few dozen milliseconds). Each word is immediately followed by a random string of letters (such as *xtwifn*) the same color as the word, and the subject's task is to name the color as quickly as possible. The string of letters "masks" the immediately preceding word, making it impossible to read consciously. Although Allison Harvey and her colleagues found that PTSD patients exhibit delayed color-naming of subliminal trauma words, my colleagues and I, and Todd Buckley and his colleagues, have failed to replicate this effect in PTSD patients.[24]

Other experiments have failed to show that Vietnam veterans with PTSD process trauma-related material outside of awareness. David Trandel and I (1987) found that trauma words inserted into an audiotape played to one ear did not disrupt PTSD patients' ability to listen to and repeat aloud a different audiotaped prose passage played to the other ear. Had patients unconsciously processed the trauma words, they would have made errors while trying to repeat the passage they were hearing in the other ear. Moreover, the PTSD patients did not exhibit heightened physiologic reactivity (skin conductance responses) to trauma words occurring outside of awareness. Indeed, in another experiment, requiring auditory identification of words against a background of white noise, our research group found that PTSD patients exhibited skin conductance responses to combat words, but only when they could consciously perceive them (McNally et al. 1987).

To the extent that patients with PTSD experience intrusive thoughts about their trauma, they ought to exhibit explicit memory biases favoring recall of trauma-related information in the laboratory. Consistent with this hypothesis, Scott Vrana and his colleagues found that Vietnam combat veterans with PTSD recalled more emotional words, such as *death* and *firefight*, relative to neutral words, such as *clock* and *windows*, and relative to combat veterans without PTSD. That is, PTSD was associated with superior recall of words related to traumatic events (Vrana, Roodman, and Beckham 1995).

Nader Amir and I did two experiments to test whether patients with combat-related PTSD exhibit implicit memory biases favoring trauma-relevant material. In our perceptual identification experiment, Vietnam combat veterans with and without PTSD viewed a series of trauma words, positive words, and neutral words on a computer screen. Shortly thereafter, they saw these "old" words intermixed with "new" distractor words drawn from the same three categories. During this second phase, each word (such as *NAPALM*) flashed on the screen for only 100 milliseconds and was followed by a visual mask comprising random characters (such as #&%@$&). Subjects were asked to identify these briefly presented words. Both groups recognized old words more often than new ones, thereby demonstrating an overall priming (implicit memory) effect. But there was no evidence of superior priming for trauma words in the PTSD group, perhaps because perceptual identification tests are more sensitive to the physical features of the stimulus, such as whether the letters are lowercase or uppercase, than to its meaning (McNally and Amir 1996).

In our second experiment, we did find evidence of enhanced priming of trauma-relevant material in PTSD patients. PTSD patients and healthy combat veterans heard a series of prerecorded sentences related either to the Vietnam war or to neutral themes. Shortly thereafter, they heard these same sentences intermixed with new trauma-relevant and neutral sentences against a background of white noise. Subjects were asked to rate the perceived volume of the noise accompanying each sentence. Previous exposure to a sentence should make it more intelligible when it later occurs against a background of white noise. If the sentence seems easier to hear and understand, then the background noise should not seem so loud. Therefore, implicit memory for sentences would be reflected in lower perceived volume ratings for noise accompanying old sentences than for noise accompanying new sentences. This is in fact what happened, and the effect was most pronounced for trauma-relevant sentences in the PTSD group (Amir, McNally, and Wiegartz 1996). This finding implies that PTSD patients more thoroughly encoded trauma-related material.[25]

Can Survivors Forget Trauma?

Some trauma therapists, such as Denise Gelinas, Lenore Terr, and Judith Herman, believe that sexually abused children develop an avoidant (or dissociative) encoding style that enables them to cope by disengaging their attention from what is happening during episodes of abuse and directing it elsewhere. Attending to innocuous cues (such as wallpaper patterns) may attenuate an otherwise very frightening experience. The experimental psychologist Jennifer Freyd believes that children molested by trusted caregivers are especially likely to acquire this cognitive style, thereby impairing their later ability to remember their abuse.[26]

Recent experiments by Michael Anderson and Collin Green (2001) have been interpreted as providing possible support for this idea. Although they did not study abuse survivors or memory for traumatic material, Anderson and Green, some psychologists believe, identified a mechanism that might allow children to inhibit memory for abuse. College students memorized pairs of unrelated words (such as *ordeal* and *roach*) before performing a "think/no-think" task. During this task, students saw the first word from a pair (*ordeal*) and said its associate (*roach*) out loud (in the "think" condition) or tried not to think about the associate (in the "no-think" condition). They had been told ahead of time which first words were to cue thinking and which were to cue cognitive avoidance. The word pairs were shown 1, 8, or 16 times (or not at all in a baseline condition). Subjects were later shown all the first words and asked to recall their associates. Strikingly, subjects had a harder time recalling associates whose first words had originally received "no-think" instructions than associates of the other words. That is, after repeatedly trying *not* to think of the associate of a word cue, subjects found it harder to recall this associate when told to do so.

Noting that deliberate attempts not to think about the associate word resulted in its inhibition from memory, the cognitive psychologist Martin Conway (2001) suggested that the inhibition might be even stronger if the material targeted for forgetting was of emotional significance and something that subjects would be highly motivated to forget. Alluding to Freud, Anderson, Green, and Conway concluded from this research that repeated attempts to forget certain material—when confronted with reminders—provide a mechanism for the repression of disturbing memories (such as memories of incest).

Their conclusions are premature. Even after repeated attempts to forget target associates, subjects in Anderson and Green's experiments still recalled approximately 75 percent of the words; "repression" was far from complete. Moreover, Anderson and Green's conclusions are inconsistent with research on memory for threatening material in people who have emotional disorders. My colleagues and I conducted experiments in which we asked psychiatric patients to try to forget negative emotional words. Contrary to Conway's conjecture, we found that patients with panic disorder were no more able than healthy control subjects to forget emotionally threatening material (McNally et al. 1999) and that patients with obsessive-compulsive disorder were *less* able than healthy control subjects to forget disturbing words (Wilhelm et al. 1996).

In fact, most research indicates that deliberate attempts to suppress emotionally disturbing thoughts tend to backfire (Wegner 1994; McNally and Ricciardi 1996). Allison Harvey and Richard Bryant (1998b) found that survivors of automobile accidents suffering from acute stress disorder experienced a marked increase in trauma-related thoughts after attempting not to think about the accidents. Likewise, Jillian Shipherd and Gayle Beck (1999) found that when rape survivors with PTSD attempted to suppress trauma-related thoughts in the laboratory, the thoughts became even more frequent.

However, none of the aforementioned studies concerned people who had been sexually abused as children—the very group that, according to Terr and others, should have the most-developed forgetting skills. Accordingly, my colleagues and I tested the ability to forget trauma-related words in women with histories of sexual abuse, either with or without PTSD, and in women with neither abuse histories nor PTSD. The subjects viewed a series of trauma-related words (such as *incest*), positive words (*celebrate*), and neutral words (*mailbox*) that appeared one at a time on a computer screen. After each word, an instruction appeared telling the subject either to remember or to forget the word. After this encoding phase, subjects were asked to write down as many of the words as they could remember, regardless of the original instructions. The abuse survivors with PTSD exhibited memory deficits, but only for positive and neutral words they were supposed to remember. They remembered trauma words very well, including those they were supposed to forget (McNally et al. 1998).

Using similar directed-forgetting methods, Lauren Korfine and Jill Hooley (2000) tested individuals with borderline personality disorder—a syndrome often linked with early childhood abuse. Relative to healthy control subjects, borderline subjects exhibited no memory deficits for negative, positive, or neutral words they had been instructed to remember. In fact, they had superior recall for negative words they were supposed to forget relative to other words and relative to control subjects.

In another directed-forgetting study, Bernet Elzinga and her colleagues (2000) found that patients with dissociative identity disorder were unable to forget words they had been instructed to forget, especially sexual words. Once again, patients who might have been expected to forget emotionally charged material had difficulty doing so.

Michelle Moulds and Richard Bryant (2002) have published the only study suggesting that trauma survivors might be good at forgetting disturbing material. Patients with acute stress disorder recalled significantly fewer trauma-related words they had been instructed to forget than did trauma-exposed people without the disorder and control subjects who had not been exposed to trauma. However, the groups did not differ in their recall of trauma-related words they had been instructed to remember. The traumatic events were recent and involved either motor vehicle accidents or nonsexual assault.

The preponderance of laboratory research confirms reports of intrusive cognition in trauma survivors with PTSD. Emotional Stroop studies show that survivors with PTSD have difficulty suppressing the meanings of trauma-related words. Moreover, despite their strong motivation to forget traumatic material—or perhaps *because of* this motivation—survivors with PTSD have trouble forgetting such material. These laboratory studies directly contradict the hypothesis that survivors are especially capable of forgetting trauma.

Judith Herman once wrote: "The ordinary response to atrocities is to banish them from consciousness" (1992: 1). But if survivors have difficulty banishing mere trauma-related *words* from consciousness, how much more difficult must it be to banish atrocities? *Attempts* to banish traumatic memories from consciousness must not be confused with *success* at doing so.

Brain Correlates of Remembering Trauma

Scientists have used positron emission tomography (PET) and functional magnetic resonance imaging (fMRI) to identify regions of the brain showing heightened activity when trauma survivors hear audiotaped scripts narrating their traumatic events or hear or see stimuli related to these events. By such methods, researchers hope to understand the neuroanatomical circuits that mediate recollection of trauma. They have also investigated whether patterns of brain activation differ between survivors who have PTSD and survivors who do not.

Interpreting this literature is not easy. Studies vary in their methods and in their subjects, and results vary from study to study. Other than making general predictions regarding the likely activation of limbic (emotional) regions of the brain, researchers have seldom been specific about the implications of their findings. Exploratory work building an empirical data base has been the order of the day. To some extent, this is true of the entire field of functional neuroimaging. It is a new field fraught with complex findings that often are not replicated and are difficult to interpret (see Uttal 2001). This is especially true when the investigations concern higher-level cognitive and emotional processes, such as remembering trauma.

Applying the script-driven imagery paradigm, several research groups have used PET to determine which brain regions show heightened activity when PTSD patients are asked to visualize their traumatic experiences while listening to audiotaped narratives of these experiences. Researchers compare these patterns of brain activation to those occurring when subjects hear audiotaped narratives of neutral experiences.

Testing eight PTSD patients who had suffered diverse traumas, Scott Rauch and his colleagues (1996) found that trauma scripts provoked heightened activity in the medial orbitofrontal cortex, the insular cortex, the anterior temporal pole, the medial temporal cortex, and the secondary visual cortex. They also detected heightened activation in the right amygdala and the anterior cingulate cortex, regions that are believed to mediate emotional experience. Moreover, a region of the brain implicated in speech production (Broca's area) exhibited decreased activation when patients listened to their trauma scripts.

Unfortunately, Rauch's group did not test any control subjects. Therefore it is impossible to tell whether these patterns of brain activation reflect traumatic *memory*. Perhaps anyone who listened to these horrific narratives would exhibit the same pattern of activation as did the patients who had actually experienced the traumatic events. Commenting on this study, Bessel van der Kolk has interpreted the deactivation in Broca's speech area as confirming his notion that for some individuals "the memories of trauma may have no verbal (explicit) component at all: the memory may be entirely organized on an implicit or perceptual level, without an accompanying narrative about what happened" (van der Kolk and Fisler 1995: 512). This makes no sense. The subjects *themselves* provided the narrative accounts of their traumatic experiences that Rauch and his colleagues used to make the audiotaped autobiographical trauma scripts. Whatever the explanation for the deactivation of Broca's area, it cannot be attributed to the subjects' inability to narrate what had happened to them.

In a project headed by Lisa Shin, our research group used PET to examine patterns of brain activation in 16 women who reported histories of childhood sexual abuse, 8 of whom had PTSD and 8 of whom did not. Subjects were asked to visualize the events narrated in the audiotaped trauma scripts and in neutral scripts, and their heart rate, blood pressure, and self-ratings of emotional responses were recorded. We found greater increases in heart rate during trauma narratives than during neutral narratives, and this effect was more pronounced in the PTSD group than in the non-PTSD group. Blood pressure differences and self-reported emotions increased in both groups. Relative to neutral narratives, trauma narratives produced heightened activation in orbitofrontal cortex and anterior temporal poles in both groups, but especially in the PTSD group. Increases in activation of the anterior cingulate gyrus were greater in the non-PTSD group than in the PTSD group, while decreases in activation of the bilateral anterior frontal regions were greater in the PTSD group than in the non-PTSD group. Only the PTSD group exhibited decreased activation in the left inferior frontal gyrus (Broca's area). The amygdala did not show heightened activation during trauma scripts in either group (Shin et al. 1999).

Also using PET, Douglas Bremner and his colleagues tested 22 women who had been sexually abused in childhood, 10 of them with PTSD, while the subjects listened to audiotaped scripts narrating traumatic experiences and neutral ones. Relative to non-PTSD subjects, PTSD subjects, while listening to trauma scripts, exhibited greater increases in activation in the anterior prefrontal cortex, the posterior cingulate, and the motor cortex; and greater decreases in activation in the subcallosal gyrus region of the anterior cingulate, the right hippocampus, the fusiform/inferior temporal gyrus, the supramarginal gyrus, and the visual association cortex. Also, PTSD patients did not show any activation in the anterior cingulate during the trauma scripts (Bremner, Narayan, et al. 1999). As in Shin's study, there was no detectable activation of the amygdala during processing of trauma scripts.

Using fMRI and script-driven imagery, Ruth Lanius and her colleagues (2001) found that six survivors of sexual abuse or assault and three survivors of motor vehicle accidents, all with PTSD, exhibited less activation in the thalamus, the anterior cingulate gyrus, and the medial frontal gyrus than did nine psychiatrically healthy trauma survivors. Again, no heightened activity in the amygdala was evident.

Patterns of brain activation in PTSD patients have been strikingly inconsistent across studies. Although all subjects were retrieving traumatic autobiographical memories prompted by audiotaped imagery scripts, results varied widely from study to study. Researchers sometimes noted activation in limbic structures associated with emotional experience (such as the anterior temporal pole), but different limbic structures showed heightened activation across different studies. The amygdala, for example, showed activation in only one of four studies. Across studies, PTSD patients exhibited increases, decreases, or no change in activation in the anterior cingulate. There is no obvious explanation for this diverse pattern of findings.

Scientists have also measured functional activity in the brain while PTSD patients view or hear trauma-related stimuli. These experiments do not require autobiographical recollection as such, but instead concern patterns of activation while patients process trauma-relevant stimuli.

In another PET project led by Lisa Shin, our group found that seven Vietnam combat veterans with PTSD had heightened activation in the right amygdala and the anterior cingulate gyrus while visualizing combat-related pictures (for example, of a sniper) which they had previously viewed. Healthy combat veterans did not show this effect, and PTSD patients did not exhibit this effect to neutral pictures (such as a building) or negative pictures (a funeral) unrelated to the war. When viewing combat pictures, PTSD subjects had decreased activation in Broca's area (Shin et al. 1997).

Also using PET, Håkan Fischer's group showed a videotape of a bank robbery to six employees who had been present during the hold-up. The subjects were not assessed for PTSD, nor was there a control group. Compared to a neutral video, the robbery video "altered activity in paralimbic and cortical brain regions of relevance for cognition and affect." Broca's area also showed decreased activity during the robbery tape, an effect that Fischer and his colleagues attributed to inhibitions of language processing caused by fear—subjects seemed scared speechless. This interpretation differs from van der Kolk's claim that trauma survivors have difficulty *describing* their trauma in narrative form (Fischer, Wik, and Fredrickson 1996: 2081).

Using PET, Douglas Bremner and his colleagues scanned Vietnam combat veterans with or without PTSD while they viewed combat pictures accompanied by combat sounds and neutral winter scenes accompanied by instrumental music. Relative to the non-PTSD veterans, those with PTSD exhibited decreased activation in the medial prefrontal cortex and the middle temporal gyrus. Control subjects had greater anterior cingulate activation during combat stimuli than did PTSD subjects. Deactivation occurred in the middle temporal gyrus, a region that inhibits amygdala activation. Bremner's group found that in PTSD subjects, but not in non-PTSD subjects, exposure to combat cues decreased activation in the medial prefrontal cortex and the middle temporal gyrus, whereas the adjacent right anterior cingulate failed to activate (Bremner, Staib, et al. 1999).

Using another imaging technique, single photon emission computerized tomography (SPECT), Israel Liberzon and his colleagues (1999) scanned Vietnam veterans with or without PTSD and nonveteran healthy control subjects while they heard three-minute audiotapes of combat-related stimuli (helicopters, gunfire) or white noise. Heightened activation occurred in the left amygdala in the PTSD group while they heard the combat tape.

Using fMRI, Scott Rauch and his colleagues (2000) reported that the medial frontal cortex may inhibit amygdala reactivity. Vietnam combat veterans, some with and some without PTSD, viewed pictures of either happy or fearful faces. Each face was presented very quickly and then immediately "masked" by a neutral face to reduce conscious registration of the facial expression. The amygdala activated more to fearful faces than to happy faces, and this effect was more pronounced in the PTSD group than in the non-PTSD group. The faces were presented too rapidly to permit any inhibitory influence arising from the medial frontal cortex. The researchers concluded that PTSD is characterized by a preconscious amygdala response to general threat (fearful face) stimuli. It is unclear whether fearful faces produced activation of the amygdala because of their fear-relevance or because of their novelty; most of us seldom encounter facial expressions of terror in everyday life.

Similar to results with script-driven, autobiographical memory studies, functional neuroimaging of the brain in PTSD patients who see or hear stimuli associated with their trauma shows no consistent pattern across studies. Sometimes the amygdala becomes activated; other times it does not.

Recent research has debunked many myths about memory, trauma, and the mechanisms underlying traumatic memory. Although many PTSD patients complain about poor overall memory, anecdotal reports of forgetfulness have seldom been substantiated by rigorous neuropsychological testing. Former prisoners of war, especially those who were tortured and starved, do show general memory problems, as do PTSD patients who also suffer from depression or other psychiatric disorders. But most PTSD patients do not exhibit objective memory impairments on standardized tests.

They do, however, have problems retrieving specific autobiographical memories, as do patients with depression. This difficulty does not imply repression or dissociation of traumatic memories themselves; rather, it indicates a general difficulty with accessing specific episodes from the past. It is unclear whether this style of remembering is a risk factor for PTSD or a consequence of the disorder. But it has been linked to failure to recover from depression.

Another myth debunked by recent research is the notion that elevated cortisol in PTSD has damaged the hippocampi of survivors. Not only is cortisol seldom elevated in PTSD, but smaller hippocampi in those with the disorder are best attributed to genetic factors, not to traumatic stress. A smaller hippocampus may constitute a vulnerability factor for the disorder among those exposed to trauma.

Cognitive experimental studies confirm the emotional Stroop interference effect as a quantitative measure of intrusive cognition, one not relying on introspective self-reports of reexperiencing the trauma. Some studies suggest that PTSD patients have enhanced ability to remember words related to trauma.

Another myth debunked is the notion that trauma survivors, especially those who were sexually abused as children, have developed skills for banishing disturbing material from awareness. Directed-forgetting experiments and thought-suppression experiments indicate that, if anything, the opposite is true: trauma survivors exhibit an impaired ability to forget disturbing material.

Attempts to map the functional neuroanatomy of remembering trauma have yielded mixed and confusing results. As of yet, few findings have been replicated across studies. Much attention has been paid to the amygdala as a key brain mechanism implicated in traumatic memory. But this structure may figure more in the encoding of traumatic memories than in their retrieval. That may be why heightened activation of the amygdala has been the exception, not the rule, in the script-driven imagery studies. Moreover, the amygdala has multiple functions in addition to participating in a brain circuit for encoding fear-related experiences. For example, using PET, Stephan Hamann and his colleagues (2002) discovered that the amygdala shows enhanced activation when people experience positive emotions and when they attend to interesting, novel stimuli. As Paul Whalen (1998) has argued, the amygdala does more than merely process fear-related information; it is activated by a range of biologically relevant, ambiguous stimuli, which may signal rewards as well as threats.

6

THEORIES OF REPRESSION AND DISSOCIATION

S IGMUND FREUD HAS SUFFERED the curious fate of being condemned by both sides of the recovered memory debate, but for entirely different reasons. One side criticizes him for retracting his seduction theory of hysteria, thereby silencing the voices of abuse survivors. Hysteria was a common neurotic syndrome afflicting nineteenth-century women, characterized by sexual difficulties, depressive symptoms, anxiety, and unexplained physical problems such as paralysis and vomiting. Early in his career, Freud believed that repressed memories of sexual abuse in early childhood caused hysteria. He later abandoned this theory, concluding instead that his patients had merely fantasized their abuse, and that few had actually been "seduced" (that is, molested). Many psychotherapists believe that Freud had it right the first time: his patients *had* been sexually abused. Moreover, they charge, Freud's subsequent psychoanalytic theorizing led his followers to dismiss genuine memories of abuse as nothing more than fantasy.

The other side of the debate condemns Freud for inspiring the recovered memory movement and for indirectly spawning an epidemic of False Memory Syndrome. Both theoretical assumptions about repressed memories of abuse and therapeutic techniques for recovering them can be traced to Freud's early work. The recovered memory movement, charge the critics, is the offspring of Freud's seduction theory of hysteria.

FREUD'S SEDUCTION THEORY

Freud expounded his seduction theory in three papers (1896a, 1896b, 1896c). The third was based on his first major professional address, delivered at a conference in Vienna. In this paper, Freud explained how his failure to cure patients with Josef Breuer's methods had led him to his new theory. Following Breuer, Freud originally believed that hysteria develops when a person experiences a sexually traumatic event after puberty, and when memory for the event and its associated emotion are repressed into the unconscious mind. Repression, Breuer and Freud thought, occurs for two reasons. In some cases, the person is in a dissociated ("altered") state of consciousness during the trauma and fails to encode it normally. In other cases, the experience is disturbingly incompatible with the person's self-concept and is therefore expelled from awareness (Breuer and Freud 1895: 214–216).

Breuer and Freud believed that repressed traumatic memories "persist for a long time with astonishing freshness and with the whole of their affective colouring." Sealed off from other memories, they remain intact indefinitely. Yet when the patient is hypnotized, the "memories emerge with the undiminished vividness of a recent event." The repressed memory of a traumatic event does not lie dormant in the unconscious, but rather "acts like a foreign body which long after its entry must continue to be regarded as an agent that is still at work." As Freud expressed it, *"hysterical patients suffer from incompletely abreacted psychical traumas."*[1]

Breuer and Freud held that hysteria patients are unable, not merely unwilling, to remember the traumas underlying their symptoms. In most cases, hypnosis is necessary to trace the path from the symptom back to the precipitating event. With this method, Breuer and Freud (1893: 6) claimed, *"each individual hysterical symptom immediately and permanently disappeared when we had succeeded in bringing clearly to light the memory of the event by which it was provoked and in arousing its accompanying affect, and when the patient had described that event in the greatest possible detail and had put the affect into words."* According to Breuer and Freud, recollection devoid of affect is insufficient to relieve symptoms. The patient must also experience an emotional catharsis while reliving the event, and must express the emotion in words. Hysterical symptoms dissipate as traumatic memory is converted into ordinary memory expressible in speech.

Despite the dramatic cures claimed by Breuer and Freud, their cases were inconsistent with their theory and their methods were far from infallible (see Freud 1896c). Sometimes the recovered memory concerned an experience too seemingly trivial to cause hysteria. One patient, for example, remembered that her illness began during adolescence, triggered by a mildly embarrassing event: overhearing someone telling a riddle whose solution might have been obscene. Sometimes the recollected trauma was incongruent with the symptom it supposedly caused. Hysterical vomiting, for example, often began after a frightening experience, not a disgusting one. But most important, identifying the trauma seldom produced a cure.

The failure of patients to improve according to theoretical expectation presented Freud with a dilemma. On the one hand, he could abandon the theory that repressed memories of trauma cause hysteria. On the other hand, he could modify the theory by assuming that he and Breuer had failed to probe deeply enough into their patients' past. Perhaps patients harbored repressed memories of trauma from their earliest childhood years, which rendered them vulnerable to developing hysteria following the stressors of adolescence. If so, then recovering memories of recent trauma would not be expected to cure hysteria. Freud chose the second alternative. Rather than abandon the repression theory altogether, he conjectured that a buried memory of early childhood "seduction"—molestation—was the root of the illness. Hence Freud (1896c: 212) continued to insist that *"hysterical symptoms are derivatives of memories which are operating unconsciously,"* but he now believed that the original pathogenic event had occurred much earlier than either he or Breuer had previously imagined.

In his classic 1896 paper, Freud triumphantly announced conclusions derived from his recent work with 18 hysteria patients. He asserted that "at the bottom of every case of hysteria there are *one or more occurrences of premature sexual experience,* occurrences which belong to the earliest years of childhood but which can be reproduced through the work of psycho-analysis in spite of the intervening decades" (1896c: 203). He said that molestation typically occurred between the ages of four and five, and produced genital excitement in the child and emotional responses ranging from indifference to "a small degree of annoyance or fright" (1896a: 155). Because of their young age, he claimed, children suffer no immediate adverse psychological consequences. But children who repress their memories of "seduction" will be at risk for developing hysteria once they reach puberty. Stressors during puberty activate dormant memories of early abuse, which are the original source of hysteria symptoms. Children who do not repress their memories of early molestation will not develop hysteria later in life.

Freud unveiled his seduction theory in an address delivered to the Society for Psychiatry and Neurology in Vienna. Expecting an enthusiastic response from his colleagues, Freud was angry and disappointed when members of the audience were unimpressed by the theory. His talk generated little interest or discussion. Writing to his close friend and fellow physician Wilhelm Fliess, Freud complained that Richard von Krafft-Ebing, head of the department of psychiatry at the University of Vienna, likened the seduction theory to "a scientific fairy tale" (quoted in Masson 1984: 9). Freud eventually repudiated the seduction theory and reinterpreted his early hysteria cases as evidence that patients harbor repressed fantasies—not memories—of sexual seduction. This emphasis on oedipal fantasy inaugurated classical psychoanalysis.

In his long career, Freud published several conflicting accounts of why he abandoned the seduction theory. Few psychoanalysts noticed or cared. They saw it as a historical curiosity, a mistaken detour on the road to orthodox psychoanalysis. But all this changed in 1981 when Jeffrey Masson, the projects director of the Sigmund Freud Archives, discovered letters from Freud to Fliess hitherto shielded from public view by the guardians of Freud's reputation who managed the Archives. Masson announced that these letters proved that Freud's patients had been sexually molested by their fathers and that Freud had covered up this fact to protect his professional reputation.[2] Masson charged that "Freud's female patients had the courage to face what had happened to them in childhood—often this included violent scenes of rape by a father—and to communicate their traumas to Freud, no doubt hesitating to believe their own memories and reluctant to remember the deep shame and hurt they had felt. Freud listened and understood and gave them permission to remember and speak of these terrible events" (1984: 9).

According to Masson, Freud had abandoned the seduction theory "not for theoretical or clinical reasons, but because of a personal failure of courage" (1984: 189). The seduction theory implied an epidemic of incest among the respectable Viennese bourgeoisie, and this scandalous implication threatened to ruin his reputation among his medical colleagues. To avoid professional ostracism, Freud retracted the theory, claiming that what his patients had told him were merely fantasies about having sex with their fathers.[3]

Masson was certainly ostracized by *his* fellow psychoanalysts. Indeed, he was promptly fired from his job at the Archives. If true, his interpretation would undercut the theoretical foundation of psychoanalysis while simultaneously impugning Freud's scientific integrity. Although Masson was condemned by orthodox analysts, his views about the accuracy of Freud's original seduction theory were embraced by therapists such as Judith Herman (1992:

12–15), who specialized in the treatment of survivors of childhood sexual abuse.

Despite the continuing influence of Masson's thesis in the trauma field, it has long been rejected by historians of psychoanalysis, who, ironically, are just as critical of Freud as Masson has been, but for different reasons. Masson erroneously believed that Freud's patients had *told* him they had been molested by their *fathers*. Indeed, if one reads only Freud's retrospective accounts of his seduction theory and why he abandoned it, one can easily understand Masson's error. For example, Freud stated: "In the period in which the main interest was directed to discovering infantile sexual traumas, almost all my women patients told me that they had been seduced by their father" (1933: 120). Freud claimed that he had been misled by "statements made by patients in which they ascribed their symptoms to passive sexual experiences in the first years of childhood—to put it bluntly, to seduction" (1914a: 17).

The notion that Freud listened while his patients remembered and disclosed memories of having been raped by their fathers is pure nonsense. As the historian of psychoanalysis Allen Esterson (2002a) points out, Freud's letters to Fliess show that Freud formulated his theory that repressed memories of infantile abuse caused hysteria *before* "uncovering" any evidence of incest. And as soon as Freud had abandoned his seduction theory, he ceased to "uncover" any more repressed memories of infantile sexual abuse.

Thus, in his most famous paper about the seduction theory, Freud wrote:

> Before they come for analysis the patients know nothing about these scenes [of early childhood sexual molestation]. They are indignant as a rule if we warn them that such scenes are going to emerge. Only the strongest compulsion of the treatment can induce them to embark on a reproduction of them. While they are recalling these infantile experiences to consciousness, they suffer under the most violent sensations, of which they are ashamed and which they try to conceal; and, even after they have gone through them once more in such a convincing manner, they still attempt to withhold belief from them, by emphasizing the fact that, unlike what happens in the case of other forgotten material, they have no feeling of remembering the scenes. (1896c: 204)

Acknowledging that hysteria patients had a reputation for lying and for fantasy-proneness, Freud emphasized that this could not account for his clinical observations. If his patients were manufacturing false reports of abuse, why would they resist acknowledging that abuse?

> But the fact is that these patients never repeat these stories spontaneously, nor do they ever in the course of a treatment suddenly present the physician with the complete recollection of a scene of this kind. One only succeeds in awakening the psychical trace of a precocious sexual event under the most energetic pressure of the analytic procedure, and against an enormous resistance. Moreover, the memory must be extracted from them piece by piece, and while it is being awakened in their consciousness they become prey to an emotion which it would be hard to counterfeit. (1896a: 153)

Freud scoffed at the possibility that his techniques were suggestive. As he stated late in his career: "The danger of our leading a patient astray by suggestion, by persuading him to accept things which we ourselves believe but which he ought not to, has certainly been enormously exaggerated." He added, "I can assert without boasting that such an abuse of 'suggestion' has never occurred in my practice" (1937: 262).[4]

In reality, as Frank Cioffi pointed out in 1974, Freud's patients never "told" him they had been sexually molested. They never made any "statements" about having been abused by anyone, and they certainly did not "ascribe their symptoms" to abuse. Once Freud had hit upon the idea that all hysteria patients harbored repressed memories of early sexual abuse, he relentlessly tried to foist this interpretation on his patients.

Other scholars who have scrutinized the evidence, such as Jean Schimek (1987), Allen Esterson (1993), and Han Israëls and Morton Schatzman (1993), have furnished further arguments in support of Cioffi's thesis. Rather than uncovering episodes of repressed trauma, Freud *constructed* such episodes by relying on material emerging during quasi-hypnotic therapy sessions. He asked his patients to close their eyes, to go deeper into their past, and to describe what they saw and remembered. Sometimes he pressed his hand on the patient's forehead while having the patient concentrate on the past. In response to his persistent psychological and physical pressure, they described fragmentary visual images, reported bodily sensations, exhibited intense affect, and gestured and squirmed while doing so. He interpreted their behavior as disguised reenactments—"scenes"—of events from childhood. But his patients adamantly denied "remembering" any abuse, insisting that the images that surfaced during therapy did not feel like real memories.

Not surprisingly, Freud's medical colleagues criticized him for attempting to implant false memories of sexual abuse in his patients (see Cioffi 1974). As one distinguished neurologist, Leopold Löwenfeld, wrote in 1899, Freud's "patients were subjected to a suggestive influence coming from the person who analysed them," and the "fantasy pictures that had arisen under the influence of the analysis were definitively denied recognition as memories of real events" (quoted in Israëls and Schatzman 1993: 43–44). Even Freud's patients accused him of using suggestive methods. He admitted that some patients had told him that "something has occurred to me now, but you obviously put it into my head" (Breuer and Freud 1895: 280). Yet he interpreted their accusations as further evidence of their denial of abuse, and therefore further confirmation of his theory.

Apparently unfamiliar with the historical scholarship debunking Masson's account, many psychotherapists continue to believe that Freud's hysteria patients were victims of father-daughter incest. But perusal of Freud's original papers about the seduction theory tells a very different story. In one paper (1896b), Freud listed the abusers of his first 13 hysteria patients—11 women and 2 men—for whom he had allegedly uncovered infantile sexual molestation. He said that 7 patients had been molested by slightly older siblings. For the remaining 6 cases, he listed nursemaids, domestic servants, governesses, and teachers as the perpetrators—but not fathers.

After adding 5 more patients to his case series, Freud again specified the assailants of his 18 hysteria patients (12 women, 6 men). His list of perpetrators now included siblings, other close relatives, nursery maids, tutors, governesses, and strangers. Fathers are never mentioned (1896c). Contrary to legend, Freud was not trying to conceal paternal incest for reasons of discretion by not identifying fathers as assailants. In fact, in a letter to Fliess written the year after he published his last seduction theory paper Freud said he was hoping to "catch" a father as a perpetrator, implying that he had not yet done so. The seduction theory required only that repressed memories of infantile sexual abuse lie at the core of every case of hysteria; it did not require that fathers be the abusers. Only later, when he advanced the theory that all children harbor fantasies of having sex with the opposite-sex parent, did Freud rewrite history by claiming that his female patients had told him they had been molested by their fathers—claims he now attributed to fantasy. This enabled Freud to claim his early seduction theory cases as confirmations of his new theory (see Esterson, submitted).

Scholars have debunked three myths concerning Freud's seduction theory and its abandonment. The first is the myth that Freud's patients told him about having been molested by their fathers. The second is that his medical colleagues were scandalized by his "findings," which seemed to imply widespread incest among the respectable Viennese bourgeoisie (Esterson 1998). The third is that he abandoned his allegedly scandalous seduction theory to restore his damaged professional reputation (Skues 1987; Cioffi 1973).

First of all, Freud did not break any taboos by discussing incest. To the contrary, sexual abuse was a major psychiatric concern in late nineteenth-century Europe. Viennese psychiatry was all too familiar with such crimes. Krafft-Ebing said shortly before Freud presented his seduction theory, "Today, rape on children is remarkably frequent" (1886: 544). Nearly a decade before Freud unveiled the seduction theory, Krafft-Ebing had described graphic cases of incest in his classic textbook on sexual deviation (1886: 626–629).

Freud's seduction theory did not get him ostracized by his colleagues. He had no problem publishing his lecture in the journal of his choice, and shortly thereafter a committee of six senior professors unanimously approved his appointment as Professor Extraordinarius at the University of Vienna in the department chaired by Krafft-Ebing, the man who had recently described the seduction theory as a scientific fairy tale. Freud anticipated that his audience would enthusiastically embrace his world-shaking new theory about the cause of hysteria. The legend of his ostracism resulted from the discrepancy between his extravagant expectations and his audience's ho-hum response.

Studying contemporary professional responses to Freud's seduction theory, historians have identified the three reasons for Freud's failure to impress his medical colleagues. First, his methods were flagrantly suggestive. Anything that might emerge during therapy was hopelessly contaminated by his biases. European psychiatrists were well aware of how suggestive hypnosis-like therapies could be, especially with hysteria patients (Macmillan 1997: 37–48; Borch-Jacobsen 1996). This is why Freud spent so much time trying to convince his audience that he was not a suggestive therapist. Second, he did not furnish any evidence for his claim that recovering repressed memories of infantile sexual abuse cured hysteria. Third, he implausibly claimed that *all* cases of hysteria were caused by repressed memories of infantile seduction, neglecting hereditary factors and other causes. Given these serious limitations in his presentation, it is little wonder that Freud's colleagues were not impressed (Esterson 2002b).

Why did Freud abandon the seduction theory? Relying on correspondence between Freud and Fliess in the Sigmund Freud Archives, the historians of psychoanalysis Han Israëls and Morton Schatzman (1993) concluded that Freud abandoned the theory because he failed to bring a single hysteria case to a successful resolution. Referring to his 18 cases, Freud proclaimed that therapeutic success confirmed his theory, but added cryptically, "where the circumstances allowed" (1896c: 199). Had Freud, in fact, produced any cures, he surely would have described them in his paper. But instead of adducing positive evidence of success, he concentrated on rebutting potential objections to his theory.

Israëls and Schatzman have convincingly shown that Freud had no cures to report. In letters to Fliess during the 18 months following the presentation of his theory, Freud described his frantic attempts to cure even a single hysteria patient. He had claimed to have recovered memories of early sexual molestation in each of his 18 hysteria cases, yet none of them had been cured in the year and a half since the presentation. Israëls and Schatzman conclude that in his claims of therapeutic success Freud was boasting of cures that he believed he was about to achieve, given that the traumatic events had been ascertained. When the cures failed to occur, rather than abandon his analytic technique entirely, he rejected the view that hysteria always arose from repressed memories of infantile sexual abuse and that reconstructing these traumatic events produced cures.[5]

Moreover, according to Frank Cioffi (1972, 1984), Freud was deeply shaken when he realized that he had misinterpreted his patients' behavior as disguised reenactments of early abuse. If Freud himself was the real source of the clinical material—fragmentary images, emotional reactions—emerging during sessions, then this would undermine the reliability of his analytic technique. Freud could either admit that his method was merely a highly suggestive variant of hypnosis or rescue his method by redefining it as a powerful tool for uncovering a patient's unconscious fantasies. He chose the latter course. The upshot, as Borch-Jacobsen (1996) has observed, is that the Freudian cover-up has nothing to do with concealing incest. The cover-up concerns Freud's claim to have discovered the Oedipus Complex, unconscious infantile sexual fantasies, and so forth in his patients, and his use of this claim to conceal the real sources of these notions: his suggestive technique and his own extravagant imagination.

Some trauma therapists interpret Freud's abandonment of the seduction theory as illustrating how the forces of patriarchy can silence the voices of survivors.[6] Others claim that the methods and assumptions of contemporary recovered memory therapy can be found in Freud's early work.[7]

Frederick Crews, a professor of literature and a trenchant critic of psychoanalysis, has summarized the striking parallels between the assumptions in Freud's early work and those of today's recovered memory therapists (1995: 216–218). For example: people repress (or dissociate) memories of events too painful to entertain consciously; these memories are not dormant, but have adverse effects on adult adjustment, despite the patient's failure to recognize this connection; sexual abuse in early childhood is especially prone to repression; trauma-exposed people are unable, not merely unwilling, to remember their traumatic experiences; patients are often in denial regarding their abuse history; special procedures, such as hypnosis, can lift the repression; unexplained physical symptoms associated with hysteria are symbolic representations of psychologically active but repressed events, and thus count as "body memories"; people resist recalling traumatic memories, and reluctance to credit the recollections as genuine counts as further evidence of their truth; for healing to occur, one must recover repressed memories, reexperience intense affect, and convert the emotional memories into narrative form.

However, there is at least one difference between Freud's patients and those of today's recovered memory therapists: Freud's patients did not disclose any memories of abuse. Freud *interpreted* their behavior during quasi-hypnotic therapy sessions as reenactments of early "scenes" of molestation. But try as he might, Freud never got his patients to recover any memories of sexual abuse.

Some clinicians, such as Phil Mollon (2000), object to Freud's being characterized as the founder of recovered memory therapy, noting that Freud addressed repressed impulses, not repressed memories, and realized that memories of childhood sexual experience were laden with fantasy.[8] Such objections entirely miss a crucial point: critics like Crews trace recovered memory therapy to the *early* Freud of the seduction theory, not to the *later* Freud of oedipal fantasies, repressed sexual and aggressive impulses, and so forth.[9]

Psychoanalysts remain deeply divided over the merits of recovered memory therapy. Some believe that Freud got it right the first time, and that he erred by abandoning his original seduction theory. Jody Davies and Mary Frawley, for example, emphasize that an important goal in the treatment of abuse survivors is "the recovery and disclosure of as many memories of early sexual abuse as possible" (1992: 23). Others, critical of recovered memory therapy, take a line that is much closer to the later Freud who cautioned that material surfacing during analysis is a mix of fantasy and memory (Gabbard, Goodman, and Richards 1995). The early Freud certainly qualifies as a recovered memory therapist, even if the later Freud may not.[10]

REPRESSION, SUPPRESSION, AND COGNITIVE SCIENCE

Varying definitions of key concepts such as *repression* and *suppression* have caused much confusion in the field of traumatic stress. The confusion has spread to the media and the courts. Vitriolic debates erupt regarding whether repression "exists" or whether people can repress and then remember their traumatic experiences. Yet the disputants on both sides often fail to clarify what they mean by "repression" and related concepts.

One key point of confusion concerns whether repression is an unconscious mechanism. Freud's daughter, the psychoanalyst Anna Freud (1936: 8), popularized the idea that psychological defense mechanisms, such as repression, always operate outside awareness. Indeed, authors have routinely distinguished *repression*, an unconscious process, from *suppression*—conscious attempts to expel disturbing material from awareness. The influential feminist psychoanalyst Alice Miller agrees: "Suppression is a *conscious* act, in contrast to repression" (1997: 56).

But Freud himself used the terms *repression* and *suppression* interchangeably. According to Freud, *"the essence of repression lies simply in turning something away, and keeping it at a distance, from the conscious"* (1915: 147). He sometimes stressed that repression was a conscious, deliberate process, as when he said that an essential prerequisite for hysteria is that "an idea must be *intentionally repressed from consciousness* and excluded from associative modification" (Breuer and Freud 1895: 116). Elsewhere he wrote that repression could operate outside awareness such that disturbing memories, impulses, and so forth could even be "stifled before they enter consciousness" (Freud 1914b: 93). Hence, according to Freud, repression could be either a conscious or an unconscious process.[11]

Some experimental psychologists have attempted to investigate repression in the laboratory. They defined repression in the narrow sense: as automatic, unconscious removal of disturbing material from consciousness. For example, some tested whether subjects would fail to remember threats to self-esteem, such as performing poorly on an "IQ test." These studies were originally celebrated as confirming Freud's ideas, until psychologists detected fatal flaws in the experimental methods. As David Holmes (1990: 96) concluded, "despite over sixty years of research involving numerous approaches by many thoughtful and clever investigators, at the present time there is no controlled laboratory evidence supporting the concept of repression."[12]

Despite Holmes's dismal conclusion about repression, Matthew Erdelyi (1990) defends the continuing relevance of psychoanalysis, arguing that many concepts in contemporary cognitive science were foreshadowed in Freud's writings. Directed forgetting and cognitive avoidance, he believes, are interpretable in Freudian terms, if one defines repression as any attempt to avoid thinking about something unpleasant. Erdelyi holds that psychoanalytic ideas are suitable for integration with contemporary cognitive science.[13]

But paring down the concept of repression to its bare bones eliminates its distinctively Freudian character. What makes Freud's repression different from the mundane notion of "trying not to think about something unpleasant" is its connection to other concepts in the psychoanalytic system. Once repression is shorn of its characteristic Freudian connotations, there will be little left to integrate with cognitive science (Crews 1995: 272).

In the spirit of Erdelyi, the clinical psychologist Drew Westen (1998) has argued that much cutting-edge research in psychology is consistent with Freud's thought. Westen mentions research on information processing occurring outside awareness and on the impact of emotion on cognition as two areas ripe for integration of cognitive science and psychoanalysis (for example, priming on implicit memory tests; depressed mood biasing what people remember). But his arguments are unconvincing. Unconscious information processing in cognitive psychology bears scant resemblance to the psychodynamic unconscious (Kihlstrom 1987), and few, if any, contemporary experiments in the cognition-emotion field have been enriched by Freud's distinctive views. The integration of emotion theory into cognitive psychology has proceeded rapidly without any detectable psychoanalytic input (for reviews see McNally 1996; Williams et al. 1997).

Defenders of Freud's lasting relevance might argue that contemporary cognitive scientists who bypass Freud's work will merely rediscover his insights about emotion, thereby reinventing the wheel. It is doubtful whether researchers will get much guidance, though, from the confusing corpus of Freud's work. As Malcolm Macmillan showed in his magisterial analysis of Freud's thought, psychoanalysis became progressively incoherent as it evolved (1997: esp. 591–627). William McDougall complained in 1936 that psychoanalytic doctrine had become "a great tangle in which Freud lashes about like a great whale caught in a net of his own contriving" (quoted in Esterson, submitted: 14). Although Mollon complained about critics who sought "to assimilate Freud into the category of 'recovered memory therapist'" (2000: 10), it is more justifiable to complain about those who seek to assimilate Freud into the category of cognitive scientist.

Advocates of integrating psychoanalysis and cognitive science issue two additional criticisms against the skeptics. First, they emphasize that psychoanalysis has evolved since Freud's day, rendering many objections obsolete. Indeed, most analysts have quietly abandoned Freud's more outrageous notions: it is difficult to find much enthusiasm today for penis envy or the death instinct. But it is unclear whether the conceptual coherence of or the empirical support for contemporary psychoanalysis is any greater than for orthodox psychoanalysis. In reference to the claim that contemporary analytic thought has transcended Freud's limitations, Macmillan asks: "Where is the evidence that it has superseded Freud's? Where is the demonstration of its superiority over the original?" Macmillan concluded his 762-page treatise on psychoanalysis on a melancholy note, asserting that contemporary versions of psychoanalysis "are just as flawed as Freud's, and the clinical and observational evidence relevant to them is just as weak" (1997: 591).

Second, advocates of integration sometimes launch ad hominem attacks against the so-called Freud bashers, insinuating that dark, neurotic, unconscious motives are driving the critics to assail Freud's legacy. Of course, whether or not unresolved oedipal conflicts, repressed hatred of one's father, and so forth energize Freud's critics has no bearing on the merit or validity of the critiques themselves.

THEORIES OF DISSOCIATIVE (TRAUMATIC) AMNESIA

The recovered memory debate concerns whether people can *repress* and later recover memories of early trauma. Many trauma therapists, however, argue that the operative mechanism is *dissociation*, not repression. Even therapists who use the terms interchangeably usually prefer to speak of dissociative (or traumatic) amnesia rather than repression. But theorists who distinguish between these mechanisms hold that repression blocks unacceptable wishes and impulses from reaching consciousness, whereas dissociation blocks disturbing memories.[14]

According to DSM-IV, dissociation is: "A disruption in the usually integrated functions of consciousness, memory, identity, or perception of the environment. The disturbance may be sudden or gradual, transient or chronic" (APA 1994: 766). Although this definition contains no reference to trauma, many therapists interpret dissociation as a defensive process that attenuates awareness of otherwise overwhelming emotional information. The vagueness of this abstract definition prompted the hypnosis scholar Campbell Perry to characterize dissociation as "a creaky and imprecise 19th century metaphor that is much in need of an overhaul" (1999: 367).

Indeed, the term has come to denote a diverse range of experiences that may have little in common. Dissociative symptoms include *derealization*, a strange, dreamlike sense that one's surroundings are unreal; *depersonalization*, a sense of being disconnected from one's body; a sense that time is either slowing down or speeding up; and *amnesia*, an inability to recall important aspects of what happened. The psychiatrist Charles Whitfield (1997) listed seemingly any kind of symptom, including intrusive memories, as a manifestation of traumatic (dissociative) amnesia. It is mystifying how vivid, intrusive recollection of a trauma might count as amnesia for the trauma. Surely, remembering a trauma all too well cannot be equated with an inability to remember it.[15]

Some theorists view dissociation as occurring on a continuum ranging from normal alterations in consciousness, such as daydreaming while driving long distances, to pathological alterations, such as an inability to remember abuse one suffered as a child. Following Freud's great rival in psychiatry, Pierre Janet (1907), other theorists regard dissociation as a pathological marker for a history of trauma (van der Kolk and Kadish 1987). Mulder and colleagues (1998), using the Dissociative Experiences Scale in a study of 1,028 randomly sampled adults, found that many people occasionally experienced dissociative symptoms, and that 6.3 percent frequently experienced three or more symptoms. Frequently experiencing these symptoms was associated with current psychiatric illness and with a history of childhood physical abuse, but not with sexual abuse.

The dissociative symptom most relevant to trauma and memory is dissociative (psychogenic) amnesia, defined in DSM-IV as "an inability to recall important personal information, usually of a traumatic or stressful nature, that is too extensive to be explained by normal forgetfulness" (APA 1994: 478). Confirming the presence of psychogenic amnesia is not easy: when trauma survivors realize that they lack memory for important aspects of the traumatic event, it is often difficult to determine whether the missing information was encoded but is inaccessible, or whether it was never encoded in the first place. Because the brain does not operate like a video recorder, preserving everything that happens to us, our memories are never complete. The challenge, then, is to estimate when memory loss is too extensive to be explained by normal, incomplete encoding and ordinary forgetting.

Lenore Terr's Theory

The work of the child psychiatrist Lenore Terr has been widely cited by theorists who believe that children often forget repeated abuse, only to recall it later as adults (see, for example, Alpert et al. 1998a). Terr proposed that trauma syndromes in children take either of two forms: Type I or Type II. The Type I syndrome results from a single, unexpected, often life-threatening event (such as kidnapping or exposure to gunfire), whereas the Type II syndrome results from repeated, predictable traumatic events (such as chronic physical or sexual abuse). Because Type I events are shocking and unexpected, children remember them in vivid detail and can readily recount them. Because Type II events are predictable, children learn to anticipate them and employ denial, psychic numbing, self-hypnosis, and psychogenic amnesia in an effort to blunt their emotional impact. These methods of coping may result in traumatic experiences being encoded in ways that render them difficult to recall later in life. Thus Terr has said that those "who experience type II traumas often forget. They may forget whole segments of childhood—from birth to age 9, for instance" (1991: 16), and that "repeated and/or variable events (as in child abuse) are less fully remembered than are single episodes of trauma" (1988: 97).

Many studies of childhood trauma support Terr's Type I syndrome, exemplified by her own classic work (1979) on the young kidnapping victims in Chowchilla, California. During the summer of 1976, 26 children were kidnapped from their school bus, transported in darkened vans for 11 hours, and then locked inside a buried truck-trailer. The children, ranging in age from 5 to 14, managed to escape unharmed. Terr's assessment of these children revealed that all of them retained vivid, detailed, narrative memories of their ordeal. Subsequent studies have confirmed that children exposed to terrifying events remember them very well. Children who witnessed parental homicide (Malmquist 1986), sexual assault of their mother (Pynoos and Nader 1988), or fatal shootings (Schwarz and Kowalski 1991) have provided vivid narratives of these experiences.[16]

The only evidence for the Type II syndrome comes from Terr's (1988) study of 20 children who had been traumatized before the age of 5. Seven had suffered prolonged or repeated abuse; the others had been exposed to a single traumatic event. Assessing the children 5 months to 12 years later, Terr found that 3 of those who had been exposed to repeated trauma were unable to verbalize what had happened to them and the other 4 retained only spotty verbal memories. Verbal recollection was much better among children exposed to a single trauma. Terr concluded that repeated traumatic events are more likely to be forgotten than a single traumatic event.

For two reasons, her conclusion is unwarranted. First, the children in the single-trauma group had been much older than those in the repeated-trauma group when the adverse events occurred. Indeed, the 3 children in the repeated-trauma group who had no verbal memories had been only 6 months, 24 months, and 28 months old when their trauma *ended*. No special mechanism is needed to explain their lack of narrative memory for events occurring prior to the offset of childhood amnesia. Second, as the memory researchers Henry Roediger and Erik Bergman (1998: 1092) observed, Terr's notion that repeated events are remembered less well than single events flies in the face of "virtually every experiment directed at this issue in the entire history of experimental psychology." Although repetitions of many similar events may make it difficult to distinguish among them, repetition does not abolish memory for the entire class of events. Yet forgetting the entire class of (abuse) events is precisely what Terr's Type II proposal implies: the more children are abused, they less likely they are to recall *ever* having been abused.

Other problems confront Terr's theory of Type II trauma. Reviews of the literature on childhood sexual abuse do not mention psychogenic amnesia as a symptom (e.g., Beitchman et al. 1991; Kendall-Tackett, Williams, and

Finkelhor 1993). If an inability to recall being abused were among the common sequelae of molestation, surely clinical researchers other than Terr would have noticed this. Daniel Brown and his colleagues (Brown, Frischholz, and Scheflin 1999) believe that amnesia never surfaced in these studies because researchers did not assess for it (psychogenic amnesia for aspects of the trauma was not an official DSM symptom of PTSD until 1987). Likewise, the sociologist Catherine Cameron asserted that "the loss and recovery of traumatic memories were everywhere assumed, but nowhere made the focus of study" (1996: 44). These speculations do not withstand scrutiny. For example, with regard to Cameron's conjecture, if everyone knew that children experience amnesia for their abuse, why was this symptom not included in the original criteria for PTSD?

The strongest arguments against Terr's Type II syndrome are empirical. Studies have revealed that children exposed to repeated trauma, such as physical abuse, chronic community violence, or the Cambodian holocaust, remember these experiences all too well.[17]

Jennifer Freyd's Betrayal Trauma Theory

The cognitive psychologist Jennifer Freyd (1996) has proposed that children are more likely to experience amnesia for abuse inflicted by their parents than for that inflicted by strangers. She holds that "analysis of evolutionary pressures and developmental needs suggests that victims of abuse may remain unaware of the abuse, not to reduce suffering, but rather to maintain an attachment with a figure vital to survival, development, and thriving" (Freyd, DePrince, and Zurbriggen 2001: 6). Her theory applies not only to incest committed by parents but also to abuse committed by any caretaker responsible for the child's well-being. Discussing similarities and differences between her theory and Terr's, Freyd has asserted "that people forget repeated traumas because the traumas that are repeated are more likely to involve betrayal by a caretaker." She and her colleagues have predicted, on the basis of Terr's work, "that repeated traumas will be associated with greater amnesia, but that perpetrator status will have a larger effect than abuse duration" (Freyd et al. 2001: 8).

Freyd's research team (2001) has conducted studies designed to test hypotheses derived from betrayal trauma theory. In a questionnaire survey, they found that 77 percent of 202 undergraduate subjects reported at least one instance of physical abuse, and 39 percent reported at least one instance of sexual abuse. One item on the questionnaire asked about "memory persistence for the event." Although few subjects reported any "memory impairment" for their abuse, those who implicated a caretaker as the abuser reported more impairment than did those who implicated noncaretakers. As the researchers acknowledged, this study has several limitations (no confirmation of the abuse, retrospective estimates of how much one forgot abuse, and so on).

In another study, Anne DePrince and Freyd (2001) tested the hypothesis that people who score high on the Dissociative Experiences Scale (DES) will exhibit superior forgetting of trauma words in the laboratory when their attention is divided by performing a concurrent cognitive task. Testing college students who scored either high or low on the DES, DePrince and Freyd obtained results consistent with their prediction. They contrasted their findings to an experiment in which my research group found that adult survivors of childhood sexual abuse who met criteria for PTSD exhibited memory impairments for nontraumatic words they had been instructed to remember, while remembering trauma words all too well, including those they were supposed to forget, whereas psychiatrically healthy sexual abuse survivors did not exhibit abnormalities in directed-forgetting performance (McNally et al. 1998). Although DePrince and Freyd presented their data as consistent with betrayal trauma theory and inconsistent with ours, the two studies are difficult to compare. DePrince and Freyd did not assess for a history of childhood sexual abuse in their subjects, let alone confirm a diagnosis of PTSD. Also, they seem to believe that a high DES score is related to trauma. This is incorrect: high DES scores are common, especially in college students. DePrince and Freyd's study may be relevant to dissociation, but it has little to do with sexual abuse, betrayal trauma, or psychiatric illness.

In fact, other evidence indicates that incest survivors do not forget the traumas of their childhood. The patients in Judith Herman's (1981) classic work on father-daughter incest remembered their abuse all too well. In Diana Russell's (1999: xxxvi) epidemiologic study, not a single incest survivor mentioned having forgotten her molestation. In a prospective, longitudinal study of verified cases of incestuous and nonincestuous abuse, Gail Goodman and her colleagues (in press) found no relationship between extent of betrayal trauma and failure to report abuse during the follow-up interview. Indeed, most subjects readily disclosed their abuse history during the survey. Although, as Freyd has noted, some retrospective surveys have suggested that individuals who report incest are sometimes more likely than other abused people to claim a period in their lives when they "could not remember" their abuse, these studies are flawed by reliance on uncorroborated reports of abuse, failure to verify that subjects had in fact been amnesic, or both.[18]

Despite the evidence against betrayal trauma theory—and the meager evidence consistent with it—this theory remains popular among therapists who are convinced that many incest survivors cannot recall ever having been abused. The discrepancy between evidential support and popularity could not be more striking.

Bessel van der Kolk's Theory

The psychiatrist Bessel van der Kolk is among the most influential theorists of traumatic amnesia. In his theoretical writings he has attempted to synthesize the concepts and findings of behavioral neuroscience with the theoretical work of Pierre Janet (1907), the early twentieth-century French psychiatrist who popularized the concept of dissociation. Although psychoanalysis eventually overshadowed Janet's contributions, van der Kolk has sought to restore Janet's reputation as a theorist important for understanding trauma (van der Kolk 1994; van der Kolk and Fisler 1995).[19]

According to Janet, memory for trauma differs qualitatively from ordinary memory. Traumatic memory can be dissociated from awareness but expressed in nonnarrative form, as exemplified by Janet's famous case of Irène (see van der Kolk and van der Hart 1991). Irène was a 20-year-old woman who had been caring for her dying mother. Her mother's death came as a terrible emotional shock despite its being fully expected. After her mother died, Irène became incapable of working and lost all interest in life. She could not remember her mother's death or anything about the three months preceding it. Yet she had spells during which she reenacted the movements she had made while tending to her mother on the day she died. Via hypnosis, Janet claimed, he had recovered the dissociated traumatic memories and aided Irène in "translating" these "implicit" traumatic memories into explicit form, thereby curing her of her amnesia and the need to reenact the traumatic experience.[20]

According to van der Kolk, cases like Irène's illustrate that memory of a traumatic experience can be "entirely organized on an implicit or perceptual level, without an accompanying narrative about what happened" (van der Kolk and Fisler 1995: 512). Van der Kolk believes "that trauma interferes with declarative memory (i.e., conscious recall of experience) but does not inhibit implicit, or nondeclarative, memory, the memory system that controls conditioned emotional responses, skills and habits, and sensorimotor sensations related to experience" (1994: 259). Unlike narrative memory, traumatic memory is "highly state-dependent and cannot be evoked at will" (van der Kolk and Fisler 1995: 520). Indeed, "state-dependent memory retrieval may also be involved in dissociative phenomena in which traumatized persons may be wholly or partially amnestic for memories or behaviors enacted while in altered states of mind" (van der Kolk 1994: 259). He believes that the distinctiveness of the extreme emotion experienced during trauma renders it difficult for people to recall when they are in different emotional states. Dissociative amnesia, then, constitutes an instance of state-dependent memory. Difficulties recalling trauma arise because the emotional, psychobiological state at retrieval differs so drastically from the one at encoding.

Van der Kolk has suggested that massive release of stress hormones is responsible for the hypothesized state dependency of traumatic memory. He believes that an inverted-U function describes the relation between release of stress hormones and declarative memory: stress improves memory, but only up to a point, after which it impairs memory. Other trauma theorists, such as Rhawn Joseph (1999), have made the same argument, citing the classic animal learning research of Yerkes and Dodson (1908) (who studied learning in stressed-out mice).

Van der Kolk, as well as other theorists such as Douglas Bremner, has cited the behavioral neuroscientist Joseph LeDoux's research on Pavlovian fear conditioning as relevant to understanding traumatic dissociative amnesia (Bremner, Krystal, et al. 1996). LeDoux (1996, 2000) discovered two pathways for activating the amygdala, a subcortical structure integral to the experience and expression of conditioned fear. One pathway rapidly transmits sensory input about fear stimuli to the amygdala via a subcortical route, whereas the second pathway passes through the cortex, taking about twice as long to reach the amygdala. Subcortical activation of the amygdala makes it possible for a fight-or-flight reaction to begin even before information about the fear-evoking stimulus has reached conscious awareness via the cortical route. Bremner and his colleagues believe that LeDoux's animal conditioning model illustrates how sexual abuse survivors might retain implicit, emotional memories of trauma while being incapable of consciously recollecting what happened.

Also, van der Kolk believes that manifestations of traumatic memory "are invariable and do not change over time," whereas narrative memory is subject to fading, distortion, and change (van der Kolk and Fisler 1995: 520). Traumatic memory is indelible; ordinary memory is not.

Van der Kolk has been very influential among psychotherapists who work with abuse survivors (see, for example, Alpert et al. 1998a). Praising van der Kolk's theory, Daniel Brown and his colleagues noted that it authorizes therapists to interpret "body memories, flashbacks, fragments, sudden intense feelings, avoidant behaviors, images, sensory processes, and dreams" as implicit expressions of dissociated traumatic memories. Following van der Kolk, Brown and his colleagues believe that these memories, in turn, can be recovered during therapy and transcribed into "an explicit, narrative form" (Brown et al. 1998: 187).

Van der Kolk's theory is plagued by conceptual and empirical problems. Implicit memory does not contain a timeless, unchanging, veridical record of the sensory features of traumatic experience that can be replayed during flashbacks. Measures of implicit memory are subject to change and distortion just like measures of explicit memory (Lustig and Hasher 2001). Moreover, as Brooks Brenneis has pointed out, "nowhere is there attached to the various habits, routines, and repetitive twitches of our lives a label that identifies them as responses to discrete past events" (1999: 615). Even if sudden intense feelings, flashbacks, and "body memories" are implicit expressions of memory, they do not contain traces of their origins. How can we ever tell whether a sudden unexplained feeling or a sensation in the body "stands for" or symbolizes a dissociated memory that might be translated into a narrative? The notion that a therapist can help someone "translate" or "recode" apparent fragments of implicit memory into narrative form is mistaken. Even if such a translation were possible, the product would be reconstructive, not reproductive. And, in the words of Roediger and Bergman: "Memories poorly encoded cannot be recovered in a more accurate narrative form 20–30 years later. No matter how great the power of retrieval cues, such cues cannot arouse memories that were not encoded well in the first place" (1998: 1104). (Consistent with Freud's early work, some therapists interpret vaginal pain and other bodily sensations as [repressed] "memories" of sexual abuse. But memories are not stored "in the body" [that is, in muscle tissue], and the notion of "body memories" is foreign to the cognitive neuroscience of memory.

Perhaps these therapists mean psychophysiologic reactivity to stimuli associated with the trauma?)

Contrary to van der Kolk's theory, trauma does not block the formation of narrative memory. That memory for trauma can be expressed as physiologic reactivity to traumatic reminders does not preclude its being expressed in narrative as well. As Lawrence Langer (1991) has thoroughly documented, survivors of the Nazi Holocaust readily provide detailed narrative accounts of their horrific experiences.

Finally, implicit memory tasks do not reflect an implicit memory *system* in the brain. They share no underlying psychobiological unity. Scientists group these phenomena under the same rubric merely because they do not require conscious recollective experience for their expression, not because they form a coherent implicit memory system (Bedford 1997).

Moreover, LeDoux's conditioning studies have doubtful relevance for traumatic amnesia. His rats undergo several trials in which a tone is followed by a "brief, mild footshock" (LeDoux 1996: 144). Because these aversive events are few, brief, and mild, they do not provide a suitable animal model for years of traumatic abuse. Furthermore, that the amygdala can be activated preconsciously does not mean that fear memories are unconscious. Even when input arrives first at the amygdala via the subcortical route, it also arrives shortly thereafter via the slower cortical route, accompanied by awareness of the feared stimulus. Hence preconscious activation of a rat's amygdala has nothing whatsoever to do with dissociated memories of trauma. And despite early reports of "indelible" emotional memories (LeDoux, Romanski, and Xagoraris 1989), subsequent research by LeDoux's group has shown that even well-established conditioned fear memories are labile and subject to alteration when retrieved (Nader, Schafe, and LeDoux 2000; see also Morrison, Allardyce, and McKane 2002; Zola 1997). Science provides no basis for assuming that emotional memories are immune to distortion or change.

Also, neuroscience research does not support van der Kolk's claim that high levels of stress hormones impair memory for traumatic experience. (In fact, research on human subjects shows that extreme stress *enhances* memory for the central aspects of an overwhelming emotional experience; see Chapter 2.) For example, in a typical experiment, a mouse first receives a single low-intensity footshock when it enters a certain compartment, and then receives an injection of the stress hormone epinephrine immediately thereafter. The length of time the mouse takes to reenter this compartment on the following day is the measure of retention: the longer it takes, the stronger the mouse's memory for the shocking experience. Injections of epinephrine enhance retention, relative to injections of saline. That is, mice receiving the drug take longer to reenter a compartment in which they got a shock. In one study, cited by the behavioral neuroscientist James McGaugh (1990), mice receiving a postshock dose of 30 µg/kg exhibited better retention than those receiving saline, whereas those receiving a dose of 300 µg/kg exhibited worse retention than those receiving saline. Yet other studies, summarized by Paul Gold (1992), show that epinephrine dosages 50 times larger than the dose that maximizes memory result in performance that is no better than that associated with saline injection. Therefore, moderate levels of stress hormones strengthen memory, but extremely high levels do not impair memory; they merely fail to enhance it.

Fear-motivated avoidance in mice does not provide a good model for impaired declarative, narrative memory for trauma in human beings. Mice, lacking language, cannot "declare" anything, and their reluctance to enter a compartment associated with shock seems more akin to a "behavioral" memory of trauma than to the narrative memories of trauma that van der Kolk believes are undermined by severe stress. In fact, the epinephrine dosages that must be injected to impair memory result in levels vastly higher than those occurring naturally when rodents encounter stressors such as forced swimming (see Mabry, Gold, and McCarty 1995). The clinical relevance of this work rests on the dubious assumption that a mouse's reluctance to enter a compartment previously associated with shock provides a convincing model for a person's inability to remember his or her history of childhood sexual abuse.

Likewise, the work of Yerkes and Dodson has dubious relevance for traumatic amnesia. Yerkes and Dodson sought to determine how intensity of punishment affects discrimination learning in mice. Mice were exposed to two passageways, one black and one white, that led to a nest box. Attempts to reach this box via the black passageway were punished with shock of either weak, medium, or strong intensity. Accordingly, the mice had to discriminate between the shocked black passageway and the unshocked white passageway. The measure of learning was the number of trials needed for a mouse to choose the white passageway consistently. Yerkes and Dodson found that the speed of learning was a linear function of the strength of shock: the stronger the shock, the fewer trials mice needed to learn the discrimination. However, their subsequent experiments indicated that the difficulty of the discrimination was an important variable. When the two passageways differed drastically in brightness, speed of learning was a linear function of shock intensity. When the two passageways differed only slightly in brightness, medium shock intensity produced faster learning than either low or high shock intensity. Yerkes and Dodson concluded that "both weak stimuli and strong stimuli result in slow habit-formation" (1908: 481). Given the absence of any evidence that stress produced amnesia for shock in these mice, one must question whether these experiments explain how people might experience amnesia for years of childhood sexual abuse.

Emotional state–dependent memory fails as a model for dissociated memories of trauma. State-dependency effects are often fragile, and even when emotional state at retrieval differs from that at encoding, subjects are not amnesic for encoded material; they merely recall less of it than when emotional states at encoding and retrieval are the same. Also, van der Kolk's model specifies state-dependency effects for implicit memories of trauma, whereas state-dependency effects, when they occur at all, concern explicit memory. State-dependency cannot explain why someone would retrieve dissociated memories of trauma during therapy, since therapy is associated with emotional states very different from the terror that occurs during trauma.

Finally, people who have experienced harrowingly close brushes with death (such as falling off a mountain) often report extreme dissociative alterations in consciousness (time slowing down, everything seeming unreal), yet they remain fully capable of providing detailed narrative accounts of their experiences (Noyes and Kletti 1976, 1977; Roberts and Owen 1988). And dissociation does not necessarily block the experience of fear. For example, novice skydivers experience dissociation before their first jump, but it neither blocks their experience of fear nor produces amnesia for skydiving (Sterlini and Bryant 2002). There is no incompatibility between dissociation and the formation of narrative memory for intense emotional experiences.

It is ironic that so much has been written about the biological mechanisms of traumatic psychological amnesia when the very existence of the phenomenon is in doubt (see Chapter 7). What we have here is a set of theories in search of a phenomenon.

MECHANISMS OF FORGETTING?

The core elements of the traumatic amnesia thesis are as follows:

1. People can experience traumatic events in childhood, but repress (or dissociate) explicit memory for those events so that they are unaware of being trauma survivors.
2. These memories of trauma are not dormant, but are expressed implicitly in emotion and behavior.
3. These memories can be recollected with reasonable fidelity and accuracy.
4. Recovering and integrating them into meaningful narratives produces therapeutic benefits.

The traumatic amnesia thesis also rests on several additional assumptions. First, the events must have been encoded into memory. Obviously, only those events stored in memory are capable of later retrieval. Second, the events must have been experienced as traumatic at the time of their occurrence; otherwise there would have been no motivation to repress them in the first place. For example, if a child fails to understand her stepfather's inappropriate touching as sexual abuse, she will lack motivation to block it from awareness. If she remembers this event years later and realizes its abusive nature, that belated realization cannot have been the reason she did not think about the experience during the intervening years.

The chief controversy over forgotten trauma concerns how best to explain the following phenomenon: A person undergoes one or more traumatic experiences during childhood, does not think about them for many years, and then begins to think about them again. According to some theorists, this sequence of events can best be explained by a defensive mechanism, either repression or dissociation, that prevents access to memories of trauma. Only when potent reminders overcome these powerful defensive mechanisms does memory for trauma resurface into awareness. A person's failure to think about the trauma, these theorists say, constitutes "amnesia," and they attribute this amnesia either to repression or to dissociation. They are reluctant to invoke "ordinary" forgetting to explain why someone who was abused in childhood might not think about the abuse for many years.

However, one cannot conclude that a person who does not think about something for a long period of time—who has "forgotten" it, in everyday parlance—is suffering from amnesia. Amnesia is an *inability* to recall information that has been encoded. We cannot assume that people have been *unable* to recall their abuse during the years when they did not think about it, and we certainly cannot conclude anything about the mechanism of forgetting (repression, dissociation, or something else) from the mere existence of a period when the abuse did not come to mind. If the person had been asked about the abuse during the period of alleged amnesia, the memories might very well have come instantly to mind.

Ascertaining the mechanisms behind someone's not thinking about trauma for many years is a difficult task. Suppose we know that someone was sexually abused as a child. If we ask her whether she was ever abused and she says no, what can we conclude? Does her answer confirm amnesia, repression, or dissociation? Not necessarily. Perhaps we did not provide adequate cues to remind her of the event. Claims that someone is unable to recall something are always relative to a retrieval context. Hence we can only say that someone failed to recall an event when presented with certain retrieval cues. We can never "prove a negative"—prove that the information is not available in the person's memory.

If we do provide presumably adequate retrieval cues, and the known abuse survivor still says she was never abused, what can we conclude? One possibility is that the memory has decayed and is no longer available in her brain. Another possibility is that she does recall the abuse when prompted by the retrieval cues but, for whatever reason, chooses to claim it never happened. We cannot tell the difference between unavailability of the memory trace and refusal to disclose the abuse. To discriminate either of these alternatives from repression or dissociation, we would have to establish a way to detect and measure the operation of these inhibitory mechanisms independent of the facts they are adduced to explain: the person's failure to report abuse. That is, we cannot invoke the mechanism of repression (or dissociation) to explain memory failure if the only evidence for the operation of the mechanism is the very data the mechanism is invoked to explain. Trauma theorists must establish methods for measuring repression and dissociation independently from recall failure itself.

Finally, it is useful to distinguish between two very different kinds of recovered memory experiences. Some people may suddenly remember abusive events they had not thought about in years. When these memories come to mind, they may say "I hadn't thought about that in ages!" or "I thought I had forgotten that." There is nothing extraordinary about such recollections. Other people may suddenly remember abusive events for the first time. They may think of themselves as having had a happy childhood, then suddenly "remember" in adulthood that they were abused. This second kind of case raises serious concerns that the "remembered" events may have been imagined, as with people who thought they had had reasonably ordinary childhoods, only to "learn" later that they had been tortured for years by members of a satanic cult. Everything else being equal, the first kind of recovered memory is more likely to be authentic than the second kind.

7

TRAUMATIC AMNESIA

B ECAUSE THE MOST CONTESTED issue in the field of trauma
concerns whether people can experience amnesia for their
traumatic experiences, it is essential to clarify what amnesia really means.
Amnesia is an inability to remember certain facts and experiences that cannot be attributed to ordinary forgetting. Merely not thinking about something for a period of time is not the same as amnesia. A diagnosis of amnesia
requires an *inability* to remember.

Amnesia is usually triggered by a precipitating event. An inability to remember facts and events that occurred before the precipitating event is
called *retrograde* amnesia. For example, a person who has received a head injury in an automobile accident and who cannot remember anything from the
period immediately preceding the crash is suffering from retrograde amnesia.
An inability to remember facts and events that occurred after the precipitating event is called *anterograde* amnesia. After his neurosurgical operation for
intractable epilepsy, H.M. could not encode any new memories (see Chapter 2). He suffered from anterograde amnesia. *Organic amnesia* is caused by
events, such as a blow to the head, that produce memory loss by damaging
the brain. *Psychogenic amnesia* is caused by events whose psychological or
emotional meaning produces memory loss without damaging the brain. Organic amnesia is relatively common; psychogenic amnesia is extremely rare
despite its frequent portrayal in films and novels (for reviews see Kihlström
and Schacter 2000; Kopelman 1987, 1995).

Disentangling organic and psychogenic causes of amnesia can be difficult,
especially when physical or psychic precipitants seem relatively minor.
Sometimes psychological stressors trigger retrograde amnesia in a person with

preexisting neurological impairment, thereby blurring the distinction between psychic and organic causation. Another challenge is distinguishing genuine from simulated psychogenic amnesia. As I discuss later in this chapter, some murderers report amnesia for their crimes. Some may fake their memory loss, hoping to gain leniency in the courtroom.[1]

Classifying a person's amnesia as psychogenic does not imply that it does not involve changes in the brain; it only implies that no physical agent has produced detectable damage. Using positron emission tomography (PET), Hans Markowitsch and his colleagues (1997) found that a patient who suffered from persistent identity loss—he had no idea who he was—and retrograde amnesia exhibited patterns of brain activation differing from those of healthy control subjects. Relying on other sources about the man's life, Markowitsch made audiotapes describing biographical events for which the patient had amnesia, and played these tapes to the patient while he was in the PET scanner. When control subjects heard descriptions of events from their past, they exhibited widespread activation of temporal and frontal regions of the right hemisphere, including the amygdala and the hippocampus (see Fink et al. 1996). In contrast, the amnesic patient exhibited activation only in a small area of the frontal and temporal regions of the left hemisphere. He responded to descriptions of important events from his past as if they were new and unfamiliar.

Classic psychogenic amnesia is characterized by sudden onset in response to stress, inability to remember precipitating events, loss of personal identity, and extensive retrograde amnesia. People with psychogenic amnesia seldom experience anterograde memory problems, whereas people with organic amnesia (like H.M.) sometimes do. And people with organic amnesia rarely experience loss of personal identity.

The antecedents of psychogenic amnesia are sometimes very stressful experiences such as becoming suicidal, attempting suicide, being raped, suffering bereavement accompanied by suicidal ideation, and mistakenly believing that one has inadvertently killed one's closest friend.[2] Yet other cases are triggered by noncatastrophic stressors, such as disappointments in love, the death of a grandparent, financial problems, family conflict, legal problems leading to job loss, or commission of adultery. In an especially interesting case, a 23-year-old man developed psychogenic retrograde amnesia for the previous six years of his life after discovering a minor, smoldering fire in his house. Several weeks later, he recalled having seen, as a 4-year-old, a man burn to death in a car wreck (a memory corroborated by the patient's mother). The otherwise trivial house fire functioned as a precipitant, apparently reminding him of a trauma from long ago (Markowitsch et al. 1998).[3]

Most people with psychogenic amnesia spontaneously recover their identity and memory within a matter of hours, days, or weeks. In rare cases, amnesia may persist for months. Recovery from psychogenic retrograde amnesia usually occurs suddenly, whereas in organic amnesia memories return gradually, if at all.[4]

Although the DSM-IV links psychogenic amnesia with dissociation, some experts in the past denied such a link. In a classic article, D. N. Parfitt and C. M. Carlyle Gall wrote: "The amnesia occurs because the patient does not wish to remember. We cannot see the need for the conception of dissociation in considering this symptom" (1944: 525). That is, rather than reflecting an automatic segregation of memory (dissociation), psychogenic amnesia reflects ordinary reluctance to think about something unpleasant.

Relevant to amnesia is the rarely assigned diagnosis of dissociative fugue—a syndrome characterized by irresistible, aimless wandering, often coupled with subsequent amnesia for at least parts of the journey (Kopelman, Christensen, et al. 1994). The philosopher and historian of psychiatry Ian Hacking (1998) characterizes fugue as a transient mental illness, one that flourishes in a specific time and place, only to vanish later. Fugue erupted in epidemic form in late nineteenth-century France, and then disappeared just as quickly before World War I.

Why, asks Hacking, is an almost never assigned diagnosis still listed in DSM-IV? The reason, he says, is that fugue provides "an extra leg (or taxonomic branch) to prop up the category of dissociative disorders" (1998: 93). The chief rationale for introducing the superordinate category of dissociative disorders in DSM-III in 1980 was to find a home for multiple personality disorder (MPD; now called dissociative identity disorder). But superordinate categories must have more than one member. For example, the anxiety disorders category includes PTSD, panic disorder, social phobia, and obsessive-compulsive disorder, along with several others. Accordingly, advocates of MPD had to find other syndromes to occupy slots under the general dissociative rubric to justify an overarching category. But in reality, none of the other dissociative disorders qualifies as a genuine syndrome—a group of symptoms that cluster together to form a coherent pattern. In fact, depersonalization disorder and dissociative amnesia are each defined by only a single symptom—recurrent feelings of unreality and memory loss, respectively. And dissociative fugue is defined by only two symptoms—unexpected travel and confusion about one's identity.

DSM-IV states that dissociative fugue usually begins after "traumatic, stressful, or overwhelming life events" (APA 1994: 482). Yet, as Hacking has shown, fugue has rarely been triggered by trauma. For example, fugue has occurred most frequently among soldiers during peacetime, not war. It was especially common in late nineteenth-century France among restless conscripts who could not tolerate the boredom and regimentation of military life. Desertion among battle-traumatized soldiers must not be confused with the aimless wandering of the fugueur (Hacking 1998: 62).

Also, other reports rarely implicate trauma in the onset of fugue. E. Stengel (1941), who described 25 cases of fugue, noted that a traumatic event seldom precipitated the person's flight. Moreover, most of his cases did not even exhibit amnesia for the period of the fugue. A seemingly irresistible urge to wander far and wide was enough to attract the attention of psychiatrists, even in the absence of trauma or memory loss. Stengel did identify other apparent risk factors for fugue, including epilepsy, depression, and having been reared by disturbed and often physically abusive parents. Others also noted vulnerability factors for fugue and psychogenic amnesia, ranging from having a "weak" personality to previous head injury, suicidal ideation, and interpersonal problems.[5]

Psychogenic Amnesia versus Traumatic Amnesia

Psychogenic amnesia must not be confused with the kind of traumatic amnesia postulated to explain why someone might not remember childhood sexual abuse. Classic psychogenic amnesia begins immediately after the precipitating event; involves loss of personal identity; involves massive retrograde memory loss, not merely loss of memory for the precipitating event; rarely lasts more than a few weeks; and usually ends suddenly rather than gradually. In addition, the restoration of memory rarely requires psychotherapy.

These features of classic psychogenic amnesia differ dramatically from those of alleged repressed and recovered memories of abuse. In the typical case, an adult has "amnesia" for sexual abuse that occurred in childhood; the amnesia lasts for many years; the amnesia never involves loss of personal identity; and the memories return in bits and pieces, often during psychotherapy. Thus the (rare) occurrences of psychogenic amnesia do not lend credence to reports of repressed and recovered memories of abuse. The two kinds of phenomena are very different.

Likewise, the DSM-IV PTSD symptom "inability to recall an important aspect of the trauma" differs from an inability to remember that one has been abused (APA 1994: 428). Furthermore, this symptom is inherently ambiguous: it does not distinguish between encoding failure and retrieval failure (amnesia). People may fail to remember aspects of traumatic events merely because their attention was directed elsewhere during the events so they did not encode these aspects. For example, a woman robbed at gunpoint may attend so closely to the assailant's weapon that she fails to encode and therefore remember his face. Assuming these aspects have been repressed (or dissociated) presupposes that they have been encoded, and this is not necessarily the case.

Evidence Adduced for Amnesia for Trauma

One side of the recovered memory debate argues that there is no convincing evidence that people can banish, and then later retrieve, memories of horrific experiences. After scrutinizing dozens of studies involving all kinds of documented traumatic events, the psychiatrist Harrison Pope and his colleagues concluded that survivors seldom forget trauma unless they suffer direct physical damage to the brain or experience the traumatic events prior to the offset of childhood amnesia (Pope et al. 1998; Pope, Oliva, and Hudson 1999). The other side of the debate, best represented by Daniel Brown and his colleagues, proclaims "overwhelming scientific support for the existence of repressed or dissociated memory" (Brown, Scheflin, and Hammond 1998: 538–539). Although Pope and Brown agree that most trauma survivors remember their horrific experiences all too well, Brown claims that a significant minority of survivors have no memory whatsoever for their traumatic experiences, but then later retrieve these memories more or less intact. Strikingly, both sides review the same scientific studies, yet arrive at opposite conclusions. How is this possible?

The answer is that traumatic amnesia theorists often misunderstand the studies they cite in support of their position. Moreover, Brown, Scheflin, and Whitfield commit an elementary logical blunder in their approach to this controversy when they assert that "the burden of proof is on them [skeptics of repressed memories] to show that repressed memories do not exist" (1999: 125). They have it precisely backward: the burden of proof is on advocates of traumatic amnesia to provide convincing evidence that people *can* repress and later recover memories of trauma. It is logically impossible for anyone to prove the null hypothesis that *any* phenomenon—repression included— never occurs. That is why careful skeptics never foolishly say that "repression of memory does not exist."

Misreadings of the literature abound in their writings. They are not reliable guides to what science says about trauma and memory. For example, they adduce studies which, they claim, "clearly offer data *in support of the existence of traumatic amnesia* but fail to report the proportion of subjects who experienced it." What these studies *do* document is the DSM-III symptom of "memory impairment or trouble concentrating" (APA 1980: 238). Brown and colleagues misunderstand this symptom, mistakenly believing that it "typically includes both hypermnesia and amnesia."[6] In reality, it refers to neither. Hypermnesia—vivid recall of the trauma—is covered by the diagnostic criterion of recurrent and intrusive recollection. The symptom of memory impairment means forgetfulness in everyday life that develops after a trauma; it does not mean difficulty remembering the trauma itself (traumatic amnesia). For example, after a trauma, survivors often notice that they frequently forget the birthdays of friends, forget to run certain errands, or forget that they have left something in the oven. Ordinary forgetfulness that develops *after* the traumatic event is not the same thing as amnesia *for* the traumatic event.

Brown, Scheflin, and Whitfield's (1999) misunderstanding becomes immediately apparent when one reads the studies they discuss. For example, among 102 witnesses of the collapse of the skywalks at the Hyatt Regency Hotel in Kansas City, 88 percent had "repeated recollections" of the disaster and 27 percent had "memory difficulties." The symptom questionnaire completed by these subjects was based on DSM-III criteria. Accordingly, their memory problems concerned everyday forgetfulness, not amnesia for the trauma itself. Some reported "efforts at repression," but their attempts to forget were unsuccessful, as their repetitive recollections indicate. The very fact that they remembered the event so vividly confirms that they had no difficulty remembering it (Wilkinson 1983). These three authors make the same mistake while reviewing other studies in which survivors complained about problems with memory or concentration. These studies concerned torture, exposure to a toxic chemical spill, an ambush during war, and the Holocaust. In each case, the survivors' memory for the trauma itself was vivid; their problems with memory were confined to everyday forgetfulness.[7]

While searching for evidence of traumatic amnesia, Brown, Scheflin, and Hammond (1998) misinterpret findings attributable to direct physical injury to the brain as relevant to psychic trauma. For example, they state that "Dollinger (1985) found that two of the 38 children studied after watching lightning strike and kill a playmate had no memory of the event" (609–610). However, they do not mention that both amnesic youngsters had themselves been struck by side flashes from the main lightning bolt, knocked unconscious, and nearly killed. Given the serious effects on the brain of being knocked unconscious by lightning, it is little wonder that these two children had no memory for the event. Psychic trauma alone was insufficient to produce amnesia; the children who had not been struck by lightning did not forget the event. Thus Dollinger's study does not provide support for the existence of traumatic amnesia. Instead, it deals with organic retrograde amnesia.

Further confusing matters, they cite a study by Willem Wagenaar and Jop Groeneweg as evidence that "amnesia for Nazi Holocaust camp experiences has also been reported" (Brown, Scheflin, and Hammond 1998: 156). Wagenaar and Groeneweg (1990) studied memory for trauma among former inmates of Camp Erika, a Nazi concentration camp. They compared the inmates' current recollections with depositions they had provided 40 years earlier when they were released from captivity. Wagenaar and Groeneweg observed "a remarkable degree of remembering" (80) for Holocaust trauma, especially remarkable because of the starvation and head injuries suffered by many inmates. "There is no doubt," they emphasized, "that almost all witnesses remember Camp Erika in great detail, even after 40 years" (84).

So why adduce this study as confirming *amnesia* for Holocaust experiences? Several of the former inmates failed to mention certain violent events (among many similar events they immediately recalled), and had forgotten certain details, such as the name of an especially sadistic guard. But even in these scattered instances of forgetting, the former inmates instantly recalled the forgotten events and details when shown their original depositions. Only one still failed to recall a specific traumatic event when he saw his original deposition—and even this man recalled the vast majority of his horrific experiences in the camp. Because memory does not operate like a video recorder, it is not surprising that survivors did not immediately recall every traumatic event that had occurred 40 years earlier. The fact that reading their original depositions prompted recollection of the forgotten events indicates that they were able to remember them when properly cued by reminders. This study has nothing to do with amnesia—an *inability* to remember one's concentration camp experiences.

Brown, Scheflin, and Whitfield cite studies reporting "*significant cognitive avoidance* of the traumatic memory" (1999: 29), apparently believing that *attempts* to avoid thinking about trauma imply the ability to repress it. Lenore Terr (1983) reassessed 25 California schoolchildren four years after they had been kidnapped and entombed in a buried truck-trailer. All had "intact and detailed" memories of the event; none had "become fully or partly amnesic" for the trauma despite their efforts to avoid thinking about it (1545, 1550). In another study, Carl Malmquist (1986) assessed 16 children, ranging from 5 to 10 years of age, who had witnessed the murder of a parent or discovered the body of a recently murdered parent. All the children suffered from vivid memories of the trauma notwithstanding their attempts to avoid "thinking or talking about it" (Terr 1983: 1544). Trying not to think about something must not be confused with being unable to remember it.

They cite another study as providing evidence of "*injury-specific amnesia, but not general amnesia* for the traumatic event itself" (1999: 29). But again, this study does not show that trauma survivors were incapable of remembering the trauma. After a fatal sniper attack on an elementary school playground, Robert Pynoos and Kathleen Nader (1989) asked each of 133 children to describe what had happened. Five children provided extremely brief accounts in which they neglected to mention their own minor gunshot wounds. However, as Pynoos and Nader stated, "when the children were directed to go over the event in slow motion, they were able to fill in gaps, sequence events correctly, add details, and elaborate on their emotional responses" (241). Apparently these children were not incapable of remembering their injuries; they were merely reluctant to discuss them.

Other cited studies also have little or nothing to do with an inability to remember trauma. For example, they cite Etzel Cardeña and David Spiegel's (1993) study of students who experienced the 1989 San Francisco earthquake, even though that study assessed "difficulties with everyday memory"—not inability to remember the earthquake. Cardeña and Spiegel did not specify what percentage of subjects had amnesia for the trauma, despite tabulating the percentages of subjects who had other dissociative symptoms.

They did say, however, that "neither partial nor full amnesia for the traumatic event was frequently reported" (477).

In two other studies, the original researchers lumped amnesia with other symptoms. In one of these, people living near the site of a gas-line explosion reported more symptoms of "amnesia, disinterest and detachment" than people living in a similar neighborhood distant from the blast (Realmuto, Wagner, and Bartholow 1991: 473). Because the researchers had used DSM-III-R criteria for PTSD, reports of "amnesia" apparently referred to subjects' having been unable to remember aspects of the disaster, perhaps because they did not encode everything that had happened. Nothing in the article, however, implies that participants had repressed their memories of the explosion. In the other study, researchers interviewed adults one year after fatal flash floods had wreaked havoc in a Puerto Rican community (Escobar et al. 1992). Flood victims reported more "pseudoneurological" symptoms (amnesia, paralysis, fainting, unusual spells, double vision) than did the control group (11 percent versus 4 percent). Unfortunately, the authors of the report on this study did not specify the percentage of subjects claiming amnesia. Moreover, the researchers did not specify what was meant by "amnesia" (everyday forgetfulness? inability to recall aspects of the flood?). Because memory is not perfect, at least some subjects are bound to say there are some things they do not recall about such disasters. Attributing their imperfect memory to traumatic amnesia or repression is unconvincing, especially because their ability to participate in these studies seems to imply that they have not repressed their memories of the trauma.

Similar interpretive issues arise in another study cited by Brown, Scheflin, and Whitfield (1999) as relevant to repression. Two years after a flood in West Virginia caused by the collapse of a dam, researchers found that 13 of 179 children, who had ranged in age from 2 to 15 when the disaster occurred, reported "an inability to recall part of the event" (Green et al. 1991: 948).

Another misinterpreted study concerned not repression of trauma but everyday memory problems associated with neurological damage. Axel Strom and his associates (1962) did extensive general medical, psychiatric, and neurologic assessments of 100 Scandinavians who had been confined to Nazi or Japanese concentration camps or prisons. Half of them had received head injuries sufficient to produce unconsciousness, and nearly all had suffered starvation. Neurologic symptoms were noted in 92 percent, and 78 percent complained of "failing memory" (78). But these organic memory problems did not involve amnesia for trauma. As Strom and his colleagues emphasized, the patients' "war experiences [were] still fresh in their minds" (61).

Brown, Scheflin, and Whitfield misread yet another study as relevant to repression of trauma. Stevan Weine and his colleagues assessed 20 Bosnian refugees who had been exposed to genocidal trauma (Weine, Becker, McGlashan, Laub, et al. 1995). All but 2 reported intrusive memories, and 16 denied having amnesia for traumatic events, whereas 2 reported some amnesia and 1 reported severe amnesia. Although no one forgot having endured genocidal horror, some subjects did experience confusion about the sequence of events. One woman failed to recall a trauma story she had recounted to investigators only three weeks earlier. But her quoted comments clearly indicate that she had not forgotten that she had been exposed to trauma. She said: "It gets mixed up and overlapping. All the memories come at the same moment and it's too much" (541). One man denied he had any "memories" of the Bosnian genocide; instead, he described a movie that kept replaying in his mind depicting all the horrors he had witnessed.

Another cited study actually documents vivid memories of trauma plus an apparent failure to encode everything that happened. Louis Najarian's research team (1996: 377) interviewed Armenian children two and a half years after a massive earthquake. Regardless of whether the children had been living near the epicenter or had merely seen horrific footage on television, nearly 100 percent of them reported vivid, intrusive memories of the event. So why cite this work as documenting amnesia for trauma? Thirty-two percent of the children near the epicenter reported the DSM-III-R symptom of an inability to remember an important aspect of the trauma. The most plausible interpretation of this fact, especially when coupled with the children's vivid memories of the earthquake, is that the children failed to encode everything that had happened. Certainly this symptom was not linked to trauma as such; the highest rate of amnesia for aspects of the trauma occurred in the group of children whose only exposure to the earthquake was on television.

Contrary to the assertions of Brown and his coauthors, the aforementioned studies do not provide convincing evidence that a significant minority of traumatized people are incapable of remembering their trauma. Most of the evidence they adduce in support of traumatic amnesia actually concerns ordinary, everyday forgetfulness, not repression of the trauma itself. Other studies probably reflect incomplete encoding—and therefore incomplete recall—of traumatic experiences. We cannot expect survivors to remember every aspect of every traumatic experience. The key point is that even when memory is not perfect, survivors do not report complete amnesia for their trauma.

Amnesia for Sexual Abuse?

The most contentious issue has been whether people experience amnesia for sexual abuse suffered in childhood. According to Brown, Scheflin, and Hammond, "approximately a third of sexually abused victims report some period of their lives where they did not remember anything about the abuse and later recovered the memory of the abuse" (1998: 196). They cite many studies in support of this claim, but fatal methodological flaws render the data of nearly every study either ambiguous or utterly uninterpretable.

An influential study by John Briere and Jon Conte (1993) exemplifies many of the problems that plague research in this area. Recruiting subjects through a national network of therapists specializing in treating abuse survivors, they obtained questionnaire data from 420 female and 30 male psychotherapy patients. All said they had experienced "psychologically or physically forced sexual contact" before their sixteenth birthday with someone at least five years older (23). In response to the question "During the period of time between when the first forced sexual experience happened and your eighteenth birthday was there ever a time when you could not remember the forced sexual experience?" 59 percent of the patients answered "yes" (24). Briere and Conte concluded that nearly 60 percent of survivors experience "sexual abuse–related repression" of their traumatic memories prior to recovering the memories later in life (26).

Briere and Conte's study was the first of many that asked subjects whether there had ever been a time when they could not remember their abuse or whether they had previously repressed their memories of abuse.[8] Investigators often failed to specify what they meant by "sexual abuse" and how long the abuse had to have been forgotten to count as having been "repressed." Moreover, few investigators established that the recalled abuse had actually happened. Admittedly, corroborating abuse is a challenging task—crimes committed in secret are difficult to verify. But subjects in some of these studies recalled abuse from early infancy, thereby undercutting their claims to credibility. Moreover, researchers were often either unclear or very liberal in what they regarded as a memory. For example, in one study, unexplained, strong bodily feelings, dreams, and visual images were counted as recovered *memories* of abuse.[9]

A serious problem in these studies is the wording of the key question: subjects were asked whether there had ever been a time when they were *unable* to remember the abuse. An affirmative answer implies that the subject has spent a period of time unsuccessfully trying to remember having been abused. But if a person has repressed all memories of abuse, on what basis would he or she attempt to remember it in the first place? How are we to make sense out of affirmative responses to this question? Some of the subjects in these surveys may have been told by their therapists that they exhibited the symptoms of a survivor of childhood sexual abuse. Subjects without any memories of abuse may have then attempted to recall their presumably repressed memories, and difficulty in doing so may have led them to say there had been a time when they could not remember their abuse. However, a more plausible interpretation is that subjects understood the question to mean "Has there ever been a time when you did not think about your abuse?" But *not thinking about* one's abuse is not the same as being *unable* to remember it. And it is an *inability* to remember that defines amnesia. One need not invoke repression, dissociation, or any other special mechanism to account for these results.

As Jonathan Schooler and his colleagues have discovered, people sometimes forget that they did recall their abuse during a period when they believe they had forgotten it. For example, in one case, a woman's husband confirmed that she had mentioned being raped on several occasions during the period in which she believed she had never thought about the rape. People often forget episodes of remembering (Schooler, Bendiksen, and Ambadar 1997).

Another problem with retrospective studies such as Briere and Conte's is that researchers have assumed that abuse survivors have worse memory for their childhoods than do other people. But unless one assesses memory for childhood among adults who have not been abused, and assesses memory for nonabusive childhood experiences among abuse survivors, this assumption remains untested.

In fact, cognitive psychologists have discovered that people's memory for childhood is not as good as they think it is. Don Read and Stephen Lindsay (2000) found that asking subjects to try to remember additional details of certain childhood experiences, such as attending a summer camp or taking a family trip, resulted in subjects' deciding that their memory for their childhood was worse than they had thought. It seems that people are most likely to believe they have had partial amnesia for the very events they have been trying hardest to remember.

Other researchers have replicated these findings. Robert Belli's research team (1998) adopted a question (from Ross et al. 1990) that psychiatrists have used to study memory gaps in patients with MPD: "Are there large parts of your childhood after age 5 that you cannot remember?" The more events undergraduate students tried to remember from their childhood, the more likely they were to respond affirmatively to this question. In another study, these researchers found that perceived difficulty in remembering predicts heightened estimates of one's amnesia for childhood (Winkielman, Schwarz, and Belli 1998). Taken together, these studies suggest that the more psychotherapy patients try to remember their childhood, including suspected incidents of abuse, the more surprised they will be by how little they remember (see also Merckelbach et al. 2001). Mistakenly believing that other people can remember their childhoods much better, these patients are likely to claim substantial amnesia for their childhood. They may conclude that something terrible must have happened that caused them to repress it.

The experience of "recovering memories" is not confined to trauma. When Don Read (1997) tested subjects at a shopping mall, 15 percent of them reported significant memory gaps for their childhood after age 5. Moreover, 60 percent reported having had a recovered memory experience in which they suddenly recalled a childhood event. About half of these subjects interpreted this experience as nothing more than not having thought about the event for a long time. Only 17 percent of the recovered memories concerned traumatic events (such as sexual abuse). As Read emphasized, reports of the percentages of sexual abuse survivors who were partially or fully amnesic for their abuse are meaningless in the absence of baseline data for amnesia for nontraumatic events. It is clear that "amnesia" for nonabusive events is far from zero.

Researchers have rectified some of the deficiencies in Briere and Conte's methods in subsequent studies. They have asked what factors might lead people not to think about their abuse for a protracted period. Some studies provide clues. Loftus, Polonsky, and Fullilove (1994) found that women who reported having entirely forgotten their abuse rated it as having been less upsetting when it occurred than did women who had never forgotten it. Indeed, a child's failure to understand these experiences as abusive may increase the likelihood that she will not think about them much until years later, when she finally recognizes them as abuse. In another study by Loftus's group, most college students who reported a period of at least several weeks during which they had not thought about their abuse, and who guessed that they probably would not have remembered it during that period even if someone had asked them about it, had not understood the experience to be sexual or abusive when it happened (Joslyn, Carlin, and Loftus 1997).

Timothy Melchert conducted three questionnaire studies on memories of abuse that illuminate why some people may not think about their abuse for periods of time. In his first survey he asked 553 college students whether there had ever been "a time when you had no memories of your physical/emotional/sexual abuse, and then later the memories came back to you" (1996: 442). Of the 553 students, 13 reported recovered memories of physical abuse, 15 of emotional abuse, and 13 of sexual abuse. However, 4 of those reporting recovered memories of sexual abuse said that they had always remembered the experience but had only belatedly realized it was abuse. Seven said the memories were too painful to think about, but all of the sexually abused subjects thought that they would have remembered the experience had someone asked them about it during the period of apparent forgetting.[10]

In his second questionnaire survey of 429 college students, Melchert found significantly higher rates of recovered memories for emotional abuse (41 percent) than for either physical (17 percent) or sexual (13 percent) abuse (Melchert and Parker 1997). Most subjects acknowledged having tried to avoid thinking about these experiences. Deliberate, conscious attempts to forget unpleasant experiences differ from an automatic, unconscious repression mechanism that removes these experiences from awareness and prevents the person from being able to recall them later. Melchert's questionnaire asked subjects to indicate the causes of their lack of memory. Not one subject chose the option "Because I simply had no memories of it ever happening."[11]

In Melchert's (1999) third questionnaire survey of 560 college students, 38 subjects reported recovered memories of abuse, and 25 of these said they deliberately tried not to think about their abuse, but affirmed that they could easily have remembered it during the period of "amnesia." Another 9 subjects believed that reminders would have enabled them to remember their abuse during that period. Only one subject believed that reminders would not have triggered retrieval of the memory. Although Brown, Scheflin, and Whitfield (1999) interpret Melchert's studies as evidence of "amnesia" for trauma, very few of Melchert's subjects believed they would have been incapable of remembering their abuse.

Two serious limitations hamper interpretation of the aforementioned studies. First, the researchers did not obtain corroboration that the abuse had, in fact, happened. Second, because subjects were not asked about their abuse during the period when they did not think about it, they are only guessing whether they would have remembered the abuse if they *had* been asked about it. Hence their retrospective accounts are difficult to evaluate.

Some researchers have attempted to address the first problem: lack of corroboration of the trauma. But, as often as not, they have merely taken their subjects' word that proof of trauma was available. Seldom have they themselves examined the corroborating evidence. For example, Judith Herman and Emily Schatzow (1987) reported data on 53 women who had participated in their incest survivor groups, of whom 14 qualified for what Herman and Schatzow called "massive repression" (12). These 14 patients said they had been entirely unaware of their abuse until memories recently emerged in or outside of therapy. Most reported remembering little of their childhood, most recalled that the abuse had begun during their preschool years, and 8 remembered it as violent. Another 19 patients said they had always remembered being abused but had recalled additional memories during therapy. Herman and Schatzow reported that 39 patients (74 percent) obtained confirmation of their abuse. What counted as confirmation? Of these patients, 21 claimed either that they had confronted the perpetrator, that another family member confirmed it, or that diaries or photographs confirmed it. The other 18 patients reported having learned that another person had been abused by the same perpetrator, and this was counted as corroboration.

Unfortunately, Herman and Schatzow relied solely on the patients' accounts of having obtained confirmation of the memories. Moreover, they failed to report whether any of the recovered memories, especially from the "massive repression" group, were among those corroborated. Finally, they included some patients in their incest survivor groups who had no memories of abuse; 16 patients had joined the groups for the purpose of recovering memories of abuse. Accordingly, social pressure to come up with abuse memories might have fostered formulation of illusory memories of events that never happened. Indeed, as Herman and Schatzow wrote: "Participation in group proved to be a powerful stimulus for recovery of memory in patients with severe amnesia. Almost all of the women who entered the group complaining of major memory deficits and who defined a goal of recovering childhood memories were able to retrieve previously repressed memories [of incest] during group treatment" (1987: 8).

In another study, Judith Herman and Mary Harvey (1997) consulted hospital medical files for 77 adult outpatients who reported childhood trauma (sexual abuse, physical abuse, or witnessing domestic violence). Most patients had always remembered their trauma; only 12 reported having once been entirely amnesic for their trauma, whereas another 13 reported having always remembered some episodes but recalled additional ones later. Herman and Harvey said that corroboration was noted in the charts of 9 of the 25 patients reporting recovered memories and 24 of the 52 patients who had always remembered their trauma, but they did not specify whether the 9 cases of corroborated recovered memory were from the group claiming total amnesia. Also, what counted as corroboration varied in probative value. For example, the records noted that 10 patients said another person had witnessed the event (for example, domestic violence), whereas in 10 cases the records stated that another person had charged the perpetrator with committing a similar offense (such as sexual abuse). Clearly, the first example counts as stronger corroboration than the second. And it appears that the patients themselves were the sources of the hospital's information about corroboration; no one obtained independent confirmation of the trauma.

Other researchers have also claimed corroboration for recovered memories without verifying their subjects' claims. The sociologist Catherine Cameron (1996) studied and compared two groups of women who sought treatment for the effects of childhood sexual abuse. One group comprised 25 patients who said they had had no memories of sexual abuse whatsoever for periods ranging from 15 to 54 years. The typical patient in this group said her long-repressed memories had returned gradually as sensory fragments which eventually came into focus as a horrifying narrative. The trauma usually began during her preschool years and extended through most of elementary school, and the alleged perpetrators were her parents. Thirteen patients told Cameron that they had corroborated their recovered memories of abuse via at least one source, including confirmation by another survivor, a relative, or the perpetrator. Cameron's second group comprised 21 patients who said that they had never forgotten their abuse, but many of them had not interpreted it as abuse until many years later. Comparing the two groups, Cameron found that more amnesic patients than nonamnesic patients had been abused by their biological mother, had been abused by their biological father, had experienced sexual violence, and had experienced penetrative abuse. For two reasons, these data must be interpreted cautiously. First, the abuse reports were not verified independently of the subjects' claims. Second, studies on documented trauma (such as the Holocaust) indicate that the more severe the violence, the less likely a victim is to forget it. Yet subjects in Cameron's study who claimed to have been amnesic for all of their abuse were those reporting the most serious sexual violence.

Failure to verify trauma independently of the subject's report also weakens a study done by Bessel van der Kolk and Rita Fisler (1995). They recruited 10 men and 36 women from the community who were haunted by memories of terrible events and who met criteria for PTSD. Thirty-six subjects reported histories of childhood trauma, and 29 reported sexual abuse. Of these 36 subjects, 15 claimed to have had "significant or total amnesia for their trauma at some point in their lives" (516), and 27 said that another person (such as a parent or sibling) or another source (such as court or hospital records, perpetrator confession or conviction) had confirmed the authenticity of the trauma memories. However, van der Kolk and Fisler did not verify the corroborating evidence themselves, and they failed to mention whether the confirming evidence pertained to traumas for which subjects had claimed prior amnesia or to traumas that subjects claimed never to have forgotten. Surprisingly, van der Kolk and Fisler said that "no subject reported having a narrative for the traumatic event as their initial mode of awareness" (517). The claim that survivors were *incapable* of describing their trauma after it happened—yet became capable of doing so years later—flies in the face of everything we know about trauma or about autobiographical memory. Autobiographical memories fade with time; they do not become progressively more vivid.

Intent on documenting that recovered memories can be corroborated, the psychiatrist Richard Kluft (1997) reported data extracted from the medical files of 34 MPD patients he had assessed or treated (19 of whom claimed to have been subjected to satanic ritual abuse). Kluft reportedly confirmed episodes of abuse for 10 patients who had never forgotten them and for 13 patients who had remembered them during psychotherapy. With regard to the recovered memories, he noted that for many of the patients, multiple sources of confirmation were available (for example, confession by perpetrator, police records, report by witness, confirmation by nonwitness). Although in at least several instances the witness, informant, or perpetrator apparently corroborated the abuse to Kluft himself, in other instances the patients themselves apparently furnished the evidence (for example, describing a deathbed scene during which the perpetrator confessed).

The psychiatric nurse Ann Burgess and her colleagues reported findings from three groups of children who were alleged to have suffered physical, psychological, and sexual abuse while attending daycare (Burgess, Hartman, and Baker 1995). Group A included 10 children whose average age was 2.6 years when they were allegedly ritualistically abused by a male teacher and his wife. Burgess and her colleagues said this teacher "was a high priest of a satanic sect" (10). Group B included 11 children whose average age was 2.7 years when the alleged abuse occurred. Four of these children said that masked, black-robed figures had inserted objects (such as pencils) into the children's vaginas and rectums. Group C included 13 children whose average age at the time of the alleged abuse was 2.9 years. All 34 children in these three groups exhibited what Burgess interpreted as behavioral and somatic indications of their trauma (for example, sleepwalking, nightmares, pouting, drawings of religious figures).

Five to 10 years after these allegations had been made and "validated through criminal proceedings in one case and civil settlements in all three cases" (10), the researchers assessed 19 of the children whose median age had been 2.5 years when the abuse was said to have occurred. According to Burgess, Hartman, and Baker, 11 of the children retained full verbal memory, 5 had fragmented verbal memory, and 3 had no memory of their abuse. The authors did not provide any details about how the memories were assessed or how the events were "validated." Moreover, because the alleged events occurred when the allegedly amnesic children were only 2.5 years of age, it is unsurprising that 3 children did not recall the events. Also, most cases of satanic abuse that were "validated" in the courts have now been overturned on appeal. Such discredited tales of satanism are now widely regarded as artifacts of overzealous, suggestive questioning of children.

Catherine Roe and Mark Schwartz (1996) administered a questionnaire concerning memory for trauma to 52 women who had been treated in an inpatient program for survivors of childhood sexual abuse. Forty respondents said they had not always remembered having been abused, and the mean duration of reported amnesia was 23 years. Of these 40, 22 described their first memory as a "flashback," and 24 reported that their memories had become increasingly vivid over time. Approximately two-thirds of the patients said their memories of abuse had surfaced under hypnosis, and 5 said that before they had any memories of abuse, their therapists had told them they might have been abused. Twenty-two respondents claimed to have gotten confirmation of their memories from at least one source. There was no corroboration, however, by the researchers independent of the patients' self- reports, nor was it clear whether the confirmed memories were among those recovered or those always remembered.

James Chu and his colleagues (1999) investigated memory for abuse in 90 female inpatients on a hospital's dissociative and posttraumatic stress disorders unit. Of these 90 women, 25 reported having been entirely amnesic for their history of childhood sexual abuse. Of these 25 women, 19 had attempted to corroborate their recovered memories, and 17 said they had secured verbal validation and 5 said they had obtained physical evidence (such as written records). Of 20 patients who also claimed to have been entirely amnesic for histories of physical abuse, 14 sought corroboration; 13 claimed to have found verbal confirmation and 5 claimed to have found physical confirmation (such as scars or records). The investigators, however, did not evaluate the evidence themselves.

Many critics have questioned the validity of studies of recovered memories whose subjects were patients who might have recovered false memories in abuse-focused psychotherapy. To avoid this criticism, some researchers have surveyed random samples of subjects drawn from nonclinical populations. While controlling for this methodological problem, researchers have failed to control for others. First, they have retrospectively asked subjects if there was ever a time when they could not remember some or all of their abuse. Not having thought about one's abuse is not the same as having been unable to remember it. Second, researchers have taken the subjects' word that corroboration of the abuse was available.

These problems plague a questionnaire study conducted by Shirley Feldman-Summers and Kenneth Pope (1994), who surveyed a national sample of psychotherapists about their own abuse histories. Among 330 respondents, 79 reported a history of abuse and 32 reported previous partial or full amnesia for the abuse. Fifteen of these 32 subjects claimed to have corroborated the abuse. Surveying a random sample of Dutch psychologists, Yvonne

Westerhof and her colleagues (2000) replicated Feldman-Summers and Pope's study, including its flaws.

The same problems undermine Diana Elliott's (1997) questionnaire study. She asked a random sample of American adults whether they had ever experienced any of 13 types of trauma, and, if so, whether there had ever been a time when they had less memory for the event than they did at the time of the study and whether there had ever been a time when they had no memory of it at all. Of the 505 people who replied, 364 reported some form of trauma. She found that 17 percent reported previous partial amnesia for a trauma, and an additional 15 percent reported previous total amnesia for a trauma. Of those reporting childhood sexual abuse, 58 percent reported continuous recall, 22 percent reported partial memory loss, and 20 percent reported complete memory loss. Sexual abuse in childhood was the event most often associated with reported complete memory loss (Elliott 1997; Elliott and Briere 1995).

The aforementioned studies are limited by the fact that researchers could not be certain that the reported traumatic events had actually occurred. To avoid this weakness, some investigators have verified trauma history by obtaining legal or medical documentation of the events.

For example, Cathy Widom and Suzanne Morris (1997) interviewed adults approximately 20 years after their sexual abuse had been documented in the courts. Respondents were shown a list of explicitly defined experiences ranging from being hugged or kissed in a sexual way to intercourse, and they were asked whether any of these experiences had happened to them before the age of 12. Thirty-two percent of the women and 58 percent of the men failed to report the abuse that had been documented in the courts (the index event). Such underreporting is common, according to Widom and Morris (citing data from A. G. Turner): within one year after having experienced rape, robbery, or assault, as many as 30 percent of victims fail to report these events to interviewers. Widom and Morris listed several possible reasons for underreporting, and said, "Whether this is due to loss of memory, denial, or embarrassment is not known" (44). (Despite this disclaimer, Daniel Brown and his colleagues adduce these data as showing amnesia for trauma.)

Widom and Robin Shepard likewise observed "substantial underreporting" of childhood physical abuse among 110 adults whose histories were court-documented (1996: 412). Approximately 40 percent of these individuals did not report their physical abuse histories when interviewed. Widom and

Shepard noted that underreporting might arise from forgetting, a sense of having deserved the abuse, a desire to protect parents, embarrassment, or a lack of rapport with the researchers.

The psychotherapist Constance Dalenberg (1996) sought corroboration for recovered memories of physical and sexual abuse in 17 of her patients. Although these women had always remembered being abused by their fathers, each had recovered additional memories while in therapy. Dalenberg obtained the cooperation of the accused fathers, who agreed to participate for various reasons ranging from wishing to expiate guilt to attempting to prove their innocence. She asked them about the abuse episodes, both continuously remembered and recovered, that their daughters had mentioned. The father-daughter dyads then discussed the evidence bearing on the truth of the accusations. Six judges, blind to whether the memories were continuous or recovered, rated the evidence as reasonably convincing for 75 percent of both the continuous and recovered memories. For example, 10 perpetrators confessed to episodes for which their daughters had continuous memory and 7 confessed to episodes for which their daughters had recovered memory. An additional 2 patients provided medical evidence corroborating recovered memories, and for another patient a sibling had witnessed the episode that had been recovered. This study indicates that among people who have always known they were abused, some will recall additional episodes that can be verified as authentic. This process has little do with repression or amnesia, however. Rather, it is akin to isolating a specific episode among many similar ones, such as sometimes can be done with repisodic memories.

In a study of memory for documented abuse, Christopher Bagley (1990) interviewed 19 women whose social service records documented that they had been sexually abused 18 years earlier. When questioned about abuse, 14 women described the index abuse in detail; 2 mentioned the index abuse but had forgotten the details; 1 did not mention it but did report having been raped at age 16; and 2 women denied that they had been abused. Bagley did not determine whether the 2 respondents who denied the abuse had forgotten it or were reluctant to mention it.

In the best-known study on this topic, the sociologist Linda Williams and her research team interviewed 129 women, aged 18–31, who had been medically evaluated for suspected sexual abuse approximately 17 years earlier (Williams 1994a). Abuse was defined as involuntary sexual contact involving force or coercion by a person at least 5 years older than the victim. Of these index episodes, 60 percent had involved reported penetration, and medical evidence had confirmed physical trauma in 34 percent and genital trauma in 28 percent of the cases. The interviewers asked about childhood sexual experiences, and recorded all events recounted by the respondents. Williams and an assistant judged whether any of the reported events matched the index event described in the hospital records. Although 38 percent (49 women) did not mention the index event or any other abuse by the named perpetrator, most of those women (33) described other episodes of sexual abuse. However, 16 women denied having suffered *any* sexual abuse. Also, 12 of those who *did* mention the index event affirmed that there had been a time when they had not remembered it (Williams 1995). Williams concluded that "for some women, having no recall of the abuse is based on more than just ordinary forgetting associated with the passage of time" (1994b: 1182).

Although Brown and his colleagues interpret these data as evidence for traumatic amnesia, other explanations are plausible. The 16 women who denied all sexual abuse may have recalled the index event but felt uncomfortable disclosing it to the interviewer, especially if the perpetrator had been a close family member. However, reluctance to mention embarrassing events cannot plausibly explain why 33 women failed to mention the index event but recounted *other* episodes of abuse. Nor can traumatic amnesia, dissociation, or repression explain the failure of these 33 women to mention the index event. Indeed, if episodes of sexual abuse in childhood were especially susceptible to dissociation, why would these women be capable of readily recounting other episodes of such abuse?

Some of the women may have been too young either to understand or to remember what had happened to them. Of the 129 women, 42 ranged in age from 0 to 6 years when the index abuse occurred, and 25 of these 42 did not report the index event. As Williams acknowledged, some of the memories disclosed by the youngest children "may be attributable to information they received from others later in life" (1994a: 1171). The events varied in their severity, and not all suspected index events were medically confirmed as having occurred. Abuse involving fondling is difficult to verify, and such abuse may not have been especially memorable. To determine whether the women who failed to mention the index event were actually unable to remember it, one would have to have done follow-up interviews.[12]

Donna Femina and her associates did such follow-up interviews in another study on documented childhood trauma. They interviewed 69 young adults who had been assessed approximately nine years earlier when incarcerated for adolescent offenses. During the original interview, many had reported histories of severe physical (and sometimes sexual) abuse, which had been verified by court, social service, and medical records. Yet when interviewed as adults, 18 of them either minimized their abuse or denied it altogether, and 8 others mentioned abuse experiences that they had not disclosed during the original assessment. Femina located, for a third interview, 11 participants whose responses during the second interview differed from their original responses: 8 of those who had minimized or denied abuse during the second interview, and 3 who reported abuse during the second interview after having denied it during the first interview. In the third interview, Femina mentioned the discrepancy between the adolescent and adult interviews and asked respondents why they thought the information differed across these two occasions.

Their responses were revealing. None of those who had denied or minimized abuse in the second interview said they had forgotten it. All said they had deliberately withheld the information, because they were too embarrassed to talk about it, because it was too upsetting to discuss, because they disliked or mistrusted the interviewer, or because they wished to protect their abusive parents (Femina, Yeager, and Lewis 1990). This small, but important, study indicates that clarification interviews are essential for distinguishing between *reluctance to disclose* abuse and *inability to remember* it.[13]

Linda Williams and Victoria Banyard (1997) published findings for 47 men whose data had been collected but not reported in Williams's original study. Their average age was 27 at the time of the study, and their medical records indicated that they had been taken to the hospital at an average age of 7.5 years, 98 percent of them for suspected penetrative abuse. Genital trauma had been confirmed in 53 percent of the boys. When Williams and Banyard asked them about sexual abuse, 26 did not mention the index episode: 13 of these denied all experiences of childhood sexual abuse; the other 13 mentioned other episodes of abuse. Seventy percent of those who had been younger than 7 at the time of the abuse, and 44 percent of those who had been aged 7–13, failed to mention it. It is unclear whether failure to mention the trauma was attributable to an inability to remember it; many men might have been reluctant to mention having been raped.

Using extensive court records to verify sexual abuse history, Gail Goodman and her colleagues (in press) conducted a similar study. They interviewed 175 subjects (81 percent female) ranging in age from 16.7 to 30.3 years. Approximately 13 years earlier, each subject had been involved in documented legal proceedings regarding having been sexually abused. The subjects' age when the documented abuse ended ranged from 3 to 16 years, and their average age when the legal proceedings began was 9.5 years. The nominal purpose of the interview was to examine attitudes and experiences concerning the law. Questions about childhood sexual abuse were inserted here and there in the interview. Of the 175 subjects, 142 (81 percent) mentioned the index abuse; 7 mentioned another abuse event; 17 (10 percent) denied ever having been abused; 2 said their parents had told them they had been abused but they had no memory of it; 5 mentioned having been abused but provided too few details to confirm that they were referring to the index event; 1 refused to answer any questions about abuse; and the mother of 1 teenaged subject requested that the researchers not ask about sexual abuse. Of the 26 who did not mention the index abuse, 12 did subsequently report it during a later phase of the research. Hence 88 percent reported the specific abuse documented in the court records. Additional analyses revealed that the older subjects had been at the time of the abuse, and the more severe the abuse, the more likely they were to report it. Contrary to clinical lore linking dissociation with forgetting of trauma, the higher subjects scored on the Dissociative Experiences Scale, the more likely they were to report the abuse, and the more self-blame subjects reported, the more likely they were to report the abuse.

As these studies indicate, claims of widespread repression and recovery of memories of childhood sexual abuse have been exaggerated by traumatic amnesia theorists. Strikingly, the better a study's methods, the less likely it is to find evidence of missing memory for trauma. Moreover, when Brown and his colleagues list studies that document amnesia for child sexual abuse, most of the studies they list suffer from the *same* methodological flaws (asking whether there was ever a time when the subject was *unable* to remember the abuse, failure to corroborate the abuse). If different studies had different flaws, and yet all pointed to the same conclusion, this would be a different matter entirely. But trying to build a case for traumatic amnesia by citing numerous studies, all sharing the same fatal flaws, is a pointless endeavor.

AMNESIA FOR OTHER KINDS OF TRAUMA

Advocates of traumatic amnesia have been at pains to emphasize that forgetting of trauma is not confined to childhood sexual abuse (Arrigo and Pezdek 1997). As Philip Coons and his colleagues asserted: "Traumatic memories can be repressed for all types of trauma, including physical and sexual childhood abuse, rape, concentration camp or hostage experiences, combat, and natural disasters, but memory loss for childhood abuse appears to be the most common" (1997: 165). How accurate is this claim?

Commission of Homicide

Between 10 and 70 percent of people charged with murder claim amnesia for the crime (Porter et al. 2001). Many of these, especially psychopathic individuals lacking a capacity for guilt, are widely believed to fake their memory loss, apparently in the hope that diminished cognitive capacity may attenuate criminal penalties (Schacter 1986). Nevertheless, some cases more convincingly suggest that murderers may indeed experience psychogenic amnesia for the crime. In the typical case of amnesia for homicide, the murder is unpremeditated, the victim is a family member, and the killer is in an extreme state of rage and may be intoxicated. Most often the suspect remembers the events leading up to the most brutal aspect of the assault, and also remembers everything that happened after the murder. Only the most emotionally violent aspect of the event is inaccessible, and it remains so, even though the person readily admits to having committed the crime (Hopwood and Snell 1933; Porter et al. 2001). For example, one case involved a 67-year-old man who beat his wife to death and then immediately phoned the police when he found himself standing over her dead body. He knew he must have killed her, but he had no recollection of doing so, and he never regained this memory. Unlike people with classic psychogenic amnesia, he did not lose his personal identity or any other memories (Gudjonsson and MacKeith 1983).

Cases like these do not seem plausibly attributable to malingering; if the person admits to the crime, why bother pretending not to remember it? But if we assume that at least some cases of amnesia for homicide are genuine, what might the mechanism be? Because approximately 50 percent of homicides occur when the killer is under the influence of alcohol (Swihart, Yuille, and

Porter 1999), perhaps missing memory is attributable to alcoholic blackout? During an alcoholic blackout, the person functions in a seemingly purposeful fashion, but is permanently incapable of recollecting what he did during the period of blackout (Goodwin, Crane, and Guze 1969).

In fact, blackouts erase all memory for the duration of time corresponding to serious intoxication, whereas most perpetrator amnesia is confined to the most violent aspects of the crime. In contrast to a blackout, details of what happened before and after the murder are retained vividly. Gayla Swihart and her colleagues (1999) coined the term *red-out* to denote memory loss corresponding to the state of violent uncontrollable rage. Red-outs, they hold, cannot be explained by reference to alcohol intoxication or other organic factors. Instead, they believe, red-outs are a form of emotional state–dependent memory; that is, to recall what happened during a red-out a person supposedly has to regain the emotional state he was in during the red-out. However, testing this hypothesis is difficult because inducing a state of rage akin to the one in which the murder was committed would be of questionable wisdom.

In their review of amnesia for homicide, J. S. Hopwood and H. K. Snell (1933) observed that the perpetrators' memory gradually returned over the course of months, apparently without any reinstatement of the extreme emotional state in which the crime had been committed. It is unclear whether these memories were genuinely recovered or whether the murderers had imagined what must have happened and then pieced together a "memory" based on this knowledge.

Genocide and Torture

Mark Pendergrast (1999) asked three distinguished Holocaust scholars—Elie Wiesel, Lawrence Langer, and Raul Hilberg—whether they were aware of any cases of massive repression of traumatic Holocaust memories. Each scholar said he was unaware of any such cases except when brain damage had occurred. Indeed, clinical research on Holocaust survivors has repeatedly emphasized the vividness of their horrific memories.[14] Hypermnesia—extreme memory vividness—has been routinely reported in these studies. This, of course, is entirely consistent with laboratory studies showing that high emotional arousal makes for vivid, detailed memories. As the psychiatrist Paul Chodoff observed, these horrific experiences are remembered "with a vivid immediacy and wealth of detail" (1963: 325).

Vivid enduring memories are remembered just as well by survivors of genocidal war in Cambodia and Bosnia. Moreover, contrary to the notions of some trauma theorists, horrific, vivid memories of the Holocaust are retained in narrative form, as evinced by oral narrative testimony provided by survivors in the Fortunoff Video Archives for Holocaust Testimonies at Yale University.[15]

Not to be confused with dissociative traumatic amnesia are occasional statements made by Holocaust survivors referring to having "repressed" memories of the concentration camps (Mazor et al. 1990; Nadler and Ben-Shushan 1989). However, as these articles make clear, no one was unable to remember having been in a concentration camp. By "repression," they merely mean that they were able to avoid dwelling on the Holocaust during the period when they were rebuilding their lives in America and elsewhere.

The same interpretation holds for survivors of the Pol Pot regime. The psychiatrist David Kinzie mentioned that "psychic amnesia and numbing often prevents patients from 'remembering' the painful events of the past" (1993: 312). But Kinzie also confirms that the Cambodian trauma survivors were not *unable* to remember what had happened to them during this regime. They simply tried not to dwell on their terrible memories of Cambodia. As further evidence of this interpretation of "repression," William Sack and his colleagues reported 12-year follow-up data on Cambodian refugees who had survived the horrors of Pol Pot's regime as children. Nearly all those qualifying for a PTSD diagnosis explicitly stressed a specific traumatic episode that haunted them again and again (for example, "I was tied to a tree in the morning and was told I would have my head chopped off that evening"; Sack, Him, and Dickason 1999: 1175). Interpreting data on victims of the Cambodian holocaust as somehow supportive of inability to remember trauma constitutes a serious misreading of the facts.

In another study confirming excellent memory for trauma in Holocaust survivors, Limor Schelach and Israel Nachson (2001) assessed memories of Auschwitz in five people who had arrived there at a young age (6, 11, 11, 18, and 22 years). The five subjects completed a standardized memory test about the camp routine and other factual details gleaned from historical documents. About 50 years after their liberation, these former inmates exhibited an impressive recall, getting 60 percent of the items correct. The group performance was lowered by the performance of the youngest subject, who had been only 6 years old at entry to the camp and had remained there only three months. Contrary to the notion that traumatic memories are most likely to be repressed, memory accuracy for emotional events was greater than that for neutral events (70 percent versus 52 percent). With the exception of one subject, deaths were remembered all too well. Moreover, their narratives were "clear, detailed, orderly, and realistic" (129).

Several studies on Holocaust survivors and torture survivors involved assessments based on DSM-III-R PTSD criteria. One diagnostic criterion is psychogenic amnesia, defined as an inability to remember an important aspect of the trauma. Reporting of this symptom probably refers to an Easterbrook-like process whereby survivors riveted their attention on the most salient aspects of danger, thereby failing to encode other aspects of the experience. Alternatively, many survivors may claim to have this symptom merely because they realize they do not remember everything that occurred during years of terror decades ago. Given that most Holocaust survivors and survivors of other torture have undergone beatings, head injuries, starvation, and solitary confinement, it would not be surprising if they reported not remembering everything that happened during their confinement. Therefore, studies reporting the DSM psychogenic amnesia symptom in 31 percent of Italian Holocaust survivors (Favaro et al. 1999), in 46 percent of Holocaust survivors who had been either in hiding or in the camps (Yehuda et al. 1997), or in 10 percent of Auschwitz survivors (Kuch and Cox 1992) must not be misread as indicating that these individuals had forgotten being persecuted by the Nazis.[16]

The same interpretation holds for studies of torture survivors. Many suffered sleep deprivation, beatings, head injury, and solitary confinement. Many complain about general memory problems in everyday life (Goldfeld et al. 1988). They do not, however, experience total amnesia for their all-too-memorable torture experiences. Studying political activists in Turkey, Metin Başoğlu and his colleagues (1994) found that 36 percent of those who had been tortured reported the DSM-III-R PTSD symptom of inability to recall an important aspect of the trauma, whereas only 2 percent of those who had not been tortured reported this symptom. Having less than perfect recall is hardly surprising given that the average tortured activist had endured nearly 300 episodes of torture during 47 months of captivity. A mechanism of dissociation or repression cannot account for these findings because it cannot explain why only some episodes are forgotten, whereas many equally horrific aspects are thoroughly remembered.[17]

Disasters and Accidents

Natural disasters and other accidents are public events that would seem difficult to forget. Indeed, people remember them well. In fact, after assessing sailors who had survived an explosion at sea, the psychiatrists Robert Leopold and Harold Dillon concluded that "repression does not appear possible" for such harrowing events (1963: 919).

However, attempts to suppress disturbing thoughts and emotional reactions may foster psychological adjustment among individuals exposed to disasters. The psychiatrist Alexander McFarlane (1988a, 1988b) interviewed firemen who had fought a major bush fire in Australia. Eight months later, 9 qualified for DSM-III PTSD, whereas 34 did not. Of the PTSD cases, 4 reported "memory disturbance," whereas only 2 of the non-PTSD cases did so. Interviewers asked about fire-related personal injuries at the 4-month and 11-month assessments. All the PTSD cases who had described their personal injuries at the 4-month assessment also did so at the 11-month assessment. In striking contrast, among the non-PTSD participants who had described their injuries at the 4-month assessment, only 43 percent mentioned injuries at the 11-month assessment. Thus the firefighters whose psychological adjustment was good were less likely to mention being injured 11 months after the fire. Authors of a study on rescue workers likewise suggested that suppression of one's emotional reactions during the disaster seems to enhance psychological adjustment in the long run (Ersland, Weisæth, and Sund 1989).

Because not everyone encodes everything about a traumatic event, some individuals will report "psychogenic amnesia" for aspects of the experience. Ingrid Carlier and Berthold Gersons (1997), assessing 136 individuals six months after they had witnessed a jet crash into an apartment building, noted that 26 percent met criteria for PTSD and 9 percent reported psychogenic amnesia for aspects of the event. No one, of course, had repressed memory of the crash.

It is important not to confuse complaints about forgetfulness in everyday life with inability to remember the disaster itself. But this is precisely what Bessel van der Kolk does when he misinterprets Sudhakar Madakasira and Kevin O'Brien's study of North Carolina tornado survivors as showing that "amnesia, with later return of memories for all, or parts, of the trauma has been noted" (van der Kolk and Fisler 1995: 509). The residents interviewed by Madakasira and O'Brien (1987) remembered the tornado quite well; indeed, 73 percent had intrusive thoughts about it. Over half of them did complain of memory impairment. But this complaint referred to the DSM-III symptom of everyday forgetfulness, not to difficulty remembering that a tornado had ravaged their community.

Combat

The literature on combat trauma has provided fertile ground for misinterpretation of reports of memory problems in soldiers as evidence of repression (for a review see van der Hart, Brown, and Graafland 1999). Dissociative amnesia theorists often confuse everyday memory complaints with difficulty remembering combat itself. For example, influential theorists, such as Bessel van der Kolk (van der Kolk and Fisler 1995), Jennifer Freyd (1996: 40), and John Briere (Briere and Conte 1993), have all incorrectly subsumed the findings of Herbert Archibald and Read Tuddenham's classic study under the rubric of dissociative amnesia. In reality, in their 20-year follow-up study of World War II veterans, Archibald and Tuddenham found that "difficulty in memory" was reported by 65 percent of combat fatigue cases, 60 percent of noncombat veterans with other diagnoses, and 5 percent of healthy combat veterans. Confirming that these memory difficulties had nothing to do with amnesia for combat, Archibald and Tuddenham emphasized that veterans with combat fatigue "cannot blot out their painful memories" (1965: 480).[18]

Repression theorists have garbled the findings of other studies as well. For example, Bertram Karon and Anmarie Widener (1997: 338) cited Charles Fisher's (1945) article on fugue states as documenting his treatment of "20 cases of amnesia caused by repressed battlefield trauma." In reality, Fisher described 6 cases, and only 1 had seen combat. The others included 4 servicemen with no combat exposure and a "housewife." Their fugues began under emotionally stressful but nontraumatic circumstances (such as anxiety in a married serviceman about his attraction to another woman) or circumstances raising the suspicion of malingering (such as a serviceman whose fugue enabled him to miss his boat destined for a war zone). In the sole combat-related case, a serviceman complained of amnesia after having survived an aerial bombing attack.

Psychiatrists have reported amnesia for battlefield experiences. However, these reports must be interpreted cautiously (see Pope, Oliva, and Hudson 1999). Many soldiers reporting large blanks in their memory had suffered from massive sleep deprivation, lack of food, and concussions or other head injuries. Moreover, their psychobiological state may have simply impaired encoding of their experiences, thereby producing blocks of missing memory (MacCurdy 1918: 63–79). Impaired encoding, of course, is very different from repression of encoded memories. A minority may have faked their amnesia, especially deserters simulating fugue states (Torrie 1944).

Describing 100 shell-shocked soldiers in World War I, M. D. Eder (1917) noted 2 cases of apparent amnesia for combat experiences. But both cases are more complex than they first appear to be. One soldier exhibited the Ganser syndrome, long linked to suspected malingering, in which the person appears to be in a fog and provides nonsensical answers to simple questions (for example, replies "Five" when asked "What is two plus two?"). The other patient lost all his memories for six weeks, including those of combat. But this was triggered not by combat itself, but rather by encountering a kindly woman who reminded him of his mother (Eder 1917: 40, 73).

After the Dunkirk retreat in World War II, William Sargant and Eliot Slater (1941) diagnosed amnesic syndromes in 144 of the first 1,000 psychiatric casualties admitted to a British hospital. Risk for amnesia for recent combat events increased as a function of the level of stress experienced. Amnesia occurred in 6 percent of those exposed to "trifling stress," in 13 percent of those exposed to "moderate stress," and in 35 percent of those exposed to "severe stress." Of the 144 cases of amnesia, 2 had epilepsy, 3 had schizophrenia, and 10 had sustained head injuries. Of the remaining 129 ("psychoneurotic") cases, 30 dated their amnesia to a concussion or being dazed by a bomb that had exploded nearby. Of these 129 cases, 39 exhibited amnesic fugue and 58 exhibited retrospective amnesia without fugue. Of the 32 who developed an amnesic syndrome in the absence of combat stress, 9 were suspected malingerers.

J. L. Henderson and Merrill Moore (1944) described the first 200 neuropsychiatric casualties admitted to an American hospital in the Pacific Theater during World War II. Of those exposed to heavy combat, 50 percent had been knocked unconscious by heavy shelling and an additional 22 percent had been dazed, and many of these patients were amnesic for the bombardment. An additional 5 percent reported amnesia for the shelling but had apparently not been knocked unconscious. The authors admitted having difficulty determining precisely what had happened, noting that records were often sketchy, as were the accounts of the patients themselves. Henderson and Moore noted that histories of head injury, previous trauma (such as car accidents), and psychological vulnerability seemingly predetermined the breakdowns they observed in the Pacific Theater.

Treating psychiatric casualties from Guadalcanal during World War II, Theodore Lidz (1946a) noted that when Marines exhibited amnesia it was usually for events occurring immediately *after* a traumatic event such as an explosion or the death of a buddy. The trauma itself was easily remembered, but preoccupation with the traumatic event had impaired encoding of events that followed soon after the shocking event.

Lidz, a psychoanalyst, expected that he would need to uncover repressed memories of horrific combat events in these patients. To his surprise, his patients began "pouring forth accounts of the episodes that had overwhelmed them with marked display of emotion." Lidz heard "interminable narrations of event after event" (1946b: 201). Lidz's findings run counter to the theory of Bessel van der Kolk and Onno van der Hart (1991: 442), who claim that traumatic experiences "cannot be organized on a linguistic level and this failure to arrange the memory in words and symbols leaves it to be organized on a somatosensory or iconic level."

Alfred Torrie reported that 9 percent of the first 1,000 cases of anxiety neurosis and hysteria admitted to hospitals in the North African campaign of World War II had amnesia (including fugue). Feigned amnesias were common: "Many cases were more aware than they would admit and recovered their lost memories with remarkable celerity" (1944: 140).

Working with World War II psychiatric casualties, Harold Rosen and Henry Myers (1947) described several cases of amnesia. For example, one patient had been defecating on the side of the road when he saw his tank take a direct hit, killing all his comrades. His memories of this experience returned when someone startled him by slamming a door. A similar case recalled all his memories via free association. Only one case temporarily lost all memories of his previous life (a case of classic psychogenic amnesia).

The primary goal of psychiatrists serving in the military is to restore the patient's functioning so that he can return to battle. Although military psychiatrists during the two world wars were psychoanalytically oriented, the sheer volume of psychiatric casualties and the pressure to return them to the battlefield as quickly as possible compelled doctors to expedite treatment. Sleep, food, and fluids did the trick for many patients, but other highly agitated patients required barbiturates. Operating under the Freudian imperative, psychiatrists sought to recover the presumably repressed traumatic memories that amnesic patients could not recall. Most recommended hypnosis, usually aided by intravenous infusion of barbiturates, as the surest and quickest method of restoring lost memories of combat. These psychiatrists believed that emotional shock was a crucial determinant of the inability to recall certain combat experiences. Most acknowledged exhaustion, predisposing personality factors, and occasionally head trauma as contributing factors. But the main emphasis was on relaxing the patient with sedatives, thereby enabling the repressed traumatic memories to rise to the surface of awareness.[19]

Intent on returning soldiers to battle, these overworked psychiatrists had scant interest in corroborating the combat memories recovered during hypnosis or barbiturate treatment. There is little doubt that these men had been exposed to intense combat. Nevertheless, many psychiatrists noted that the material recovered via these methods was not necessarily accurate. As Sargant and Slater (1941: 763) warned, information obtained from patients in this state "will often be a mixture of truth and fantasy," a view echoed by the psychiatrist Lawrence Kubie (1943). Although many patients reported relief at recovering lost memories, Sargant and Slater noted that these patients could improve without direct attempts to recover memories. Nevertheless, the consensus was that restoring combat memories to amnesic patients would hasten their recovery from combat neurosis.

Many scholars have questioned the validity of the combat memories reportedly forgotten and then regained under hypnosis. Confirming Sargant and Slater's (1941) suspicions that material produced under hypnosis is a mixture of fact and fantasy, subsequent research has indicated that hypnotized individuals are just as likely to generate false "memories" as to recover true ones, and that supplementing hypnosis with barbiturates only makes matters worse. Several clinicians have noted that memories retrieved under hypnosis reflect fears of what might have happened in battle as much as what did happen. Indeed, hypnotically recovered combat memories have been reported in men who have never been to war. In most cases, however, there has been little reason to doubt that the patients were exposed to some combat, and in some instances witnesses have corroborated the events. But as Scott Lilienfeld and Elizabeth Loftus (1998) pointed out, the doctors conducting the hypnotic retrieval sessions knew what these events were, and hence may have inadvertently shaped the patients' reports. In fact, the hypnotic techniques described by military psychiatrists were extremely suggestible.[20] To confirm that hypnosis was permitting access to genuine memories, the doctors would have to be blind to the corroborating evidence of the trauma, and independent raters would have to compare the evidence to the material obtained in hypnosis. This type of study has not been done. Finally, the claim that hypnosis fostered psychological healing is unwarranted. Uncontrolled observations, such as those reported in this extensive literature, do not rule out the obvious competing explanation that patients would have improved no matter what was done.

The most salient cognitive disturbance in psychologically traumatized combat veterans is the intrusive recollection of terrifying events: vivid, unbidden thoughts and nightmares about combat. (They remember traumatic events extremely well.) Like many people with psychiatric disorders, veterans with chronic stress reactions often complain of problems with everyday memory and concentration. Studies have also shown that some combat veterans report amnesia for combat experiences, and some reports suggest that these memories may be recollected under hypnosis or with the help of barbiturates. Nevertheless, reports of amnesia and recollection of combat experiences have significant interpretive limitations. Many events during combat may not have been encoded, because of head injury, exhaustion, and so forth, and thus the "memories" regained from these amnesic periods may well be confabulated accounts of what might have happened or of the soldiers' fears of what might have happened. Finally, some cases of alleged amnesia for combat may have arisen from malingering.

Case Studies of Recovered Memories

Case studies provide some of the best evidence that people can recall traumatic events after not thinking about them for many years. One cannot assume, of course, that failing to think about a traumatic event is equivalent to being unable to remember it (amnesia) attributable to repression, dissociation, or some other mechanism. But case studies have confirmed that some people may experience traumatic events, not think about them for a long period of time, and then suddenly remember them years later.

Some scholars question the probative import of case studies (see Wagenaar 1997). The psychiatrist August Piper (1999), for example, likened isolated case reports of recovered traumatic memories to isolated "sightings" of Elvis Presley. The psychiatrist Harrison Pope (1997: 31–35) argued that isolated cases of corroborated recovered memories may reflect nothing more than measurement error. That is, if the rate of false positives—false accounts of corroborated recovered memories—were one per thousand patients, we would expect to see many cases of corroborated repressed memory each year, given that the number of patients seen yearly is in the millions.

These arguments are too extreme. First, comparing cases of corroborated recovered memories to Elvis sightings ignores the fact that the first has external evidence, whereas the second does not.

Second, estimates of measurement error apply to *instruments* for measuring phenomena, not to the phenomena themselves. Pope's point about measurement error *does* apply to methods such as hypnosis used for recovering accurate memories. We can ask what proportion of memories recovered under hypnosis are accurate and what proportion are inaccurate and how these "hit" and "false positive" rates compare to ordinary recall without hypnosis. We can estimate the measurement error associated with the method of hypnosis but not that associated with the memories themselves.

Third, just as it takes only one confirmed case of a black swan to disconfirm the generalization "all swans are white," it takes only one case of recovered memory to disconfirm the generalization that people cannot recover memories of traumatic events. Moreover, replications of confirmed cases increase confidence in the reality of the phenomena.

Fourth, scientific knowledge does not come only from large studies, or experimental ones. Indeed, most of our knowledge in clinical neuropsychology comes from single cases, such as that of H.M., and even single cases can be studied with great rigor (see Caramazza 1986). To be sure, Pope and Piper are right to call for large-scale longitudinal studies of trauma-exposed children to determine whether they retain their memories over time or repress them. But well-documented case reports are not "scientifically meaningless," as Piper believes (1999: 279).

However, the probative import of case studies depends entirely on the quality of the evidence. Not all have equal value. For example, ever since Freud's abandonment of the seduction theory, psychoanalysts have been prone to attribute adults' recollections of childhood sexual abuse to incestuous fantasy, not genuine trauma (see Wolf and Alpert 1991). But in recent years psychoanalysts have been increasingly willing to credit the authenticity of memories of incest, including ones previously allegedly repressed (see Simon 1992). Case studies have been appearing that purportedly indicate recovered memories of repressed incidents of incest. After years of psychoanalysis, one man recovered memories of having enjoyed sexual intercourse with his mother when he was an adolescent, memories his analyst deemed genuine because of their clarity (Shengold 1980). After more than 10 years on the couch, another patient remembered his mother molesting him on many occasions when he was between 3 and 4 years of age (Silber 1979).

The controversy over recovered memory has sensitized psychoanalysts to the importance of corroborating memories that either resurface or are constructed during analysis. But some analysts are still insufficiently rigorous in what they count as corroboration. Stanley Friedman, for example, described a woman who remembered a long history of violent sadistic abuse by her grandfather and other men, all of which had been entirely repressed until she was in psychoanalysis. While acknowledging the lack of external evidence, Friedman nevertheless judged this horrific account to be credible, noting "its quality of authenticity and my own empathic response" (1997: 119). As further evidence of its veracity, he cited "the internal consistency, continuity, and emotional authenticity of the psychotherapeutic process" (121). That is, because the patient experienced intense affect while recounting a long series of similar sadistic abuses committed against her from early childhood until adolescence, the memories were probably authentic. Similarly, discussing recovered memories of trauma, Ethel Person and Howard Klar state that "their vividness, imagery, and unchangeability mark them as veridical" (1994: 1077).

Other psychoanalysts have attempted to furnish more dependable evidence of the authenticity of recovered memories of trauma.[21] Unfortunately, even reports involving some kind of corroboration have rarely withstood close scrutiny (Brenneis 2000).

Psychologists, too, sometimes regard certain phenomena as manifestations of explicit memory that do not appear to qualify. Sunita Duggal and Alan Sroufe (1998) reported the case of Laura, a subject in a longitudinal study of child development. When Laura was a preschooler, her parents divorced and shared custody. Her mother was addicted to stimulants, and her father abused alcohol. Her mother worked as a children's advocate at a shelter for battered women. Laura exhibited sexualized play at preschool, and her interactions with an anatomically correct doll sparked concerns that she was being abused. She was distressed about visiting her father, who denied abusing her. Several years later, in third grade, Laura told a friend that she had been sexually abused. The friend told someone else, and Laura was referred for counseling services.

In a survey when she was 16, Laura indicated that she had never been abused. In a research interview the following year, she denied having been exposed to traumatic events, including abuse. When Laura was nearly 19, she participated in a research interview conducted by a graduate student who was blind to her history. When the student asked whether she had been sexually abused, Laura mentioned having been kissed on the cheek by her father. When she remembered this event she became extremely upset and assumed that something more must have happened, something she could not remember.

Despite Duggal and Sroufe's characterization, this is not a straightforward case of "recovered memory of childhood sexual trauma" (301). Laura recovered a memory of her father kissing her on the cheek, and this recollection was accompanied by distress and fear that he had done something else to her which she was unable to recall, try as she might. Whether she had been abused, and if so, by whom, was never established.

Michael Nash (1994) described a 40-year-old male patient who sought psychotherapy for depression, social withdrawal, erectile dysfunction, and other problems. The man recalled a scene from when he was 10 years old: he was lying down with his buttocks exposed, frightened, and surrounded by older boys who were masturbating. One of the boys was his cousin. Determined to check the accuracy of this recovered memory, he phoned his 45-year-old cousin, who admitted that several boys had rubbed their penises on the patient without penetrating him. These boys, the cousin recalled with great embarrassment, had been gathering to engage in sex play and masturbation when the patient discovered them. The older boys had incorporated the 10-year-old, who was unwilling, into their activities. The cousin said he had been surprised that after this incident his younger cousin acted as if nothing had happened. Nash himself did not speak to the corroborator.

The political scientist Ross Cheit recovered memories of sexual abuse that had occurred 24 years earlier (see Freyd 1996: 6–9). He awoke one day thinking about the administrator of a summer camp he had attended as a boy, whom he had liked and admired. Cheit had not thought about this man in years. But prompted by several cues, including learning that his 10-year-old nephew was about to attend a similar camp, he recalled being abused by the administrator.

Cheit has since constructed a website archive of corroborated cases of re-covered memories of trauma. He lists 38 cases that have surfaced in legal pro-ceedings, 19 cases discussed in mainly scholarly publications, and 23 others culled from newspaper reports. Many cases cited in the newspapers involved legal proceedings that failed to go forward, sometimes because of statutes of limitations. Most of the cases Cheit lists concern recovered memories of sex-ual abuse; a few concern murder.[22]

Cheit's recovered memory project is an important contribution, but sev-eral caveats about the evidence are warranted. First, because of statutes of limitations, state laws seldom permit people to file suit against alleged perpe-trators unless the memories were entirely repressed. Hence, if a person always remembered having been abused, but was too fearful to come forward and file suit until many years later, the suit would not go forward because the statute of limitations would have expired. The laws, then, are biased against abuse victims who have always remembered the abuse. Stated differently, the laws favor people who claim to have repressed their memories, even if in fact they always remembered them. This is a serious problem for many of Cheit's legal cases. The plaintiffs may very well have been abused, but justice would be unavailable to them if they admitted they had always remembered the abuse. Second, the quality of what Cheit counts as corroboration varies. In some cases the perpetrator confessed. An out-of-court settlement, however, cannot be deemed corroboration because some innocent defendants settle out of court to avoid being bankrupted by a prolonged legal battle. Cheit also re-gards as corroboration evidence that the alleged offender committed similar acts against another person (such as the sister of the person who has recov-ered the memory). Finally, Cheit's cases do not establish repression or trau-matic, dissociative amnesia as the basis for forgetting. Many people who were genuinely abused, such as Cheit himself, may have managed to avoid think-ing about their experiences until reminded of them many years later. Despite these caveats, Cheit's work is an important step toward providing evidence for recovered memories of trauma.

The perils of relying mainly on legal cases as evidence of recovered memo-ries of abuse are illustrated by the psychiatrist David Corwin's case of "Jane Doe." During a child custody dispute between divorced parents, Corwin as-sessed their 6-year-old daughter ("Jane Doe"), who had accused her mother of multiple instances of sexual abuse (digital penetration of her vagina while bathing her). Corwin videotaped his interview with the 6-year-old, and 11 years later the girl asked to view the tapes. Before showing her the tapes, Corwin interviewed her, asking her what she remembered about the original interviews and about the abuse allegations against her mother. With her consent, Corwin also videotaped this interview. When he asked whether she remembered anything about sexual abuse, she first said she did not, but moments later she exhibited intense emotion as she said she recollected being digitally penetrated by her mother in the bathtub. Her recollection, however, was not fully in accord with the original interview. As a 17-year-old, she said that she remembered her mother taking pornographic photographs of her and her brother, a charge she had not made at age 6, and she recalled only a single episode of vaginal penetration rather than the multiple episodes she had originally reported. She told Corwin that she had always known there had been allegations of sexual abuse against her mother, but that she had not remembered the content of the allegations (the abuse itself) until Corwin asked her about it 11 years later (Corwin and Olafson 1997).

Although Corwin's "Jane Doe" case has been widely hailed in the clinical literature and in the courtroom as proof of repressed and recovered memory of sexual abuse, subsequent investigation of the case by Elizabeth Loftus and Mel Guyer (2002a, 2002b) has undermined this claim. Indeed, the preponderance of documentary evidence strongly implies that her father, as part of his fight for custody, had coached her to accuse her mother of having abused her. Corwin's videotape captured not the recovery of a memory of trauma, but rather the recovery of the content of the dubious accusations.

Ironically, the most convincing evidence that people can forget about their traumatic experiences, not think about them for a long time, and then suddenly remember them years later comes from an experimental, not a clinical, psychologist. Jonathan Schooler, with his colleagues Miriam Bendiksen and Zara Ambadar (1997), has published the most sophisticated case study research on recovered memory of trauma. They stress that three points must be confirmed: evidence that the event happened, evidence that it was forgotten, and evidence that it was remembered. They have documented several cases of recovered memory. Case #1 was a 39-year-old man (JR) who, at the age of 30, had recovered memories of being fondled at the age of 12 by a parish priest. The first memory occurred suddenly, with great vividness, as he was lying in bed after seeing a movie about someone who struggled with memories of molestation. During subsequent months he recollected approximately 10 more episodes of genital fondling by the priest. JR told Schooler that he had confronted the priest and that the priest had admitted the abuse, saying that he (the priest) had been in therapy after being accused of abuse by someone else. JR's former therapist (a colleague of Schooler's) confirmed JR's account of the events subsequent to his memory recovery. Despite having discussed other intimate matters with his therapist, JR had never mentioned being abused. Apparently, he had forgotten it. JR himself claimed that if someone had asked him, during his teens or twenties, whether he had ever been abused he would have honestly denied it.

Case #2 was a 40-year-old woman (WB) who was referred to Bendiksen for therapy after having recovered her traumatic memory. At a party, WB heard a man justify his advances to a young woman by asserting that she was not exactly a virgin. WB became enraged and left the party, and that night she had nightmares. Upon awakening the next morning, she suddenly remembered having been raped at knifepoint while hitchhiking as a 16-year-old. Shortly after the rape, she had told several people, including a man she later married and divorced, that she had had an involuntary sexual experience akin to rape. Schooler's research team interviewed her ex-husband. During the period in which WB alleged that she had forgotten the rape, she had mentioned it to her husband several times, with little emotion. She was startled to learn this, having forgotten ever mentioning it. In effect, she had forgotten that she had remembered during the period of alleged forgetting. What made her experience of memory recovery so striking was the full cognitive and emotional realization that the unpleasant sexual experience had undeniably been rape. In fact, WB suggested that she had probably repressed the meaning of the event rather than the memory of the event itself. Coincidentally, Bendiksen, WB's therapist, was also the therapist of the man at the party who had provoked WB's outrage, and the man confirmed WB's angry reaction to his remark. This case illustrates the complexities of studying recovered memory. WB had recalled the rape on several occasions during the period of alleged forgetting, but she forgot that she had remembered. And what seemed to have been the recovery of a memory appears to be a stimulus-cued recollection of an event that she now interpreted in a different, emotionally devastating light.

Case #3 involved a 51-year-old woman (TW) who told Schooler about her memory recovery approximately 17 years after it occurred. When a co-worker asked TW whether she was interested in attending a lecture on sexual molestation, she was suddenly stunned by a vivid, shocking memory of having been molested at the age of 9. She had told her mother about the abuse shortly after it happened, and she believed she had not thought about it since. However, TW's former husband said she had mentioned it to him several times during their marriage, in a matter-of-fact fashion. TW was shocked to learn that she had forgotten these conversations, just as she was shocked when she recovered the memory after her co-worker mentioned the lecture on molestation. Her feeling that she had recovered an inaccessible memory was based on her failure to remember having previously accessed the memory during the period of apparent "amnesia."

Case #4 was a 41-year-old woman (DN) who recounted a memory recovery that had occurred approximately six years earlier. DN had been attending group therapy for survivors of childhood sexual abuse. She had always remembered this abuse. During one session, the therapist remarked that people who were abused in childhood are often revictimized as adults. While driving home from this session, DN suddenly recalled having been raped 13 years earlier, at the age of 22, and having testified in court against the rapist, who had been convicted. She was so stunned that she had to pull over to the side of the road. DN was convinced that she had remembered these events for two years after they had occurred, but had forgotten about them ever since. Her former lawyer verified the facts of the case, and DN had failed to mention the rape during an extensive intake interview before she started therapy. She was amazed that she could have forgotten the rape and the trial.

Several points about these cases warrant emphasis. First, the remembered experiences include a single event (WB, TW), multiple events (JR), and an extended trauma (rape plus trial; DN). Second, the memories returned suddenly in complete form, not gradually in fragments. That is, these cases differ from cases in which recovered memory therapists help patients gradually retrieve trauma memories, bit by bit. All of Schooler's cases retained their memory in a narrative form; they simply had not thought about the memories in many years. Third, each subject expressed shock at the return of the memory and great surprise that it had ever been forgotten. Fourth, each recovery was prompted by a trigger outside of psychotherapy. Fifth, subjects were not very good at ascertaining the prior state of their memory. Some thought they had never recollected the event during a certain period, when in fact they had discussed it with others. They had forgotten that they had remembered, perhaps because previous recalls had not been accompanied by much emotion, or because the full significance of the event had not been apparent ("it wasn't really rape"). Schooler and his colleagues have called this the "forgot-it-all-along" effect.

The "forgot-it-all-along" effect is fully congruent with research showing that people are not very accurate at assessing how good or bad their memories are. Attempts to validate questionnaires designed to test how well people can evaluate their own memories have shown that asking people whether they did not or could not remember some event in the past is essentially worthless (Herrmann 1982).

Most evidence adduced in support of traumatic amnesia either is seriously flawed or can be more plausibly explained in ways other than an *inability* to remember. Not every study, of course, suffers from all of these flaws. The most common flaws are:

- asking subjects whether there was ever a time—duration often unspecified—when they were *unable* to remember their traumatic experience;
- misinterpreting not thinking about a trauma for a long time as being unable to remember it;
- failing to realize that people who believe they forgot certain events for a long period may have simply forgotten that they remembered those events;
- failing to appreciate that most people have gaps in their memory for childhood and that efforts to remember result in the illusion of heightened amnesia for childhood;
- failing to realize that some molested children do not understand their experience as sexual abuse when it occurs, but later reconceptualize it as such;
- failing to verify that the trauma actually happened or merely relying on subjects' claims that corroboration is available;
- failing to distinguish between failure to report traumatic experiences and inability to remember them;
- failing to conduct follow-up interviews to determine why subjects did not mention traumatic experiences known to have occurred;
- confusing forgetfulness in everyday life following a traumatic event with inability to remember the traumatic event itself;

- confusing reporting of the psychogenic amnesia symptom with inability to remember the trauma itself;
- failing to realize that the DSM symptom "psychogenic amnesia" may reflect a failure to encode certain aspects of the traumatic event, rather than an inability to access memories of them—that memory is not a video recorder and survivors cannot encode and remember all aspects of their trauma;
- failing to rule out starvation, head injury, sleep deprivation, and malingering as possible sources of reported amnesia for traumatic events.

8

FALSE MEMORIES OF TRAUMA

To the casual observer, the notion that someone might remember having experienced a trauma that never actually occurred seems absurd. Yet people have been remembering atrocities that never happened and have been experiencing the emotional distress congruent with belief in their authenticity.

Some of the more remarkable traumatic events for which people claim to have recovered memories in recent years concern abduction by space aliens (Mack 1994) and ritualistic abuse at the hands of satanic cults (Noblitt and Perskin 2000; Scott 2001). Most of these memories have surfaced with the help of mental health professionals. Many people are reluctant to conclude that these memories are false. Several arguments are made in defense of their authenticity: that anything is possible; that skeptics are blinded by a narrow positivistic world view; that skeptics are in denial about the secret horrors lurking in society; that scientists have never shown that false memories of trauma can be "implanted"; that no one has yet proven that satanic cults and alien abductors do not exist; and that refusing to believe such stories is on a par with denying the Holocaust. "Open-minded" believers insist that "the jury is still out" regarding the credibility of these recovered memories.

Although cognitive psychologists have shown that minor experimental manipulations can distort memory in the laboratory, many traumatic amnesia theorists regard such work as largely irrelevant to debates about false memories of trauma. They warn about extrapolating from the laboratory to the clinic. They emphasize that implanting a false memory of having been lost in a shopping mall as a child is not the same thing as implanting false memories of years of brutal incest. As Daniel Brown and his colleagues have argued: "Until a sufficient database is collected from studies measuring memory performance in traumatized as compared to nontraumatized individuals, we are not in a position to generalize the findings from laboratory studies on normal memory to memory for traumatic experiences" (Brown, Scheflin, and Hammond 1998: 98).

Although psychotherapists do rightly warn about reckless extrapolation from the laboratory to the clinic, they must be careful about categorical dismissal of research as artificial and irrelevant to memory for trauma. As Katharine Shobe and John Kihlstrom (1997) have cogently argued, psychotherapists cannot simply assume that memory for trauma is exempt from the principles that govern memory for nontraumatic events. One must demonstrate, not merely assert, that traumatic memory differs dramatically from nontraumatic memory. In fact, some findings suggest that principles discovered in the laboratory may apply even more to traumatic events than to the ones studied in experimental research. For example, laboratory studies have shown that moderate levels of stress enhance memory for the central aspects of the stressful experience, and field research concerning shocking events confirms that this memory principle applies just as much to traumatic events as to laboratory stressors. Also, brief, trivial manipulations can produce memory distortion for minor things in the laboratory. These effects may be even more pronounced in the context of suggestive psychotherapy in which therapist and patient collaborate in an attempt to uncover memories of abuse over many sessions and with the aid of techniques such as hypnosis. And the fact that scientific principles are often discovered in controlled settings does not mean they do not apply to the real world. Airplanes fly because the laws of physics apply outside the artificial, controlled settings in which they were discovered.

It is a logical truism that one cannot "prove the null hypothesis" when framed as a universal generalization. Hence, one cannot prove that repression never occurs, and one cannot prove that someone has never been abused—unless a definitive marker of specific trauma is missing. Only under very unusual circumstances have clinicians been able to prove that certain traumatic memories were false. For example, one woman vividly remembered the surgical removal of her clitoris when she was a child, a memory refuted by her gynecologist (Good 1994). Another, whose hymen was intact, remembered being gang-raped by satanists (Ross 1995: 57). Still others have re-called the sacrificial killing of certain individuals who later turned out to be alive and well (Nathan and Snedeker 1995: 101; Ross 1995: 57).

Many people have asked, Why would people ever want to believe they had been sexually abused if it were not true? Why would someone embrace the identity of "abuse survivor" if it were not true? A possible answer was pro-vided by Ellen Bass and Laura Davis in their book *The Courage to Heal:* "When you first remember your abuse or acknowledge its effects, you may feel tremendous relief. Finally there is a reason for your problems. There is some-one, and something to blame" (1988: 173). If faced with a choice between being miserable and not knowing why, and being miserable and being able to blame someone else, many people will choose the latter.

Some psychotherapists have pointed out that no controlled, experimental evidence confirms that memories of genuine trauma can be implanted in nontraumatized subjects. This statement is true but disingenuous. Ethics pro-hibit the experimental implantation of traumatic memories. Experiments demonstrating such implantation will never be done. Experiments are the strongest basis for inferring causation, but scientific inference does not rest solely on experimentation (manipulation of independent variables), and in some disciplines, like astronomy and geology, experiments are seldom feasi-ble. The claim that some people develop false memories of trauma is a war-ranted *abductive inference* derived from multiple, converging nonexperi-mental sources of evidence. An abductive inference—"an inference to the best explanation"—is a form of reasoning whereby one accepts a hypothesis as (likely to be) true because it provides a better explanation for the phenom-ena of interest than any rival hypothesis. Abductive inferences are used by scientists, historians, detectives, and people in everyday life as they strive to make sense of their world (Harman 1965; Josephson and Josephson 1996: esp. 1–30).

Abduction by Space Aliens

To the best of my knowledge, no one has ever been abducted by a space alien. However, many people believe otherwise. A 1997 Yankelovich poll revealed that 34 percent of Americans believe that space aliens have landed on earth and 17 percent believe that aliens have abducted human beings for use in medical experiments. This poll also revealed that 80 percent of Americans believe the government knows more about extraterrestrials than it is letting on (Handy 1997).

Most interesting are the people who report that they themselves have been abducted by space aliens. Their narratives provide undeniable evidence that people can remember traumatic experiences that never happened. Most of these individuals prefer to be called "experiencers" rather than "alien abductees." However, the opaque circumlocution "experiencer" merely refers to someone who has experienced alien abduction.

As the psychiatrist John Mack (1994) has reported, most experiencers recover their memories of alien abduction while undergoing hypnosis or quasi-hypnotic procedures designed to regress them back to the moment when the abduction occurred or the moment when they experienced a missing block of time. The methods of helping people remember alien abduction are identical to those of recovered memory therapy.

My colleagues and I have assessed "alien abductees" in our research program (described in Chapter 9). We have not, however, "helped" them recover any memories. Rather, we have studied the memories they have already recovered under hypnosis by other clinicians. We have noted a remarkable consistency across our subjects. The typical abductee is someone with long-standing interests in "New Age" practices and beliefs such as astral projection, reincarnation, alternative healing practices, "energy" therapies, mental telepathy, and astrology. Nearly all describe themselves as very spiritual, but they no longer practice mainstream religion.

Their experience with "aliens" begins with an episode of sleep paralysis. Sleep paralysis typically occurs as a person is awakening from REM sleep (see Hufford 1982). During REM sleep, when dreaming occurs, people experience full body paralysis. This is a good thing: otherwise dreamers would hurt themselves acting out their dreams. In sleep paralysis, the mental and physical aspects of REM become desynchronized for a few seconds or minutes. The person awakens from REM before the paralysis has waned, and becomes fully conscious of an inability to move. In some episodes of sleep paralysis, people continue to experience fragments of REM cognition after they open their eyes, dreaming with their eyes open. They experience hypnopompic ("upon awakening") hallucinations, most commonly of shadowy figures lurking about the bedroom. Sometimes people see flashing lights and hear sounds ranging from footsteps in the hallway to buzzing and humming. They may also experience tactile hallucinations of electricity shooting throughout their body and a sense of levitating above their bed. The hallucinations vanish and the paralysis wanes as soon as the mental and physical components re-align upon full awakening.

No more pathological than a hiccup, sleep paralysis is a relatively common experience, especially for people whose sleep patterns have been disrupted by jet lag, shift work, or fatigue. Approximately 30 percent of the general popu-lation has experienced an episode of sleep paralysis, but only about 5 percent of the population has experienced hallucinations while paralyzed. When the full experience occurs, the emotion reported by about 95 percent of people is terror. Different cultures have interpreted the experience in diverse ways. The incubus and succubus of the late Middle Ages, being "ridden by the witch" in the southern United States, being visited by the "old hag" in New-foundland, and being haunted by ghosts are among the most common cul-tural glosses. But sometimes hypnopompic visual hallucinations of figures in the bedroom are interpreted as aliens (Cheyne, Newby-Clark, and Rueffer 1999).

Our typical subject, then, begins with a set of beliefs about the likelihood of alien abduction, experiences at least one episode of sleep paralysis with hypnopompic hallucinations, and then consults a mental health professional who uses quasi-hypnotic methods to help the person uncover presumably re-pressed memories of "what happened next" after the sleep episode. Our sub-jects have told us about experiences they have recalled under hypnosis: being whisked to space ships to have their sperm and ova forcibly extracted for the purpose of a hybrid human-alien breeding program, being forced to have sex with aliens, and so forth. Several subjects have recovered presumably re-pressed memories of meeting their hybrid children on the spacecraft.

Consistent with John Mack's claim that experiencers are not mentally ill, we have uncovered very little psychopathology during psychiatric diagnostic interviews with our subjects. Only one of them had ever met criteria for a psychotic illness, and even he had experienced sleep paralysis accompanied by hypnopompic visual hallucinations. One could, of course, diagnose them as delusional because they misinterpret hypnopompic hallucinations as alien beings. But such an unilluminating diagnostic appraisal would merely re-describe the phenomenon without explaining it. More to the point, subjects have not exhibited other symptoms (such as hearing voices) that suggest a diagnosis of schizophrenia. According to Brendan Maher (1999), delusions are attempts to make sense of anomalous experiences. For example, a schizo-phrenic person who experiences auditory hallucinations might explain them by concluding that the CIA has implanted a radio transmitter in his head. Sleep paralysis accompanied by hypnopompic hallucinations certainly qual-ifies as an anomalous experience, which our subjects are interpreting as a visi-tation from aliens.

However, there is one important difference between these alien abductees and typical trauma survivors. Every abductee I have interviewed reported be-ing glad the abduction had occurred. Several noted that among all the people on Earth, they were chosen to serve as breeders for a new race of hybrid be-ings. The subjects acknowledged how frightening and disorienting it was to realize that they had been subjected to (usually) repeated abduction by aliens for the purpose of medical experimentation. But all of them said the experi-ence had deepened their spiritual awareness of the universe, thereby making the "trauma" worth it in the end.

Satanic Ritual Abuse

Throughout the 1980s, increasing numbers of psychotherapy patients claimed to have recovered memories of having been abused as part of the rit-uals of secret satanic cults. Their trauma was not solely sexual. They also re-membered being forced to consume urine, blood, and feces; to worship the devil in ceremonies featuring satanic paraphernalia, dancing, and chanting; to participate in human sacrifice; to serve as baby breeders furnishing fresh infants for ritual murder; to eat the remains of sacrificed infants; and to en-dure brutal tortures designed to make them forget everything they had expe-rienced.[1]

Before beginning psychotherapy, few were aware that they had been vic-timized by satanists. Most patients sought help for depression, but as treat-ment progressed, increasingly horrific memories surfaced, beginning with childhood sexual abuse and culminating with infant sacrifice and cannibal-ism.[2] Retrieving these dissociated memories was deemed vital for recovery. As the therapists David Sakheim and Susan Devine asserted, patients "can only begin to heal by remembering as best they can the traumatic events that led to the creation of their symptoms" (1992: xvii).

Remembering ritual abuse, however, was accompanied by severe psychiat-ric decompensation (for example, suicidal depression). In one series of 20 patients who had undergone months of memory recovery work, all became suicidal when they eventually remembered satanic abuse, and 10 attempted suicide. All had initially sought treatment for depressive, anxiety, or dissociative symptoms, but the focus of therapy had soon shifted to the recovery of presumably dissociated memories of trauma (Young 1992; Schaffer and Cozolino 1992).

As their symptoms intensified, many patients qualified for diagnoses of multiple personality disorder (MPD) and posttraumatic stress disorder (PTSD) (Young et al. 1991). Their mental status was congruent with the horrors reported. As the psychiatrist Sandra Bloom affirmed, "we can say with a high degree of certainty that their symptom picture is consistent only with trauma of monumental proportions" (1994: 463).

During the 1990s, specialists in dissociative disorders began to articulate theories of ritual abuse. The most detailed theory was developed by D. Corydon Hammond, a psychologist who has published written guidelines on the proper use of clinical hypnosis. Using hypnosis on his patients, Hammond supposedly learned that individuals with MPD are survivors of ritual abuse, torture, and mind-control programming. They are victims of a vast international cult consisting of secretive, tightly organized cells of multigenerational satanists whose avowed aim is world domination. The conspiracy, says Hammond, is masterminded by one "Dr. Greenbaum," a Jewish doctor who once worked for Nazi Germany and now conspires with the CIA and other governmental agencies to advance the cause of the cult. Hammond discovered this conspiracy during hypnotic treatment of his MPD patients, who, he believes, have been enslaved by the cult.[3]

Hammond and other specialists in ritual abuse emphasized that it is difficult to unmask cult members. Many members are professionals who manage to coordinate their satanic activities with busy careers as politicians, lawyers, doctors, and teachers. According to Hammond, cult indoctrination begins early in life. Adult members torture, sexually abuse, and brainwash their own children and other youngsters. Horrific abuse is designed to activate mechanisms of dissociative amnesia, which in turn generate "alter" personalities who commit crimes on behalf of the cult. Among these crimes are drug trafficking, prostitution, and the production and distribution of pornography.[4] By applying advanced mind-control techniques, the cult implants programs in these individuals that ensure robotic obedience to its commands. By hypnotizing his patients, Hammond claimed to have discovered the secret trigger words that activate the mind-control programs which drive cult victims to commit murder and other crimes. Experts on ritual abuse assert that the vast illegal income generated by these "Manchurian candidates" has enabled the cult to infiltrate the media, government, and law enforcement agencies (Gould 1995). Having been mind-programmed, patients are utterly oblivious of their crimes until therapists restore their memories under hypnosis. Ritual abuse experts were not surprised that none of their patients knew anything about the cult before commencing psychotherapy. As the psychotherapist Catherine Gould affirmed, "the normative response to severe trauma, especially in early childhood, is dissociation and amnesia for the traumatic events" (1995: 337). That is, the very fact that patients were entirely unaware of having been victimized by the cult was interpreted as further evidence of the cult's powerful mind-control programming.

According to specialists in ritual abuse, striking similarities among the memories recovered from patients across North America and Europe enhanced their credibility, especially when obvious motives to fabricate were absent. They were impressed when hospitalized patients, treated in special dissociative disorders units, provided "satanic" word associations (such as *chanting*) to seemingly neutral cue words (such as *circle*). These responses were interpreted as signifying a possible history of cult involvement.[5]

In the face of skepticism about these dramatic claims, mental health professionals specializing in trauma and dissociation presented additional arguments in favor of the ritual abuse theory of multiple personality. The memories of satanic abuse, they said, concerned activities no less credible than the well-documented atrocities of vicious individuals such as the Marquis de Sade or Jeffrey Dahmer (Goodwin 1994), or the organized violence of the Nazis or the Catholic Inquisitors (Ross 1995: 34–36). Moreover, asserted the psychiatrist Colin Ross, the existence of large, affluent religious organizations, such as the Reverend Sun Myung Moon's Unification Church, "make it conceivable that Satanic human-sacrifice cults could be operating in secrecy through a combination of bribery, financial power, political connections, and intelligence expertise" (1995: 53). Citing European historical sources, the psychotherapists Sally Hill and Jean Goodwin claimed that "certain satanic cult practices have been documented over many centuries" (1989: 40). Colin Ross concluded: "It would be a historical anomaly if there were no secret societies practising ritual human sacrifice in North America today" (1995: 82).

Ritual abuse therapists were also quick to attack the skeptics. According to Sandra Bloom (1994), those who questioned the reality of ritual abuse were in danger of making the same mistake as those who had once denied the reality of incest. Expressing skepticism was akin to silencing the voices of survivors. The social worker E. Sue Blume (1995) likened the skeptics to Holocaust deniers, and Ross wondered whether skeptics were merely struggling to deny their own histories of abuse. Questioning ritual abuse narratives, he warned, might trigger a "flight into health" on the part of patients. He urged clinicians to seek a "balanced middle ground" when considering the reality of satanic ritual abuse, and to avoid extreme skepticism as well as unconditional belief (Ross 1995: 87, 79, 89). Bloom spoke for many therapists when she concluded: "But for us to believe that satanic, organized, ritual abuse does not occur, someone is going to have to offer us an explanation that is at least as credible as the eyewitness accounts of our adult patients and the child patients of our colleagues" (1994: 469).

Hammond's theory of ritual abuse and MPD has gained considerable attention, even far outside the field of trauma studies.[6] In part, this attention is due to his stature in the field. Hammond is a past president of the American Society of Clinical Hypnosis, and he and his coauthors Daniel Brown and Alan Scheflin recently won the prestigious Guttmacher Award from the American Psychiatric Association for their book *Memory, Trauma Treatment, and the Law.*

Despite Hammond's prominence in the field of dissociative disorders, not all experts endorsed his "Dr. Greenbaum" theory of ritual abuse and MPD. For example, one Christian therapist hypothesized that "alters" were not personality fragments at all, but rather demons that had possessed the patient. To facilitate assessment and treatment, he proposed a new diagnosis, complete with DSM-style criteria, entitled "oppressive supernatural states disorder" (Friesen 1992: 197). The American Psychiatric Association has yet to adopt his proposal.

Other specialists in dissociative disorder questioned the credibility of the satanic abuse theory of MPD. These skeptics did not doubt that patients had been severely abused as children. But they were skeptical of the claim that organized satanists were the culprits (Coons 1994; Putnam 1991b).

The controversy about the reality of satanic abuse prompted studies by social scientists. Bette Bottoms and her colleagues (1996) conducted the largest investigation into satanic abuse allegations in the United States. They sent a random sample of clinical members of the American Psychological Association a postcard asking whether they had encountered any cases of children or adults who claimed to have experienced either satanic ritual abuse or abuse motivated by religious ideology. Among the 2,722 respondents, 13 percent had seen a child whose case involved allegations of satanic ritual abuse, and 11 percent had seen an adult who recalled having been satanically abused as a child. Although several psychologists said they had encountered more than 100 cases each, most of those who had encountered any cases of alleged satanic abuse had seen only one or two. A detailed questionnaire was sent to those who reported cases, asking them to describe up to eight cases they had seen.[7]

Although many trauma specialists have emphasized the similarity between children's and adults' reports, Bottoms's respondents were more impressed by the differences. Adults described far more elaborate, severe, and bizarre forms of abuse than children did, and 95 percent of the adults had recovered their memories during psychotherapy. Although 67 percent of the adults had initially sought help for depression, 49 percent eventually received a diagnosis of MPD. Alleged survivors were far more likely to accuse their parents than others of satanic abuse (53 percent versus 2 percent; Qin et al. 1998).

Adults' claims to have completely repressed the abuse were positively related to its reported severity, the number of other victims, and the number of perpetrators: the more violent the abuse, the more victims, and the more satanists involved, the more likely a patient was to claim to have forgotten every bit of it. The respondents reported having encountered a total of 287 adult and 457 child survivors of ritual abuse. In only three of these cases did the clinicians claim to have obtained corroboration of the satanic aspects of the allegations. But what they regarded as corroboration was not convincing: one patient owned a voodoo doll, another had satanic symbols etched in his (or her) skin, and a third had merely described satanic rituals in great detail. As Bottoms and her colleagues concluded, given the severity of the remembered abuse, "the evidence was astonishingly weak and ambiguous." Startlingly, therapists' belief in ritualistic abuse "was not related to the amount of evidence provided but to the bizarreness and extremity of the allegations." The stranger the allegations, the more likely the therapists were to believe them (Qin et al. 1998: 276, 279).

Kirk Weir and M. S. Wheatcroft (1995) assessed children in the United Kingdom who had made allegations of ritualistic sexual abuse. In 75 percent of the cases, they concluded that the evidence did not support the allegations and that the allegations were false. However, they concluded that ritualistic sexual abuse probably had occurred in five of the cases. In three of these cases, children spontaneously provided detailed accounts, and in four, they exhibited marked behavioral disturbance. Unfortunately, Weir and Wheatcroft published only one complete case history. The adults in this case were a man who had twice been convicted of sexual assault, his wife, the wife's sister, and her husband. The main perpetrator and his sister-in-law were interested in the occult, and eventually got their spouses involved. The four adults began having sexual intercourse with their own teenaged children as well as with other adolescents. Sexual activities were accompanied by occult rituals and paraphernalia. One of the teenaged girls, who had been seeing a psychiatrist and exhibiting behavioral problems, disclosed these activities. Other girls followed suit, and medical examination supported the allegations of sexual intercourse and penetration by knives. All four perpetrators confessed.

This case concerned four socially isolated, antisocial adults, who had incorporated occult paraphernalia into their sexual abuse of adolescents. It differed dramatically from the typical narrative of satanic ritual abuse. The offenders were not highly educated professionals who functioned as part of an international conspiracy. Mind-control programming, ingestion of urine and feces, baby breeding, infant sacrifice, and cannibalism were notably absent. Finally, there was no evidence that the young victims were unable or unwilling to disclose their abuse. They did not repress or dissociate their memories of trauma.

The anthropologist Jean La Fontaine (1998) conducted the most comprehensive study yet done on satanic abuse allegations in the United Kingdom. Studying 84 cases, all involving children, she found corroborating evidence of sexual abuse in 35 of them. However, in only 3 cases was there any evidence of occult rituals, and none involved any evidence of satanic cult involvement or any of the standard features of the prototypic narrative (cannibalism, human sacrifice, and so on). Although the sexual abuse aspects of a significant minority of these cases turned out to be accurate, the satanic features were not. La Fontaine concluded that there is no convincing evidence that satanic cults have ritually abused children.

Ironically, the only case of a convicted, self-confessed satanic sexual abuser is apparently a case of false memory (Wright 1994). The daughters of Paul

Ingram, a fundamentalist Christian and law enforcement officer, recovered memories of him abusing them. During an intensive quasi-hypnotic interrogation, he recovered memories not only of having brutally raped his own children for many years, but also of having led a satanic cult for nearly two decades and having coordinated the sacrificial murders of hundreds of babies. The interrogators assured him that it is not unusual for people to repress all memories of their criminal careers, and that the visual images surfacing during interrogation were memories of genuine events. Despite the absence of *any* evidence of crime—there were no missing babies, and the bodies of allegedly sacrificed infants were never found—Ingram confessed and was sentenced to prison. Although he has long recanted his coerced confession, he remains imprisoned for crimes he almost certainly did not commit. His case provides a vivid illustration of how suggestive interviewing techniques can create bizarre false memories.[8]

The Ingram case is far from unique. The psychologist Saul Kassin (1997a) has described other cases of *internalized false confession* wherein an innocent individual—confused, fatigued, and anxious—is exposed to psychologically coercive interrogation by police who claim to know he is guilty. When exposed to such pressure, the person may begin to doubt his own memory. While acknowledging the drastic differences between the purposes of "recovered memory" therapy and police interrogation, Kassin (1997b) nevertheless emphasizes their disturbing similarities:

> In both sets of cases, an authority figure claims to have privileged insight into an experience in the individual's past. In both, the individual is in a state of heightened vulnerability or malleability with regard to his or her memory. In both, the interactions between expert and individual take place in a private, socially isolated environment devoid of external reality cues. And in both, the expert ultimately convinces the individual to accept a negative and painful self-insight—in the absence of memory—by invoking the concept of repression. (301)

Opinions vary regarding the veracity of recovered memories of satanic ritual abuse. Reviewing the literature on such abuse, Brown, Scheflin, and Hammond concluded that these reports "may be mostly fictitious, a blending of internal and external sources, but sometimes mostly genuine" (1998: 64).

However, the evidence adduced in support of the reality of satanic abuse crumbles upon inspection. For example, the notion of a top-secret, conspiratorial cult, run by apparently upstanding members of society, does not fit any available facts. In hundreds of investigations, the FBI has failed to uncover a single shred of evidence corroborating the existence of a satanic cult. The absence of evidence is especially noteworthy because violent criminals almost always leave traces of their deeds. Having investigated many horrible crimes in his career, the supervisory FBI agent Kenneth Lanning (1991, 1992) originally thought the satanic allegations might be true. But in view of the absence of evidence, he eventually concluded that mental health professionals must explain why patients "are alleging things that don't seem to be true" (1992: 146).

Staunch believers in the existence of the cult have offered two reasons for rejecting Lanning's conclusion. First, the absence of evidence, they say, merely confirms how cleverly the cult conceals its activities. Second, some therapists have even accused Lanning himself of being a satanist who has infiltrated the FBI to advance the cause of the cult.[9]

Other features of the ritual abuse narrative are criminologically implausible. Contrary to the beliefs of some therapists, the existence of organized crime networks does not confirm the existence of satanic cults. Victims shot dead in public places, for example, provided plenty of physical evidence of the Cosa Nostra, however secret its inner workings might have been. Unlike organized crime, the alleged satanic cult has never left any evidence of its misdeeds. Moreover, the cult supposedly has hundreds—perhaps thousands—of members, yet no one has defected. Complex conspiracies are almost impossible to keep secret for very long; conflicts among conspirators are inevitable, and sooner or later somebody defects and turns state's evidence (Lanning 1992).

The cult allegedly involves both women and men, who participate in coed sadistic sexual abuse. Women were accused in 100 percent of the daycare cases involving allegations of ritualistic abuse (Finkelhor, Williams, and Burns 1988: 60). However, epidemiologic data indicate that very few women sexually abuse children, let alone in large groups that include men (Finkelhor et al. 1990). In a study based on a random sample of American adults, female perpetrators were mentioned by only 1 percent of female victims of child sexual abuse and only 17 percent of male victims. In another study involving a random sample of women, only 5 percent of those who had suffered incest mentioned a female perpetrator (Russell 1986: 389). Moreover, although the cult supposedly involves countless sexual sadists, such deviants are extremely rare and usually operate alone. Approximately two-thirds of sexually sadistic offenders committed their crimes without accomplices, and the others had only a single accomplice (Dietz, Hazelwood, and Warren 1990).

Despite offers of rewards, not a single piece of child pornography has surfaced in any of the ritual abuse cases investigated in the United States (Finkelhor, Williams, and Burns 1988: 90–91; Nathan 1991). FBI and Interpol agents have searched throughout America and Europe for the child pornography allegedly produced and distributed by ritual abusers, but to no avail (Nathan and Snedeker 1995: 116). In fact, within several years after pornography involving children began to appear in adult bookstores in the 1970s, public outcry and legislative action eradicated its production and commercial distribution throughout America (Stanley 1989). The market for child pornography was always minuscule anyway, compared to the market for adult pornography.

Moreover, the "snuff film"—a type of violent pornography said to feature actual murders of women or children—is now recognized as an urban legend. No such film has ever been found (Stine 1999). Many sociologists specializing in folklore consider the entire satanic ritual abuse scare nothing more than an urban (or contemporary) legend (Victor 1993, 1998). Features of the ritual abuse narrative resemble other long-debunked legends having no basis in fact. Among these are stories about how Americans kidnap and butcher Central American children, selling their organs on a medical black market (Campion-Vincent 1990, 1997), and stories about anonymous sadists who gave poisoned candy and apples containing razor blades to trick-or-treaters on Halloween (Best and Horiuchi 1985). Such legends spread widely because they resonate with common anxieties about the welfare of children.[10]

Unbeknownst to ritual abuse therapists, the historical sources they cite concerning Satan-worshipping cults throughout European history are devoid of any factual basis (see Noll 1989). The distinguished historian Norman Cohn has thoroughly demolished this legend. After exhaustive review of the primary sources, Cohn concluded: "There is in fact no serious evidence for the existence of such a sect of Devil-worshippers anywhere in medieval Europe. One can go further: there is serious evidence to the contrary" (1993: 78). Nearly every feature of the contemporary ritual abuse narrative (with the exception of CIA mind-control programming) can be found in legends that originated in late antiquity and developed through the Reformation.

Accumulated folklore provided the basis for specific questions put to accused satanists and witches during the late Middle Ages. Under torture, suspected witches would answer yes to questions about satanic rituals, incest, orgies, baby breeding, cannibalism, and so forth (Cohn 1993: 65). Affirmative replies to detailed questions were thought to provide confirmation of the existence of witchcraft and satanism. Not everyone who claimed to be a witch did so under torture (ibid. 210). Some psychotic individuals incorporated folklore about copulating with the devil, flying through the air, and so forth into their delusional systems of belief.[11]

Contrary to Colin Ross's belief that human sacrifice cults are flourishing today, such practices have always been rare in North America. Several Native American tribes did practice ritual human sacrifice, but no group has ritually sacrificed human beings since the Pawnee of Nebraska abandoned the practice in the early nineteenth century.[12]

Although cannibalism figures very prominently in satanic abuse narratives, convincing evidence of institutionalized cannibalism has been surprisingly scarce (Arens 1979, 1998; Pickering 1999). Most documented cases of cannibalism have involved isolated psychopathic individuals (such as Jeffrey Dahmer) or people in danger of starvation such as the pioneers in the Donner party or mariners lost at sea. The most recent documented case of institutionalized cannibalism in North America occurred nearly a thousand years ago (about 1150 CE) in what is now the southwestern United States (Marlar et al. 2000). Many other reports throughout history merely amounted to certain groups of people accusing outsiders of the practice: pagan Romans accused Christians; Christians accused Jews; tribal groups have accused one another; colonized people have accused colonizers and vice versa. After reviewing these accounts, the anthropologist William Arens concluded: "I have been unable to uncover adequate documentation of cannibalism as a custom in any form for any society" (1979: 21). The confirmed cases documented since Arens's review, however, do not buttress the credibility of contemporary accounts of otherwise well-fed North American satanists who devour infants during their ceremonies.[13]

Documents released under the Freedom of Information Act confirm that the CIA spent millions of dollars on secret mind-control research during the Cold War. Fearing that its Communist rivals had already devised sophisticated brainwashing techniques, the CIA sought to develop a truth serum and other methods for prying secrets from enemy agents. The agency also sought methods for inducing robotic obedience in persons who would then conduct covert operations in foreign lands. For more than two decades, the CIA studied the effects of LSD, marijuana, sensory deprivation, hypnosis, and other methods for inducing zombie-like obedience in witting and unwitting participants. Their bumbling attempts to develop "mind-control" methods failed, such as their plan to spray unsuspecting people with LSD from an aerosol can. When Senator Edward Kennedy's committee investigated these antics years later, one of his staffers referred to the operatives as the "Gang That Couldn't Spray Straight" (Marks 1979: 108).

Given the absence of evidence to support allegations of satanic ritual abuse, how did belief in the phenomenon spread so rapidly among highly educated mental health professionals?[14] To answer this question, the anthropologist Sherrill Mulhern (1991, 1992) attended 14 continuing education seminars designed to teach professionals how to diagnose and treat survivors of ritual abuse. The proselytizing presenters exhorted, threatened, and admonished attendees to believe in the reality of satanic cults. Questioning survivors' memories of sexual torture, ritual murder, cannibalism, and mind-control programming, they said, was tantamount to repeating the grievous error of the past when professionals denied the reality of sexual abuse. To convince attendees of the reality of the satanic cults, they wove together bits and pieces of information from diverse sources, including drawings done by patients featuring satanic symbols (such as pentagrams), album covers from heavy metal rock groups, historical folklore about devil-worshipping cults, and photographs of mutilated animals. Patients who recalled having been victims of ritual abuse gave moving presentations about their harrowing experiences. Presenters stressed the importance of memory recovery work for healing. Never did they warn attendees about the risks of fostering illusory memories of trauma. Seminars like these provided fertile ground for the rapid dissemination of urban legends about the cult.

Therapists who treat ritual abuse invariably mention their "shock" at the "disclosures" made by patients. But it is important to realize how these "disclosures" occur. To gain access to dissociated traumatic memories, the therapist hypnotizes the patient after telling the patient how to use "ideomotor signals." For example, the patient might be told to lift one finger to signal a "yes" response to the therapist's questions, and to lift another finger to signal a "no" response. After inducing trance, the therapist might ask questions like

"Were hooded figures present at the ceremony?" "Was there a bonfire?" Lifting the yes-finger in response to one of these leading questions is interpreted as a "disclosure" regarding a detail of the satanic ceremony. It takes little imagination to see how the preconceptions of the therapist could shape the "disclosures" of the patient, thereby producing a spurious similarity among "disclosures" across many patients.[15]

The entire saga of alleged ritual abuse provides one long argument for the reality of false memories of trauma. In nearly every case, the memories return only in psychotherapy. The proportion of patients who have no recollection of their ritual abuse until they begin psychotherapy ranges from 95 to 100 percent across studies.[16] Moreover, hypnosis and memory recovery techniques figure prominently in the emergence of these memories; rates range from 93 to 100 percent of cases (Coons 1994; Young et al. 1991). Because hypnosis researchers are ethically barred from implanting false memories of trauma, there will never be any direct experimental laboratory evidence that hypnosis can foster false memories of satanic abuse in patients. However, individuals have recovered even more bizarre "memories" under hypnosis, thereby lending credence to the idea that memories discovered while hypnotized may be false. For example, during past-life hypnotic regression, both patients and research subjects have recalled "memories" from previous "lives" (Stevenson 1994; Spanos et al. 1991). Subjects who are told before they are hypnotized that children were often abused throughout history tend to recover memories of their "own" sexual abuse during "past-life" regressions. Hypnotized young adults have even recovered memories from their personal future—middle age (Rubenstein and Newman 1954).

People vary in their ability to become hypnotized. Dissociative disorder patients, however, appear to be among the most hypnotizable. The psychiatrist George Ganaway (1989) reported that nearly all of the 82 patients assessed in his dissociative disorders program qualified as Grade-5 on the Hypnotic Induction Profile. As the psychiatrist Herbert Spiegel (1974) emphasized, extremely hypnotizable, Grade-5 individuals drift in and out of trance even without formal hypnotic induction. They exhibit characteristics rendering them vulnerable to the formation of false memories, such as a trusting eagerness to please the therapist, suspension of critical judgment, and vivid, but not necessarily accurate, memories. Between 10 and 20 percent of the general population qualifies as highly hypnotizable (Baars and

McGovern 1995; Spiegel 1974). These individuals do not even require for-mal hypnotic induction to exhibit false memory formation (Barnier and McConkey 1992).

Patients who recover memories of ritual abuse often develop PTSD during the course of therapy. Rates have ranged from 28 percent to 84 percent and 100 percent.[17] Although some ritual abuse therapists argue that exacerbation of symptoms is a necessary step on the road to recovery—that patients must get worse before they can get better—a more likely explanation is that these therapists are unwittingly inducing the very disorder that they intend to treat.

Ritual Abuse of Children

Beginning in the 1980s, children began accusing daycare workers of sexually abusing them (see Nathan and Snedeker 1995). However, in only 16 of 43 cases studied in depth did a child directly disclose sexual abuse. In the re-maining cases, a parent noted an increase in fears or nightmares, a mysterious rash, a change in attitude, or unusual behavior (such as "French-kissing" a parent). Worried parents took their children to psychotherapists or pediatri-cians, who diagnosed sexual abuse (Finkelhor et al. 1988: 103, 105–106).

Formal investigations followed. Most daycare cases, though, did not in-volve charges of ritualistic abuse. Among 270 cases in which at least some in-vestigators believed abuse had occurred, only 36 involved allegations of rit-ual abuse (ibid.: 59). Like their adult counterparts, these youngsters did not spontaneously disclose their ritual abuse. They did so only after having been in psychotherapy (Gonzalez et al. 1993). Because of the children's presumed inability or unwillingness to disclose abuse, experts urged therapists to use structured, leading questions to uncover the underlying victimization (Gould 1992). While acknowledging the risks of this approach, Kee MacFarlane, who played a major role in fueling the panic about satanic abuse at the McMartin preschool in California in the mid-1980s, nevertheless main-tained that "leading questions may sometimes be necessary in order to enable frightened young children to respond and talk about particular subjects" (1985: 155).

Children often denied having been abused for significant periods of time, but persistent questioning unlocks their presumably dissociated memories of trauma. In addition to describing their participation in pornographic activities, children revealed a range of abuses that broadly resembled those remembered by adults in psychotherapy (consumption of urine and feces, murder of infants, and so forth). Therapists were impressed by how well-adjusted these children first appeared to be in spite of the horrors they had so recently experienced. As the therapists Barbara Snow and Teena Sorensen argued, "the appearance of normalcy was facilitated by the children's ability to dissociate, compartmentalize, and repress" their traumatic experiences (1990: 485). Although they rarely exhibited dramatic psychiatric symptoms before disclosing the abuse, their clinical decompensation following disclosure seemed to confirm suspicions that they had been severely traumatized. Children in ritual abuse cases eventually exhibited more psychiatric symptoms than did children in nonritualistic cases, and having been allegedly exposed to ritualistic abuse significantly predicted severity of psychiatric symptoms (Finkelhor, Williams, and Burns 1988). Citing unpublished data, Susan Kelley, Renee Brant, and Jill Waterman (1993) reported that 83 percent of children exposed to ritualistic sexual abuse, but only 36 percent of those exposed to nonritualistic sexual abuse, met criteria for a diagnosis of PTSD. Noting that children seldom disclose ritual abuse until well into evaluation or treatment, these authors also mentioned that PTSD symptoms erupt when memories of ritualistic abuse become conscious. These observations strongly suggest that the treatment itself is causing the PTSD.[18]

Two kinds of errors threaten the integrity of child abuse investigations. Some children may falsely claim to have been abused ("false positives"), whereas others may falsely deny it ("false negatives"). Although the relative frequency of these errors is unknown, some child welfare advocates fear that the risk of false negatives is greater than the risk of false positives (on false negatives, see MacFarlane 1985; Sorensen and Snow 1991). This fear has been heightened by the popularity of the psychiatrist Roland Summit's (1983) concept of the *child sexual abuse accommodation syndrome*. Theorizing from his clinical experience, Summit argued that abused children often deny having been abused, and that many who do disclose abuse subsequently retract their allegations and then reinstate them again. According to Summit, professionals investigating suspicions of abuse must be skeptical of initial denials and later retractions, for these are often components of a frightening and complex process of disclosure.

There are several reasons why children might deny their abuse, according to those who believe in the child sexual abuse accommodation syndrome.

First, trauma-induced dissociation may render memories of abuse relatively inaccessible to awareness. Persistent questioning in a safe, supportive context may be necessary to penetrate these dissociative defenses, enabling the children to remember and disclose their trauma. Second, even if children are fully aware of the abuse, they may fail to disclose it because they fear retaliation from the perpetrator. Third, children may harbor positive as well as negative feelings toward the perpetrator, making them unwilling to disclose and send the offender to jail. Fourth, children may be reluctant to disclose embarrassing experiences. Fifth, for very young children, immature verbal skills may hamper their ability to convey what happened to them.

When interviewed properly, even preschoolers can provide accurate testimony.[19] Unfortunately, after reviewing hundreds of forensic interview transcripts, Stephen Ceci and his colleagues concluded that "the vast majority of these do contain highly improper interviewing techniques" likely to foster false allegations of abuse (Ceci, Bruck, and Rosenthal 1995: 501). Quoting from transcripts from a widely publicized case, Maggie Bruck and Ceci (1995) showed that interviewers repeatedly asked a child the same questions in multiple interviews occurring over weeks and months, implying dissatisfaction with the child's initial denial of abuse. Questions were suggestively phrased, implying the guilt of the alleged perpetrator. Interviewers also used anatomically correct dolls in suggestive ways. In one example, the interviewer asked the child to use a doll and utensils to demonstrate *how* the alleged offender had hurt the child with a spoon, although the child had not made any such allegation. Interviewers applied peer pressure, telling children how their friends had already disclosed, urging them to do so as well. Interviewers conveyed negative stereotypes of the alleged offender, reassuring children that the perpetrator was safely behind bars. Interviewers bullied reticent children, calling them "babies" when they failed to disclose, and offered them candy and other rewards for disclosing. Children eager to end the interview were told that they could leave as soon as they told what the alleged offender had done to them. Assuming the validity of the child sexual abuse accommodation syndrome, investigators were reluctant to conclude that children who initially denied any abuse had not, in fact, been abused.

The child sexual abuse accommodation syndrome provided the justification for this persistent, suggestive style of questioning. Sorensen and Snow (1991) reported that 72 percent of 116 children and adolescents, aged 3–17, who were referred for psychotherapy originally denied having been sexually abused. Corroboration of the abuse was available in each case (confession or plea bargain by offender, 80 percent; conviction of offender, 14 percent; medical evidence, 6 percent), 22 percent had retracted their allegations at some point, but 96 percent of them eventually acknowledged having been abused.

But most studies are clearly inconsistent with the child sexual abuse accommodation syndrome. In one series of 309 cases of confirmed abuse, only 9 percent of the children retracted their allegations (Jones and McGraw 1987). In another series of 234 cases of confirmed abuse, only 6 percent of the children denied the abuse and only 4 percent retracted their allegations (Bradley and Wood 1996). Therefore, as Ceci and his colleagues have observed, the notion that children routinely deny or recant their abuse appears to be little more than a "stubborn urban legend" (Bruck, Ceci, and Hembrooke 1998: 138).

Allegations of abuse in daycare centers prompted research on children's suggestibility, studies designed to mimic aspects of these problematic forensic interviews. Ethics prohibit experimental attempts to implant memories of abuse in children, but if mild forms of suggestive interviewing distort children's recollective reports in experimental contexts, then surely the far more aggressive methods characteristic of the sexual abuse investigations might, indeed, foster false memories, beliefs, or allegations of trauma. Experimental psychologists who study memory in children have provided ample evidence that the methods of interviewing in many of the abuse cases probably fostered false memories (or at least false allegations) of sexual abuse.[20]

Early studies inspired by concerns about the unreliability of preschoolers' testimony indicated that children seldom provided seriously incorrect statements about, for example, a medical examination (Saywitz et al. 1991). These studies were largely irrelevant to the controversial daycare cases in which interviewers made numerous interviewing errors that were likely to lead to erroneous reports of abuse. For ethical reasons, researchers in subsequent studies did not test whether young children could be coaxed to provide false reports of abuse. But these studies did show that features that were common in the inappropriate forensic interviews could produce similar memory distortions in the laboratory for nonabusive events.

In their "Sam Stone study," Michelle Leichtman and Ceci (1995) tested the effects of stereotype induction plus repeated, suggestive questioning on children's eyewitness testimony. For one month, preschoolers heard anecdotes exemplifying the clumsiness of a stranger named Sam Stone. Then

Sam Stone made a brief, uneventful visit to their daycare center. During four subsequent weekly interviews, researchers questioned children about Sam's visit, repeatedly insinuating that he had gotten a teddy bear dirty and ripped a book. Ten weeks after Sam's visit, a new interviewer asked children to describe what had happened. Forty-six percent of those aged 3–4 and 30 percent of those aged 5–6 spontaneously mentioned that Sam had committed one or both misdeeds, and 72 percent and 35 percent did so when asked whether anything had happened concerning a teddy bear or a book. Forty-four percent of the younger children claimed to have witnessed these events, and 21 percent continued to do so despite the interviewer's gentle challenges. Children in the control group, who had received neither a stereotype induction nor misleading suggestions, accurately described Sam's visit in response to the open-ended question.

Bruck and her colleagues found that repeated, misleading interviews can distort children's reports of a stressful personal event involving their own bodies. Seventy-five 5-year-olds received an inoculation from their pediatrician and then heard a story and received treats from a research assistant who made either a neutral, a distress-denying, or a distress-affirming comment. The single suggestive comment about how the child responded to the shot did not affect children's reports of their distress one week later. About 11 months later, 63 of the children received either three suggestive or three nonsuggestive interviews concerning the pediatric visit, then took a memory test. During the suggestive interviews, the interviewer emphasized how little the child had cried and how little the shot had hurt, and made misleading comments about the actions of the doctor and the research assistant. In the memory test, children who had received suggestive interviews reported having cried less and experienced less pain than did those who had received nonsuggestive interviews. The former group also more often misreported details of the pediatric visit (for example, said the assistant had given them the shot). In summary, providing a single suggestion during a single interview had no impact on the reporting of a stressful event one week later, but several suggestive interviews about 11 months later did alter the children's reports. This procedure mimics the repetitive interviews experienced by many children in the forensic setting, interviews that frequently occur long after the abuse allegedly happened (Bruck, Ceci, Francoeur, and Barr, 1995).

In another study, Bruck, Hembrooke, and Ceci (1997) tested whether repeated suggestive interviews comprising peer pressure, selective reinforcement, leading questions, guided imagery, and enactment with puppets could implant a false positive and a false negative memory in 16 preschoolers. The false positive event was helping a woman find her lost pet monkey, and the false negative event was seeing a man steal food from the daycare center. A true positive event and a true negative event were staged at the daycare center to provide benchmarks for recall. During the first, baseline interview, the researcher merely asked each child about the four events; in the next three interviews, the researcher used the suggestive techniques; and in the last interview a new interviewer merely asked questions about each event. About 80 percent of the children claimed to have witnessed the false events, and their recounting of these events had the same spontaneity and detail as did their narratives of the true events. There was no control group of children who were merely exposed to repeated, nonsuggestive interviews.

In another study, Jodi Quas and her associates (1999) asked children a series of suggestive questions about a (fictitious) operation on their nose. Parents affirmed that no child had ever had such surgery, and yet 8 of the 11 children aged 3–5, 8 of the 17 children aged 6–8, and 1 of the 12 children aged 9–14 claimed to have had this experience. Of the entire group of 17 who claimed to have had this surgery, 13 provided additional details of this false memory.

During many forensic interviews, children who denied having been abused were asked to imagine what it would have been like to have been molested in certain ways by the alleged perpetrator (Bruck and Ceci 1995). This type of question is intended to enable reticent children to disclose suspected abuse. Unfortunately, young children are especially prone to confuse the results of perception with those of imagination. After several guided imagery sessions, children may believe that images of abuse arose from genuine events, rather than from the sessions themselves.

Ceci and his colleagues (1994) conducted a study to address the effects of such repeated guided imagery. They interviewed parents of preschoolers about positive (such as a surprise birthday party), neutral (such as wearing a blue sweater to school), and negative (such as the death of a pet) events that had happened to their children, plus a neutral event that the child had witnessed (such as seeing one's brother wear a blue sweater to school). They developed several corresponding fictional events that parents confirmed had never happened to their children. Presenting the procedure as a "picture-in-the-head" game, researchers told all the children that their mothers had said each event had happened to them, and asked the children to imagine and describe the 8 events during 11 weekly sessions. For the twelfth session, a new interviewer told the child that the previous interviewer had mistakenly said that all the events were genuine when in fact only some were. After each session, children were asked whether they thought each event had happened. Nearly all children correctly affirmed the genuine events. Children aged 3–4 were more prone to assent to false events than were children aged 5–6, and negative events were the least likely category of false event to be affirmed. The proportion of children affirming the false negative event increased from the first to the eleventh session for both younger (from 17 to 31 percent) and older children (from 10 to 28 percent). False assent rates dropped slightly after session 12, when the new interviewer informed the child that some events were not authentic. Unfortunately, Ceci's group did not test whether this increase over time was statistically significant. They emphasized that it is impossible to tell whether guided imagery sessions, especially those using anatomically correct dolls as props, would result in more or fewer false assents than did their experiment.

One question that arises from these studies on children's suggestibility is whether they document false *memories* or merely false *reports*. Do children really believe that the fictional events happened? Or do they merely say so to please the interviewers? Consistent with the false memory interpretation, approximately one-third of the children in these studies continued to insist that particular events had really happened to them even after they were told those events were not real (Ceci and Huffman 1997). Lacking any obvious motivation to lie, these children appeared to have developed false memories, perhaps confusing the products of their repeated attempts to visualize the events with the products of direct experience. Indeed, Ceci and his colleagues have shown videotapes of children giving accurate and inaccurate accounts of Sam Stone's visit to their classroom and of real and false events in the other studies. Professionals were no better than chance at discriminating false from true reports. The credibility of a child's account was related to the amount of perceptual detail mentioned in the child's narrative. The more details, the more professionals tended to believe the narrative, regardless of whether it was true.

Other studies have shown that some people who are pressured to answer questions about fictional events subsequently believe the events actually happened. Jennifer Ackil and Maria Zaragoza (1998) had college students, first-graders, and third/fourth-graders view a brief film excerpt and then answer questions about it. Subjects were required to answer all questions, including those concerning events that had not occurred in the film. For example, one character had slipped off his chair unhurt, but subjects had to specify (confabulate) what part of his body had begun to bleed after the fall. One week later, subjects were given a memory test. Approximately 55 percent of the confabulated "facts" provided by the first-graders, 35 percent of those provided by the third/fourth graders, and 20 percent of those provided by the college students were incorrectly attributed to the film. Despite having knowingly provided false statements about nonevents, one week later some subjects believed they had witnessed these confabulated events in the film. Strikingly, this false memory effect occurred even though subjects were warned before the memory test that some of the postevent questions had contained inaccurate information.

Adopting the suggestive techniques used in the McMartin preschool investigation, Sena Garven and her colleagues found that 58 percent of preschoolers exposed to suggestive questions, social influence, and reinforcement could be persuaded to make accusations against a visitor to their classroom, whereas 17 percent of children exposed only to suggestive questions did so. In their second study, they found that positive reinforcement led 52 percent of children to make fantastic allegations such as being taken from their school in a helicopter, whereas only 5 percent of children not exposed to this influence made fantastic allegations (Garven et al. 1998; Garven, Wood, and Malpass 2000).

No feature of forensic interviewing has received more empirical scrutiny than anatomically correct (AC) dolls. More than 90 percent of professionals use AC dolls to evaluate children for possible sexual abuse (Conte et al. 1991). The dolls have three main purposes. First, investigators use them to ascertain the child's labels for various body parts. Second, investigators watch the child play with the dolls to see whether he or she exhibits behavior believed typical of abused children. Third, investigators use the dolls as props during interviews, asking children to show, rather than merely tell, what happened to them. Many professionals believe that the dolls cue memory, compensate for immature verbal skills, and facilitate disclosure of potentially embarrassing experiences (Everson and Boat 1994).

Authorities agree that AC dolls are useful for learning a child's labels for body parts. This uncontroversial application facilitates subsequent communication between the child and the interviewer. The other two applications, however, have sparked considerable controversy (Skinner and Berry 1993). Although formal guidelines caution against diagnosing abuse solely on the basis of the child's interaction with the dolls (Everson and Boat 1994), some clinicians suspect that abused children will interact with the dolls in diagnostically revealing ways. Unfortunately, opinions vary regarding what counts as normal, exploratory doll play and what signals a possible history of abuse. For example, in one survey of professionals who investigate allegations of child sexual abuse, half claimed that fearful avoidance of AC dolls signified a possible history of abuse, whereas the others disagreed. Moreover, there was not a single behavioral indicator (such as touching the doll's genitalia) that all respondents agreed would constitute normal exploratory behavior among nonabused children aged 2–5 (Boat and Everson 1988). In fact, professionals watching children interact with these dolls cannot reliably distinguish abused from nonabused children (Realmuto, Jensen, and Wescoe 1990; Realmuto and Wescoe 1992).

To provide an empirical basis for clinical assessments, researchers have compared the play of children referred for treatment for suspected abuse with nonreferred, and presumably nonabused, children. Several studies indicate that children referred for sexual abuse evaluations exhibit more sexualized play with AC dolls than do nonreferred children, but other studies do not. As many as 50 percent of nonreferred children inspect the dolls' genitalia (Everson and Boat 1990), but very few directly simulate sexual activities between the dolls or between dolls and themselves.[21]

In the largest study of nonreferred children, Mark Everson and Barbara Boat (1990) reported that only 6 percent of 223 children aged 2–5 engaged in explicitly sexual play with the dolls, but rates varied among demographic subgroups. For black children, for example, 22 percent of the lower-income boys and 50 percent of the lower-income girls simulated intercourse between the dolls when the interviewer had stepped out of the room; the corresponding rates for children from middle- and upper-income families were 11 percent for boys and 0 percent for girls. It may be that cramped living arrangements in low-income families increase the likelihood of children witnessing sexual behavior.

Further studying whether use of AC dolls facilitates accurate reporting, Maggie Bruck and her colleagues tested the accuracy of 40 3-year-olds' reporting of routine pediatric examinations. Half of the children received a genital examination, during which the doctor gently touched them on the genitals and buttocks, whereas the others did not. Immediately after the visit to the doctor, a researcher asked direct questions (such as "Did Dr. F touch you here?") while pointing to body parts on the AC doll. Children were next asked to demonstrate on the doll where the doctor had touched them, and then to demonstrate on themselves where the doctor had touched them. Use of the dolls did not increase the accuracy of the children's reports of genital touching. In response to the doll-assisted questions, only 47 percent of the children who received genital examinations and 50 percent of the other children provided correct answers. Accuracy rates were 25 percent for those who had had the genital exam and 50 percent for the others when children were asked to demonstrate on the doll. Only children who had received the genital exam were asked to demonstrate on their bodies how the doctor had touched them, and their accuracy rate was only 35 percent.

In a second study, Bruck's group had 20 children who had undergone the genital examination demonstrate first on their own bodies and then on the AC dolls how the doctor had touched them. Once again, children made many errors of commission as well as omission, and the dolls failed to increase accuracy of responses. Several children shoved their fingers into the dolls' vaginal and anal orifices when asked how the doctor had touched them (Bruck, Ceci, Francoeur, and Renick, 1995).

Other studies have also shown that AC dolls fail to enhance the accuracy of preschoolers' recollective reports (Goodman and Aman 1990). In fact, few children younger than 4 years are capable of conceptualizing AC dolls as representations of themselves. Ironically, the dolls were intended to overcome preschoolers' verbal limitations, yet the children's immature cognitive abilities prevent them from understanding doll-assisted assessments. An inability to conceptualize a doll as a representation for oneself probably explains why doll-assisted interviews yield reports that are less accurate than interviews without dolls (DeLoache and Marzolf 1995).

AC dolls rarely provoke explicit sexual play in nonreferred children, and referred children frequently exhibit more sexual play with the dolls than do nonreferred children. Moreover, interrater reliability ratings of children's interactions with AC dolls are usually excellent (Skinner and Berry 1993). On these grounds, some scholars defend the use of AC dolls as part of a comprehensive professional evaluation of children for sexual abuse (Everson and Boat 1994). Others disagree (Skinner and Berry 1993; Wolfner, Faust, and

Dawes 1993). The problem is that no one has yet demonstrated the *incremental validity* of AC dolls: a procedure has incremental validity only if it increases the validity and accuracy of judgments (see Garb 1984, 1998). As Glenn Wolfner, David Faust, and Robyn Dawes emphasized, use of dolls would be clinically and ethically justified only if the addition of dolls to evaluation protocols produced significantly more accurate judgments than protocols lacking the dolls. AC dolls would have diagnostic utility only if abused children interacted with them differently from nonabused children who were suspected (incorrectly) of having been abused.

Moreover, Wolfner, Faust, and Dawes pointed out, adding a procedure, such as AC doll play, to an assessment battery in order to get a "full clinical picture" violates professional ethics if the procedure lacks incremental validity for the intended purpose (such as identifying sexual abuse). Adding components of unknown validity to a comprehensive evaluation can *detract* from the accuracy of the resultant judgments. Needless to say, tests lacking incremental validity—let alone having *negative* incremental (decremental?) validity—have no business being part of any clinical assessment protocol. As Wolfner, Faust, and Dawes concluded, "there is simply no scientific evidence available that would justify clinical or forensic diagnosis of abuse on the basis of doll play" (1993: 9).

Retractors

Another source of evidence for false memories of trauma is the increasing number of former patients who have retracted their allegations of sexual abuse. The modal case involves an adult who seeks psychotherapy for depression and who recovers memories of child sexual abuse during the therapy, but who later comes to believe that the "memories" were merely products of therapeutic suggestion (de Rivera 2000).[22]

Recovered memory therapists have found retractors' accounts unconvincing. Brown, Scheflin, and Hammond (1998: 398), for example, insinuated that adults with recovered memories of genuine abuse may retract these memories when lured by the prospect of winning a lucrative lawsuit against former therapists. Blume (1995) interprets retractors as people easily swayed by social pressure, in this case, pressure from their families who are in denial regarding the abuse.

Frederick Crews, in contrast, sees retractors' accounts as providing compelling evidence for false memories of trauma: "Even if one were to insist that the retractor was 'right the first time' about having been molested," Crews asserts, "the point still holds, for in that case the pseudomemory would be the new, exculpating one. But no one who has spoken at length with a number of retractors can doubt that they have *returned* to a healthy sense of reality" (1996: 241). Like Crews, Diana Russell, a feminist activist and sociologist whose controlled research documented the prevalence of incest, interprets retraction as evidence that the original memories of abuse are often false. Indeed, she notes that "retraction often results in a radical improvement in the mental health of former clients" (1986: xxv).

Most published accounts of retractors constitute gripping case stories. However, researchers have begun to study the phenomenon more systematically. Eric Nelson and Paul Simpson (1994) conducted a telephone survey with 19 women and 1 man who had recovered memories of abuse and subsequently rejected them as illusory. All but one of the respondents had recovered their memories during treatment; 63 percent had initiated litigation against their former therapists; 90 percent reported that their therapy had included trance-induction techniques to aid memory recovery, including hypnosis (85 percent), regression (30 percent), trance writing (15 percent), sodium amytal (15 percent), relaxation/imagery (5 percent), and dream work (5 percent). Therapists and group therapy members had suggested abuse memories to 85 percent of the retractors, and 70 percent reported feeling pressure to remember. Books on recovering from sexual abuse, such as *The Courage to Heal*, were mentioned by 70 percent. All the retractors said they had doubted their memories, and that their expressions of doubt had been rebutted by therapists, who told them that doubt is common and expected, not a sign that the memories are illusory. Others had been told that doubt proves the memories are authentic.

Harold Lief and Janet Fetkewicz (1996) obtained questionnaire replies from 40 percent of 100 retractors whose names were provided by the False Memory Syndrome Foundation. Of those responding, 48 percent had remembered satanic ritual abuse and 38 percent had remembered witnessing murder. Half of the respondents had recalled abuse beginning between the ages of three months and five years, and three retractors had recalled prenatal abuse. Most (92 percent) had recovered their memories in therapy, and 82 percent said therapists had suggested that they had been abused before they had recovered any such memories. Hypnosis (68 percent), age regression

(75 percent), guided imagery (72 percent), and dream interpretation (70 percent) were common methods of memory retrieval. Some retractors remarked that they had been searching for meaning in their lives or for an explanation of their emotional problems. Many had gotten worse during therapy, often becoming very dependent on their therapists, telephoning them daily.

James Ost, Alan Costall, and Ray Bull (2002) studied 20 retractors identified via false memory societies. Contrary to the notion that people retract their recovered memories under pressure from family and others, these subjects reported having felt far more pressure to recover trauma memories in the first place than to retract them. Indeed, several subjects had felt pressure from their therapists not to retract their memories. Only 15 percent reported some pressure from family or friends to retract their recovered memories of abuse. Half of the retractors had been advised to sever ties with the alleged abusers (usually family members); hence diminished contact with family may partly explain why few experienced pressure to recant. On average, retractors had taken about two months to recover their first memories of abuse in psychotherapy, and about five years to conclude that the memories were false. If outside pressure to retract played little or no role in their recantations, what convinced them that their memories were false? Most noted that recovered memories seemed "different" from ordinary memories and from abuse memories they had always remembered. Some noted that recovered memories were abnormally clear and vivid and became more so with time, unlike normal memories that tend to fade with time. Others said their recovered memories seemed vague or dreamlike. In any event, these recollections were not experienced as genuine recollections. Hence, experiential qualities of the memories themselves, not outside pressure from family members, eventually convinced these individuals that their recollections of abuse were not authentic.

It would be easy to get the impression that recovered memories of childhood sexual abuse usually surface during psychotherapy. This is certainly true for extravagant material, such as satanic ritual abuse. But it is far from invariably the case for ordinary memories of sexual molestation in childhood. Indeed, researchers have found proportions of subjects who report recovering their memories during psychotherapy ranging from 14 to 68 percent.[23] The popular notion that recovered memory therapy is needed for one to be reminded of unpleasant childhood experiences is simply not true. Subjects in these studies have cited many different kinds of cues (such as beginning a family, returning to one's former neighborhood) that reminded them of abuse they had not thought about in years. Of course, the fact that a trauma memory surfaces outside therapy does not guarantee its accuracy. But it can eliminate one possible source of memory contamination—suggestive psychotherapy.

The evidence that some people develop false memories of horrific trauma is overwhelming. The strongest evidence comes from the strange saga of satanic ritual abuse. Calling recollected memories of satanic abuse "the Achilles' heel of the recovered memory movement," the sociologist Richard Ofshe and his coauthor Ethan Watters point out that therapists who believe in the recovery of "non-satanic memories of abuse are in a predicament: If they admit that these stories of satanic abuse aren't true, they would have to admit that their therapy methods have produced false accounts that clients have mistaken for memory. By doing so, they would call into question all memories, believable or unbelievable, satanic or not, that have been recovered through the very particular procedures of this type of treatment" (1994: 194–195). Ironically, Colin Ross, one of the major theorists of ritual abuse, seems to agree. If satanic cults do not exist, he says, then "the survivor pseudo-memories pose a serious problem about the reality of all childhood trauma memories" (1995: 72).

9

A VIEW FROM THE LABORATORY

ONE STRIKING ASPECT of the debate about recovered memory has been the absence of any research on cognitive functioning in the people at the heart of the debate: those who report repressed and recovered memories of childhood sexual abuse. Until very recently, participants on both sides of this controversy have argued their case by adducing evidence from either clinical experience, surveys of abuse survivors, or studies done on college students. Laboratory studies of the cognitive functioning of people reporting recovered memories of abuse have been surprisingly absent. Are these individuals better at forgetting trauma-related information than those who have always remembered their abuse, and can such heightened forgetting skills be observed in the laboratory? Alternatively, are such individuals more likely than other people to form false memories in the laboratory?

For ethical reasons, experimentalists cannot attempt to create false memories of abuse, but they can test whether certain people are more prone than others to form false memories of nontraumatic events. Although such experiments cannot resolve the recovered memory debate, they can illuminate the issues. More specifically, one can test hypotheses about cognitive mechanisms that ought to be operative if people can repress and then recover memories and if some people are more prone than others to form false memories. My colleagues and I have been conducting laboratory experiments designed to test such hypotheses. We have tested hypotheses derived from both sides of the recovered memory debate.

Several years ago we were recruiting women who had been sexually abused in childhood for a neuroimaging study on traumatic memory. I was one of the clinicians conducting psychiatric diagnostic interviews for this project. Our purpose was to recruit survivors with and without PTSD, and to use positron emission tomography to investigate the functional neuroanatomy of recollecting autobiographical trauma memories (Shin et al. 1999).

During the course of about ten days, I had three odd interviews, all alike. When I asked these interviewees about the details of the abuse—when it had occurred, the identity of the perpetrator, and so forth—each of them said she did not know. When I gently asked why they had responded to an advertisement recruiting sexual abuse survivors if they had no memories of having been abused, they all furnished similar explanations. They mentioned that they had been having many problems—chronically depressed mood, problems with men, drinking too much, feeling tense when near an older male relative—that they could not explain. The source of their problems remained mysterious, they said, until they realized that they must have been sexually abused, but had repressed their memories of the abuse. The forgotten trauma must be the source of their present difficulties.

These three women did not qualify for our neuroimaging project, which required that subjects provide narratives of their abuse experiences to be incorporated into a script-driven imagery protocol. However, they provided the spark for our new line of research: the cognitive psychology of repressed and recovered memories of trauma. I discussed these three interviewees with a colleague, the memory expert Daniel Schacter. To test our suspicion that my encountering three cases of alleged repressed memory was not a fluke—that there might be many more such cases—we decided to recruit subjects on the basis of their memory status. A graduate student, Susan Clancy, and the biological psychiatrist Roger Pitman soon joined us as we mapped out plans to study the cognitive psychology of people reporting repressed and recovered memories of being sexually abused in childhood (McNally 2001d).

CLINICAL AND PERSONALITY CHARACTERISTICS

After recruiting through newspapers and other community announcements, we tested four groups of women. The *repressed memory group* comprised subjects who believed they had been sexually abused as children, but who had no memory of these events. Approximately one-third had begun to believe they were abuse survivors while they were in psychotherapy. Some described what they believed were memory flashbacks of abuse; these were brief visual images (for example, of a penis) lacking any narrative content. Some interpreted their aches, pains, or panic attacks as "body memories" of trauma they could not consciously remember. One subject interpreted her frequent need to urinate as a body memory of abuse. Another interpreted her dreams as evidence of repressed memories of molestation. Needless to say, we had no way of determining whether any of these individuals did harbor repressed memories of abuse. It was impossible to corroborate their abuse when they had no memories to corroborate.

The *recovered memory group* comprised subjects who reported having remembered abuse after long periods of not thinking about it. Unlike the repressed memory subjects, these subjects could recount episodes of abuse. Unable to obtain corroboration of the recovered memories, we could not determine whether they were true, false, or a mixture of both. Many subjects had never told anyone about the abuse; in other cases, potential corroborators had died. About half of the subjects mentioned having recovered their memories during the course of psychotherapy, but only one subject had recalled her abuse while in a therapy session.

The recovered memories varied in credibility. During an emotionally difficult period in her life, one subject suddenly recalled having been fondled by her pediatrician when she was approaching puberty. She had told her mother about it, but her mother had refused to believe her. She was reminded of her doctor's abuse of her while working at a medical conference. Another subject, when asked by her aunt whether she had ever been sexually abused, suddenly remembered being forced to perform fellatio on a relative when she was 8 years old. Other recovered memories were less credible. One subject reported recollections of being molested in her crib, and another of being raped and beaten by her father when she was only 3 years old.

The *continuous memory group* comprised subjects who reported never having forgotten their abuse. They had participated in a previous study on the psychophysiology of traumatic memory (Orr et al. 1998), and 80 percent had furnished the name of a person who could confirm the abuse. Like our other subjects, this group had been recruited from the community.

The *control group* comprised subjects who said they had never been sexually abused.

One of our first aims was to get a better sense of the personalities and clinical features of people who report repressed and recovered memories of abuse (McNally, Clancy, et al. 2000a). To accomplish this, we asked our subjects to complete a battery of questionnaires. Our measure of normal personality variation was Auke Tellegen's (1982) Multidimensional Personality Questionnaire (MPQ), a comprehensive inventory that includes an absorption scale (Tellegen and Atkinson 1974). People scoring high on the trait of absorption easily become disengaged from their surroundings, becoming enraptured by striking sunsets, engrossed in novels, or lost in daydreams. Their vivid imaginations may render them prone to confuse fantasy with reality. They may be at risk for developing false memories, including memories of abuse. Subjects also completed questionnaires measuring depressive symptoms, dissociative symptoms, and posttraumatic stress symptoms.[1]

The questionnaire results revealed that the people who believed they harbored repressed memories of childhood sexual abuse were the most psychologically distressed, the most prone to experience negative emotions, the most dissociative, and the most prone to fantasize (absorption). Strikingly, subjects who had always remembered their abuse were indistinguishable from those who had never been abused on every personality and clinical measure. However, some subjects who reported continuous memories mentioned having benefited from psychotherapy for their abuse-related distress. Successful therapy would be likely to lower their scores on questionnaires that measure psychological problems. Subjects reporting recovered memories of childhood sexual abuse tended to fall midway between the continuous memory and repressed memory subjects on most measures.

Statistically significant differences emerged in terms of personality traits and clinical symptoms. The personality profiles of the control and continuous memory groups were indistinguishable, as were the personality profiles of the repressed and recovered memory groups. The repressed memory group scored higher than the control and continuous memory groups, but not significantly higher than the recovered memory group, on the MPQ negative affectivity scale. (The higher a person is on negative affectivity, the more frequently and intensely the person experiences anger, guilt, anxiety, and sadness.) The control and continuous memory groups were indistinguishable on measures of dissociation, depression, and PTSD, whereas the repressed memory group scored higher than these groups on each measure, and higher than the recovered memory group on PTSD and depressive symptoms. Hence, believing one harbors repressed memories of abuse is associated with greater psychopathology than always having remembered one's abuse. The recovered memory group also reported more symptoms of dissociation and PTSD than the control group, but not significantly more than the continuous memory group. The repressed and recovered memory groups had similar scores on the absorption scale that were significantly higher than those of the continuous memory group and the control group. The elevated absorption scores in the repressed and recovered memory groups indicated a greater tendency to fantasize.

These findings are consistent with three interpretations. First, to make sense of their psychological distress, some people may come to believe that repressed memories of abuse lie at the root of their problems. Consistent with this interpretation, the repressed and recovered memory subjects had higher-than-normal absorption scores, indicative of fantasy proneness. Second, the pattern of scores on the dissociation measure might be interpreted as indicating that some people repress memories of abuse. The repressed memory subjects, whose abuse memories had yet to surface, had the highest scores on the dissociation measure, followed by the recovered memory subjects, whose memories of abuse had been repressed but then had broken through into awareness, followed by the continuous memory subjects, whose low scores on the dissociation measure might signal difficulty repressing disturbing material. Finally, a psychoanalytically inclined theorist might argue that unconscious, automatic efforts to prevent disturbing emotional memories from resurfacing into awareness occur at a cost. If the price of repression is suffering from inexplicable symptoms of distress, then the repressed memory subjects should report more symptoms than the continuous memory subjects—as indeed they did.

GUIDED IMAGERY

Many psychologists have worried that certain therapeutic methods designed to recover repressed memories of abuse may inadvertently create false memories of abuse. One such method is guided imagery (see Loftus and Ketcham 1994). Patients who are uncertain whether they have been abused are asked to close their eyes and visualize episodes of abuse that might have happened.

This exercise is intended to trigger recollection of dissociated memories of abuse, especially if the imagined scenario approximates the patient's genuine, but repressed, experiences. Unfortunately, researchers have found that guided imagery, at least in college students, can produce an imagination-inflation effect. That is, laboratory studies indicate that having subjects imagine unusual childhood events inflates their confidence that the events actually happened to them (Garry et al. 1996; Heaps and Nash 1999).

Might people who have recovered memories of childhood sexual abuse be especially susceptible to this imagination-inflation effect? Of course, ethics prevent researchers from trying to implant additional memories of abuse in these subjects. But if these people have a general tendency to believe imagined things actually happened to them, then they ought to exhibit large imagination-inflation effects even for benign childhood events.

Adopting a procedure developed by Elizabeth Loftus's group (Garry et al. 1996), we investigated this possibility by comparing subjects who reported recovered memories of childhood sexual abuse with nonabused control subjects. Subjects first rated their confidence about whether certain events had happened to them in childhood. No event on the list concerned abuse or was traumatic; for example, one event was finding a $10 bill in a parking lot. On a subsequent visit to our laboratory, the subjects performed a guided imagery task in which they vividly imagined certain events from the original list, but not others. For example, for finding a $10 bill, the subject was asked to imagine what emotions she would have felt, who else would probably have been present, and what she would have done with the money. After this task, subjects spent about 30 minutes completing other tasks, then again rated their confidence about whether each event on the list had happened to them. Despite falling short of statistical significance, the data suggested that merely having imagined certain events boosted confidence that the events had in fact occurred. But this effect was more than twice as large for control subjects as for recovered memory subjects: in other words, the *opposite* of what we had predicted (Clancy, McNally, and Schacter 1999). Interestingly, several subjects in the recovered memory group asked if we were trying to see whether guided imagery would lead them to develop false memories. They seemed especially vigilant to guard against this effect. It is possible that their sensitivity to the controversy about the authenticity of recovered memories counteracted the otherwise memory-distorting effects of guided imagery. Indeed, none of our control subjects expressed suspicions about the purpose of the study, and they were even more prone to the imagination-inflation effect than were subjects in Garry's original research.[2]

THE DRM PARADIGM

Guided imagery may not be the best technique with which to investigate proneness to form false memories. For anyone sensitive to current controversies about false memories, its purpose may be too apparent. Therefore, in our next experiment, we used a less transparent method: the Deese/Roediger/ McDermott (DRM) paradigm (Deese 1959; Roediger and McDermott 1995). In the standard DRM paradigm, subjects hear a series of word lists during the study phase. Each list consists of semantically related words (such as *candy*, *sour*, *bitter*, *sugar*) that are strongly related to another word that is not listed—the "false target" (such as *sweet*). Subjects later are given recognition tests for all the listed words plus other distractor words, including the false target. Subjects often falsely "recognize" false targets as having been presented during the study phase.

We tested whether subjects reporting recovered memories of childhood sexual abuse would be more prone than others to exhibit false recognition in the DRM paradigm. Subjects reporting either repressed, recovered, or continuous memories of abuse or no abuse participated. They were presented with lists of words, none of them related to abuse or trauma. In this experiment, the recovered memory group exhibited more false memory effects than the other groups, and the more dissociative symptoms a person reported, the stronger was the false memory effect (Clancy et al. 2000).

The results of our guided imagery and DRM studies have two main clinical implications. First, psychotherapy patients may be able to counteract the otherwise memory-distorting effects of guided imagery. Of course, our guided imagery procedure differs in important ways from "recovered memory therapy": our procedure was brief, was done in only one session, and was not explicitly designed to recover repressed memories of trauma. Second, relative to other subjects, those reporting recovered memories of abuse exhibited higher rates of false memory in the DRM paradigm. More than other subjects, they affirmed having encountered words that were not presented but that shared a common theme with those that were presented. That is, they relied more on memory for gist than on memory for specific words. However, none of the word categories was related to abuse or to negative emotional themes, and it is unclear whether this false memory effect would have been larger or smaller had the material been related to trauma.

It is also unclear whether these individuals rely on gist memory in everyday life to decide, for example, whether certain experiences (such as sexual or physical abuse) must have happened. That one falsely remembers having encountered a word in an experiment does not necessarily mean that one will falsely remember having been sexually abused simply because the gist of one's memory for childhood is negative.

Two other studies, one by Lori Zoellner and her colleagues (2000) and one by Douglas Bremner and his colleagues (Bremner, Shobe, and Kihlstrom 2000), reported enhanced false memory effects in the DRM paradigm in people reporting traumatic experiences. In Zoellner's study, adult survivors of rape or nonsexual assault exhibited higher rates of false recall than nontraumatized subjects, regardless of whether the survivors met criteria for PTSD. In Bremner's study, women who had been sexually abused as children (all with continuous memories) and who had PTSD exhibited higher rates of false recognition than those without PTSD or those who had not been abused. However, in both of these studies, the groups with higher rates of false memories had poor memory performance overall. In our experiments, by contrast, the recovered memory subjects differed from other groups only in rates of false recall, not in other measures of memory functioning such as rates of correct recall.

DIRECTED FORGETTING

Some clinical theorists, such as Lenore Terr (1991), believe sexually abused children cope by developing an avoidant encoding style that enables them to disengage their attention from threatening events and direct it elsewhere. The ability to attend to benign aspects of their immediate environment, or to pretend they are somewhere else, may attenuate abuse that would otherwise be overwhelmingly upsetting. If children do disengage emotionally and cognitively when they are being sexually abused, this may impoverish their autobiographical memory.

In our first experiment on this topic, we administered a directed-forgetting task to three groups of subjects: childhood sexual abuse survivors with PTSD, childhood sexual abuse survivors without PTSD, and nonabused control subjects. Subjects viewed a series of words on a computer screen. There were three categories of words: trauma-related (such as *incest*), positive (such as *carefree*), and neutral (such as *banister*). Immediately after each word, instructions appeared on the screen, telling the subject either to forget or to remember the word. Half of the words in each category received "remember" instructions. Subjects knew that their memory for the remember-words would later be tested, but in fact we later asked them to write down as many of the words as they could remember, regardless of the original instructions. If abuse survivors with PTSD have a superior ability to disengage attention from abuse cues and to forget disturbing events, they ought to exhibit impaired memory for trauma-related words. That is, they should be readily capable of forgetting trauma-related words—mere pale proxies for the actual abuse memories. However, in contradiction to the avoidant encoding hypothesis, abuse survivors with PTSD exhibited memory deficits for neutral and positive words they were supposed to remember, but they recalled trauma words very well, including those they had been told to forget. If anything, trauma-related words were intrusive, not easily forgettable, in the PTSD group (McNally et al. 1998).

In our second experiment on this topic, we used the same directed-forgetting procedure to test three groups: subjects reporting recovered memories of childhood sexual abuse, subjects reporting repressed memories of childhood sexual abuse, and subjects reporting no history of abuse. We did not assess for PTSD. If anyone should exhibit superior forgetting of trauma cues, it should be subjects with repressed and recovered memories of abuse. The results, however, revealed entirely normal memory functioning in these individuals: they recalled trauma, positive, and neutral words they were told to remember more often than trauma, positive, and neutral words they were told to forget, and they exhibited neither better nor worse memory for trauma-related material than the subjects who reported no history of abuse (McNally, Clancy, and Schacter 2001).

In these two directed-forgetting experiments, *none* of the groups exhibited the predicted superior ability to forget information related to abuse. Sexual abuse survivors with PTSD remembered trauma-related words all too well, and those reporting repressed or recovered memories of sexual abuse exhibited neither enhanced nor impaired ability to forget these words. To be sure, the directed-forgetting paradigm concerns mere words, not autobiographical memories of trauma. Nevertheless, if survivors were capable of forgetting memories of abuse, they should have been capable of forgetting words related to their trauma.

The Emotional Stroop Task

The most robust cognitive effect in the PTSD field is selective processing of trauma cues in the emotional Stroop color-naming paradigm (for a review see McNally 1998). In this paradigm, subjects view words of varying emotional significance, and are asked to name the colors in which the words appear while ignoring the meanings of the words. Delays in color-naming ("Stroop interference") occur when the meaning of the word captures the subject's attention despite efforts to attend to its color. Traumatized individuals who qualify for PTSD exhibit more Stroop interference for words related to their traumatic experiences than for neutral or other emotional words, and they exhibit more interference for words related to trauma than do trauma-exposed people who do not qualify for PTSD (see Chapter 5). Emotional Stroop interference may provide a quantitative index of intrusive cognition. This effect has been replicated many times in survivors of rape, combat, and childhood sexual abuse. Accordingly, we were curious about whether subjects reporting repressed or recovered memories of sexual abuse would likewise exhibit delayed color-naming for words related to abuse.

Subjects reporting either repressed, recovered, or continuous memories of childhood sexual abuse and control subjects reporting no history of abuse were shown a series of words in different colors on a computer screen. They were asked to name the color of each word as quickly as possible while ignoring the word's meaning. The words were either trauma-related (such as *molested*), positive (such as *elation*), or neutral (such as *carpet*). Neither the continuous, recovered, nor repressed memory subjects exhibited the delayed color-naming of trauma words that occurs in people with PTSD. On this task, they did not look like psychiatrically impaired trauma survivors. Of course, the absence of trauma-related interference on the emotional Stroop task does not mean that repressed and recovered memory subjects had not been abused. But it does indicate an important difference between these subjects and PTSD patients in their processing of trauma cues (McNally, Clancy, et al. 2000b).

ALIEN ABDUCTION

The most important limitation of the aforementioned studies is that we were unable to determine how many of our subjects had, in fact, been sexually abused. The unavailability of corroboration presents an interpretive challenge. In our new wave of studies, we are formally attempting to corroborate as many of the recovered as well as continuous memories as possible. But even here, ambiguities remain, for the absence of corroboration does not mean that a memory is false.

So our next step was to investigate memories we strongly suspect to be false, studying people who report recovered memories of abduction by space aliens. We tested three groups of subjects, recruited through advertisements and referrals from a local group interested in alien abduction. The *recovered memory* group comprised six men and five women who recalled having been abducted by aliens, usually more than once. These subjects had (apparent) episodes of sleep paralysis during which they had hypnopompic ("upon awakening") hallucinations of figures hovering by their bed, electrical tingling sensations, flashing lights, and buzzing sounds. Many had sought hypnotic exploration to recover presumably repressed memories of "what had happened next." Typical "memories" recalled during these sessions included visiting spaceships, having sex with aliens, being medically probed while lying on metal tables, and having sperm (or ova) extracted for the production of human/alien hybrids. The *repressed memory* group comprised five men and four women who believed they had been abducted by aliens, but who had no memories of abduction. They assumed they must have been abducted by space aliens because of what they regarded as telltale signs, such as finding unexplained marks on their bodies, waking up in the morning in awkward positions, having a passion for reading science fiction, or becoming suddenly fearful upon seeing drawings of "typical" space aliens with their bulbous gray heads and large black eyes. Some believed that they had repressed their memories of abduction, others that they could not remember because the aliens controlled their memories. The *control group* comprised people who said they had never been abducted by space aliens.

Using a DRM paradigm and neutral material (words such as *tooth* and *taste*) we found that people who recalled alien abduction, or who thought they had been abducted but could not remember it, were much more prone to exhibit false recall and false recognition in the laboratory than were control subjects. The groups did not differ in rates of correct recall and recognition. The strongest predictor of false recall effects was score on the absorption scale ($r = .56$)—a measure of proneness to fantasize (Clancy et al. 2002).

People who recover memories of either sexual abuse or abduction by space aliens seem to have a tendency to exhibit false memory effects in the DRM paradigm. So there may be a connection between formation of false memories in the laboratory and recovery of traumatic memories outside the laboratory. We can be fairly certain that none of our subjects had been abducted by space aliens. But we have no way of knowing how many—if any—subjects who reported recovered memories of childhood sexual abuse had formed false memories of abuse.

We next conducted a script-driven psychophysiology study involving six women and four men who reported that they had been abducted by space aliens (one of the women and three of the men had also participated in our DRM study) and eight control subjects who said they had not been abducted by aliens (McNally, Lasko, et al. 2002). (All the "abductees" had "memories" of abduction; none had only "repressed memories.") The purpose was to test whether people who said they had been abducted would exhibit the heightened physiologic reactivity (heart rate, skin conductance, muscle tension in the face) that constitutes the emotional signature of reliving trauma in PTSD patients. Would believing that one had been abducted suffice to produce physiologic reactions similar to those associated with remembering rape, combat, and other traumatic events?

Before testing our subjects in the laboratory, we interviewed them about their abduction experiences and assessed them for psychiatric illness. All the abductees reported at least one episode of apparent sleep paralysis accompanied by hypnopompic hallucinations, which they interpreted as contact with alien beings. Typical hallucinations were figures hovering near their beds, flashing lights, buzzing sounds, and tingling sensations. Although all abductees affirmed that these experiences had been frightening, all ultimately regarded them as positive and none wished they had never been abducted. Nine of the abductees viewed themselves as very spiritual, and they tended to interpret their abductions as disclosing a profound spiritual dimension of the universe. Eight abductees reported that, with the aid of memory recovery techniques such as guided imagery and hypnosis, they had recovered detailed memories of alien encounters (such as being whisked up into spacecraft and subjected to medical probing by aliens). Seven abductees reported recovering memories of either having sexual intercourse with aliens or having sperm or ova extracted for the purpose of breeding hybrid human-alien babies. Four abductees mentioned recovering memories of meeting their hybrid offspring.

Three abductees fell short, by one or two symptoms, of qualifying for past PTSD related to their alien abduction experiences, and one still had sub-threshold PTSD. Otherwise, the group was nearly free of current or past psychiatric disorders. For example, one subject had panic disorder, another had a specific phobia for insects, and two had suffered major depression in the past. The abductees' average score on the absorption scale was as elevated as those of subjects in our previous studies who reported repressed or recovered memories of childhood sexual abuse. The scores on measures of PTSD and depression were very low.

None of the control subjects had either a current or a past psychiatric disorder. One control subject had experienced an episode of sleep paralysis, but without any accompanying hypnopompic hallucinations. She had first thought that her inability to move upon awakening indicated a possible neurological disease. The absence of recurrent episodes of sleep paralysis had eliminated this worry.

Following our standard PTSD protocol, abductees heard "autobiographical" scripts describing their two most terrifying abduction experiences (for example, being probed on a space ship; having aliens climb on top of one's bed), a real-life stressful experience (such as hearing news about the violent death of a loved one), a real-life positive experience (such as the birth of one's child), and a real-life neutral experience (such as mowing the lawn). Each control subject heard the scripts of one of the abductees. The controls hardly responded at all physiologically when listening to these scripts. In contrast, the abductees exhibited heightened physiologic reactivity to their abduction scripts similar to that provoked by their other stressful scripts. Using a mathematical model (discriminant function analysis), we examined how many subjects would have been classified as having PTSD on the basis of their psychophysiologic reactivity alone. As we expected, no control subject looked like a PTSD patient, but 6 of the 10 abductees did. Between 50 and 60 percent of people who are diagnosed with PTSD on psychiatric interviews exhibit a profile of heightened physiologic reactivity to trauma scripts. However, unlike PTSD patients, who rarely respond to stressful but nontraumatic scripts or to positive ones, the abductees responded to other stress-ful scripts and somewhat to positive ones.

Mean levels of psychophysiologic responsivity of alien abductees to their abduction scripts resembled the response levels of PTSD subjects to their personal trauma scripts. For abductees, the mean skin conductance response was 1.82 μS; my colleagues have found it to be 1.30 μS for sexual abuse survivors with PTSD (Orr et al. 1998) and 0.60 μS for combat veterans with PTSD (Pitman et al. 1987). For abductees, the mean heart rate response was 7.8 bpm; my colleagues have found it to be 7.8 bpm for sexual abuse survivors (Orr et al. 1998) and 5.9 bpm for combat veterans with PTSD (Pitman et al. 1987).

The fact that people who believe they have been abducted by space aliens respond like PTSD patients to audiotaped scripts describing their alleged ab-ductions underscores the power of belief to drive a physiology consistent with actual traumatic experience. It does not, however, impugn the veracity of the memories evoked in previous script-driven imagery studies on PTSD.

Some psychotherapists have claimed that recovered memories of child-hood (or other) trauma must be authentic because the emotional intensity of recollection is so great. Our study indicates the fallacy in this argument. In-deed, the abductees we studied evinced objective signs of emotional, psychophysiologic reactivity while recollecting memories of traumatic events that almost certainly had not happened.

The studies summarized in this chapter constitute the first attempts to inves-tigate cognitive processing in people reporting either repressed or recovered memories of trauma. They suggest several conclusions. First, such individuals typically exhibit symptoms of psychological distress, and they are character-ized by elevated scores on measures of absorption and dissociation. These ele-vations may reflect either a propensity for repressing traumatic memories, a propensity for forming false memories of trauma, or a consequence of abuse itself (assuming it occurred). (Subjects who had always remembered their abuse did not have elevated scores on these measures.) Second, individuals reporting recovered memories of sexual abuse are capable of guarding against the memory-distorting effects of guided imagery, but fall prey to false memory effects in the less transparent DRM paradigm, as do those reporting recov-ered memories of alien abduction. Third, we have found no evidence that subjects reporting either repressed or recovered memories of sexual abuse have a superior ability to forget trauma-related material. If abuse survivors do not exhibit superior ability to forget mere words related to trauma, one must question their ability to forget autobiographical traumatic memories. Fourth, subjects reporting either recovered or repressed memories of sexual abuse performed very differently from sexual abuse survivors with PTSD on our experimental tasks.

None of our studies can answer the question, Were the subjects who believed they had repressed memories of abuse and those who reported having recovered memories of abuse actually abused as children? Nevertheless, the methods of cognitive psychology may help resolve this controversy by enabling scientists to test hypotheses about how people may either forget traumatic events or come to believe they have been traumatized when, in fact, they have not.

10

CONTROVERSIES ON THE HORIZON

W HAT HAS CLINICAL RESEARCH taught us about memory for trauma? Events that trigger overwhelming terror are memorable, unless they occur in the first year or two of life or the victim suffers brain damage. The notion that the mind protects itself by repressing or dissociating memories of trauma, rendering them inaccessible to awareness, is a piece of psychiatric folklore devoid of convincing empirical support. To be sure, people may deliberately try not to think about disturbing experiences, and sometimes they succeed, especially if the experiences were unpleasant but not catastrophic. They may get on with their lives, concentrating on other matters and not dwelling on their early adverse experiences. When later reminded of these experiences, they may say they had "forgotten" them, meaning they had not thought about them for many years. But failing to think about something is not the same as being unable to remember it. Not having something come to mind for a period of time is not the same as having amnesia for the experience.

Moreover, because the mind does not operate like a video recorder, not every aspect of a traumatic event will be encoded in memory and therefore potentially recallable later. It is a mistake to assume that someone has amnesia for an experience if the person never encoded the experience into memory in the first place.

Finally, some experiences are reclassified as traumatic many years after they occur. Some molested children are too young to understand sexual abuse for what it is, and only years later realize what they experienced. But their failure to think about it and classify it as abuse cannot be attributed to repression or dissociation of their memories if the emotional realization that they were abused occurs in adulthood.

Is memory for trauma different from memory for nontraumatic experiences? In one sense, this is true by definition: in the first case the content of the memory is trauma, and in the second case it is not. But this question concerns whether the causal mechanisms that mediate memory for traumatic experiences are different from those which mediate memory for nontraumatic ones. A better way to frame the question is, What are the similarities and the differences between memory for trauma and memory for nontraumatic experiences?

Investigators have found little reason to believe that distinct psychobiological mechanisms unique to trauma come into play when people either encode or recall traumatic events. Traumatic events are a subset of events that trigger terror. As with all extremely negative emotional events, stress hormones interacting with an activated amygdala enhance the hippocampus's capacity to establish vivid, relatively durable memories of the experience—or at least its salient, central features. High levels of emotional stress enhance explicit, declarative memory for the trauma itself; they do not impair it. When people with PTSD recall traumatic events, recollection is accompanied by emotional arousal that creates the illusion of reliving the event. None of these reactions requires any special "trauma" mechanisms in the brain; the mechanisms of intense emotional encoding and retrieval suffice to explain traumatic memory as well as memory for other emotionally intense experiences.

EMERGING CONTROVERSIES

The debate about repressed and recovered memories of sexual abuse is not the only controversy about how people remember trauma. There are several other contentious issues concerning PTSD that bear on memory for trauma (for a review see McNally 2003).

"Phony Combat Vets"

Much of what we know about PTSD is based on the self-reports of Vietnam veterans diagnosed with the disorder. Two potentially serious problems threaten the integrity of this data base. One is the deliberate exaggeration of symptoms by veterans seeking to obtain the PTSD diagnosis (Frueh et al. 2000). As many as 94 percent of veterans diagnosed with PTSD apply for financial compensation for their illness, and the incentive to do so is strong, especially for those with limited occupational opportunities (McGrath and Frueh 2002). As the former Department of Veterans Affairs psychiatrist Douglas Mossman (1994) bluntly put it, "At the VA, it pays to be sick." In addition to free treatment for PTSD, the government provides varying amounts of compensation, depending on the degree of social and occupational impairment attributed to the disorder. A veteran who secures a service-connected disability rating of 100 percent for PTSD can earn more than $36,000 per year, tax-free and indexed to inflation for life (Burkett and Whitley 1998: 236). Recovery from PTSD thus results in a substantial loss of income for the veteran. This does not mean that most veterans diagnosed with PTSD are malingerers. But the ease of exaggerating or faking symptoms and the incentives for doing so should worry researchers who need to confirm that subjects in their studies really do have the disorder.

Some men report combat-related PTSD symptoms even though they either never experienced combat, never served in Vietnam, or never served in the military at all. In their book *Stolen Valor*, which won an award for military historical scholarship, the Vietnam veteran B. G. Burkett and the investigative journalist Glenna Whitley (1998) document many cases of "phony combat vets." Thanks to the Freedom of Information Act, Burkett and Whitley obtained the military records of men who had identified themselves as combat veterans (such as men appearing in television documentaries about PTSD). They discovered massive fraud. For example, they learned that nearly 30 percent of the members of the American Ex-POW Association had never been prisoners of war (1998: 502–503). These men did not merely fake symptoms; they faked their exposure to traumatic stress. Burkett and Whitley estimate that as many as 75 percent of those "receiving PTSD compensation are pretenders" (279).

Burkett and Whitley recommend that researchers studying combat-related PTSD obtain each veteran's military records from the National Personnel Records Center and other official sources to verify self-reports of combat exposure rather than merely rely on a photocopy of the DD-214 provided by the veteran himself. The DD-214 is a military transcript issued to veterans upon their discharge from the service. Contrary to a widespread misconception in the field of traumatic stress studies, a fire that erupted in 1973 at the National Personnel Records Center did not destroy any records from the Vietnam era (Stender and Walker 1974).[1]

Burkett and Whitley argue that many studies of combat-related PTSD are contaminated by the inadvertent inclusion of subjects who have lied about their combat trauma. They are especially critical of the National Vietnam Veterans Readjustment Study (NVVRS), an epidemiologic survey that yielded a lifetime PTSD prevalence rate of 30.9 percent among men who had served in Vietnam (Kulka et al. 1990: 53). This rate of PTSD is surprisingly high, given that only about 15 percent of the men who served in Vietnam were assigned to combat units (Dean 1997: 209). To be sure, men with non-combat assignments (such as truck drivers) sometimes got in harm's way and developed PTSD. But even after we allow for ambushed truck drivers and so forth, explaining the 30.9 percent PTSD prevalence rate is not easy. Burkett and Whitley observe that the NVVRS researchers did not avail themselves of military archives for each subject's unit and did not obtain each subject's complete military file (223–233). Had they done so, they would have been able to verify self-reported traumatic events. Instead, the research team took a subject's word for it when he described events in Vietnam that had triggered his symptoms. The NVVRS researchers may have an opportunity to correct this oversight: a multimillion-dollar follow-up study of the PTSD veterans is being planned. Therefore, the researchers will have a chance to compare traumatic events recalled by subjects with the archival records.

Although many clinicians believe they can spot a phony combat veteran a mile away, they are not necessarily right. Consider the strange case of Edward Daily, a veteran of the Korean war who claimed to have earned a battlefield commission, several Purple Hearts, and a Distinguished Service Cross, and to have escaped after being detained as a POW by the North Koreans. He was diagnosed with PTSD and received nearly half a million dollars in total compensation from the VA for his disorder. Several years ago he came to national attention when he confessed that he had machine-gunned hundreds of South Korean civilians near the village of No Gun Ri. But as the military historian Robert Bateman (2002) has shown, Daily was a mechanic in Korea and never saw a moment of combat, and the alleged massacre apparently never happened. Daily has pleaded guilty to having defrauded the VA by faking his traumatic events and his PTSD (Vines and Cohen 2002).

It is entirely possible that the number of "phony veterans" is much lower among subjects participating in epidemiologic, clinical, and basic science research than among the publicity-seeking individuals studied by Burkett, Whitley, and Bateman.[2] "Phony veterans" may be reluctant to volunteer for research studies, knowing that they will be carefully assessed by the investigators. But unless we avail ourselves of the historical archival material to verify self-reported traumatic events we will never know how widespread this problem is or how much it has infected the data base on PTSD. To ensure the integrity of the data, psychologists and psychiatrists need to consult military archives to supplement traditional interview and questionnaire methods of assessing exposure to trauma.

What Counts as Trauma?

One unintended consequence of peace and prosperity is a liberalized definition of what counts as a traumatic stressor. The threshold for classifying an experience as traumatic is lower when times are good. In the absence of catastrophic stressors such as war, specialists in traumatic stress turn their attention elsewhere, discovering new sources of victims of hitherto unrecognized trauma.

Consider a survey by the RAND Corporation designed to gauge America's psychiatric response to the terrorist attacks of September 11, 2001. On the weekend after the attacks, phone interviewers assessed a representative sample of 560 adults who resided throughout the United States. The researchers concluded that 44 percent of Americans "had substantial symptoms of stress," ominously adding that these effects of terrorism "are unlikely to disappear soon" and that "clinicians should anticipate that even people far from the attacks will have trauma-related symptoms" (Schuster et al. 2001: 1507, 1511, 1512). How did they arrive at this dire conclusion about mental health in America? They asked respondents whether they had experienced any of five symptoms, such as anger and irritability or concentration problems, "since Tuesday" (September 11). Respondents were asked to rate each symptom on a five-point scale ranging from one ("not at all") to five ("extremely"). A person qualified as "substantially stressed" if he or she assigned a rating of at least four ("quite a bit") to one of the five symptoms. For example, anyone who experienced "quite a bit" of anger at Osama bin Laden qualified as substantially stressed.

As Jerome Wakefield and Robert Spitzer (2002) have rightly argued, such surveys medicalize expectable human reactions by failing to discriminate between genuine symptoms of disorder and normal distress reactions. Along these lines, Wakefield (1996) has cogently criticized the diagnosis of acute stress disorder. The diagnostic criteria do not identify a genuine disorder arising from dysfunction in an internal psychobiological mechanism. Instead they appear to pathologize normal responses to horrific events. Wakefield does not deny or minimize the suffering of people who receive this diagnosis. But he questions whether they should be called mentally ill.

The broadening definition of traumatic stressors threatens to undermine any chance of elucidating the psychobiological mechanisms that give rise to PTSD symptoms. To place this issue in perspective, consider the stressors of fighting in the Pacific Theater during World War II, especially for those who became prisoners of the Japanese. The counseling psychologist Brian Engdahl and his colleagues (1997) found that 84 percent of American fighting men who were held as POWs by the Japanese developed PTSD, and 59 percent still had the disorder more than half a century later. Engdahl described a typical case. After experiencing ferocious combat in the Philippines, this soldier was captured by the Japanese, survived the Bataan Death March, saw many fellow POWs capriciously murdered by their captors, endured starvation and torture, nearly drowned on two occasions when the prison ship sank, and was nearly worked to death in a coal mine. Like all POWs, he expected to be executed once the invasion of Japan began. The invasion was aborted when Japan surrendered after the dropping of the second atomic bomb.[3]

Many experiences now being adduced as traumatic, especially in the courtroom—fender benders, overhearing obnoxious sexual jokes in the workplace, being fired—are unlikely to produce the same kind of psychobiological consequences as the horrors endured by Engdahl's POW subjects. To be sure, many people will develop PTSD following far less traumatic experiences than those suffered by the men who fought in the Pacific. Nevertheless, the more we broaden the category of traumatic stressors, the less credibly we can assign causal significance to a given stressor itself and the more weight we must place on personal vulnerability factors. And shifting the causal emphasis away from the event and toward the survivor undercuts the rationale for having a diagnosis of posttraumatic stress disorder in the DSM in the first place. The more we identify noncatastrophic events as stressors deemed capable of producing PTSD, the less likely it is that we will ever discover any common mechanisms that mediate PTSD symptoms.

PTSD in the Courtroom

This conceptual bracket creep in the definition of trauma continues apace, and it has legal as well as epidemiologic implications. Claudia Avina and William O'Donohue (2002) have proposed that under some circumstances a woman who has repeatedly overheard sexual jokes in the workplace may qualify for a diagnosis of PTSD and therefore deserve financial compensation for her joke-induced stress disorder. Being exposed to offensive jokes and more serious forms of sexual harassment may, indeed, justify legal action by the victim. But whether these experiences produce the same psycho-biological consequences as violent rape and other PTSD-inducing stressors is questionable.

Forensic psychologists have sounded the alarm about abuse of the PTSD diagnosis in civil litigation. Gerald Rosen and his colleagues have pointed out that lawyers have been coaching litigants on what symptoms to mention when they are being assessed by clinicians prior to bringing suit for psycho-logical damages linked to PTSD (Rosen 1995; Aronson, Rosenwald, and Rosen 2001). Faking these symptoms is easy, and there is no objective stan-dard test for the disorder as there is for many serious physical injuries that figure in litigation (Burges and McMillan 2001; Sparr and Pankratz 1983). The forensic clinical psychologist Paul Lees-Haley (1999) describes diverse cases he has encountered in which the plaintiff reportedly suffered from PTSD. The PTSD-inducing stressors have included being fired from a job, one-mile-per-hour fender benders, age discrimination, living within a few miles of an explosion (although unaware that it had happened), and being kissed in public.

Rosen's concerns about the effects of compensation on the incidence of PTSD invite comparison to concerns about compensation for whiplash in-jury resulting from traffic accidents. There is no financial compensation for whiplash in Lithuania, and the incidence of neck pain is no higher among people who experience rear-end collisions than among uninjured people in the general population (Schrader et al. 1996). After Saskatchewan switched from a tort-compensation system that included payments for pain and suffer-ing to a no-fault system that did not, the incidence of whiplash injury dropped by 43 percent in men and by 15 percent in women. The prognosis for recovery brightened, too; those who did file claims under the new system recovered much faster from their whiplash than had victims under the former one. The decrease in the incidence of whiplash occurred despite an increase in the rate of traffic accidents. The researchers who reported these findings concluded that a system that provides financial compensation for continued disability presents a serious barrier to recovery (Cassidy et al. 2000).

Is PTSD a Social Construction?

Ever since the ratification of PTSD as a formal diagnosis in 1980, it has been haunted by a reputation for being little more than an idiom of distress shaped by social and political forces. PTSD researchers have sought to dispel this impression by arguing that PTSD has been discovered in nature by astute clinicians, not invented by them. More specifically, they have sought to document its biological basis, its occurrence in diverse cultures throughout the world, and its occurrence throughout history.

Discovering a biological "basis" for PTSD would put it on a par with other diseases in medicine, undermining the claim that it is merely a socially constructed idiom of distress. This task has been made difficult by marked biological variability among groups of individuals who qualify for the disorder on the basis of self-report. For example, the proportion of diagnosed PTSD subjects who exhibit psychophysiologic reactivity to reminders of their trauma has varied widely from study to study: from 60 percent to 90 percent. And this effect is the most replicable biological one we have (Orr, Metzger, and Pitman 2002). Moreover, people reporting abduction by space aliens are just as reactive, complicating interpretation somewhat.

A second approach involves attempts to identify PTSD in non-Western cultures. No one disputes the reality of bacterial infection; people around the world suffer from it in the same way. Accordingly, if PTSD can be detected among diverse peoples, then perhaps it is more than merely an artifact of Western culture. A universal psychobiological response to trauma would go a long way toward countering skeptical critiques of the validity of the PTSD diagnosis.

Psychiatric anthropologists have had little difficulty identifying sources of trauma throughout the world. But debate abounds regarding how well Western concepts of PTSD fit the response to horrific events in other cultures. In fact, many human rights advocates vigorously object to diagnosing PTSD among torture survivors because they believe that medicalizing the problem misdirects attention away from the perpetrators of institutionalized violence (Desjarlais et al. 1995: 47–50).

Treatment issues aside, there are genuine questions about how well Western psychiatric concepts apply in non-Western cultures. For example, the fact that female genital surgery horrifies Westerners who regard it as institutionalized mutilation and abuse, but is valued by African women (Shweder 2000), reminds us not to ignore culture when investigating trauma. It is questionable whether the Western concept of PTSD captures the essence of the human response to trauma wherever and whenever it occurs. Moreover, many attempts to provide psychotherapeutic services to war-traumatized people throughout the developing world have failed, in part because the entire Western framework of diagnosis and psychotherapeutic treatment for trauma is utterly foreign to their cultures (Bracken and Petty 1998). Accordingly, many experts are urging that humanitarian efforts be directed toward fostering the reconstitution of communities and supporting indigenous efforts rather than importing Western trauma discourse and psychotherapies.

A third approach is to identify PTSD in other historical eras. One psychiatrist interpreted entries in Samuel Pepys's famous diary as evidence that he suffered from PTSD after witnessing the Great Fire of London in 1666 (Daly 1983). The psychiatrist Jonathan Shay diagnosed PTSD in one of Shakespeare's characters, the soldier Hotspur (1994: 165–166). In *Henry IV, Part I*, Hotspur's wife complains about his loss of interest in formerly pleasurable activities, his exaggerated startle response, his sweat-drenched nightmares, and his fitful sleep during which he tends to "murmur tales of iron wars" (II.iii.48). In his book *Achilles in Vietnam*, Shay even drew parallels between the vengeful, traumatized Achilles, grief-stricken by the death of his friend Patroclus, and the behavior of Vietnam combat veterans who described atrocities they had supposedly committed in Vietnam.[4]

Retrospective historical diagnoses of PTSD constitute a psychiatric version of the Whig interpretation of history. The historian Herbert Butterfield (1931) criticized the nineteenth-century British Whigs for viewing the past through the lens of modernity and for celebrating their political ancestors as having anticipated their Whiggish (liberal) views. PTSD researchers run the same risk when they diagnose Achilles, Hotspur, or Pepys as having PTSD and when they scrutinize old texts for anticipations of today's views of PTSD as set forth in DSM-IV. To understand how people responded to trauma in the past, we have to understand how it was viewed from their perspective, not our own.

The notion of PTSD as a universal, timeless response to trauma is coming under increasing attack from medical anthropologists, historians, and philosophers (Bracken and Petty 1998; Hacking 1999; Young 1995; see also Summerfield 1999, 2000, 2001). Unfortunately, these authors are often misunderstood as downplaying or even denying psychological pain or the reality of trauma. This is not the case. Instead, as Allan Young has argued, "The disorder is not timeless, nor does it possess an intrinsic unity. Rather, it is glued together by the practices, technologies, and narratives with which it is diagnosed, studied, treated, and represented and by the various interests, institutions, and moral arguments that mobilized these efforts and resources" (1995: 5). The concept of traumatic memory has nineteenth-century origins, and before that, there were "unhappiness, despair, and disturbing recollections, but no traumatic memory, in the sense that we know it today" (141).

Does this mean that PTSD is not "real"—that it is merely a "social construction"? Not exactly. As Ian Hacking has pointed out (1999: 100–124), many mental disorders are best construed as *interactive kinds* rather than *natural kinds* that exist independently of human culture. Unlike infectious diseases, elements in the periodic table, and other kinds discovered in nature by scientists, interactive kinds are affected by the very process of classification. This process has been especially evident for multiple personality disorder. No one doubts that people diagnosed with MPD suffered psychologically, but the form of their suffering and how it was expressed were shaped by diagnostic practices. Switching from one personality to another was a phenomenon that flourished only when the culture authorized people to express their unhappiness in this way. As the psychoanalyst Otto Kernberg (2002) has noted, the epidemic of MPD at his clinic suddenly ceased. Patients who once expressed their unhappiness by creating alternate personalities no longer do so. Widespread criticism of the MPD diagnosis has apparently encouraged individuals to be distressed in different ways.

SCIENCE AND ADVOCACY

The ultimate purpose of research on trauma and memory is to deepen our understanding of how trauma affects people's lives and to learn how science can inform good clinical practice to help survivors overcome trauma's consequences. Therapists and researchers can easily lose sight of this purpose. Many professionals involved in recent controversies about how people remember trauma are either clinicians or laboratory scientists. Some of us are both. And many people specializing in the field of traumatic stress view themselves as advocates for survivors as well as scientists or healers.

Occasionally these dual roles can produce tension, as when scientific data are perceived as clashing with efforts on behalf of victims. Researchers who have identified factors that make certain individuals vulnerable to PTSD are often accused of "blaming victims" for their plight. Others who have expressed concern about exaggeration of symptoms or outright fabrication of trauma histories have been accused of "betraying veterans." Attempts to confirm that trauma has biological consequences (such as hippocampal shrinkage) have been celebrated, whereas attempts to explain such phenomena as preexisting vulnerability factors have been condemned. The involvement of leading figures in the field of traumatic stress studies in the congressional condemnation of Bruce Rind and his meta-analysis is perhaps the most egregious example of (perceived) advocacy trumping science.

David Hume (1740: 302) famously emphasized that one cannot derive an *ought* from an *is*. Advocates who condemn scientific data on moral grounds make the opposite, but equally illogical, mistake: they attempt to derive an *is* from an *ought*. Ultimately the best form of advocacy is a commitment to pursuing the truth about trauma wherever it may lead us.

NOTES

1. The Politics of Trauma

1 For feminists who raised public awareness about incest, see Herman (1981); Rush (1977); Russell (1986). Gorey and Leslie (1997) reviewed prevalence studies on sexual abuse. The most reliable data emerged from Russell's survey of 930 randomly selected San Francisco women. Russell, a sociologist, found that 16 percent of women had experienced incest (defined as any sexual contact between relatives) before age 18, and 6 percent had suffered forcible genital intercourse. Although women were eight times more likely to have been abused by a stepfather than by a biological father, 2.9 percent had experienced some form of incestuous abuse at the hands of their biological fathers (Russell 1986: 388, 99, 234).

2 For other therapeutic goals unrelated to memory recovery see Brown, Scheflin, and Hammond (1998: 436–497).

3 This concept was embodied in van der Kolk's (1994) memorable slogan "The body keeps the score."

4 Bass and Davis published two later editions of *The Courage to Heal*. I quote from the first edition because it has been the most influential of the three.

5 Finkelhor, Williams, and Burns (1988) reviewed daycare studies. Nathan and Snedeker (1995: 115–116) described the disclosures extracted from the children and how they became symptomatic during the investigations.

6 See Shephard (2001) for a history of the conceptualization of combat trauma. Wilson (1994) discussed traumatic diagnoses in the DSMs. Bloch (1969: 290) reported that in his psychiatric service in Vietnam "noncombat troops far outnumber fighting ones (the estimated ratio is 7:1)." Scott (1990) discussed the politicking surrounding the ratification of PTSD.

7 For a review of research on the validity of DSM-IV PTSD, see McNally (1999a).

8 "Eve" did, however, report having been battered by her husband.

9 The clinically trained cognitive psychologist John Kihlstrom defined False Memory Syndrome as "a condition in which a person's identity and interpersonal relationships are centered around a memory of traumatic experience which is objectively false but in which the person strongly believes. Note that the syndrome is not characterized by false memories as such. We all have memories that are inaccurate. Rather, the syndrome may be diagnosed when the memory is so deeply ingrained that it orients the individual's entire personality and lifestyle, in turn disrupting all sorts of other adaptive behavior. The analogy to personality disorder is intentional. False Memory Syndrome is especially destructive because the person assiduously avoids confrontation with any evidence that might challenge the memory. Thus it takes on a life of its own, encapsulated and resistant to correction. The person may become so focused on memory that he or she may be effectively distracted from coping with the real problems in his or her life" (quoted in False Memory Syndrome Foundation 1995: 1; see also Kihlstrom 1997b). For case studies of the effects on families, see Goldstein and Farmer (1994: 1–181).

10 Although renowned hypnosis researchers conclude that there is no evidence that hypnosis enhances accuracy of recollection (e.g., Kihlstrom 1997a; Lynn et al. 1997), some trauma therapists disagree. Because most research on hypnotically refreshed memory concerns nonemotional material, Brown, Scheflin, and Hammond assert that *"although hypnosis does not aid in the recall of meaningless stimuli, it may facilitate recall of personally meaningful information or material associated with emotional situations or aid recall where strong or traumatic emotion impedes memory retrieval"* (1998: 316). Unfortunately, their speculation that hypnosis "may" facilitate retrieval of repressed or dissociated memories of trauma is based on ambiguous clinical anecdotes from World Wars I and II that are open to alternative explanations, not on acceptable scientific evidence (see Chapter 7).

Leavitt (1997) found that patients reporting recovered memories of childhood sexual abuse (CSA) scored significantly *lower* on the Gudjonsson Suggestibility Scale (Gudjonsson 1987) than did women who denied a history of CSA. Brown, Scheflin, and Hammond (1998: 539) interpret this study as evidence against the hypothesis that patients often develop false memories of abuse in therapy. There are two problems with this interpretation. First, scores on this scale did not correlate with those on the Dissociative Experiences Scale (Bernstein and Putnam 1986), a measure known to predict false memory formation (see Chapter 2, p. 74). This raises questions about the Gudjonsson scale's relevance as a measure of proneness to develop false memories. Second, even if the Gudjonsson scale is relevant, Leavitt's results imply that any false memories that do develop are probably attributable to the therapeutic methods themselves rather than to personal characteristics of the patients (e.g., heightened suggestibility).

11 For a history of the MPD movement, see Acocella (1999); for its connection to false memories, e.g., McHugh (1992).

12 Lilienfeld et al. (1999); Spanos (1994). Lilienfeld et al.'s article was a rebuttal to Gleaves's (1996) critique of Spanos's exposition of the sociocognitive model of dissociative identity disorder.

13 Citing Taub (1996), Brown, Scheflin, and Hammond (1998: 16) wrote that "there are an estimated 800 malpractice suits against therapists concerning memory issues, with many more expected to follow." In reality, Taub wrote that there were approximately 800 lawsuits filed *against parents (and others) by psychotherapy patients* on the basis of recovered memories of abuse. Taub was citing Lipton's data on lawsuits against parents whose grown children had initiated legal action on the basis of recovered memories of abuse, not lawsuits against therapists for malpractice. Lawsuits against therapists by third parties are controversial among legal scholars because the therapist is ordinarily seen as having a duty of care only toward the patient, not the relatives of the patient (Bowman and Mertz 1996). A landmark case in California permitted a father to sue his grown daughter's therapists for malpractice for having allegedly implanted false memories that he had sexually abused her.

14 For those interpreting critiques of recovered memory as antifeminist, see Brown (1995a, 1997); Enns et al. (1995). The notion that critiques of "recovered memory therapy" mask a reactionary antifeminist bias is odd. Many leading critics are themselves liberal feminists (e.g., Loftus, Milo, and Paddock 1995; Russell 1986; Tavris 1993).

15 Others have made similar assertions: Alpert (1997: 987) stated that "there is no scientific support to indicate that numerous therapists are creating false memories"; Enns et al. (1995) denied any evidence that members of incest survivor groups feel pressure to confabulate abuse memories.

16 Examples include Post-Incest Syndrome (Blume 1990: xiv), post-Vietnam syndrome (Shatan 1973), repressed memory syndrome (Fredrickson 1992: 40), rape trauma syndrome (Burgess and Holmstrom 1974), and child sexual abuse accommodation syndrome (Summit 1983).

17 These results have often been misconstrued by parties on both sides of the recovered memory debate (Lindsay and Poole 1998).

18 APA Working Group on Investigation of Memories of Childhood Abuse
    (1998); Alpert, Brown, and Courtois (1998a, 1998b, 1998c); Ornstein, Ceci,
    and Loftus (1998a, 1998b, 1998c).

19 Meta-analysis is an established statistical technique for combining results of
    similar studies, thereby enhancing the reliability of the conclusions. As Rind
    and his colleagues emphasized, their findings did "not imply that moral or legal
    definitions of or views on behaviors currently classified as CSA should be
    abandoned or even altered" (47).

20 For multiple perspectives on the controversy, see Baird (2002); Garrison and
    Kobor (2002); Lilienfeld (2002a, 2002b); Rind, Bauserman, and Tromovitch
    (2000a); Rind, Tromovitch, and Bauserman (2000); Sher and Eisenberg
    (2002). Some observers questioned whether studies of college students are
    generalizable to the population at large. But as Rind and his colleagues pointed
    out, college students are not statistically atypical; 50 percent of American
    adults have attended college. Moreover, the results were similar to those of a
    previous meta-analysis done on national population samples (Rind and
    Tromovitch 1997). In fact, the Rind, Tromovitch, and Bauserman (1998)
    meta-analysis may provide a less biased estimate of the association between
    CSA and maladjustment than do studies based on psychiatric samples (e.g.,
    Beitchman et al. 1992).

21 U.S. House of Representatives (1999). The vote was 355–0. An additional 13
    members voted "present" (i.e., abstained from voting). Congressman Brian
    Baird, a clinical psychologist who had treated sexual abuse survivors, described
    why he refused to vote in support of the condemnation (Baird 2002).

22 For critiques of Rind, Tromovitch, and Bauserman, see Dallam et al. (2001);
    Ondersma et al. (2001); Spiegel (2000). For rejoinders, Rind, Bauserman, and
    Tromovitch (2000a, 2000b); Rind, Tromovitch, and Bauserman (2000, 2001).
    For the editors' perspective, Sher and Eisenberg (2002).

2. How We Remember

1   On H.M. see Parkin (1996); Scoville (1954); Milner (1966); Scoville and
    Milner (1957).

2   Parkin (1998) questioned the rigor of the central executive concept. In reply,
    Baddeley (1998) agreed that the central executive is a kind of homunculus—a
    little man in the head who makes all the decisions and performs the cognitive
    duties not performed by the other working-memory subsystems. However, he
    stressed, the central executive is useful as a transitional concept that denotes
    functions that have yet to be fully understood. Once we understand the com-

plex working-memory tasks as well as we do the simpler ones (e.g., phonological loop), we will no longer need to posit a central executive. Just as the concept of the atom fractionated into the concepts of subatomic particles, we can expect the central executive to fractionate into its constituent elements.

3 For critiques, see Manns, Clark, and Squire (2002); Wiens and Öhman (2002). For a cogent rejoinder, Shanks and Lovibond (2002).

4 Brewin, Andrews, and Gotlib (1993) reviewed the literature on the reliability of autobiographical memory.

5 See Roediger and Guynn (1996) for studies on the physical environment and other factors as contextual retrieval cues.

6 On perceptual details, see Johnson et al. (1988) and McGinnis and Roberts (1996); on the effect of thinking or talking about events, Suengas and Johnson (1988); on the effects of imagery ability and dissociation, Hyman and Billings (1998); on emotional focus and source confusion, Johnson, Nolde, and De Leonardis (1996).

7 For a review of childhood amnesia, see White and Pillemer (1979). On visual imagery in early memories, see Kihlstrom and Harackiewicz (1982); on their "snapshot" quality, Eacott (1999); on their emotional content, Dudycha and Dudycha (1933). Eacott and Crawley (1998) and Usher and Neisser (1993) reported adults' memories of salient events that occurred when they were 30 months old.

8 Childhood amnesia, however, is not confined to linguistically represented memories. Three years after leaving preschool, children have great difficulty recognizing photographs of their preschool classmates. Lie and Newcombe (1999) found that children correctly recognized only 28 percent of their former classmates with high certainty, whereas preschool teachers recognized 88 percent of their former students with high certainty.

9 See, e.g., Bauer (1996); Fivush and Hamond (1989); McDonough and Mandler (1994).

10 On the archeology museum trip, see Fivush, Hudson, and Nelson (1984); on the birth of a sibling, Sheingold and Tenney (1982); on distinctive events, Fivush, Gray, and Fromhoff (1987).

11 For arguments in favor of the explicit memory interpretation, see Bauer, Hertsgaard, and Dow (1994); Meltzoff (1995).

12 Psychologists have investigated flashbulb memories for the assassination of Sweden's Prime Minister Olof Palme (Christianson 1989), the explosion of the *Challenger* space shuttle (Bohannon 1988; Bohannon and Symons 1992; McCloskey, Wible, and Cohen 1988; Neisser and Harsch 1992; Warren and Swartwood 1992), the resignation of Britain's Prime Minister Margaret

Thatcher (Conway et al. 1994; Wright, Gaskell, and O'Muircheartaigh 1998), the onset of the Persian Gulf War (Weaver 1993), the accidental death of 95 spectators at a British soccer match (Wright 1993), and a Scandinavian ferry disaster (Christianson and Engelberg 1999).

13 Cohen, McCloskey, and Wible (1988); McCloskey et al. (1988). But see Schmidt and Bohannon (1988) for a dissenting view.

14 Vandermaas, Hess, and Baker-Ward (1993) found that behavioral ratings of higher anxiety among 4- and 5-year-olds predicted enhanced memory for a dental visit, whereas the opposite was true for 7- and 8-year-olds.

15 Reanalyzing Peterson and Bell's data, Peterson and Biggs (1997) found that preschoolers' responses to wh- questions (Who? What? Where?), which require content-laden substantive responses, are more likely to be accurate than their responses to yes/no questions, especially when the child responds "no." Slightly less than half of the "no" responses were correct (i.e., chance level). "Yes" responses were 80–92 percent correct depending on the child's age.

16 Bernstein and Blacher (1967) related an anecdote about a 2-year-old who appeared to recollect a traumatic event she had experienced at the age of 3 months—a painful pneumoencephalogram requiring insertion of a needle into the lower spine for two hours, during which she screamed continuously. Construction work at the hospital resulted in much hammering in a nearby room. At 28 months she exhibited fear when hearing a neighbor hammering nails into a wall. Upon questioning, she described what had happened to her in the hospital when she was much younger: "Man stuck me in the tushie and knocked my head off" (158–159)—a claim she clarified by saying that her head hurt. Bernstein and Blacher speculated that the neighbor's hammering reminded her of the painful hospital episode when she was 3 months old.

17 On these complexities, see Lewontin (1998) for cognition in general and McNally (2001a) for psychopathology.

18 Roediger and McDermott (2000) review research on memory distortion. Memory "errors" are often by-products of otherwise adaptive mechanisms (Schacter 2001). Bruce and Winograd (1998) discuss how social controversies sparked interest in the laboratory study of false memories.

19 Loftus's (1979) book summarizes her initial series of studies, exemplified by Loftus, Miller, and Burns (1978).

20 On subjects' remembering things they have not seen, see, e.g., Roediger, Jacoby, and McDermott (1996); Zaragoza and Mitchell (1996). On confidence in distorted memories, Loftus et al. (1989); Zaragoza and Mitchell (1996). On the effect despite forewarnings, Ackil and Zaragoza (1998); Belli et al. (1994); Lindsay (1990). On repeated exposure to suggestive questions, Mitchell and

Zaragoza (1996); Zaragoza and Mitchell (1996). On questions that likely prompt imagery, Fiedler et al. (1996). On interpolated delays, Belli et al. (1992); Higham (1998).

21 For the consensus on multiple causes, see Loftus and Hoffman (1989); Ayers and Reder (1998). For the memory alteration hypothesis, Loftus and Palmer (1974). For the source confusion hypothesis, Lindsay and Johnson (1989). For the endorse-by-default hypothesis, McCloskey and Zaragoza (1985).

22 Koriat et al. (2000) review the literature on false memory effects in the laboratory. False recall matched true recall in Read (1996), and false recognition matched true recognition in Schacter, Verfaellie, and Pradere (1996). Several studies have shown that false recall persists or even increases over time, whereas veridical recall declines (McDermott 1996; Payne et al. 1996; Toglia, Neuschatz, and Goodwin 1999); but see Lampinen and Schwartz (2000) for an exception. On false recognition for pictures, see Koutstaal and Schacter (1997); on stereotypical scenes, Miller and Gazzaniga (1998).

23 For studies showing *remember* responses for critical lures as often as for studied words, see, e.g., Gallo, Roberts, and Seamon (1997); Payne et al. (1996); Schacter et al. (1996). For studies not showing this effect, see, e.g., Mather, Henkel, and Johnson (1997); Read (1996). False memories were associated with less detail in Norman and Schacter (1997) and endorsed with less confidence in Mather et al. (1997).

24 Multiple retrieval attempts (Payne et al. 1996), increased number of associated words (Robinson and Roediger 1987), emotional stress (Payne et al. 2002), and grouping words by gist (Mather et al. 1997) all increase false memories. Unawareness of the forthcoming test (Tussing and Greene 1997), forewarning about false memory (Gallo et al. 1997; McDermott and Roediger 1998), seeing the study words (Smith and Hunt 1998), and presenting pictures with study words (Israel and Schacter 1997) reduce false memories.

25 Roediger and McDermott (1996) published a rejoinder to Freyd and Gleaves's critique.

26 Some critics have misunderstood James Coan's project as an "experiment" (e.g., K. S. Pope 1995: 304). In reality, it was part of a homework assignment (see Coan 1997). The actual research came later, and was conducted by Loftus and Pickrell. See Loftus (1999) for correction of other misunderstandings of this research (Crook and Dean, 1999a, 1999b).

27 Critics might argue that certain target events actually did occur to certain subjects when they were very young, but that parents had forgotten these events and were unable to recall them even when the researchers asked, for example, "Was your child ever hospitalized overnight with a high fever?" It seems ex-

traordinarily unlikely that parents would have forgotten such emotionally disturbing events. Hence this critique has little merit.

28 The measures were the Dissociative Experiences Scale (Bernstein and Putnam 1986) and the Creative Imagination Scale (Wilson and Barber 1978).

3. What Is Psychological Trauma?

1 On the dose-response model, see March (1993). For conditioning formulations, Keane, Zimering, and Caddell (1985); Pitman, Shalev, and Orr (2000). Foa, Zinbarg, and Rothbaum (1992), and van der Kolk et al. (1985) proposed animal conditioning models of PTSD.

2 On World War II veterans, see Sutker, Allain, and Winstead (1993); on Vietnam veterans, Kulka et al. (1990: 54); on the Armenian earthquake, Pynoos et al. (1993); on Mount St. Helens, Shore, Tatum, and Vollmer (1986); on the Oklahoma City bombing, North et al. (1999).

3 Survival guilt, a symptom of PTSD in DSM-III (APA 1980: 238), differs from guilt over having committed atrocities. On guilt over having enjoyed killing, see Bourke (1999: 203–229); Nadelson (1992). On guilt over having committed atrocities, Haley (1974); Shatan (1973). Breslau and Davis (1987) found that atrocity commission increases risk for PTSD beyond that attributable to combat. For atrocity involvement predicting PTSD severity, see Beckham, Feldman, and Kirby (1998); Yehuda, Southwick, and Giller (1992). Although military archives document atrocities (technically, war crimes) committed by American personnel in Vietnam, one historian who has studied declassified military documents and other sources believes that many atrocity narratives are untrue (Lewy 1978: 307–331). One frequently heard story was that Americans would interrogate groups of suspected Viet Cong (VC) in helicopters. If the prisoners refused to answer questions, one suspected VC would be pushed out of the helicopter to his death to encourage the others to speak. But there has never been a corroborated case of this kind of war crime in Vietnam. Some members of Vietnam Veterans Against the War who claimed to have witnessed atrocities during the war were later discovered never to have served in Vietnam.

4 For Turkish prisoners, see Başoğlu and Mineka (1992); for murderers, Harry and Resnick (1986); for assault survivors, Andrews et al. (2000).

5 Yehuda and McFarlane (1995) provide an excellent critique of the original conceptual foundations of PTSD.

6 Brewin, Andrews, and Valentine (2000); Yehuda (1999). Risk factor research cited here concerns individuals who have always remembered their trauma

(e.g., combat veterans) as opposed to individuals who report having recovered previously repressed memories of trauma.

7 E.g., Boscarino (1995); Keane et al. (1985); Solomon, Mikulincer, and Avitzur (1988).

8 For lower intelligence, see McNally and Shin (1995); Vasterling et al. (1997, 2002). For neuroticism, Breslau et al. (1991); McFarlane (1989). For neurologic soft signs, Gurvits et al. (2000).

9 For family instability, see King et al. (1996). For preexisting mood or anxiety disorder, Breslau et al. (1991); Smith et al. (1990). For family history of mood or anxiety disorders, Breslau et al. (1991); Davidson et al. (1985). For CSA, Engel et al. (1993); Nishith, Mechanic, and Resick (2000). For childhood physical abuse, Bremner, Southwick, et al. (1993); Breslau, Chilcoat, Kessler, and Davis (1999).

10 For Israeli accident victims, see Shalev et al. (1996); for French crime victims, Birmes et al. (2001). For accident victims in Australia, see Harvey and Bryant (1998a); in America, Ursano et al. (1999). Johnson, Pike, and Chard (2001) reported that peritraumatic dissociation predicted severity of PTSD symptoms among women seeking treatment for effects of CSA. But these data were collected retrospectively, not immediately after the trauma.

11 For a review of behavior genetic methods as applied to psychopathology, see Faraone, Tsuang, and Tsuang (1999).

12 The degree of concordance (both twins agreeing that the abuse had occurred) was impressive (weighted kappa = 0.40).

13 For combat veterans see King et al. (1995); for torture survivors, Başoğlu et al. (1994); for burn victims, Perry et al. (1992); for accident survivors, Blanchard et al. (1995); Ehlers, Mayou, and Bryant (1998); Schnyder et al. (2001).

14 For panic disorder, see McNally and Lukach (1992); for spousal infidelity, Helzer, Robins, and McEvoy (1987); for divorce, Burstein (1985a); for miscarriage, Engelhard, van den Hout, and Arntz (2001); for childbirth, Czarnocka and Slade (2000); for *The Exorcist*, Bozzuto (1975); for the frogs, Thyer and Curtis (1983).

15 See Dunmore, Clark, and Ehlers (1999); Ehlers and Clark (2000); Ehlers, Mayou, and Bryant (1998); Mayou, Bryant, and Ehlers (2001).

16 See, e.g., Bremner, Steinberg, et al. (1993); Carlson and Rosser-Hogan (1991); Chu and Dill (1990).

17 On *Chlamydia trachomatis*, see Hammerschlag et al. (1988); on *Neisseria gonorrhoeae*, Whittington et al. (1988).

18 Foster and Huber (1999: 115–117) cite a population sample of 3,825,368 that yielded 1,325 true positives (infected individuals scoring HIV-positive), 23

false negatives (infected individuals scoring HIV-negative), 7,648 false positives (noninfected individuals scoring HIV-positive), and 3,816,372 true negatives (noninfected individuals scoring HIV-negative). The *predictive value* of a test reflects how likely it is to identify individuals correctly. The predictive value is the number of true positives (1,325) divided by the total number of individuals who test positive (1,325 + 7,648). It indicates the percentage of people selected from the general population who test HIV-positive and who are actually infected: $1,325 \div 8,973 = .148$. A predictive value of 14.8 percent means that approximately 6 out of 7 individuals, drawn from the general population, who test positive for HIV will not be infected. See Grove and Barden (1999) on these issues as they apply to expert testimony by psychologists.

4. Memory for Trauma

1 See Sutker, Alain, and Winstead (1993) for POWs and combat veterans; Başoğlu et al. (1994) for Turkish activists; Realmuto et al. (1992) for Cambodians; Foa et al. (1993) for assault victims.

2 Among Kurdish refugees who survived harrowing escapes from (mainly) Iraq, 88.9 percent had had at least one nightmare reminiscent of their trauma during the six months before they were interviewed. The frequency of traumatic nightmares, however, declined as a function of years since the escapes (Husni et al. 2001).

3 Hefez, Metz, and Lavie (1987); Schlosberg and Benjamin (1978); van der Kolk et al. (1984). More specifically, traumatic nightmares can erupt during Stage 2 of non-REM sleep.

4 Glaubman et al. (1990); Greenberg, Pearlman, and Gampel (1972); Lavie et al. (1979). One laboratory study indicated that Vietnam veterans with combat-related PTSD woke up anxiously from REM sleep, often with increases in respiration and heart rate, but without any recall of a preceding dream (Mellman et al. 1995).

5 See MacCurdy (1918: 29) and Rivers (1918) for World War I veterans; Grinker and Spiegel (1945: 92) for World War II veterans; Terr (1979) for kidnapped children.

6 Actually, according to Freud, the white animals symbolized the parents' white underclothes, not the white linen. But I quibble.

7 See Burstein (1985b) on visual imagery and duration; Mellman and Davis (1985) on panic attacks; Burstein (1984) on dream disturbances; Bryant and Harvey (1996) on imagery ability.

8 Mayer and Pope (1997) described the veteran; Grunert et al. (1988) published

data on hand injuries; Merckelbach et al. (1998) studied the traumatized college students.

9 Rynearson and McCreery (1993) studied people who had lost loved ones to murder; Cella et al. (1988) described the man who had flashbacks of his son's scalding; Zeanah (1988) described the woman who had flashbacks of her father's corpse.

10 Terr (1979, 1981, 1988). There are a smattering of case histories regarding memory for early trauma in preverbal children or children who were just beginning to speak. Hewitt (1994) described two children who had been sexually abused, one at 2 years, 7 months, and the other at 2 years, 1 month, when their verbal skills were extremely limited. They later described the events accurately at ages 4 and 6. Both had been referred to therapy for behavioral problems attributed to their abuse. Sugar (1992) described three cases. In one, a girl had survived an airplane accident at 16 months, one month after she had started to speak. In therapy, she spontaneously described the crash at 26 months of age. The second case involved a boy who had begun to speak at 15 months and was in an automobile accident at 24 months. He described the accident again and again. The third case was a woman in her thirties who recalled an anxiety-laden image from the age of 18 months, before she could speak, of her mother standing next to some material on the floor. Her mother confirmed that the toddler had witnessed a miscarriage. She had retained a salient visual image and then described it years later.

11 Terr (1989) does not confine her interpretations to her patients. She has published a detailed exegesis of the life and writings of the novelist Stephen King in which she attributes his career to the fact that a train killed one of his friends when King was a preschooler. Indeed, she stated: "I think it is clear that Stephen King currently suffers many of the symptoms and signs of posttraumatic stress disorder of childhood" (375). She does not make it clear whether King was present when his friend was killed.

12 On heart rate reactivity to audiovisual stimuli, see Blanchard et al. (1982, 1986, 1991); Malloy, Fairbank, and Keane (1983); Pallmeyer, Blanchard, and Kolb (1986). However, exposure to trauma-relevant audiovisual stimuli has not produced larger increases in electrodermal activity (e.g., skin conductance reactivity) in PTSD subjects than in control subjects (Blanchard et al. 1982; Malloy et al. 1983; Pallmeyer et al. 1986).

13 Lang (1985) developed the script-driven imagery paradigm. Studying Vietnam veterans, Pitman et al. (1987) found that skin conductance and EMG were significantly higher in the PTSD group than in a group of healthy combat vet-

erans when subjects in both groups heard scripts depicting their own combat experience. Heart rate showed a nonsignificant trend in the same direction. Studying World War II and Korean war veterans, Orr et al. (1993) used heart rate and skin conductance as the measures of physiologic reactivity. In their study of veterans with anxiety disorders, Pitman et al. (1990) found significant effects for skin conductance and EMG, and heart rate showed a nonsignificant trend in the same direction. Heart rate, EMG, and skin conductance were the measures in the Vietnam nurses study (Carson et al. 2000). Autobiographical trauma scripts have produced greater psychophysiologic reactivity than generic trauma scripts in people with PTSD related to motor vehicle accidents (Blanchard et al. 1994), war-related nursing (Carson et al. 2000), and combat (Orr et al. 1993; Pitman et al. 1987).

14 Studies of accident survivors have shown significant effects for heart rate (Blanchard et al. 1994, 1996) and heart rate and EMG (Shalev, Orr, and Pitman 1993).

15 Patients with panic disorder and agoraphobia—a group known for fearing bodily arousal—also do not respond physiologically to threatening imagery scripts (Zander and McNally 1988).

16 Twenty-eight patients had definitely not lost consciousness but claimed to recall nothing of the accident. Alcohol intoxication, concerns about being prosecuted, and so forth apparently figured in these cases.

17 The proportions of the 96 patients reporting symptoms were: intrusive memories, 19.2 percent; nightmares, 23.1 percent; sense of reliving trauma, 30.8 percent; emotional reactivity, 96.2 percent; physiological reactivity, 50 percent.

18 See Brewin (2001); Brewin, Dalgleish, and Joseph (1996); Joseph and Masterson (1999).

19 Lovibond and Shanks (2002); Shanks and Lovibond (2002).

5. Mechanisms of Traumatic Memory

1 Axelrod and Milner did not assess for PTSD in their subjects. For cognitive impairments in PTSD, see Buckley, Blanchard, and Neill (2000).

2 Stein et al. used the California Verbal Learning Test (CVLT) and the Benton Visual Retention Task; 77.3 percent of the abuse survivors had PTSD. Jenkins et al. used the CVLT.

3 Studying Vietnam veterans, Bremner's group used items from the Wechsler Memory Scale (WMS) that require subjects to recount two stories in logical order. Other tests required subjects to learn and recall a list of words and to view and then reproduce designs (Bremner, Scott, et al. 1993). Studying Vietnam veterans, Yehuda, Keefe, et al. (1995) detected a very specific memory

deficit on the CVLT. Subjects were exposed to Word List A five times, trying to recall the words immediately after each presentation. They then attempted to learn Word List B, then tried to recall List A immediately and again 20 minutes later. Relative to healthy control subjects, those with PTSD had difficulty recalling Word List A after having learned Word List B. Bremner's group tested abuse survivors. The verbal test was the logical memory task from the Wechsler Adult Intelligence Scale (WAIS), and the visual test required subjects to draw designs that they had viewed only briefly. Deficits were not apparent on the visual test. Nonabused control subjects did not exhibit deficits on either task (Bremner, Randall, Scott, Capelli, et al. 1995). Beers and De Bellis (2002) studied children who had either been physically or sexually abused or witnessed domestic violence. These children exhibited attentional problems, but not memory difficulties.

4 Barrett et al. used the CVLT. They used the Rey-Osterrieth Complex Figure Drawing Test to assess visual memory.

5 Sutker et al. (1990) found that on the immediate recall index of the WMS, high-weight-loss subjects performed worse than POWs who had lost less weight, who in turn performed worse than non-POW combat veterans. The high-weight-loss group also performed worse than other combat veterans on the delayed recall index.

6 Verbal memory was tested by the CVLT, and visual memory by the Rey-Osterrieth Complex Figure Drawing Test.

7 Eich et al. (1997); Nissen et al. (1988); Peters et al. (1998).

8 Healthy combat veterans never wore military regalia to the laboratory. Although our PTSD group exhibited overgeneral retrieval, this was especially true for the 7 of 19 PTSD subjects who wore regalia.

9 Severity of dissociative symptoms was negatively related to memory specificity when subjects were asked to recall memories from any period in their lives, $r = -.45$. However, both groups easily recalled specific memories from the accident period in response to negative cues (88.3 percent for those with ASD; 91.7 percent for the others).

10 Reviere and Bakeman (2001) found few differences in autobiographical memory functioning between college students with and without early trauma histories. However, they used different methods from those used in the overgeneral memory studies.

11 The British terms for norepinephrine and epinephrine are noradrenaline and adrenaline. CRF is also known as corticotropin releasing hormone (CRH). Adrenocorticotropic hormone is also known as corticotropin.

12 Bremner et al. did not control statistically for possible differences in whole

brain volume between patients and controls. Instead, they directly compared hippocampal volumes between patients and control subjects. This approach is entirely justifiable on statistical and logical grounds, assuming that one has controlled for height and sex. "Correcting" statistically for differences in overall brain volume can produce highly misleading results for a variety of mathematical reasons (Arndt et al. 1991). Bremner and colleagues (Bremner, Randall, Scott, Bronen, et al. 1995: 979) suggested that "dysfunction of the hippocampus may offer an explanation for the fragmentation of memories into single sensory phenomena that are seen clinically in patients with PTSD."

13 Twelve of the PTSD patients were men. The volume of the left amygdala was 15 percent smaller in patients than in controls, but this difference fell just short of statistical significance.

14 The abused and control groups were matched in terms of age, handedness, height, weight, education, and socioeconomic status. The measure of dissociative symptoms was the Dissociative Experiences Scale, and the measure of explicit memory was the CVLT. Hippocampal volumes were computed as a percentage of brain slice volume. Sapolsky cited a personal communication from Stein.

15 There were no differences between PTSD subjects and control subjects in terms of whole brain volume, amygdaloid volume, ventricular volume, or ventricular-brain ratio. Self-reported extent of combat exposure, however, predicted smaller hippocampal volume, suggesting that this variable, rather than PTSD per se, may figure in any hippocampal atrophy ($r = .72$). But severity of PTSD symptoms was also highly correlated with extent of combat exposure ($r = .82$).

16 The researchers controlled for overall brain volume differences by entering the volume of the prosencephalon as a covariate.

17 For critiques of the atrophy hypothesis, see Kihlstrom and Schacter (2000); Pitman (2001); Yehuda (2001).

18 Pitman and Orr (1990) found elevated levels in veterans, and Lemieux and Coe (1995) in women with childhood sexual abuse histories. Although values are not invariably in the low-normal range, even when PTSD patients show high levels of cortisol they rarely get as high as those with endocrinological disorders.

19 Finally, risk for PTSD is higher among victims of motor vehicle accidents (McFarlane, Atchison, and Yehuda 1997) or rape (Resnick et al. 1995) whose plasma cortisol levels are *low* shortly after the trauma. Resnick et al.'s subjects, however, had histories of previous assault.

20 Gilbertson's results are not the only evidence of genetic influence on hippo-

campal volume. Studying monkeys, Lyons et al. (2001) found that volume differences were related to genetic differences among the monkeys, not to differences in the stressfulness of their environments. Lyons et al. concluded that small hippocampi "reflect an inherited characteristic of the brain" (1145).

21 For emotional Stroop studies on people with PTSD related to combat, see also Kaspi, McNally, and Amir (1995); Litz et al. (1996); McNally, English, and Lipke (1993); McNally, Amir, and Lipke (1996); Vrana, Roodman, and Beckham (1995). On sexually abused children see Dubner and Motta (1999); on motor vehicle accident survivors, Bryant and Harvey (1995b); on survivors of a sea disaster, Thrasher, Dalgleish, and Yule (1994).

22 Riemann and McNally (1995) found that congruence between Stroop words and current personal concerns produces interference, even among nonclinical subjects. Consistent with reports of overall concentration impairments, subjects with PTSD often are slower to color-name words overall than are healthy trauma survivors (Cassiday et al. 1992; Kaspi et al. 1995; Metzger et al. 1997). But they are slowest when it comes to naming the colors of trauma words. Among rape survivors, Stroop interference was more strongly correlated with self-reported intrusive reexperiencing symptoms of PTSD ($r = .41$) than with self-reported avoidance and numbing symptoms ($r = .14$; Cassiday et al. 1992; McNally 1998).

23 Stroop interference for personally significant emotional material is not confined to PTSD. For example, people with either generalized anxiety disorder (Mathews and MacLeod 1985) or panic disorder (McNally, Riemann, and Kim 1990) exhibit delayed color-naming of threat words relevant to their concerns. Just as people afraid of snakes, but not of spiders, exhibit physiologic arousal only to the former, so do people exhibit emotional Stroop interference. Nevertheless, the magnitude of emotional Stroop interference appears much higher in PTSD patients than in patients with other disorders, let alone in healthy control subjects (Williams et al. 1996).

Metzger et al. (1997) had PTSD patients and healthy control subjects perform an emotional Stroop task while monitoring their brain wave activity (EEG). They measured the amplitude and latency of each P3 response to each Stroop word. P3 is a positive EEG response that occurs 300 milliseconds following stimulus onset, usually triggered by either novel or personally relevant stimuli. Metzger found that although PTSD patients exhibited the trauma-related Stroop interference effect, there were no P3 latency differences as a function of word type (trauma, positive, or neutral). If encoding of stimulus color were disrupted by primed trauma concepts in memory, then the P3 latencies to trauma words should have been slowed down just as the color-naming of these words was slowed down. Because this did not happen, Metzger concluded that trauma-related interference occurs because PTSD patients have difficulty suppressing the meanings of trauma words once they are activated. Intrusive cognition in PTSD may be more strongly related to difficulty removing disturbing material from working memory than to the ease with which it enters working memory in the first place.

24 Harvey, Bryant, and Rapee (1996); Buckley, Blanchard, and Hickling (2002); McNally et al. (1996). For the varied meanings of automatic cognitive processing in the study of anxiety, see McNally (1995).

25 However, the effect reached statistical significance only when PTSD patients heard trauma-related sentences against the loudest of three levels of white noise.

26 Gelinas (1983); Terr (1991); Herman and Schatzow (1987); Freyd (1996).

6. *Theories of Repression and Dissociation*

1 Breuer and Freud (1893: 9, 10–12, 9, 6); Freud (1893: 38). The terms "abreaction" and "catharsis," often used by Breuer and Freud, refer to the expression of previously repressed emotion.

2 On changes in Freud's story over time, see Cioffi (1974); Israëls and Schatzman (1993); Schimek (1987). For the revisionist account, see Masson (1984), and for its impact among psychoanalysts, see Malcolm (1984).

3 Freud never denied the reality of incest or its pathogenic potential. As he remarked in a 1924 footnote added to a reprinted version of one of his early seduction papers, "Seduction retains a certain aetiological importance" (Freud 1896b: 168). What he did retract was the notion that all cases of hysteria arise from repressed memories of seduction.

Masson's theory was foreshadowed by Florence Rush (1977), a feminist scholar who likewise accused Freud of attempting to conceal the prevalence of incest. In Rush's opinion, Freud detected symptoms of hysteria in himself and his siblings, and was reluctant to conclude that his father had been a child molester.

4 See also Breuer and Freud (1895: 295); Freud (1937).

5 Skues (1998) has expressed concern that critics of Freud's seduction theory have relied on Strachey's authorized English translation of Freud's works rather than reading them in the original German. But Esterson (2001) has shown that Skues's concern is unfounded. For example, leading scholars *did* consult the original German edition of Freud's works, even when their English-language publications quote from Strachey's translation (e.g., Israëls and Schatzman 1993). Moreover, the alleged "mistranslations" are best viewed as

"free" translations, especially because they do not alter the main points being made by Freud.

6 Herman (1992: 18–20). See Gleaves and Hernandez (1999) for a recent version of Masson's thesis, and Esterson (2002a) for a devastating critique of Gleaves and Hernandez's scholarship.

7 See Bowers and Farvolden (1996); Crews (1995); Kihlstrom (1995).

8 For a cogent critique of Mollon's book, see Esterson (submitted). Among the many claims made by Mollon debunked by Esterson is that concerning Freud's alleged corroboration of several recovered "memories" from his hysteria patients.

9 Mollon (2000) and Talbot (1999) are two authors who make these mistakes.

10 For a thorough psychoanalytic critique of recovered memory therapy, see Brenneis (1997b).

11 According to one dictionary of psychology, "Repression should not be confused with suppression or inhibition. Both of the latter processes are voluntary. The essential mechanism of repression was held by Freud to be unconscious and involuntary" (Chaplin 1968: 423). The entry for *suppression* reads: "conscious inhibition of impulses or ideas which are incompatible with the individual's evaluation of himself according to his ego ideal. *Contr.* REPRESSION" (490). See Erdelyi (1990); Erdelyi and Goldberg (1979).

12 Some trauma therapists dismiss Holmes's (1974, 1990) conclusion, stressing that his was a minority view among the contributors to an edited book on the topic of repression and dissociation (e.g., Brown, Scheflin, and Hammond 1998: 609). However, given that the contributors were chosen for their interest in repression, it is unsurprising that Holmes's view was atypical.

13 On directed forgetting, see Bjork (1972); on cognitive avoidance, Foa and Kozak (1986).

14 Brown and van der Hart (1998); van der Hart and Friedman (1989); van der Hart (1996); and van der Kolk and van der Hart (1989) favor *dissociation* over *repression*. Brown, Scheflin, and Hammond (1998: 538–539) use these terms interchangeably, but prefer *dissociation*.

15 Whitfield listed "*intrusive* memories, *unconscious* memories, *abreactions* (dramatic reexperiencing of the trauma) and *flashbacks, psychological* memories, *somatic* (physical) memories, *avoidance of the experience* of memories, and *partial or total amnesia* for the event or events" (1997: 108–109).

16 For reviews of the literature on childhood PTSD, see McNally (1991, 1993).

17 For physical abuse, see Pelcovitz et al. (1994); for chronic community violence, Fitzpatrick and Boldizar (1993); for the Cambodian holocaust, Kinzie et al. (1986).

18 For example, Freyd (1996: 152–153) cited Cameron's (1994, 1996) research as showing that people who have been sexually abused by their parents experience complete amnesia for their trauma more often than people abused by noncaretakers. But Cameron verified neither abuse history nor amnesia, and also mentioned that 10 percent of her cases were victims of ritualistic abuse, raising questions about the reliability of the recovered memories.

19 Other theorists who have sought to explain forgetting of trauma in neuroscientific terms include Bremner, Krystal, et al. (1996), Jacobs and Nadel (1998), and Joseph (1999).

20 However, as Brenneis (1997a) has pointed out, the case of Irène is ambiguous, at best. No one else was present at her mother's death, so it is impossible to tell whether her odd behavior was a reenactment of her actions that night. Moreover, Janet's knowledge about her mother's death may have skewed his interpretation of Irène's actions as reenactments.

An irony of the Janet revival is his use of hypnosis to implant false memories of a nontraumatic past. Using his "substitution technique," Janet claimed to have replaced a traumatic memory with a nontraumatic version of the same event in 26 patients who suffered from intrusive recollections (van der Hart 1996).

7. *Traumatic Amnesia*

1 For disentangling organic from psychogenic amnesia, see De Renzi et al. (1995); Lucchelli, Muggia, and Spinnler (1995); Markowitsch (1999). For psychological stressors triggering retrograde amnesia, Kopelman, Green, et al. (1994). For distinguishing genuine from simulated amnesia, Barbarotto, Laiacona, and Cocchini (1996).

2 For suicidal ideation, see Abeles and Schilder (1935). For attempted suicide, Gudjonsson and Haward (1982); Takahashi (1988). For rape, Christianson and Nilsson (1989); Kaszniak et al. (1988). For bereavement with suicidal ideation, Domb and Beaman (1991). For believing one has killed a friend, Fisher and Joseph (1949).

3 For disappointments in love, see Kanzer (1939); for death of a grandparent, Schacter et al. (1982); for financial problems, Wilson, Rupp, and Wilson (1950); for family conflict, Abeles and Schilder (1935); for legal problems, Gudjonsson and Taylor (1985); for adultery, Geleerd, Hacker, and Rapaport (1945).

4 For timing of recovery, see Abeles and Schilder (1935); Kanzer (1939); Wilson, Rupp, and Wilson (1950). For persistent amnesia, Markowitsch et al. (1997); Sengupta, Jena, and Saxena (1993).

5 For "weak personality," see Abeles and Schilder (1935); for head injury, Berrington, Liddell, and Foulds (1956); for suicidal ideation, Stengel (1941); for interpersonal problems, Kapur (1991). As discussed later in this chapter, several psychiatrists during World War II did report cases of apparent fugue during the evacuation of Dunkirk and other engagements. As these doctors sometimes noted, it was unclear whether the accompanying amnesia was genuine or feigned.

6 Brown, Scheflin, and Whitfield (1999: 28, 27). All emphasis in quotations is from the original.

7 Like Brown, Bessel van der Kolk routinely confuses everyday memory problems with an inability to remember the trauma itself. For example, van der Kolk and Fisler (1995) misinterpret Wilkinson's study as showing that "amnesia, with later return of memories for all, or parts, of the trauma, has been noted following natural disasters and accidents" (509). On torture survivors, see Goldfeld et al. (1988). On the toxic spill, Bowler et al. (1994) note that widespread media attention "undoubtedly served to imprint and solidify the memory of the disaster" (617). On ambushed soldiers, see Feinstein (1989). Eaton, Sigal, and Weinfeld (1982) reported that 15 percent of the Holocaust survivors said they had a "memory problem," but so did 11 percent of the control group.

8 For example: Of 228 sexual abuse survivors in a questionnaire study, 65 said they had repressed their memories of unwanted sexual experiences that occurred before age 16 (Roesler and Wind 1994). Of 23 college students who reported sexual abuse, 11 said there had been a time when they had "been unable to remember" the abuse (Sheiman 1993: 16). Of 234 college students who reported unwanted sexual contact during childhood in a questionnaire study, 71 said there had been a time when they "could not remember" the abuse (Epstein and Bottoms 1998: 1224). In a survey of 613 college students, 9 percent of men and 14 percent of women reported having recovered a "repressed memory," and 23 percent of the recovered memories concerned sexual assault (Golding, Sanchez, and Sego 1996). Of 55 women in a substance abuse program who reported histories of childhood sexual abuse (CSA), 10 reported having entirely forgotten the abuse and another 6 reported having forgotten parts of it (Loftus, Polonsky, and Fullilove 1994). Of 45 women seeking treatment for effects of CSA, 25 reported having been "amnesic for their abuse" (Rodriguez et al. 1997: 56). When 105 patients seeking treatment for effects of CSA were asked in an interview whether there had ever been a period of time lasting at least one year when they were unable to remember any or all of their abuse, 31 said they had completely blocked it out; 10 said they had had a

vague sense or suspicion that they had been abused, but no definite memory; 15 said they had had only partial memory; 17 said they had remembered at least one entire episode, but not all of them; and 32 said they had always had fairly complete memory for most or all of their abuse episodes (Gold, Hughes, and Hohnecker 1994). When 160 women in a program for adult survivors of CSA were asked "At the present time, to what degree are you able to remember the sexual abuse that occurred in your childhood?" and "Was there ever a period of time when for at least 1 full year you were unable to remember any or all of the abuse?" 47 reported having entirely repressed all memories of their abuse; 21 had suspected they might have been abused but had no explicit memories; 18 had only partial "memories," such as flashback images; 29 entirely remembered at least one episode of abuse, but had forgotten others; and 45 had fairly complete memories of all their abuse experiences; only 9 patients still had no definite memories of abuse at the time of the intake interview; 46.3 percent of the patients reported that their memories of abuse had increased, rather than faded, over time; and memory—or lack thereof—for abuse was unrelated to its reported severity (Gold, Hughes, and Swingle 1999). Of 32 women in group treatment for CSA, 37 percent "reported that they forgot the abuse for a period of their lives" (Koopman, Gore-Felton, and Spiegel 1997: 74). Coons, Bowman, and Milstein (1997) reported that relative to patients with affective disorders, such as depression, those with dissociative disorders, such as MPD, more often reported having partially or fully forgotten traumatic events (96 percent versus 24 percent), including CSA (36 percent versus 3 percent). Of 173 counseling and clinical psychologists who returned a mailed questionnaire about their abuse histories, 34 women and 24 men reported having been sexually abused in childhood, and all of these except 1 woman and 1 man remembered at least some of the traumatic events (the 2 subjects claiming to have been totally amnesic had recovered their memories during psychotherapy; Polusny and Follette 1996). In a survey of counselors, 32 percent of those reporting CSA claimed to have had a period of time when they "could not remember" any of the abuse (Fish and Scott 1999).

9 Binder, McNiel, and Goldstone (1994) cited 11 subjects (among 30 recruited from the community) who reported having been entirely amnesic for their sexual abuse. Six credited psychotherapy with aiding memory retrieval, but not all recovered memories were credible. One subject remembered having been sexually molested between the ages of 18 months and $3\frac{1}{2}$ years. In another study (Cameron 1994), 10 percent of subjects recalled memories of ritualistic abuse. In another study (Dale and Allen 1998), what subjects considered recovered memories included feelings, dreams, and visual images.

10 In contrast, Hovdestad and Kristiansen (1996) reported that 51 of 113 sexual abuse survivors recruited from the community reported having recovered memories of CSA which they believed they would not have been able to recall previously.

11 Likewise, Albach, Moormann, and Bermond (1996) reported that 86 of 97 sexual abuse survivors said they intentionally avoided thinking about the abuse.

12 See Loftus, Garry, and Feldman (1994) for other nonrepression explanations for Williams's data.

13 This research group also studied 12 convicted murderers (one a woman) with dissociative identity disorder. They located social service, legal, and medical records documenting physical and sexual abuse suffered by the murderers when they were children. Four subjects for whom documented abuse was very severe denied ever having been physically or sexually abused. Seven other subjects acknowledged having been abused but said their memories were fragmentary. Three interpretive issues are relevant. First, the researchers state that their subjects denied or minimized their abuse when "in their usual personality states" (Lewis et al. 1997: 1707), thereby raising the question of whether memories of documented abuse were accessible to "alters." Second, for some subjects, the abuse had occurred when they were very young (for example, 3 years old). Accordingly, it is not surprising that memories of the abuse would be vague or nonexistent many years later. Third, this study did not include a clarification interview in which subjects were asked about the discrepancy between documentation of trauma and their later denial. Hence it is unclear whether the 4 subjects who denied having been abused failed to remember the abuse or merely failed to disclose it.

14 See Robinson et al. (1990); Robinson, Rapaport-Bar-Sever, and Rapaport (1994); Wagenaar and Groeneweg (1990).

15 See Savin et al. (1996) for Cambodia; Weine, Becker, McGlashan, Laub, et al. (1995) for Bosnia; Langer (1991) for testimony archived at Yale.

16 Strom et al. (1962) noted memory complaints in Holocaust survivors, many with head injuries. Eaton et al. (1982) compared memory complaints of Holocaust survivors with those of other immigrants, and Wagenaar and Groeneweg (1990) documented vivid, accurate memories for concentration camp experiences. Van der Hart and Brom (2000) reviewed the literature on memory for the Holocaust. Also, Weine, Becker, McGlashan, Vojvoda, et al. (1995) reported that only 2 of 12 Bosnian survivors of the 1990s genocide reported a "little bit" of amnesia, whereas the others reported no amnesia.

17 Weisæth (1989) noted that 4 of 13 Norwegian seamen who had been tortured

as spies by the Libyan government complained of "amnesia." Because none of them forgot having been tortured, it is unclear what was meant by amnesia.

18 In another study, Solomon et al. (1994) administered questionnaires to 164 Israelis who had been POWs of the 1973 Yom Kippur War, 112 soldiers suffering combat stress reaction, and 184 combat veterans as controls. About 60 percent of the combat stress reaction group, 50 percent of the control group, and 45 percent of the POWs reported "difficulty remembering aspects of the war." Given that the assessments occurred about 20 years after the war, it is not surprising that about half of all participants had problems remembering parts of it. Whether these respondents would have reported difficulty remembering aspects of other experiences that had happened 20 years previously is unknown.

19 For military psychiatry, see Fisher (1943); Grinker and Spiegel (1944); Henderson and Moore (1944); Kubie (1943); MacCurdy (1918: 93); Myers (1915); Thom and Fenton (1920); Torrie (1944); Sargant and Slater (1940, 1941).

20 For doubts about the reports' validity, see Lilienfeld and Loftus (1998); Pendergrast (1998); Piper (1998). For false memories emerging under hypnosis, Lynn et al. (1997). On barbiturates, Piper (1993). On memories versus fears of what might have happened, Grinker and Spiegel (1945: 61–62). On combat memories in men who did not go to war, Pendergrast (1998). For corroborated war events, Myers (1915). For evidence of suggestive interventions, Fisher (1945); Grinker and Spiegel (1944). Cassiday and Lyons (1992) described a 66-year-old World War II veteran who began to experience PTSD symptoms after his son suffered a severe head injury. After suffering four strokes, the veteran began recalling memories of having been an intelligence officer in the Far East following the war, and of having been captured, tortured, and given intravenous hallucinogenic drugs. He also recalled his escape, his debriefing by the American military, and having received medications and undergone many hypnosis sessions designed to make him forget his traumatic experiences. The purpose of these sessions, he said, was to help him form a new identity that excluded memories of his secret intelligence work. Consulting his military records, Cassiday and Lyons found no record of classified assignments. This virtually assures that his stories were confabulations: as Burkett and Whitley (1998: 285–286) point out, only the specific details of covert assignments are redacted from a veteran's military record, leaving the dates and the phrase "Classified Assignment."

21 See, e.g., Szajnberg (1993); Rosen (1955); Viederman (1995).

22 For Cheit's archive, see <www.brown.edu/Departments/Taubman_Center/ Recovmem/Archive.html>. See also Cheit (1998, 1999).

8. *False Memories of Trauma*

1 Eighteen percent of the cases in the files of the False Memory Syndrome Foundation concerned allegations of satanic ritual abuse (False Memory Syndrome Foundation, 1995). The American Bar Association reported that approximately 25 percent of prosecuting attorneys had handled such cases as of 1991 (Qin et al. 1998, citing Smith, Elstein, Trost, and Bulkley 1993). The terms *satanic ritual abuse*, *ritual abuse*, and *sadistic ritual abuse* refer to essentially the same thing. The similarities among these alleged phenomena greatly exceed the differences (such as whether Satan is directly worshipped). For examples of memories of satanic abuse, see Ross (1995); Smith and Pazder (1980).

2 For confirmation that few reported satanic abuse before beginning therapy, see Young (1992); Young et al. (1991). For depression as the presenting complaint, Bottoms, Shaver, and Goodman (1996); for infant sacrifice and cannibalism, Schaffer and Cozolino (1992).

3 Alpert, Brown, and Courtois (1998b) discuss Hammond's hypnosis guidelines, and Ofshe and Watters (1994: 187–193) quote Hammond on his theory of multiple personality. Hammond (1992) expounded his theory in a lecture given at a conference on abuse and multiple personality. An audiotape of his lecture had been sold by Audio Transcripts of Alexandria, VA.

4 Therapists who concur with Hammond include Blume (1995), and Gould and Cozolino (1992).

5 Bloom (1994) emphasizes similarities across accounts; Jonker and Jonker-Bakker (1997) stress the absence of fabrication motives; Leavitt and Labott (1998) studied responses to "cult" words.

6 For example, professors of English literature (Showalter 1997: 182–183) and of sociology (Ofshe and Watters 1994: 187–193; Victor 1993: 294–295) have discussed Hammond's theory.

7 The 2,722 psychologists who returned legible, valid replies constituted 46 percent of those who had been contacted. In a study of San Diego County therapists, Bucky and Dalenberg (1992) found that only a handful of therapists saw the bulk of cases of ritual abuse. Unfortunately the response rate for their questionnaire was only 10 percent.

8 On the Ingram case see Wright (1994). Some psychotherapists, such as Olio and Cornell (1998), believe Ingram did commit the crimes he recalled during his interrogation. For a critique of this view, see Ofshe (1992, 1994); for a case in which an innocent person was cajoled into confessing to a murder, Gudjonsson, Kopelman, and MacKeith (1999).

9 He mentions this accusation in Lanning (1992). Bottoms and Davis (1997),

who also observed that believers in satanic abuse suspected skeptics of being members of the cult, wrote: "These kinds of beliefs are nothing short of paranoid and would seem to be dangerous guides for professional therapy" (124).

10 Some dissociative disorder specialists object to the comparison, noting that urban legends are rarely traceable to anyone providing first-hand testimony of having experienced the events in question, whereas ritual abuse survivors are recounting their own direct experience of satanic atrocities (Ross 1995: 91). Of course, this objection presupposes the truth of the satanic "memories" that surface in therapy.

11 Although some people did practice magic during the Middle Ages, Cohn stresses that they were not satanists (131).

12 Osborn (2000: 34). Although the Pawnee leader Petalesharo formally abolished the "Morning Star" human sacrifice ritual in 1817, the last (unauthorized) documented case occurred in 1838. See <www.nativepubs.com/nativepubs/Apps/bios/0225Petalesharo.asp?pic=nor>.

13 At an Anasazi site (dated 1150 CE), scientists discovered traces of human myoglobin, a protein common in muscle cells, in fossilized human feces. This discovery confirmed osteological evidence that human beings had been defleshed, cooked, and eaten at this site. For accusations of cannibalism, see Arens (1979); for Dahmer, Keppel, and Birnes (1997: 263–290); for the Donner party, Stewart (1960); for lost mariners, Philbrick (2000).

14 Attendees at these seminars came from all mental health disciplines, and in fact belief in satanic ritual abuse is not confined to poorly trained paraprofessionals: level of professional training is unrelated to belief in satanic cults (Bucky and Dalenberg 1992; Qin et al. 1998).

15 Mulhern (1992) witnessed these methods being taught at the continuing education seminars.

16 For these rates see Bottoms, Shaver, and Goodman (1996); Leavitt and Labott (1998); Schaffer and Cozolino (1992); Young et al. (1991).

17 These rates are from Bottoms, Shaver, and Goodman (1996); Lawrence, Cozolino, and Foy (1995); Young et al. (1991).

18 For persistent denial followed by disclosure, see Jonker and Jonker-Bakker (1997); Snow and Sorensen (1990). For similarities to adult ritual abuse reports, see Finkelhor, Williams, and Burns (1988). For symptoms developing after disclosure, see Gould (1992); Kelley, Brant, and Waterman (1993); Snow and Sorenson (1990).

19 See Ceci and Bruck 1993; Ceci and Friedman 2000; Ceci and Huffman 1997.

20 Bruck and Ceci (1995); Ceci, Bruck, and Rosenthal (1995). Ceci and Friedman (2000) rebut Lyon's (1999) critique.

21 Researchers reporting sexualized play were August and Forman (1989); Jampole and Weber (1987); White et al. (1986). Cohn (1991) did not find it. For rarity of simulated sexual play with the dolls, see Sivan et al. (1988); White et al. (1986); Cohn (1991); Jampole and Weber (1987); Glaser and Collins (1989).

22 For case studies of retractors, see Goldstein and Farmer (1993); Pendergrast (1996: 344–397).

23 The proportions are: 56.2 percent (Feldman-Summers and Pope 1994); 68 percent (Westerhof et al. 2000); 28 percent (Herman and Harvey 1997); 54 percent (Binder, McNiel, and Goldstone 1994); 28 percent (Chu et al. 1999); 60.8 percent (Hovdestad and Kristiansen 1996); 27 percent (Cameron 1996); 16 percent (Rodriguez et al. 1997); 41 percent (Orr et al. 1998); 68 percent (Andrews et al. 1999); and 14 percent (Elliott 1997).

9. A View from the Laboratory

1 The measures we used were the Beck Depression Inventory (Beck and Steer 1987); the Dissociative Experiences Scale (Bernstein and Putnam 1986); and the civilian version (Vreven et al. 1995) of the Mississippi Scale for Combat-Related Posttraumatic Stress Disorder (Keane, Caddell, and Taylor 1988).

2 Using a variant of the imagination-inflation paradigm, Mazzoni et al. (1999) found that having a clinician interpret a student's dream as indicative of a repressed memory of a mildly traumatic experience that had occurred before the age of 3 (such as being lost in a public place) boosted the subject's subsequent confidence that the event had actually occurred, even though the subject had denied it on the baseline assessment. This study suggests that an authority figure, such as a clinical psychologist, might foster false memories by interpreting a patient's dreams as evidence of repressed memories.

10. Controversies on the Horizon

1 The DD-214 lists the veteran's military occupational specialty, awards, and dates of service. Most PTSD researchers have required no more corroboration of traumatic exposure than a photocopy of the DD-214. But it is easy to forge combat exposure on a DD-214 by simply, for example, typing "Purple Heart" on the form. Moreover, the clerk-typists responsible for filling out these discharge papers sometimes omit important items such as Air Medals earned by a helicopter pilot. Hence a DD-214 can either overestimate or underestimate exposure to trauma. A veteran's official military file is much less vulnerable to either of these problems.

2 Following Burkett and Whitley's lead, I obtained military records from the Na-

tional Personnel Records Center for 34 of my PTSD subjects. I found no case of a phony Vietnam veteran; for example, there were no "infantrymen" who spent the war as a cook in Fort Riley, Kansas. Although details of the files varied, evidence of exposure to combat was clear for most of them (e.g., Combat Infantryman's Badge, Purple Hearts). The absence of "phony vets" in this small pilot study suggests that men who volunteer for research studies may differ from those who have caught the attention of Burkett and Whitley, who studied men whose public statements and actions seemed suspicious in the first place.

3 For the savagery of the Pacific Theater, see Manchester (1979); O'Donnell (2002); Pearson (2001).

4 However, some critics have argued that Shay's patients have hoodwinked him by telling wild, fabricated atrocity tales (see Burkett and Whitley 1998: 283–288; Farrell 1995; Spinrad 1995).

WORKS CITED

Abeles, M., and Schilder, P. 1935. Psychogenic loss of personal identity: Amnesia. *Archives of Neurology and Psychiatry, 34,* 587–604.

Ackil, J. K., and Zaragoza, M. S. 1998. Memorial consequences of forced confabulation: Age differences in susceptibility to false memories. *Developmental Psychology, 34,* 1358–72.

Acocella, J. 1999. *Creating hysteria: Women and multiple personality disorder.* San Francisco: Jossey-Bass.

Adler, A. 1943. Neuropsychiatric complications in victims of Boston's Cocoanut Grove disaster. *JAMA, 123,* 1098–1101.

Adolphs, R., Tranel, D., and Denburg, N. 2000. Impaired emotional declarative memory following unilateral amygdala damage. *Learning and Memory, 7,* 180–186.

Agartz, I., Momenan, R., Rawlings, R. R., Kerich, M. J., and Hommer, D. W. 1999. Hippocampal volume in patients with alcohol dependence. *Archives of General Psychiatry, 56,* 356–363.

Albach, F., Moormann, P. P., and Bermond, B. 1996. Memory recovery of childhood sexual abuse. *Dissociation, 9,* 261–273.

Alexander, D. A., and Wells, A. 1991. Reactions of police officers to body-handling after a major disaster: A before-and-after comparison. *British Journal of Psychiatry, 159,* 547–555.

Alexander, E. R. 1988. Misidentification of sexually transmitted organisms in children: Medicolegal implications. *Pediatric Infectious Disease Journal, 7,* 1–2.

Alpert, J. 1994. Analytic reconstruction in the treatment of an incest survivor. *Psychoanalytic Review, 81*, 217–235.

Alpert, J. L. 1997. Unsubstantiated claims of false memory and essential responsibilities. *American Psychologist, 52*, 987.

Alpert, J. L., Brown, L. S., and Courtois, C. A. 1998a. Symptomatic clients and memories of childhood abuse: What the trauma and child sexual abuse literature tells us. *Psychology, Public Policy, and Law, 4*, 941–995.

———— 1998b. Reply to Ornstein, Ceci, and Loftus (1998): The politics of memory. *Psychology, Public Policy, and Law, 4*, 1011–24.

———— 1998c. Comment on Ornstein, Ceci, and Loftus (1998): Adult recollections of childhood abuse. *Psychology, Public Policy, and Law, 4*, 1052–67.

American Psychiatric Association (APA). 1980. *Diagnostic and statistical manual of mental disorders.* 3rd ed. [DSM-III.] Washington.

———— 1987. *Diagnostic and statistical manual of mental disorders.* 3rd ed., rev. [DSM-III-R.] Washington.

———— 1994. *Diagnostic and statistical manual of mental disorders.* 4th ed. [DSM-IV.] Washington.

Amir, N., McNally, R. J., and Wiegartz, P. S. 1996. Implicit memory bias for threat in posttraumatic stress disorder. *Cognitive Therapy and Research, 20*, 625–635.

Amir, N., Stafford, J., Freshman, M. S., and Foa, E. B. 1998. Relationship between trauma narratives and trauma pathology. *Journal of Traumatic Stress, 11*, 385–392.

Anderson, M. C., and Green, C. 2001. Suppressing unwanted memories by executive control. *Nature, 410*, 366–369.

Andrews, B., Brewin, C. R., Ochera, J., Morton, J., Bekerian, D. A., Davies, G. M., and Mollon, P. 1999. Characteristics, context and consequences of memory recovery among adults in therapy. *British Journal of Psychiatry, 175*, 141–146.

Andrews, B., Brewin, C. R., Rose, S., and Kirk, M. 2000. Predicting PTSD symptoms in victims of violent crime: The role of shame, anger, and childhood abuse. *Journal of Abnormal Psychology, 109*, 69–73.

APA Working Group on Investigation of Memories of Childhood Abuse. 1998. Final conclusions of the American Psychological Association Working Group on Investigation of Memories of Childhood Abuse. *Psychology, Public Policy, and Law, 4,* 933–940.

Archibald, H. C., and Tuddenham, R. D. 1965. Persistent stress reaction after combat: A 20-year follow-up. *Archives of General Psychiatry, 12,* 475–481.

Arens, W. 1979. *The man-eating myth.* New York: Oxford University Press.

——— 1998. Rethinking anthropophagy. In F. Barker, P. Hulme, and M. Iversen, eds., *Cannibalism and the colonial world,* 39–62. Cambridge: Cambridge University Press.

Arndt, S., Cohen, G., Alliger, R. J., Swayze, V. W., II, and Andreasen, N. C. 1991. Problems with ratio and proportion measures of imaged cerebral structures. *Psychiatry Research: Neuroimaging, 40,* 79–89.

Arntz, A., Meeren, M., and Wessel, I. 2002. No evidence for overgeneral memories in borderline personality disorder. *Behaviour Research and Therapy, 40,* 1063–68.

Aronson, R. H., Rosenwald, L., and Rosen, G. M. 2001. Attorney-client confidentiality and the assessment of claimants who allege posttraumatic stress disorder. *Washington Law Review, 76,* 313–347.

Arrigo, J. M., and Pezdek, K. 1997. Lessons from the study of psychogenic amnesia. *Current Directions in Psychological Science, 6,* 148–152.

Atkinson, R. C., and Shiffrin, R. M. 1968. Human memory: A proposed system and its control processes. In K. W. Spence and J. T. Spence, eds., *The psychology of learning and motivation: Advances in research and theory,* vol. 2, 89–195. New York: Academic Press.

August, R. L., and Forman, B. D. 1989. A comparison of sexually abused and nonsexually abused children's behavioral responses to anatomically correct dolls. *Child Psychiatry and Human Development, 20,* 39–47.

Avina, C., and O'Donohue, W. 2002. Sexual harassment and PTSD: Is sexual harassment diagnosable trauma? *Journal of Traumatic Stress, 15,* 69–75.

Axelrod, B. N., and Milner, I. B. 1997. Neuropsychological findings in a sample of Operation Desert Storm veterans. *Journal of Neuropsychiatry and Clinical Neurosciences, 9,* 23–28.

Ayers, M. S., and Reder, L. M. 1998. A theoretical review of the misinformation effect: Predictions from an activation-based memory model. *Psychonomic Bulletin and Review, 5,* 1–21.

Baars, B. J., and McGovern, K. 1995. Steps toward healing: False memories and traumagenic amnesia may coexist in vulnerable populations. *Consciousness and Cognition, 4,* 68–74.

Baddeley, A. 1998. The central executive: A concept and some misconceptions. *Journal of the International Neuropsychological Society, 4,* 523–526.

———— 2000. Short-term and working memory. In Tulving and Craik, eds., 2000, 77–92.

Baddeley, A. D., and Hitch, G. 1974. Working memory. In *The psychology of learning and motivation: Advances in research and theory,* vol. 8, 47–89. New York: Academic Press.

Bagley, C. 1990. Validity of a short measure of child sexual abuse for use in adult mental health surveys. *Psychological Reports, 66,* 449–450.

Baird, B. N. 2002. Politics, operant conditioning, Galileo, and the American Psychological Association's response to Rind et al. 1998. *American Psychologist, 57,* 189–192.

Barbarotto, R., Laiacona, M., and Cocchini, G. 1996. A case of simulated, psychogenic or focal pure retrograde amnesia: Did an entire life become unconscious? *Neuropsychologia, 34,* 575–585.

Barnier, A. J., and McConkey, K. M. 1992. Reports of real and false memories: The relevance of hypnosis, hypnotizability, and context of memory test. *Journal of Abnormal Psychology, 101,* 521–527.

Barrett, D. H., Green, M. L., Morris, R., Giles, W. H., and Croft, J. B. 1996. Cognitive functioning and posttraumatic stress disorder. *American Journal of Psychiatry, 153,* 1492–94.

Bartlett, F. C. 1932. *Remembering: A study in experimental and social psychology.* Cambridge: Cambridge University Press.

Başoğlu, M., and Mineka, S. 1992. The role of uncontrollable and unpredictable stress in post-traumatic stress responses in torture survivors. In M. Başoğlu, ed., *Torture and its consequences: Current treatment approaches,* 182–225. Cambridge: Cambridge University Press.

Başoğlu, M., Mineka, S., Paker, M., Aker, T., Livanou, M., and Gök, Ş. 1997. Psychological preparedness for trauma as a protective factor in survivors of torture. *Psychological Medicine, 27*, 1421–33.

Başoğlu, M., Paker, M., Paker, Ö., Özmen, E., Marks, I., Incesu, C., Şahin, D., and Sarımurat, N. 1994. Psychological effects of torture: A comparison of tortured with nontortured political activists in Turkey. *American Journal of Psychiatry, 151*, 76–81.

Bass, E., and Davis, L. 1988. *The courage to heal: A guide for women survivors of child sexual abuse.* New York: Harper and Row.

Bateman, R. L. 2002. *No Gun Ri: A military history of the Korean War incident.* Mechanicsburg, PA: Stackpole Books.

Bauer, P. J. 1996. What do infants recall of their lives? Memory for specific events by one- to two-year-olds. *American Psychologist, 51*, 29–41.

Bauer, P. J., Hertsgaard, L. A., and Dow, G. A. 1994. After 8 months have passed: Long-term recall of events by 1- to 2-year-old children. *Memory, 2*, 353–382.

Bays, J., and Chadwick, D. 1993. Medical diagnosis of the sexually abused child. *Child Abuse and Neglect, 17*, 91–110.

Bechara, A., Tranel, D., Damasio, H., Adolphs, R., Rockland, C., and Damasio, A. R. 1995. Double dissociation of conditioning and declarative knowledge relative to the amygdala and hippocampus in humans. *Science, 269*, 1115–18.

Beck, A. T., and Steer, R. A. 1987. *Beck Depression Inventory manual.* San Antonio: Psychological Corporation.

Beckham, J. C., Feldman, M. E., and Kirby, A. C. 1998. Atrocities exposure in Vietnam combat veterans with chronic posttraumatic stress disorder: Relationship to combat exposure, symptom severity, guilt, and interpersonal violence. *Journal of Traumatic Stress, 11*, 777–785.

Bedford, F. L. 1997. False categories in cognition: The Not-The-Liver Fallacy. *Cognition, 64*, 231–248.

Beers, S. R., and De Bellis, M. D. 2002. Neuropsychological function in children with maltreatment-related posttraumatic stress disorder. *American Journal of Psychiatry, 159*, 483–486.

Behnke, S. H., and Hilliard, J. T. 1998. *The essentials of Massachusetts mental health law: A straightforward guide for clinicians of all disciplines.* New York: Norton.

Beitchman, J. H., Zucker, K. J., Hood, J. E., daCosta, G. A., and Akman, D. 1991. A review of the short-term effects of child sexual abuse. *Child Abuse and Neglect, 15,* 537–556.

Beitchman, J. H., Zucker, K. J., Hood, J. E., daCosta, G. A., Akman, D., and Cassavia, E. 1992. A review of the long-term effects of child sexual abuse. *Child Abuse and Neglect, 16,* 101–118.

Belicki, K. 1992. Nightmare frequency versus nightmare distress: Relations to psychopathology and cognitive style. *Journal of Abnormal Psychology, 101,* 592–597.

Belli, R. F., Lindsay, D. S., Gales, M. S., and McCarthy, T. T. 1994. Memory impairment and source misattribution in postevent misinformation experiments with short retention intervals. *Memory and Cognition, 22,* 40–54.

Belli, R. F., Windschitl, P. D., McCarthy, T. T., and Winfrey, S. E. 1992. Detecting memory impairment with a modified test procedure: Manipulating retention interval with centrally presented event items. *Journal of Experimental Psychology: Learning, Memory, and Cognition, 18,* 356–367.

Belli, R. F., Winkielman, P., Read, J. D., Schwarz, N., and Lynn, S. J. 1998. Recalling more childhood events leads to judgments of poorer memory: Implications for the recovered/false memory debate. *Psychonomic Bulletin and Review, 5,* 318–323.

Bernstein, A. E. H., and Blacher, R. S. 1967. The recovery of a memory from three months of age. *Psychoanalytic Study of the Child, 22,* 156–161.

Bernstein, E. M., and Putnam, F. W. 1986. Development, reliability, and validity of a dissociation scale. *Journal of Nervous and Mental Disease, 174,* 727–735.

Berntsen, D. 1996. Involuntary autobiographical memories. *Applied Cognitive Psychology, 10,* 435–454.

——— 1998. Voluntary and involuntary access to autobiographical memory. *Memory, 6,* 113–141.

——— 2001. Involuntary memories of emotional events: Do memories of traumas and extremely happy events differ? *Applied Cognitive Psychology, 15,* S135–S158.

Berrington, W. P., Liddell, D. W., and Foulds, G. A. 1956. A re-evaluation of the fugue. *Journal of Mental Science, 102,* 280–286.

Best, J., and Horiuchi, G. T. 1985. The razor blade in the apple: The social construction of urban legends. *Social Problems, 32,* 488–499.

Binder, R. L., McNiel, D. E., and Goldstone, R. L. 1994. Patterns of recall of childhood sexual abuse as described by adult survivors. *Bulletin of the American Academy of Psychiatry and Law, 22,* 357–366.

Birmes, P., Carreras, D., Charlet, J.-P., Warner, B. A., Lauque, D., and Schmitt, L. 2001. Peritraumatic dissociation and posttraumatic stress disorder in victims of violent assault. *Journal of Nervous and Mental Disease, 189,* 796–798.

Bjork, R. A. 1972. Theoretical implications of directed forgetting. In A. W. Melton and E. Martin, eds., *Coding processes in human memory,* 217–236. Washington: V. H. Winston and Sons.

Blanchard, E. B., and Buckley, T. C. 1999. Psychophysiological assessment of posttraumatic stress disorder. In P. A. Saigh and J. D. Bremner, eds., *Posttraumatic stress disorder: A comprehensive text,* 248–266. Needham Heights, MA: Allyn and Bacon.

Blanchard, E. B., Hickling, E. J., Buckley, T. C., Taylor, A. E., Vollmer, A., and Loos, W. R. 1996. Psychophysiology of posttraumatic stress disorder related to motor vehicle accidents: Replication and extension. *Journal of Consulting and Clinical Psychology, 64,* 742–751.

Blanchard, E. B., Hickling, E. J., Galovski, T., and Veazey, C. 2002. Emergency room vital signs and PTSD in a treatment seeking sample of motor vehicle accident survivors. *Journal of Traumatic Stress, 15,* 199–204.

Blanchard, E. B., Hickling, E. J., Mitnick, N., Taylor, A. E., Loos, W. R., and Buckley, T. C. 1995. The impact of severity of physical injury and perception of life threat in the development of post-traumatic stress disorder in motor vehicle accident victims. *Behaviour Research and Therapy, 33,* 529–534.

Blanchard, E. B., Hickling, E. J., Taylor, A. E., Loos, W. R., and Gerardi, R. J. 1994. The psychophysiology of motor vehicle accident related posttraumatic stress disorder. *Behavior Therapy, 25,* 453–467.

Blanchard, E. B., Kolb, L. C., Gerardi, R. J., Ryan, P., and Pallmeyer, T. P. 1986. Cardiac response to relevant stimuli as an adjunctive tool for diagnosing post-traumatic stress disorder in Vietnam veterans. *Behavior Therapy*, *17*, 592–606.

Blanchard, E. B., Kolb, L. C., Pallmeyer, T. P., and Gerardi, R. J. 1982. A psychophysiological study of post-traumatic stress disorder in Vietnam veterans. *Psychiatric Quarterly*, *54*, 220–229.

Blanchard, E. B., Kolb, L. C., Prins, A., Gates, S., and McCoy, G. C. 1991. Changes in plasma norepinephrine to combat-related stimuli among Vietnam veterans with posttraumatic stress disorder. *Journal of Nervous and Mental Disease*, *179*, 371–373.

Bliss, E. L. 1980. Multiple personalities: A report of 14 cases with implications for schizophrenia and hysteria. *Archives of General Psychiatry*, *37*, 1388–97.

Bloch, H. S. 1969. Army clinical psychiatry in the combat zone: 1967–1968. *American Journal of Psychiatry*, *126*, 289–298.

Bloom, S. L. 1994. Hearing the survivor's voice: Sundering the wall of denial. *Journal of Psychohistory*, *21*, 461–477.

Blume, E. S. 1990. *Secret survivors: Uncovering incest and its aftereffects in women.* New York: Wiley.

—— 1995. The ownership of truth. *Journal of Psychohistory*, *23*, 131–140.

Boat, B. W., and Everson, M. D. 1988. Use of anatomical dolls among professionals in sexual abuse evaluations. *Child Abuse and Neglect*, *12*, 171–179.

Bohannon, J. N., III. 1988. Flashbulb memories for the Space Shuttle disaster: A tale of two theories. *Cognition*, *29*, 179–196.

Bohannon, J. N., III, and Symons, V. L. 1992. Flashbulb memories: Confidence, consistency, and quantity. In E. Winograd and U. Neisser, eds., *Affect and accuracy in recall: Studies of "flashbulb" memories*, 65–91. Cambridge: Cambridge University Press.

Bonne, O., Brandes, D., Gilboa, A., Gomori, J. M., Shenton, M. E., Pitman, R. K., and Shalev, A. Y. 2001. Longitudinal MRI study of hippocampal volume in trauma survivors with PTSD. *American Journal of Psychiatry*, *158*, 1248–51.

Borch-Jacobsen, M. 1996. Neurotica: Freud and the seduction theory. *October, 76* (spring), 15–43.

———— 1997. Sybil—The making of a disease: An interview with Dr. Herbert Spiegel. *New York Review of Books, 44*, no. 7 (April 24), 60–64.

Boscarino, J. A. 1995. Post-traumatic stress and associated disorders among Vietnam veterans: The significance of combat exposure and social support. *Journal of Traumatic Stress, 8,* 317–336.

———— 1996. Posttraumatic stress disorder, exposure to combat, and lower plasma cortisol among Vietnam veterans: Findings and clinical implications. *Journal of Consulting and Clinical Psychology, 64,* 191–201.

Bottoms, B. L., and Davis, S. L. 1997. The creation of satanic ritual abuse. *Journal of Social and Clinical Psychology, 16,* 112–132.

Bottoms, B. L., Shaver, P. R., and Goodman, G. S. 1996. An analysis of ritualistic and religion-related child abuse allegations. *Law and Human Behavior, 20,* 1–34.

Bourke, J. 1999. *An intimate history of killing: Face-to-face killing in twentieth-century warfare.* New York: Basic Books.

Bourne, P. G., Rose, R. M., and Mason, J. W. 1967. Urinary 17-OHCS levels: Data on seven helicopter ambulance medics in combat. *Archives of General Psychiatry, 17,* 104–110.

———— 1968. 17-OHCS levels in combat: Special Forces "A" Team under threat of attack. *Archives of General Psychiatry, 19,* 135–140.

Bower, G. H. 1981. Mood and memory. *American Psychologist, 36,* 129–148.

Bower, G. H., and Mayer, J. D. 1985. Failure to replicate mood-dependent retrieval. *Bulletin of the Psychonomic Society, 23,* 39–42.

———— 1989. In search of mood-dependent retrieval. *Journal of Social Behavior and Personality, 4,* 121–156.

Bower, G. H., Monteiro, K. P., and Gilligan, S. G. 1978. Emotional mood as a context for learning and recall. *Journal of Verbal Learning and Verbal Behavior, 17,* 573–585.

Bowers, J. S., and Schacter, D. L. 1990. Implicit memory and test awareness. *Journal of Experimental Psychology: Learning, Memory, and Cognition, 16,* 404–416.

Bowers, K. S., and Farvolden, P. 1996. Revisiting a century-old Freudian slip—From suggestion disavowed to the truth repressed. *Psychological Bulletin, 119,* 355–380.

Bowler, R. M., Mergler, D., Huel, G., and Cone, J. E. 1994. Psychological, psychosocial, and psychophysiological sequelae in a community affected by a railroad chemical disaster. *Journal of Traumatic Stress, 7*, 601–624.

Bowman, C. G., and Mertz, E. 1996. A dangerous direction: Legal intervention in sexual abuse survivor therapy. *Harvard Law Review, 109*, 549–639.

Bowman, M. 1997. *Individual differences in posttraumatic response: Problems with the adversity-distress connection.* Mahwah, NJ: Erlbaum.

——— 1999. Individual differences in posttraumatic distress: Problems with the DSM-IV model. *Canadian Journal of Psychiatry, 44*, 21–33.

Bozzuto, J. C. 1975. Cinematic neurosis following "The Exorcist": Report of four cases. *Journal of Nervous and Mental Disease, 161*, 43–48.

Bracken, P. J., and Petty, C., eds. 1998. *Rethinking the trauma of war.* London: Free Association Books.

Bradley, A. R., and Wood, J. M. 1996. How do children tell? The disclosure process in child sexual abuse. *Child Abuse and Neglect, 20*, 881–891.

Brainerd, C. J., and Reyna, V. F. 1998. Fuzzy-trace theory and children's false memories. *Journal of Experimental Child Psychology, 71*, 81–129.

Bramsen, I., Dirkzwager, A. J. E., and van der Ploeg, H. M. 2000. Predeployment personality traits and exposure to trauma as predictors of posttraumatic stress symptoms: A prospective study of former peacekeepers. *American Journal of Psychiatry, 157*, 1115–19.

Bramsen, I., Dirkzwager, A. J. E., van Esch, S. C. M., and van der Ploeg, H. M. 2001. Consistency of self-reports of traumatic events in a population of Dutch peacekeepers: Reason for optimism? *Journal of Traumatic Stress, 14*, 733–740.

Bremner, J. D. 1999. Does stress damage the brain? *Biological Psychiatry, 45*, 797–805.

——— 2001. Hypotheses and controversies related to effects of stress on the hippocampus: An argument for stress-induced damage to the hippocampus in patients with posttraumatic stress disorder. *Hippocampus, 11*, 75–81.

Bremner, J. D., Innis, R. B., Ng, C. K., Staib, L. H., Salomon, R. M., Bronen, R. A., Duncan, J., Southwick, S. M., Krystal, J. H., Rich, D., Zubal, G., Dey, H., Soufer, R., and Charney, D. S. 1997. Positron emission tomography measurement of cerebral metabolic correlates of yohimbine administration in combat-related posttraumatic stress disorder. *Archives of General Psychiatry, 54,* 246–254.

Bremner, J. D., Krystal, J. H., Charney, D. S., and Southwick, S. M. 1996. Neural mechanisms in dissociative amnesia for childhood abuse: Relevance to the current controversy surrounding the "False Memory Syndrome." *American Journal of Psychiatry, 153,* FS71–82.

Bremner, J. D., Narayan, M., Staib, L. H., Southwick, S. M., McGlashan, T., and Charney, D. S. 1999. Neural correlates of memories of childhood sexual abuse in women with and without posttraumatic stress disorder. *American Journal of Psychiatry, 156,* 1787–95.

Bremner, J. D., Randall, P., Scott, T. M., Bronen, R. A., Seibyl, J. P., Southwick, S. M., Delaney, R. C., McCarthy, G., Charney, D. S., and Innis, R. B. 1995. MRI-based measurement of hippocampal volume in patients with combat-related posttraumatic stress disorder. *American Journal of Psychiatry, 152,* 973–981.

Bremner, J. D., Randall, P., Scott, T. M., Capelli, S., Delaney, R., McCarthy, G., and Charney, D. S. 1995. Deficits in short-term memory in adult survivors of childhood abuse. *Psychiatry Research, 59,* 97–107.

Bremner, J. D., Randall, P., Vermetten, E., Staib, L., Bronen, R. A., Mazure, C., Capelli, S., McCarthy, G., Innis, R. B., and Charney, D. S. 1997. Magnetic resonance imaging-based measurement of hippocampal volume in posttraumatic stress disorder related to childhood physical and sexual abuse—A preliminary report. *Biological Psychiatry, 41,* 23–32.

Bremner, J. D., Scott, T. M., Delaney, R. C., Southwick, S. M., Mason, J. W., Johnson, D. R., Innis, R. B., McCarthy, G., and Charney, D. S. 1993. Deficits in short-term memory in posttraumatic stress disorder. *American Journal of Psychiatry, 150,* 1015–19.

Bremner, J. D., Shobe, K. K., and Kihlstrom, J. F. 2000. False memories in women with self-reported childhood sexual abuse: An empirical study. *Psychological Science, 11,* 333–337.

Bremner, J. D., Southwick, S. M., Johnson, D. R., Yehuda, R., and Charney, D. S. 1993. Childhood physical abuse and combat-related posttraumatic stress disorder in Vietnam veterans. *American Journal of Psychiatry, 150,* 235–239.

Bremner, J. D., Staib, L. H., Kaloupek, D., Southwick, S. M., Soufer, R., and Charney, D. S. 1999. Neural correlates of exposure to traumatic pictures and sound in Vietnam combat veterans with and without posttraumatic stress disorder: A positron emission tomography study. *Biological Psychiatry*, 45, 806–816.

Bremner, J. D., Steinberg, M., Southwick, S. M., Johnson, D. R., and Charney, D. S. 1993. Use of the Structured Clinical Interview for DSM-IV Dissociative Disorders for systematic assessment of dissociative symptoms in posttraumatic stress disorder. *American Journal of Psychiatry*, 150, 1011–14.

Brenneis, C. B. 1994. Can early childhood trauma be reconstructed from dreams? On the relation of dreams to trauma. *Psychoanalytic Psychology*, 11, 429–447.

———— 1997a. Final Report of APA Working Group on Investigation of Memories of Childhood Abuse: A critical commentary. *Psychoanalytic Psychology*, 14, 531–547.

———— 1997b. *Recovered memories of trauma: Transferring the present to the past.* Madison, CT: International Universities Press.

———— 1999. [Review of *Remembering trauma: A psychotherapist's guide to memory and illusion.*] *International Journal of Psycho-analysis*, 80, 614–616.

———— 2000. Evaluating the evidence: Can we find authenticated recovered memory? *Journal of the American Psychoanalytic Association*, 17, 61–77.

Breslau, N., Chilcoat, H. D., Kessler, R. C., and Davis, G. C. 1999. Previous exposure to trauma and PTSD effects of subsequent trauma: Results from the Detroit Area Survey of Trauma. *American Journal of Psychiatry*, 156, 902–907.

Breslau, N., Chilcoat, H. D., Kessler, R. C., Peterson, E. L., and Lucia, V. C. 1999. Vulnerability to assaultive violence: Further specification of the sex difference in post-traumatic stress disorder. *Psychological Medicine*, 29, 813–821.

Breslau, N., and Davis, G. C. 1987. Posttraumatic stress disorder: The etiologic specificity of wartime stressors. *American Journal of Psychiatry*, 144, 578–583.

Breslau, N., Davis, G. C., and Andreski, P. 1995. Risk factors for PTSD-related traumatic events: A prospective analysis. *American Journal of Psychiatry*, 152, 529–535.

Breslau, N., Davis, G. C., Andreski, P., and Peterson, E. 1991. Traumatic events and posttraumatic stress disorder in an urban population of young adults. *Archives of General Psychiatry, 48,* 216–222.

Breslau, N., Kessler, R. C., Chilcoat, H. D., Schultz, L. R., Davis, G. C., and Andreski, P. 1998. Trauma and posttraumatic stress disorder in the community: The 1996 Detroit Area Survey of Trauma. *Archives of General Psychiatry, 55,* 626–632.

Breuer, J., and Freud, S. 1893. On the psychical mechanism of hysterical phenomena: Preliminary communication. In J. Strachey, ed. and trans., *The standard edition of the complete psychological works of Sigmund Freud [Standard edition],* vol. 2, 3–17. London: Hogarth Press, 1955.

———— 1895. Studies on hysteria. In *Standard edition,* vol. 2, 21–319. London: Hogarth Press, 1955.

Brewin, C. R. 2001. A cognitive neuroscience account of posttraumatic stress disorder and its treatment. *Behaviour Research and Therapy, 39,* 373–393.

Brewin, C. R., Andrews, B., and Gotlib, I. H. 1993. Psychopathology and early experience: A reappraisal of retrospective reports. *Psychological Bulletin, 113,* 82–98.

Brewin, C. R., Andrews, B., and Valentine, J. D. 2000. Meta-analysis of risk factors for posttraumatic stress disorder in trauma-exposed adults. *Journal of Consulting and Clinical Psychology, 68,* 748–766.

Brewin, C. R., Dalgleish, T., and Joseph, S. 1996. A dual representation theory of posttraumatic stress disorder. *Psychological Review, 103,* 670–686.

Brewin, C. R., Watson, M., McCarthy, S., Hyman, P., and Dayson, D. 1998. Intrusive memories and depression in cancer patients. *Behaviour Research and Therapy, 36,* 1131–42.

Briere, J. 1995. Science versus politics in the delayed memory debate: A commentary. *Counseling Psychologist, 23,* 290–293.

Briere, J., and Conte, J. 1993. Self-reported amnesia for abuse in adults molested as children. *Journal of Traumatic Stress, 6,* 21–31.

Brittlebank, A. D., Scott, J., Williams, J. M. G., and Ferrier, I. N. 1993. Autobiographical memory in depression: State or trait marker? *British Journal of Psychiatry, 162,* 118–121.

Brown, D., Frischholz, E. J., and Scheflin, A. W. 1999. Iatrogenic dissociative identity disorder—An evaluation of the scientific evidence. *Journal of Psychiatry and Law, 27,* 549–637.

Brown, D., Scheflin, A. W., and Hammond, D. C. 1998. *Memory, trauma treatment, and the law.* New York: Norton.

Brown, D., Scheflin, A. W., and Whitfield, C. L. 1999. Recovered memories: The current weight of the evidence in science and in the courts. *Journal of Psychiatry and Law, 27,* 5–156.

Brown, L. S. 1995a. Toward not forgetting: The science and politics of memory. *Counseling Psychologist, 23,* 310–314.

——— 1995b. Comment. *Consciousness and Cognition, 4,* 130–132.

——— 1997. The private practice of subversion: Psychology as tikkun olam. *American Psychologist, 52,* 449–462.

——— 1998. The prices of resisting silence: Comments on Calof, Cheit, Freyd, Hoult, and Salter. *Ethics and Behavior, 8,* 189–193.

Brown, P., and van der Hart, O. 1998. Memories of sexual abuse: Janet's critique of Freud, a balanced approach. *Psychological Reports, 82,* 1027–43.

Brown, R., and Kulik, J. 1977. Flashbulb memories. *Cognition, 5,* 73–99.

Bruce, D., and Winograd, E. 1998. Remembering Deese's 1959 articles: The Zeitgeist, the sociology of science, and false memories. *Psychonomic Bulletin and Review, 5,* 615–624.

Bruck, M., and Ceci, S. J. 1995. Amicus brief for the case of *State of New Jersey v. Michaels* presented by Committee of Concerned Social Scientists. *Psychology, Public Policy, and Law, 1,* 272–322.

Bruck, M., Ceci, S. J., Francoeur, E., and Barr, R. 1995. "I hardly cried when I got my shot!" Influencing children's reports about a visit to their pediatrician. *Child Development, 66,* 193–208.

Bruck, M., Ceci, S. J., Francoeur, E., and Renick, A. 1995. Anatomically detailed dolls do not facilitate preschoolers' reports of a pediatric examination involving genital touching. *Journal of Experimental Psychology: Applied, 1,* 95–109.

Bruck, M., Ceci, S. J., and Hembrooke, H. 1998. Reliability and credibility of young children's reports: From research to policy and practice. *American Psychologist, 53,* 136–151.

Bruck, M., Hembrooke, H., and Ceci, S. 1997. Children's reports of pleasant and unpleasant events. In Read and Lindsay, eds., 1997, 199–213.

Bryant, R. A. 1995. Autobiographical memory across personalities in dissociative identity disorder: A case report. *Journal of Abnormal Psychology, 104,* 625–631.

——— 1996. Posttraumatic stress disorder, flashbacks, and pseudomemories in closed head injury. *Journal of Traumatic Stress, 9,* 621–629.

——— 2001. Posttraumatic stress disorder and traumatic brain injury: Can they co-exist? *Clinical Psychology Review, 21,* 931–948.

Bryant, R. A., and Harvey, A. G. 1995a. Acute stress response: A comparison of head injured and non-head injured patients. *Psychological Medicine, 25,* 869–873.

——— 1995b. Processing threatening information in posttraumatic stress disorder. *Journal of Abnormal Psychology, 104,* 537–541.

——— 1996. Visual imagery in posttraumatic stress disorder. *Journal of Traumatic Stress, 9,* 613–619.

——— 1998. Traumatic memories and pseudomemories in posttraumatic stress disorder. *Applied Cognitive Psychology, 12,* 81–88.

——— 2000. *Acute stress disorder: A handbook of theory, assessment, and treatment.* Washington: American Psychological Association.

Bryant, R. A., Marosszeky, J. E., Crooks, J., and Gurka, J. A. 2000. Posttraumatic stress disorder after severe traumatic brain injury. *American Journal of Psychiatry, 157,* 629–631.

Buchanan, T. W., Denburg, N. L., Tranel, D., and Adolphs, R. 2001. Verbal and nonverbal emotional memory following unilateral amygdala damage. *Learning and Memory, 8,* 326–335.

Buchanan, T. W., and Lovallo, W. R. 2000. Enhanced memory for emotional material following stress-level cortisol treatment in humans. *Psychoneuroendocrinology, 26,* 307–317.

Buckley, T. C., Blanchard, E. B., and Hickling, E. J. 2002. Automatic and strategic processing of threat stimuli: A comparison between PTSD, panic disorder, and nonanxiety controls. *Cognitive Therapy and Research, 26,* 97–115.

Buckley, T. C., Blanchard, E. B., and Neill, W. T. 2000. Information processing and PTSD: A review of the literature. *Clinical Psychology Review, 28,* 1041–65.

Bucky, S. F., and Dalenberg, C. 1992. The relationship between training of mental health professionals and the reporting of ritual abuse and multiple personality disorder symptomatology. *Journal of Psychology and Theology, 20,* 233–238.

Burges, C., and McMillan, T. M. 2001. The ability of naive participants to report symptoms of post-traumatic stress disorder. *British Journal of Clinical Psychology, 40,* 209–214.

Burgess, A. W., Hartman, C. R., and Baker, T. 1995. Memory presentations of childhood sexual abuse. *Journal of Psychosocial Nursing, 33,* 9–16.

Burgess, A. W., and Holmstrom, L. L. 1974. Rape trauma syndrome. *American Journal of Psychiatry, 131,* 981–986.

Burke, A., Heuer, F., and Reisberg, D. 1992. Remembering emotional events. *Memory and Cognition, 20,* 277–290.

Burkett, B. G., and Whitley, G. 1998. *Stolen valor: How the Vietnam generation was robbed of its heroes and its history.* Dallas: Verity Press.

Burstein, A. 1984. Dream disturbances and flashbacks. *Journal of Clinical Psychiatry, 45,* 46.

———— 1985a. Posttraumatic stress disorder. *Journal of Clinical Psychiatry, 46,* 300–301.

———— 1985b. Posttraumatic flashbacks, dream disturbances, and mental imagery. *Journal of Clinical Psychiatry, 46,* 374–378.

Butler, L. T., and Berry, D. C. 2001. Implicit memory: Intention and awareness revisited. *Trends in Cognitive Sciences, 5,* 192–197.

Butterfield, H. 1931. *The Whig interpretation of history.* New York: Norton, 1965.

Cahill, L. 2000. Modulation of long-term memory storage in humans by emotional arousal: Adrenergic activation and the amygdala. In J. P. Aggleton, ed., *The amygdala: A functional analysis,* 2nd ed., 425–445. Oxford: Oxford University Press.

Cahill, L., Babinsky, R., Markowitsch, H. J., and McGaugh, J. L. 1995. The amygdala and emotional memory. *Nature, 377,* 295–296.

Cahill, L., Haier, R. J., Fallon, J., Alkire, M. T., Tang, C., Keator, D., Wu, J., and McGaugh, J. L. 1996. Amygdala activity at encoding correlated with long-term free recall of emotional information. *Proceedings of the National Academy of Sciences, 93,* 8016–21.

Cahill, L., Haier, R. J., White, N. S., Fallon, J., Kilpatrick, L., Lawrence, C., Potkin, S. G., and Alkire, M. T. 2001. Sex-related difference in amygdala activity during emotionally influenced memory storage. *Neurobiology of Learning and Memory, 75,* 1–9.

Cahill, L., Prins, B., Weber, M., and McGaugh, J. L. 1994. ß-adrenergic activation and memory for emotional events. *Nature, 371,* 702–704.

Cameron, C. 1994. Women survivors confronting their abusers: Issues, decisions, and outcomes. *Journal of Child Sexual Abuse, 3,* 7–35.

——— 1996. Comparing amnesic and nonamnesic survivors of childhood sexual abuse: A longitudinal study. In K. Pezdek and W. P. Banks, eds., *The recovered memory/false memory debate,* 41–68. San Diego: Academic Press.

Campion-Vincent, V. 1990. The baby-parts story: A new Latin American legend. *Western Folklore, 49,* 9–25.

——— 1997. Organ theft narratives. *Western Folklore, 56,* 1–37.

Canli, T., Zhao, Z., Brewer, J., Gabrieli, J. D. E., and Cahill, L. 2000. Event-related activation in the human amygdala associates with later memory for individual emotional experience. *Journal of Neuroscience, 20:* RC99, 1–5.

Caramazza, A. 1986. On drawing inferences about the structure of normal cognitive systems from the analysis of patterns of impaired performance: The case for single-patient studies. *Brain and Cognition, 5,* 41–66.

Cardeña, E., and Spiegel, D. 1993. Dissociative reactions to the San Francisco Bay area earthquake of 1989. *American Journal of Psychiatry, 150,* 474–478.

Carlier, I. V. E., and Gersons, B. P. R. 1997. Stress reactions in disaster victims following the Bijlmermeer plane crash. *Journal of Traumatic Stress, 10,* 329–335.

Carlson, E. B., and Rosser-Hogan, R. 1991. Trauma experiences, posttraumatic stress, dissociation, and depression in Cambodian refugees. *American Journal of Psychiatry, 148,* 1548–51.

Carson, M. A., Paulus, L. A., Lasko, N. B., Metzger, L. J., Wolfe, J., Orr, S. P., and Pitman, R. K. 2000. Psychophysiologic assessment of posttraumatic stress disorder in Vietnam nurse veterans who witnessed injury or death. *Journal of Consulting and Clinical Psychology, 68,* 890–897.

Cassiday, K. L., and Lyons, J. A. 1992. Recall of traumatic memories following cerebral vascular accident. *Journal of Traumatic Stress, 5,* 627–631.

Cassiday, K. L., McNally, R. J., and Zeitlin, S. B. 1992. Cognitive processing of trauma cues in rape victims with post-traumatic stress disorder. *Cognitive Therapy and Research, 16,* 283–295.

Cassidy, J. D., Carroll, L. J., Côté, P., Lemstra, M., Berglund, A., and Nygren, Å. 2000. Effect of eliminating compensation for pain and suffering on the outcome of insurance claims for whiplash injury. *New England Journal of Medicine, 342,* 1179–86.

Ceci, S. J., and Bruck, M. 1993. Suggestibility of the child witness: A historical review and synthesis. *Psychological Bulletin, 113,* 403–439.

Ceci, S. J., Bruck, M., and Rosenthal, R. 1995. Children's allegations of sexual abuse: Forensic and scientific issues: A reply to commentators. *Psychology, Public Policy, and Law, 1,* 494–520.

Ceci, S. J., and Friedman, R. D. 2000. The suggestibility of children: Scientific research and legal implications. *Cornell Law Review, 86,* 33–108.

Ceci, S. J., and Huffman, M. L. C. 1997. How suggestible are preschool children? Cognitive and social factors. *Journal of the American Academy of Child and Adolescent Psychiatry, 36,* 948–958.

Ceci, S. J., and Loftus, E. F. 1994. "Memory work": A royal road to false memories? *Applied Cognitive Psychology, 8,* 351–364.

Ceci, S. J., Loftus, E. F., Leichtman, M. D., and Bruck, M. 1994. The possible role of source misattributions in the creation of false beliefs among preschoolers. *International Journal of Clinical and Experimental Hypnosis, 42,* 304–320.

Cella, D. F., Perry, S. W., Kulchycky, S., and Goodwin, C. 1988. Stress and coping in relatives of burn patients: A longitudinal study. *Hospital and Community Psychiatry, 39,* 159–166.

Chaplin, J. P. 1968. *Dictionary of psychology*. New York: Dell.

Cheit, R. E. 1998. Consider this, skeptics of recovered memory. *Ethics and Behavior*, 8, 141–160.

———— 1999. Junk skepticism and recovered memory: A reply to Piper. *Ethics and Behavior*, 9, 295–318.

Chen, E., Zeltzer, L. K., Craske, M. G., and Katz, E. R. 2000. Children's memories for painful cancer treatment procedures: Implications for distress. *Child Development*, 71, 933–947.

Cheyne, J. A., Newby-Clark, I. R., and Rueffer, S. D. 1999. Relations among hypnagogic and hypnopompic experiences associated with sleep paralysis. *Journal of Sleep Research*, 8, 313–317.

Chodoff, P. 1963. Late effects of the Concentration Camp Syndrome. *Archives of General Psychiatry*, 8, 323–333.

Christianson, S.-Å. 1984. The relationship between induced emotional arousal and amnesia. *Scandinavian Journal of Psychology*, 25, 147–160.

———— 1989. Flashbulb memories: Special, but not so special. *Memory and Cognition*, 17, 435–443.

———— 1992. Emotional stress and eyewitness memory: A critical review. *Psychological Bulletin*, 112, 284–309.

Christianson, S.-Å., and Engelberg, E. 1999. Memory and emotional consistency: The MS *Estonia* ferry disaster. *Memory*, 7, 471–482.

Christianson, S.-Å., and Hübinette, B. 1993. Hands up! A study of witnesses' emotional reactions and memories associated with bank robberies. *Applied Cognitive Psychology*, 7, 365–379.

Christianson, S.-Å., and Loftus, E. F. 1987. Memory for traumatic events. *Applied Cognitive Psychology*, 1, 225–239.

———— 1991. Remembering emotional events: The fate of detailed information. *Cognition and Emotion*, 5, 81–108.

Christianson, S.-Å, and Nilsson, L.-G. 1984. Functional amnesia as induced by a psychological trauma. *Memory and Cognition*, 12, 142–155.

———— 1989. Hysterical amnesia: A case of aversively motivated isolation of memory. In T. Archer and L.-G. Nilsson, eds., *Aversion, avoidance, and anxiety*:

Perspectives on aversively motivated behavior, 289–310. Hillsdale, NJ: Erlbaum.

Chu, J. A., and Dill, D. L. 1990. Dissociative symptoms in relation to childhood physical and sexual abuse. *American Journal of Psychiatry*, *147*, 887–892.

Chu, J. A., Frey, L. M., Ganzel, B. L., and Matthews, J. A. 1999. Memories of childhood abuse: Dissociation, amnesia, and corroboration. *American Journal of Psychiatry*, *156*, 749–755.

Cioffi, F. 1972. Wollheim on Freud. In Cioffi 1998, 143–160.

———— 1973. The myth of Freud's hostile reception. In Cioffi 1998, 161–181.

———— 1974. Was Freud a liar? In Cioffi 1998, 199–204.

———— 1984. From Freud's "scientific fairy tale" to Masson's politically correct one. In Cioffi 1998, 205–209.

———— 1998. *Freud and the question of pseudoscience*. Chicago: Open Court.

Clancy, S. A., McNally, R. J., and Schacter, D. L. 1999. Effects of guided imagery on memory distortion in women reporting recovered memories of childhood sexual abuse. *Journal of Traumatic Stress*, *12*, 559–569.

Clancy, S. A., McNally, R. J., Schacter, D. L., Lenzenweger, M. F., and Pitman, R. K. 2002. Memory distortion in people reporting abduction by aliens. *Journal of Abnormal Psychology*, *111*, 455–461.

Clancy, S. A., Schacter, D. L., McNally, R. J., and Pitman, R. K. 2000. False recognition in women reporting recovered memories of sexual abuse. *Psychological Science*, *11*, 26–31.

Clark, R. E., and Squire, L. R. 1998. Classical conditioning and brain systems: The role of awareness. *Science*, *280*, 77–81.

Clifford, B. R., and Hollin, C. R. 1981. Effects of the type of incident and the number of perpetrators on eyewitness memory. *Journal of Applied Psychology*, *66*, 364–370.

Clifford, B. R., and Scott, J. 1978. Individual and situational factors in eyewitness testimony. *Journal of Applied Psychology*, *63*, 352–359.

Coan, J. A. 1997. Lost in a shopping mall: An experience with controversial research. *Ethics and Behavior*, *7*, 271–284.

Cohen, N. J., McCloskey, M., and Wible, C. G. 1988. There is still no case for a flashbulb-memory mechanism: Reply to Schmidt and Bohannon. *Journal of Experimental Psychology: General, 117*, 336–338.

Cohn, D. S. 1991. Anatomical doll play of preschoolers referred for sexual abuse and those not referred. *Child Abuse and Neglect, 15*, 455–466.

Cohn, N. 1993. *Europe's inner demons: The demonization of Christians in medieval Christendom*, rev. ed. Chicago: University of Chicago Press.

Colegrove, F. W. 1899. Individual memories. *American Journal of Psychology, 10*, 228–255.

Conte, J. R., Sorenson, E., Fogarty, L., and Dalla Rosa, J. 1991. Evaluating children's reports of sexual abuse: Results from a survey of professionals. *American Journal of Orthopsychiatry, 61*, 428–437.

Conway, M. A. 1996. Autobiographical memory. In E. L. Bjork and R. A. Bjork, eds., *Memory*, 165–194. San Diego: Academic Press.

———— 2001. Repression revisited. *Nature, 410*, 319–320.

Conway, M. A., Anderson, S. J., Larsen, S. F., Donnelly, C. M., McDaniel, M. A., McClelland, A. G. R., Rawles, R. E., and Logie, R. H. 1994. The formation of flashbulb memories. *Memory and Cognition, 22*, 326–343.

Conway, M. A., Collins, A. F., Gathercole, S. E., and Anderson, S. J. 1996. Recollections of true and false autobiographical memories. *Journal of Experimental Psychology: General, 125*, 69–95.

Conway, M. A., and Pleydell-Pearce, C. W. 2000. The construction of autobiographical memories in the self-memory system. *Psychological Review, 107*, 261–288.

Coons, P. M. 1994. Reports of satanic ritual abuse: Further implications about pseudomemories. *Perceptual and Motor Skills, 78*, 1376–78.

Coons, P. M., Bowman, E. S., and Milstein, V. 1997. Repressed memories in patients with dissociative disorder: Literature review, controlled study, and treatment recommendations. In D. Spiegel, ed., *Repressed memories*, 153–172. Washington: American Psychiatric Press.

Corwin, D. L., and Olafson, E. 1997. Videotaped discovery of a reportedly unrecallable memory of child sexual abuse: Comparison with a childhood interview videotaped 11 years before. *Child Maltreatment, 2*, 91–112.

Courtois, C. A. 1992. The memory retrieval process in incest survivor therapy. *Journal of Child Sexual Abuse*, *1*, 15–31.

Crews, F. 1995. *The memory wars: Freud's legacy in dispute*. New York: New York Review of Books.

——— 1996. Forward to 1896? Commentary on papers by Harris and Davies. *Psychoanalytic Dialogues*, *6*, 231–250.

Crombag, H. F. M., Wagenaar, W. A., and van Koppen, P. J. 1996. Crashing memories and the problem of "source monitoring." *Applied Cognitive Psychology*, *10*, 95–104.

Crook, L. S., and Dean, M. C. 1999a. "Lost in a shopping mall"—A breach of professional ethics. *Ethics and Behavior*, *9*, 39–50.

——— 1999b. Logical fallacies and ethical breaches. *Ethics and Behavior*, *9*, 61–68.

Cutshall, J., and Yuille, J. C. 1989. Field studies of eyewitness memory of actual crimes. In D. C. Raskin, ed., *Psychological methods in criminal investigation and evidence*, 97–124. New York: Springer.

Czarnocka, J., and Slade, P. 2000. Prevalence and predictors of post-traumatic stress symptoms following childbirth. *British Journal of Clinical Psychology*, *39*, 35–51.

Dale, P., and Allen, J. 1998. On memories of childhood abuse: A phenomenological study. *Child Abuse and Neglect*, *22*, 799–812.

Dalenberg, C. J. 1996. Accuracy, timing and circumstances of disclosure in therapy of recovered and continuous memories of abuse. *Journal of Psychiatry and Law*, *24*, 229–275.

Dallam, S. J., Gleaves, D. H., Cepeda-Benito, A., Silberg, J. L., Kraemer, H. C., and Spiegel, D. 2001. The effects of child sexual abuse: Comment on Rind, Tromovitch and Bauserman 1998. *Psychological Bulletin*, *127*, 715–733.

Daly, R. J. 1983. Samuel Pepys and post-traumatic stress disorder. *British Journal of Psychiatry*, *143*, 64–68.

Davidson, J., Swartz, M., Storck, M., Krishnan, R. R., and Hammett, E. 1985. A diagnostic and family study of posttraumatic stress disorder. *American Journal of Psychiatry*, *142*, 90–93.

Davies, J. M., and Frawley, M. G. 1992. Dissociative processes and transference-countertransference paradigms in the psychoanalytically oriented treatment of adult survivors of childhood sexual abuse. *Psychoanalytic Dialogues*, 2, 5–36.

Dean, E. T., Jr. 1997. *Shook over hell: Post-traumatic stress, Vietnam, and the Civil War*. Cambridge, MA: Harvard University Press.

De Bellis, M. D., Baum, A. S., Birmaher, B., Keshavan, M. S., Eccard, C. H., Boring, A. M., Jenkins, F. J., and Ryan, N. D. 1999. Developmental traumatology, Part I: Biological stress systems. *Biological Psychiatry*, 45, 1259–70.

De Bellis, M. D., Keshavan, M. S., Clark, D. B., Casey, B. J., Giedd, J. N., Boring, A. M., Frustaci, K., and Ryan, N. D. 1999. Developmental traumatology, Part II: Brain development. *Biological Psychiatry*, 45, 1271–84.

Deese, J. 1959. On the prediction of occurrence of particular verbal intrusions in immediate recall. *Journal of Experimental Psychology*, 58, 17–22.

Deffenbacher, K. A. 1983. The influence of arousal on reliability of testimony. In S. M. A. Lloyd-Bostock and B. R. Clifford, eds., *Evaluating witness evidence*, 235–251. Chichester, UK: Wiley.

DeLoache, J. S., and Marzolf, D. P. 1995. The use of dolls to interview young children: Issues of symbolic representation. *Journal of Experimental Child Psychology*, 60, 155–173.

DePrince, A. P., and Freyd, J. J. 2001. Memory and dissociative tendencies: The roles of attentional context and word meaning in a directed forgetting task. *Journal of Trauma and Dissociation*, 2, 67–82.

de Quervain, D. J.-F., Roozendaal, B., Nitsch, R. M., McGaugh, J. L., and Hock, C. 2000. Acute cortisone administration impairs retrieval of long-term declarative memory in humans. *Nature Neuroscience*, 3, 313–314.

De Renzi, E., Lucchelli, F., Muggia, S., and Spinnler, H. 1995. Persistent retrograde amnesia following a minor trauma. *Cortex*, 31, 531–542.

de Rivera, J. 2000. Understanding persons who repudiate memories recovered in therapy. *Professional Psychology: Research and Practice*, 31, 378–386.

Desjarlais, R., Eisenberg, L., Good, B., and Kleinman, A. 1995. *World mental health: Problems and priorities in low-income countries*. Oxford: Oxford University Press.

Dietz, P. E., Hazelwood, R. R., and Warren, J. 1990. The sexually sadistic criminal and his offenses. *Bulletin of the American Academy of Psychiatry and Law,* *19,* 163–178.

Dohrenwend, B. P. 2000. The role of adversity and stress in psychopathology: Some evidence and its implications for theory and research. *Journal of Health and Social Behavior, 41,* 1–19.

Dohrenwend, B. P., and Shrout, P. E. 1985. "Hassles" in the conceptualization and measurement of life stress variables. *American Psychologist, 40,* 780–785.

Dolan, R. J., Lane, R., Chua, P., and Fletcher, P. 2000. Dissociable temporal lobe activations during emotional episodic memory retrieval. *NeuroImage, 11,* 203–209.

Dollinger, S. J. 1985. Lightning-strike disaster among children. *British Journal of Medical Psychology, 58,* 375–383.

Domb, Y., and Beaman, K. 1991. Mr X—A case of amnesia. *British Journal of Psychiatry, 158,* 423–425.

Domino, M. L., and Boccaccini, M. T. 2000. Doubting Thomas: Should family members of victims watch executions? *Law and Psychology Review, 24,* 59–75.

Dorahy, M. J. 2001. Dissociative identity disorder and memory dysfunction: The current state of experimental research and its future directions. *Clinical Psychology Review, 21,* 771–795.

Driessen, M., Herrmann, J., Stahl, K., Zwaan, M., Meier, S., Hill, A., Osterheider, M., and Petersen, D. 2000. Magnetic resonance imaging volumes of the hippocampus and the amygdala in women with borderline personality disorder and early traumatization. *Archives of General Psychiatry, 57,* 1115–22.

Dubner, A. E., and Motta, R. W. 1999. Sexually and physically abused foster care children and posttraumatic stress disorder. *Journal of Consulting and Clinical Psychology, 67,* 367–373.

Dudycha, G. J., and Dudycha, M. M. 1933. Some factors and characteristics of childhood memories. *Child Development, 4,* 265–278.

Duggal, S., and Sroufe, L. A. 1998. Recovered memory of childhood sexual trauma: A documented case from a longitudinal study. *Journal of Traumatic Stress,* *11,* 301–321.

Dunmore, E., Clark, D. M., and Ehlers, A. 1999. Cognitive factors involved in the onset and maintenance of posttraumatic stress disorder (PTSD) after physical or sexual assault. *Behaviour Research and Therapy, 37,* 809–829.

Eacott, M. J. 1999. Memory for the events of early childhood. *Current Directions in Psychological Science, 8,* 46–49.

Eacott, M. J., and Crawley, R. A. 1998. The offset of childhood amnesia: Memory for events that occurred before age 3. *Journal of Experimental Psychology: General, 127,* 22–33.

Easterbrook, J. A. 1959. The effect of emotion on cue utilization and the organization of behavior. *Psychological Review, 66,* 183–201.

Eaton, W. W., Sigal, J. J., and Weinfeld, M. 1982. Impairment in Holocaust survivors after 33 years: Data from an unbiased community sample. *American Journal of Psychiatry, 139,* 773–777.

Ebbinghaus, H. 1885. *Memory: A contribution to experimental psychology,* trans. H. A. Ruger and C. E. Bussenius. New York: Teachers College, Columbia University, 1913.

Eder, M. D. 1917. *War-shock.* London: William Heinemann.

Ehlers, A., and Clark, D. M. 2000. A cognitive model of posttraumatic stress disorder. *Behaviour Research and Therapy, 38,* 319–345.

Ehlers, A., Mayou, R. A., and Bryant, B. 1998. Psychological predictors of chronic posttraumatic stress disorder after motor vehicle accidents. *Journal of Abnormal Psychology, 107,* 508–519.

Eich, E. 1995. Searching for mood dependent memory. *Psychological Science, 6,* 67–75.

Eich, E., Macaulay, D., Loewenstein, R. J., and Dihle, P. H. 1997. Memory, amnesia, and dissociative identity disorder. *Psychological Science, 8,* 417–422.

Elliott, D. M. 1997. Traumatic events: Prevalence and delayed recall in the general population. *Journal of Consulting and Clinical Psychology, 65,* 811–820.

Elliott, D. M., and Briere, J. 1995. Posttraumatic stress associated with delayed recall of sexual abuse: A general population study. *Journal of Traumatic Stress, 8,* 629–647.

Elzinga, B. M., de Beurs, E., Sergeant, J. A., van Dyck, R., and Phaf, R. H. 2000. Dissociative style and directed forgetting. *Cognitive Therapy and Research, 24*, 279–295.

Engdahl, B., Dikel, T. N., Eberly, R., and Blank, A., Jr. 1997. Posttraumatic stress disorder in a community group of former prisoners of war: A normative response to severe trauma. *American Journal of Psychiatry, 154*, 1576–81.

Engel, C. C., Jr., Engel, A. L., Campbell, S. J., McFall, M. E., Russo, J., and Katon, W. 1993. Posttraumatic stress disorder symptoms and precombat sexual and physical abuse in Desert Storm veterans. *Journal of Nervous and Mental Disease, 181*, 683–688.

Engelhard, I., van den Hout, M. A., and Arntz, A. 2001. Posttraumatic stress disorder after pregnancy loss. *General Hospital Psychiatry, 23*, 62–66.

Enns, C. Z., Campbell, J., Courtois, C. A., Gottlieb, M. C., Lese, K. P., Gilbert, M. S., and Forrest, L. 1998. Working with adult clients who may have experienced childhood abuse: Recommendations for assessment and practice. *Professional Psychology: Research and Practice, 29*, 245–256.

Enns, C. Z., McNeilly, C. L., Corkery, J. M., and Gilbert, M. S. 1995. The debate about delayed memories of child sexual abuse: A feminist perspective. *Counseling Psychologist, 23*, 181–279.

Epstein, M. A., and Bottoms, B. L. 1998. Memories of childhood sexual abuse: A survey of young adults. *Child Abuse and Neglect, 22*, 1217–38.

Erdelyi, M. H. 1990. Repression, reconstruction, and defense: History and integration of the psychoanalytic and experimental frameworks. In J. L. Singer, ed., *Repression and dissociation: Implications for personality theory, psychopathology, and health,* 1–31. Chicago: University of Chicago Press.

Erdelyi, M. H., and Becker, J. 1974. Hypermnesia for pictures: Incremental memory for pictures but not words in multiple recall trials. *Cognitive Psychology, 6,* 159–171.

Erdelyi, M. H., and Goldberg, B. 1979. Let's not sweep repression under the rug: Toward a cognitive psychology of repression. In J. F. Kihlstrom and F. J. Evans, eds., *Functional disorders of memory,* 355–402. Hillsdale, NJ: Erlbaum.

Ersland, S., Weisæth, L., and Sund, A. 1989. The stress upon rescuers involved in an oil rig disaster: "Alexander L. Kielland" 1980. *Acta Psychiatrica Scandinavica, 80* (Suppl. 355), 38–49.

Escobar, J. I., Canino, G., Rubio-Stipec, M., and Bravo, M. 1992. Somatic symptoms after a natural disaster: A prospective study. *American Journal of Psychiatry, 149,* 965–967.

Esposito, K., Benitez, A., Barza, L., and Mellman, T. 1999. Evaluation of dream content in combat-related PTSD. *Journal of Traumatic Stress, 12,* 681–687.

Esterson, A. 1993. *Seductive mirage: An exploration of the work of Sigmund Freud.* Chicago: Open Court.

———— 1998. Jeffrey Masson and Freud's seduction theory: A new fable based on old myths. *History of the Human Sciences, 11,* 1–21.

———— 2001. The mythologizing of psychoanalytic history: Deception and self-deception in Freud's accounts of the seduction theory. *History of Psychiatry, 12,* 329–352.

———— 2002a. Freud's seduction theory: A reply to Gleaves and Hernandez. *History of Psychology, 5,* 85–91.

———— 2002b. The myth of Freud's ostracism by the medical community in 1896–1905: Jeffrey Masson's assault on truth. *History of Psychology, 5,* 115–134.

———— Submitted. Freud's theories of repression and memory: A critique of Mollon's *Freud and False Memory Syndrome.*

Evans, J., Williams, J. M. G., O'Loughlin, S., and Howells, K. 1992. Autobiographical memory and problem-solving strategies of parasuicide patients. *Psychological Medicine, 22,* 399–405.

Everson, M. D., and Boat, B. W. 1990. Sexualized doll play among young children: Implications for the use of anatomical dolls in sexual abuse evaluations. *Journal of the American Academy of Child and Adolescent Psychiatry, 29,* 736–742.

———— 1994. Putting the anatomical doll controversy in perspective: An examination of the major uses and criticisms of the dolls in child sexual abuse evaluations. *Child Abuse and Neglect, 18,* 113–129.

Fabiani, M., Stadler, M. A., and Wessels, P. M. 2000. True but not false memories produce a sensory signature in human lateralized brain potentials. *Journal of Cognitive Neuroscience, 12,* 941–949.

False Memory Syndrome Foundation. 1995. *Frequently asked questions*. Philadelphia.

Fanon, F. 1961. *The wretched of the earth*, trans. Constance Farrington. New York: Grove, 1963.

Faraone, S. V., Tsuang, M. T., and Tsuang, D. W. 1999. *Genetics of mental disorder: A guide for students, clinicians, and researchers*. New York: Guilford.

Farrell, A. 1995. [Review of] *Achilles in Vietnam*, Jonathan Shay. *Viet Nam Generation, 6*, 192–193.

Favaro, A., Rodella, F. C., Colombo, G., and Santonastaso, P. 1999. Post-traumatic stress disorder and major depression among Italian Nazi concentration camp survivors: A controlled study 50 years later. *Psychological Medicine, 29*, 87–95.

Feinstein, A. 1989. Posttraumatic stress disorder: A descriptive study supporting DSM-III-R criteria. *American Journal of Psychiatry, 146*, 665–666.

Feldman-Summers, S., and Pope, K. S. 1994. The experience of "forgetting" childhood abuse: A national survey of psychologists. *Journal of Consulting and Clinical Psychology, 62*, 636–639.

Femina, D. D., Yeager, C. A., and Lewis, D. O. 1990. Child abuse: Adolescent records vs. adult recall. *Child Abuse and Neglect, 14*, 227–231.

Fiedler, K., Walther, E., Armbruster, T., Fay, D., and Naumann, U. 1996. Do you *really* know what you have seen? Intrusion errors and presuppositions effects on constructive memory. *Journal of Experimental Social Psychology, 32*, 484–511.

Fink, G. R., Markowitsch, H. J., Reinkemeier, M., Bruckbauer, T., Kessler, J., and Heiss, W.-D. 1996. Cerebral representation of one's own past: Neural networks involved in autobiographical memory. *Journal of Neuroscience, 16*, 4275–82.

Finkelhor, D., Hotaling, G., Lewis, I. A., and Smith, C. 1990. Sexual abuse in a national survey of adult men and women: Prevalence, characteristics, and risk factors. *Child Abuse and Neglect, 14*, 19–28.

Finkelhor, D., Williams, L. M., and Burns, N. 1988. *Nursery crimes: Sexual abuse in day care*. Newbury Park, CA: Sage Publications.

Finkenauer, C., Luminet, O., Gisle, L., El-Ahmadi, A., van der Linden, M., and Philippot, P. 1998. Flashbulb memories and the underlying mechanisms of their formation: Toward an emotional-integrative model. *Memory and Cognition, 26,* 516–531.

Fischer, H., Wik, G., and Fredrikson, M. 1996. Functional neuroanatomy of robbery re-experience: Affective memories studied with PET. *NeuroReport, 7,* 2081–86.

Fish, V., and Scott, C. G. 1999. Childhood abuse recollections in a nonclinical population: Forgetting and secrecy. *Child Abuse and Neglect, 23,* 791–802.

Fisher, C. 1943. Hypnosis in treatment of neuroses due to war and to other causes. *War Medicine, 4,* 565–576.

——— 1945. Amnesic states in war neuroses: The psychogenesis of fugues. *Psychoanalytic Quarterly, 14,* 437–468.

Fisher, C., and Joseph, E. D. 1949. Fugue with awareness of loss of personal identity. *Psychoanalytic Quarterly, 18,* 480–493.

Fitzpatrick, K. M., and Boldizar, J. P. 1993. The prevalence and consequences of exposure to violence among African-American youth. *Journal of the American Academy of Child and Adolescent Psychiatry, 32,* 424–430.

Fivush, R., Gray, J. T., and Fromhoff, F. A. 1987. Two-year-olds talk about the past. *Cognitive Development, 2,* 393–409.

Fivush, R., and Hamond, N. R. 1989. Time and again: Effects of repetition and retention interval on 2 year olds' event recall. *Journal of Experimental Child Psychology, 47,* 259–273.

Fivush, R., Hudson, J., and Nelson, K. 1984. Children's long-term memory for a novel event: An exploratory study. *Merrill-Palmer Quarterly, 30,* 303–316.

Foa, E. B., Feske, U., Murdock, T. B., Kozak, M. J., and McCarthy, P. R. 1991. Processing of threat-related information in rape victims. *Journal of Abnormal Psychology, 100,* 156–162.

Foa, E. B., and Kozak, M. J. 1986. Emotional processing of fear: Exposure to corrective information. *Psychological Bulletin, 99,* 20–35.

Foa, E. B., McNally, R., and Murdock, T. B. 1989. Anxious mood and memory. *Behaviour Research and Therapy, 27,* 141–147.

Foa, E. B., Molnar, C., and Cashman, L. 1995. Change in rape narratives during exposure therapy for posttraumatic stress disorder. *Journal of Traumatic Stress, 8,* 675–690.

Foa, E. B., Riggs, D. S., Dancu, C. V., and Rothbaum, B. O. 1993. Reliability and validity of a brief instrument for assessing post-traumatic stress disorder. *Journal of Traumatic Stress*, 6, 459–473.

Foa, E. B., Zinbarg, R., and Rothbaum, B. O. 1992. Uncontrollability and unpredictability in post-traumatic stress disorder: An animal model. *Psychological Bulletin*, 112, 218–238.

Foster, J. K., and Jelicic, M., eds. 1999. *Memory: Systems, process, or function?* Oxford: Oxford University Press.

Foster, K. R., and Huber, P. W. 1999. *Judging science: Scientific knowledge and the federal courts*. Cambridge, MA: MIT Press.

Foulkes, W. D. 1962. Dream reports from different stages of sleep. *Journal of Abnormal and Social Psychology*, 65, 14–25.

Fowler, R. D. 1999. *APA letter to the Honorable Rep. DeLay (R-TX)*. June 9. Available at <www.apa.org/releases/delay.html>.

Frankel, F. H. 1994. The concept of flashbacks in historical perspective. *International Journal of Clinical and Experimental Hypnosis*, 42, 321–336.

Fredrickson, R. 1992. *Repressed memories: A journey to recovery from sexual abuse*. New York: Simon and Schuster.

Freud, A. 1966. *The ego and the mechanisms of defense*, rev. ed. Madison, CT: International Universities Press.

Freud, S. 1893. On the psychical mechanism of hysterical phenomena: A lecture. In J. Strachey, ed. and trans., *The standard edition of the complete psychological works of Sigmund Freud [Standard edition]*, vol. 3, 27–39. London: Hogarth Press, 1962.

——— 1896a. Heredity and the aetiology of the neuroses. In *Standard edition*, vol. 3, 143–156. London: Hogarth Press, 1962.

——— 1896b. Further remarks on the neuro-psychoses of defence. In *Standard edition*, vol. 3, 162–185. London: Hogarth Press, 1962.

——— 1896c. The aetiology of hysteria. In *Standard edition*, vol. 3, 191–221. London: Hogarth Press, 1962.

——— 1914a. On the history of the psycho-analytic movement. In *Standard edition*, vol. 14, 7–66. London: Hogarth Press, 1957.

———— 1914b. On narcissism: An introduction. In *Standard edition*, vol. 14, 73–102. London: Hogarth Press, 1957.

———— 1915. Repression. In *Standard edition*, vol. 14, 146–158. London: Hogarth Press, 1962.

———— 1918. From the history of an infantile neurosis. In *Standard edition*, vol. 17, 7–122. London: Hogarth Press, 1955.

———— 1933. New introductory lectures on psycho-analysis. In *Standard edition*, vol. 22, 5–157. London: Hogarth Press, 1964.

———— 1937. Constructions in analysis. In *Standard edition*, vol. 23, 257–269. London: Hogarth Press, 1964.

Freyd, J. J. 1996. *Betrayal trauma: The logic of forgetting childhood abuse*. Cambridge, MA: Harvard University Press.

Freyd, J. J., DePrince, A. P., and Zurbriggen, E. L. 2001. Self-reported memory for abuse depends upon victim-perpetrator relationship. *Journal of Trauma and Dissociation, 2*, 5–16.

Freyd, J. J., and Gleaves, D. H. 1996. "Remembering" words not presented in lists: Relevance to the current recovered/false memory controversy. *Journal of Experimental Psychology: Learning, Memory, and Cognition, 22*, 811–813.

Freyd, P. 1999. About the False Memory Syndrome Foundation. In S. Taub, ed., *Recovered memories of child sexual abuse: Psychological, social, and legal perspectives on a contemporary mental health controversy*, 17–39. Springfield, IL: Charles C. Thomas.

Friedman, M. J., Schneiderman, C. K., West, A. N., and Corson, J. A. 1986. Measurement of combat exposure, posttraumatic stress disorder, and life stress among Vietnam combat veterans. *American Journal of Psychiatry, 143*, 537–539.

Friedman, S. 1997. On the "true-false" memory syndrome: The problem of clinical evidence. *American Journal of Psychotherapy, 51*, 102–122.

Friesen, J. G. 1992. Ego-dystonic or ego-alien: Alternate personality or evil spirit? *Journal of Psychology and Theology, 20*, 197–200.

Frueh, B. C., Hamner, M. B., Cahill, S. P., Gold, P. B., and Hamlin, K. L. 2000. Apparent symptom overreporting in combat veterans evaluated for PTSD. *Clinical Psychology Review, 20*, 853–885.

Gabbard, G. O., Goodman, S. M., and Richards, A. D. 1995. Psychoanalysis after Freud: A response to Frederick Crews and other critics. *Psychoanalytic Books*, 6, 155–173.

Galea, S., Ahern, J., Resnick, H., Kilpatrick, D., Bucuvalas, M., Gold, J., and Vlahov, D. 2002. Psychological sequelae of the September 11 terrorist attacks. *New England Journal of Medicine*, 346, 982–987.

Galea, S., Boscarino, J., Resnick, H., and Vlahov, D. In press. Mental health in New York City after the September 11 terrorist attacks: Results from two population surveys. In R. W. Manderscheid and M. J. Henderson, eds., *Mental health, United States, 2001*. Washington: Superintendent of Documents, Government Printing Office.

Gallo, D. A., Roberts, M. J., and Seamon, J. G. 1997. Remembering words not presented in lists: Can we avoid creating false memories? *Psychonomic Bulletin and Review*, 4, 271–276.

Ganaway, G. K. 1989. Historical versus narrative truth: Clarifying the role of exogenous trauma in the etiology of MPD and its variants. *Dissociation*, 2, 205–220.

Garb, H. N. 1984. The incremental validity of information used in personality assessment. *Clinical Psychology Review*, 4, 641–655.

——— 1998. *Studying the clinician: Judgment research and psychological assessment.* Washington: American Psychological Association.

Garrison, E. G., and Kobor, P. C. 2002. Weathering a political storm: A contextual perspective on a psychological research controversy. *American Psychologist*, 57, 165–175.

Garry, M., Manning, C. G., Loftus, E. F., and Sherman, S. J. 1996. Imagination inflation: Imagining a childhood event inflates confidence that it occurred. *Psychonomic Bulletin and Review*, 3, 208–214.

Garven, S., Wood, J. M., and Malpass, R. S. 2000. Allegations of wrongdoing: The effects of reinforcement on children's mundane and fantastic claims. *Journal of Applied Psychology*, 85, 38–49.

Garven, S., Wood, J. M., Malpass, R. S., and Shaw, J. S., III. 1998. More than suggestion: The effect of interviewing techniques from the McMartin Preschool case. *Journal of Applied Psychology*, 83, 347–359.

Geleerd, E. R., Hacker, F. J., and Rapaport, D. 1945. Contribution to the study of amnesia and allied conditions. *Psychoanalytic Quarterly, 14,* 199–220.

Gelinas, D. J. 1983. The persisting negative effects of incest. *Psychiatry, 46,* 312–332.

Gil, T., Calev, A., Greenberg, D., Kugelmass, S., and Lerer, B. 1990. Cognitive functioning in post-traumatic stress disorder. *Journal of Traumatic Stress, 3,* 29–45.

Gilbertson, M. W., Gurvits, T. V., Lasko, N. B., Orr, S. P., and Pitman, R. K. 2001. Multivariate assessment of explicit memory function in combat veterans with posttraumatic stress disorder. *Journal of Traumatic Stress, 14,* 413–432.

Gilbertson, M. W., Shenton, M. E., Ciszewski, A., Kasai, K., Lasko, N. B., Orr, S. P., and Pitman, R. K. 2002. Smaller hippocampal volume predicts pathologic vulnerability to psychological trauma. *Nature Neuroscience, 5,* 1242–47.

Glaser, D., and Collins, C. 1989. The response of young, non-sexually abused children to anatomically correct dolls. *Journal of Child Psychology and Psychiatry, 30,* 547–560.

Glaubman, H., Mikulincer, M., Porat, A., Wasserman, O., and Birger, M. 1990. Sleep of chronic post-traumatic patients. *Journal of Traumatic Stress, 3,* 255–263.

Gleaves, D. H. 1996. The sociocognitive model of dissociative identity disorder: A reexamination of the evidence. *Psychological Bulletin, 120,* 42–59.

Gleaves, D. H., and Hernandez, E. 1999. Recent reformulations of Freud's development and abandonment of his seduction theory: Historical/scientific clarification or a continued assault on truth? *History of Psychology, 2,* 324–354.

Gloor, P., Olivier, A., Quesney, L. F., Andermann, F., and Horowitz, S. 1982. The role of the limbic system in experiential phenomena of temporal lobe epilepsy. *Annals of Neurology, 12,* 129–144.

Godden, D. R., and Baddeley, A. D. 1975. Context-dependent memory in two natural environments: On land and underwater. *British Journal of Psychology, 66,* 325–331.

Gold, P. E. 1992. A proposed neurobiological basis for regulating memory storage for significant events. In E. Winograd and U. Neisser, eds., *Affect and accuracy in recall: Studies of "flashbulb" memories*, 141–161. Cambridge: Cambridge University Press.

Gold, S. N., Hughes, D., and Hohnecker, L. 1994. Degrees of repression of sexual abuse memories. *American Psychologist, 49,* 441–442.

Gold, S. N., Hughes, D. M., and Swingle, J. M. 1999. Degrees of memory of childhood sexual abuse among women survivors in therapy. *Journal of Family Violence, 14,* 35–46.

Goldfeld, A. E., Mollica, R. F., Pesavento, B. H., and Faraone, S. V. 1988. The physical and psychological sequelae of torture: Symptomatology and diagnosis. *JAMA, 259,* 2725–29.

Golding, J. M., Sanchez, R. P., and Sego, S. A. 1996. Do you believe in repressed memories? *Professional Psychology: Research and Practice, 27,* 429–437.

Goldstein, E., and Farmer, K. 1993. *True stories of false memories.* Boca Raton, FL: Upton Books.

———— 1994. *Confabulations: Creating false memories, destroying families.* Boca Raton, FL: Upton Books.

Gonzalez, L. S., Waterman, J., Kelly, R. J., McCord, J., and Oliveri, M. K. 1993. Children's patterns of disclosures and recantations of sexual and ritualistic abuse allegations in psychotherapy. *Child Abuse and Neglect, 17,* 281–289.

Good, M. I. 1994. The reconstruction of early childhood trauma: Fantasy, reality, and verification. *Journal of the American Psychoanalytic Association, 42,* 79–101.

Goodman, G. S., and Aman, C. 1990. Children's use of anatomically detailed dolls to recount an event. *Child Development, 61,* 1859–71.

Goodman, G. S., Ghetti, S., Quas, J. A., Edelstein, R. S., Alexander, K. W., Redlich, A. D., Cordon, I. M., and Jones, D. P. H. In press. A prospective study of memory for child sexual abuse: New findings relevant to the repressed/lost memory controversy. *Psychological Science.*

Goodman, G. S., Hirschman, J. E., Hepps, D., and Rudy, L. 1991. Children's memory for stressful events. *Merrill-Palmer Quarterly, 37,* 109–158.

Goodman, G. S., Quas, J. A., Batterman-Faunce, J. M., Riddlesberger, M. M., and Kuhn, J. 1994. Predictors of accurate and inaccurate memories of traumatic events experienced in childhood. *Consciousness and Cognition*, 3, 269–294.

Goodwin, D. W., Crane, J. B., and Guze, S. B. 1969. Phenomenological aspects of the alcoholic "blackout." *British Journal of Psychiatry*, 115, 1033–38.

Goodwin, J. M. 1994. Credibility problems in sadistic abuse. *Journal of Psychohistory*, 21, 479–496.

Gorey, K. M., and Leslie, D. R. 1997. The prevalence of child sexual abuse: Integrative review adjustment for potential response and measurement biases. *Child Abuse and Neglect*, 21, 391–398.

Gould, C. 1992. Diagnosis and treatment of ritually abused children. In Sakheim and Devine, eds., 1992.

——— 1995. Denying ritual abuse of children. *Journal of Psychohistory*, 22, 329–339.

Gould, C., and Cozolino, L. 1992. Ritual abuse, multiplicity, and mind-control. *Journal of Psychology and Theology*, 20, 194–196.

Gould, E., Tanapat, P., McEwen, B. S., Flügge, G., and Fuchs, E. 1998. Proliferation of granule cell precursors in the dentate gyrus of adult monkeys is diminished by stress. *Proceedings of the National Academy of Sciences*, 95, 3168–71.

Graf, P., and Schacter, D. L. 1985. Implicit and explicit memory for new associations in normal and amnesic subjects. *Journal of Experimental Psychology: Learning, Memory, and Cognition*, 11, 501–518.

Gray, M. J., and Lombardo, T. W. 2001. Complexity of trauma narratives as an index of fragmented memory in PTSD: A critical analysis. *Applied Cognitive Psychology*, 15, S171–S186.

Green, B. 1990. Defining trauma: Terminology and generic stressor dimensions. *Journal of Applied Social Psychology*, 20, 1632–42.

Green, B. L., Korol, M., Grace, M. C., Vary, M. G., Leonard, A. C., Gleser, G. C., and Smitson-Cohen, S. 1991. Children and disaster: Age, gender, and parental effects on PTSD symptoms. *Journal of the American Academy of Child and Adolescent Psychiatry*, 30, 945–951.

Greenberg, R., Pearlman, C. A., and Gampel, D. 1972. War neuroses and the adaptive function of REM sleep. *British Journal of Medical Psychology, 45,* 27–33.

Greenwald, A. G. 1980. The totalitarian ego: Fabrication and revision of personal history. *American Psychologist, 35,* 603–618.

Grinker, R. R., and Spiegel, J. P. 1944. Brief psychotherapy in war neuroses. *Psychosomatic Medicine, 6,* 123–131.

———— 1945. *Men under stress.* Philadelphia: Blakiston.

Grossman, D. 1995. *On killing: The psychological cost of learning to kill in war and society.* Boston: Little, Brown.

Grove, W. M., and Barden, R. C. 1999. Protecting the integrity of the legal system: The admissibility of testimony from mental health experts under *Daubert/Kumho* analyses. *Psychology, Public Policy, and Law, 5,* 224–242.

Grunert, B. K., Devine, C. A., Matloub, H. S., Sanger, J. R., and Yousif, N. J. 1988. Flashbacks after traumatic hand injuries: Prognostic indicators. *Journal of Hand Surgery, 13A,* 125–127.

Gudjonsson, G. H. 1987. A parallel form of the Gudjonsson Suggestibility Scale. *British Journal of Clinical Psychology, 26,* 215–221.

———— 1997. Accusations by adults of childhood sexual abuse: A survey of the members of the British False Memory Society (BFMS). *Applied Cognitive Psychology, 11,* 3–18.

Gudjonsson, G. H., and Haward, L. R. C. 1982. Case report—Hysterical amnesia as an alternative to suicide. *Medicine, Science and Law, 22,* 68–72.

Gudjonsson, G. H., Kopelman, M. D., and MacKeith, J. A. C. 1999. Unreliable admissions to homicide: A case of misdiagnosis of amnesia and misuse of abreaction technique. *British Journal of Psychiatry, 174,* 455–459.

Gudjonsson, G. H., and MacKeith, J. A. C. 1983. A specific recognition deficit in a case of homicide. *Medicine, Science and Law, 23,* 37–40.

Gudjonsson, G. H., and Taylor, P. J. 1985. Cognitive deficit in a case of retrograde amnesia. *British Journal of Psychiatry, 147,* 715–718.

Gurvits, T. V., Gilbertson, M. W., Lasko, N. B., Tarhan, A. S., Simeon, D., Macklin, M. L., Orr, S. P., and Pitman, R. K. 2000. Neurologic soft signs in chronic posttraumatic stress disorder. *Archives of General Psychiatry, 57,* 181–186.

Gurvits, T. V., Lasko, N. B., Schachter, S. C., Kuhne, A. A., Orr, S. P., and Pitman, R. K. 1993. Neurological status of Vietnam veterans with chronic posttraumatic stress disorder. *Journal of Neuropsychiatry and Clinical Neurosciences, 5,* 183–188.

Gurvits, T. V., Shenton, M. E., Hokama, H., Ohta, H., Lasko, N. B., Gilbertson, M. W., Orr, S. P., Kikinis, R., Jolesz, F. A., McCarley, R. W., and Pitman, R. K. 1996. Magnetic resonance imaging study of hippocampal volume in chronic, combat-related posttraumatic stress disorder. *Biological Psychiatry, 40,* 1091–99.

Hacking, I. 1995. *Rewriting the soul: Multiple personality and the sciences of memory.* Princeton: Princeton University Press.

———— 1998. *Mad travelers: Reflections on the reality of transient mental illness.* Charlottesville: University Press of Virginia.

———— 1999. *The social construction of what?* Cambridge, MA: Harvard University Press.

Haley, S. A. 1974. When the patient reports atrocities: Specific treatment considerations of the Vietnam veteran. *Archives of General Psychiatry, 30,* 191–196.

Hamann, S. 2001. Cognitive and neural mechanisms of emotional memory. *Trends in Cognitive Sciences, 5,* 394–400.

Hamann, S. B., Ely, T. D., Grafton, S. T., and Kilts, C. D. 1999. Amygdala activity related to enhanced memory for pleasant and aversive stimuli. *Nature Neuroscience, 2,* 289–293.

Hamann, S. B., Ely, T. D., Hoffman, J. M., and Kilts, C. D. 2002. Ecstasy and agony: Activation of the human amygdala in positive and negative emotion. *Psychological Science, 13,* 135–141.

Hammerschlag, M. R., Rettig, P. J., and Shields, M. E. 1988. False positive results with the use of chlamydial antigen detection tests in the evaluation of suspected sexual abuse of children. *Pediatric Infectious Disease Journal, 7,* 11–14.

Hammond, D. C. 1992. Lecture delivered at the Fourth Annual Regional Meeting on Abuse and Multiple Personality. Audiotapes of this lecture were available from Audio Transcripts, Alexandria, VA.

Hamond, N. R., and Fivush, R. 1991. Memories of Mickey Mouse: Young children recount their trip to Disney World. *Cognitive Development, 6,* 433–448.

Handy, B. 1997. Roswell or bust. *Time, 149* (June 23), 62–67.

Haritos-Fatouros, M. 1988. The official torturer: A learning model for obedience to the authority of violence. *Journal of Applied Social Psychology, 18,* 1107–20.

Harman, G. 1965. The inference to the best explanation. *Philosophical Review, 74,* 88–95.

Harry, B., and Resnick, P. J. 1986. Posttraumatic stress disorder in murderers. *Journal of Forensic Science, 31,* 609–613.

Harvey, A. G., and Bryant, R. A. 1998a. The relationship between acute stress disorder and posttraumatic stress disorder: A prospective evaluation of motor vehicle accident survivors. *Journal of Consulting and Clinical Psychology, 66,* 507–512.

———— 1998b. The effect of attempted thought suppression in acute stress disorder. *Behaviour Research and Therapy, 36,* 583–590.

———— 2000. Memory for acute stress disorder symptoms: A two-year prospective study. *Journal of Nervous and Mental Disease, 188,* 602–607.

———— 2001. Reconstructing trauma memories: A prospective study of "amnesic" trauma survivors. *Journal of Traumatic Stress, 14,* 277–282.

Harvey, A. G., Bryant, R. A., and Dang, S. T. 1998. Autobiographical memory in acute stress disorder. *Journal of Consulting and Clinical Psychology, 66,* 500–506.

Harvey, A. G., Bryant, R. A., and Rapee, R. M. 1996. Preconscious processing of threat in posttraumatic stress disorder. *Cognitive Therapy and Research, 20,* 613–623.

Harvey, P. D., and Yehuda, R. 1999. Strategies to study risk for the development of PTSD. In R. Yehuda, ed., *Risk factors for posttraumatic stress disorder,* 1–22. Washington: American Psychiatric Press.

Heaps, C., and Nash, M. 1999. Individual differences in imagination inflation. *Psychonomic Bulletin and Review, 6,* 313–318.

Hefez, A., Metz, L., and Lavie, P. 1987. Long-term effects of extreme situational stress on sleep and dreaming. *American Journal of Psychiatry, 144,* 344–347.

Helzer, J. E., Robins, L. N., and McEvoy, L. 1987. Post-traumatic stress disorder in the general population: Findings of the Epidemiologic Catchment Area Survey. *New England Journal of Medicine, 317,* 1630–34.

Henderson, D., Hargreaves, I., Gregory, S., and Williams, J. M. G. 2002. Autobiographical memory and emotion in a non-clinical sample of women with and without a reported history of childhood sexual abuse. *British Journal of Clinical Psychology*, *41*, 129–141.

Henderson, J. L., and Moore, M. 1944. The psychoneuroses of war. *New England Journal of Medicine*, *230*, 273–278.

Herman, J. L. 1981. *Father-daughter incest*. Cambridge, MA: Harvard University Press.

———— 1992. *Trauma and recovery*. New York: Basic Books.

Herman, J. L., and Harvey, M. R. 1997. Adult memories of childhood trauma: A naturalistic clinical study. *Journal of Traumatic Stress*, *10*, 557–571.

Herman, J. L., and Schatzow, E. 1987. Recovery and verification of memories of childhood sexual trauma. *Psychoanalytic Psychology*, *4*, 1–14.

Herrmann, D. J. 1982. Know thy memory: The use of questionnaires to assess and study memory. *Psychological Bulletin*, *92*, 434–452.

Heuer, F., and Reisberg, D. 1990. Vivid memories of emotional events: The accuracy of remembered minutiae. *Memory and Cognition*, *18*, 496–506.

Hewitt, S. K. 1994. Preverbal sexual abuse: What two children report in later years. *Child Abuse and Neglect*, *18*, 821–826.

Higham, P. A. 1998. Believing details known to have been suggested. *British Journal of Psychology*, *89*, 265–283.

Hill, S., and Goodwin, J. 1989. Satanism: Similarities between patient accounts and pre-Inquisition historical sources. *Dissociation*, *2*, 39–44.

Holmes, D. S. 1974. Investigations of repression: Differential recall of material experimentally or naturally associated with ego threat. *Psychological Bulletin*, *81*, 632–653.

———— 1990. The evidence for repression: An examination of sixty years of research. In J. L. Singer, ed., *Repression and dissociation: Implications for personality theory, psychopathology, and health*, 85–102. Chicago: University of Chicago Press.

Hopwood, J. S., and Snell, H. K. 1933. Amnesia in relation to crime. *Journal of Mental Science*, *79*, 27–41.

Hovdestad, W. E., and Kristiansen, C. M. 1996. A field study of "false memory syndrome": Construct validity and incidence. *Journal of Psychiatry and Law,* *24,* 229–338.

Howard, J. M., Olney, J. M., Frawley, J. P., Peterson, R. E., Smith, L. H., Davis, J. H., Guerra, S., and Dibrell, W. H. 1955. Studies of adrenal function in combat and wounded soldiers: A study in the Korean theatre. *Annals of Surgery,* *141,* 314–320.

Howe, M. L., and Courage, M. L. 1993. On resolving the enigma of infantile amnesia. *Psychological Bulletin, 113,* 305–326.

Howe, M. L., Courage, M. L., and Peterson, C. 1995. Intrusions in preschoolers' recall of traumatic childhood events. *Psychonomic Bulletin and Review, 2,* 130–134.

Hufford, D. J. 1982. *The terror that comes in the night: An experience-centered study of supernatural assault traditions.* Philadelphia: University of Pennsylvania Press.

Hume, D. 1740. *A treatise of human nature.* Oxford: Oxford University Press, 2000.

Huntjens, R. J. C., Postma, A., Peters, M., Hamaker, E. L., Woertman, L., and van der Hart, O. In press. Perceptual and conceptual priming in patients with dissociative identity disorder. *Memory and Cognition.* [update in proof]

Huntjens, R. J. C., Postma, A., Peters, M. L., Woertman, L., and van der Hart, O. In press. Inter-identity amnesia for neutral, episodic information in dissociative identity disorder. *Journal of Abnormal Psychology.*

Husni, M., Cernovsky, Z. Z., Koye, N., and Haggarty, J. 2001. Nightmares of refugees from Kurdistan. *Journal of Nervous and Mental Disease, 189,* 557–559.

Hyman, I. E., Jr., and Billings, F. J. 1998. Individual differences and the creation of false childhood memories. *Memory, 6,* 1–20.

Hyman, I. E., Jr., Husband, T. H., and Billings, F. J. 1995. False memories of childhood experiences. *Applied Cognitive Psychology, 9,* 181–197.

Hyman, I. E., Jr., and Pentland, J. 1996. The role of mental imagery in the creation of false childhood memories. *Journal of Memory and Language, 35,* 101–117.

Ignatieff, M. 2002. The torture wars. *New Republic, 226* (April 22), 40–43.

Israel, L., and Schacter, D. L. 1997. Pictorial encoding reduces false recognition of semantic associates. *Psychonomic Bulletin and Review, 4*, 577–581.

Israëls, H., and Schatzman, M. 1993. The seduction theory. *History of Psychiatry, 4*, 23–59.

Jacobs, W. J., and Nadel, L. 1998. Neurobiology of reconstructed memory. *Psychology, Public Policy, and Law, 4*, 1110–34.

Jacoby, L. L., and Dallas, M. 1981. On the relationship between autobiographical memory and perceptual learning. *Journal of Experimental Psychology: General, 110*, 306–340.

Jacoby, L. L., and Hayman, C. A. G. 1987. Specific visual transfer in word identification. *Journal of Experimental Psychology: Learning, Memory, and Cognition, 13*, 456–463.

Jampole, L., and Weber, M. K. 1987. An assessment of the behavior of sexually abused and nonsexually abused children with anatomically correct dolls. *Child Abuse and Neglect, 11*, 187–192.

Janet, P. 1907. *The major symptoms of hysteria.* New York: Macmillan.

Jenkins, M. A., Langlais, P. J., Delis, D., and Cohen, R. 1998. Learning and memory in rape victims with posttraumatic stress disorder. *American Journal of Psychiatry, 155*, 278–279.

Jenkins, P. 1998. *Moral panic: Changing concepts of the child molester in modern America.* New Haven: Yale University Press.

Johnson, D. M., Pike, J. L., and Chard, K. M. 2001. Factors predicting PTSD, depression, and dissociative severity in female treatment-seeking childhood sexual abuse survivors. *Child Abuse and Neglect, 25*, 179–198.

Johnson, M. K., Foley, M. A., Suengas, A. G., and Raye, C. L. 1988. Phenomenal characteristics of memories for perceived and imagined autobiographical events. *Journal of Experimental Psychology: General, 117*, 371–376.

Johnson, M. K., Hashtroudi, S., and Lindsay, D. S. 1993. Source monitoring. *Psychological Bulletin, 114*, 3–28.

Johnson, M. K., Nolde, S. F., and De Leonardis, D. M. 1996. Emotional focus and source monitoring. *Journal of Memory and Language, 35*, 135–156.

Johnson, M. K., and Raye, C. L. 1981. Reality monitoring. *Psychological Review, 88*, 67–85.

Jones, B., Heard, H., Startup, M., Swales, M., Williams, J. M. G., and Jones, R. S. P. 1999. Autobiographical memory and dissociation in borderline personality disorder. *Psychological Medicine, 29,* 1397–1404.

Jones, D. P. H., and McGraw, J. M. 1987. Reliable and fictitious accounts of sexual abuse in children. *Journal of Interpersonal Violence, 2,* 27–45.

Jonker, F., and Jonker-Bakker, I. 1997. Effects of ritual abuse: The results of three surveys in the Netherlands. *Child Abuse and Neglect, 21,* 541–556.

Joseph, R. 1999. The neurology of traumatic "dissociative" amnesia: Commentary and literature review. *Child Abuse and Neglect, 23,* 715–727.

Joseph, S., and Masterson, J. 1999. Posttraumatic stress disorder and traumatic brain injury: Are they mutually exclusive? *Journal of Traumatic Stress, 12,* 437–453.

Josephson, J. R., and Josephson, S. G., eds. 1996. *Abductive inference: Computation, philosophy, technology.* Cambridge: Cambridge University Press.

Joslyn, S., Carlin, L., and Loftus, E. F. 1997. Remembering and forgetting childhood sexual abuse. *Memory, 5,* 703–724.

Kagan, J. 1998. Animal fear and human guilt. *Cerebrum, 1,* 16–21.

Kaminer, H., and Lavie, P. 1991. Sleep and dreaming in Holocaust survivors: Dramatic decrease in dream recall in well-adjusted survivors. *Journal of Nervous and Mental Disease, 179,* 664–669.

Kanzer, M. 1939. Amnesia: A statistical study. *American Journal of Psychiatry, 96,* 711–716.

Kaplan, Z., Weiser, M., Reichenberg, A., Rabinowitz, J., Caspi, A., Bodner, E., and Zohar, J. 2002. Motivation to serve in the military influences vulnerability to future posttraumatic stress disorder. *Psychiatry Research, 109,* 45–49.

Kapur, N. 1991. Amnesia in relation to fugue states: Distinguishing a neurological from a psychogenic basis. *British Journal of Psychiatry, 159,* 872–877.

Karon, B. P., and Widener, A. J. 1997. Repressed memories and World War II: Lest we forget! *Professional Psychology: Research and Practice, 28,* 338–340.

Kaspi, S. P., McNally, R. J., and Amir, N. 1995. Cognitive processing of emotional information in posttraumatic stress disorder. *Cognitive Therapy and Research, 19,* 433–444.

Kassin, S. M. 1997a. The psychology of confession evidence. *American Psychologist,* *52,* 221–233.

——— 1997b. False memories turned against the self. *Psychological Inquiry, 8,* 300–302.

Kaszniak, A. W., Nussbaum, P. D., Berren, M. R., and Santiago, J. 1988. Amnesia as a consequence of male rape: A case report. *Journal of Abnormal Psychology, 97,* 100–104.

Keane, T. M., Caddell, J. M., and Taylor, K. L. 1988. Mississippi Scale for Combat-Related Posttraumatic Stress Disorder: Three studies in reliability and validity. *Journal of Consulting and Clinical Psychology, 56,* 85–90.

Keane, T. M., Kolb, L. C., Kaloupek, D. G., Orr, S. P., Blanchard, E. B., Thomas, R. G., Hsieh, F. Y., and Lavori, P. W. 1998. Utility of psychophysiological measurement in the diagnosis of posttraumatic stress disorder: Results from a Department of Veterans Affairs Cooperative Study. *Journal of Consulting and Clinical Psychology, 66,* 914–923.

Keane, T. M., Scott, W. O., Chavoya, G. A., Lamparski, D. M., and Fairbank, J. 1985. Social support in Vietnam veterans with posttraumatic stress disorder: A comparative analysis. *Journal of Consulting and Clinical Psychology, 53,* 95–102.

Keane, T. M., Zimering, R. T., and Caddell, J. T. 1985. A behavioral formulation of posttraumatic stress disorder in Vietnam veterans. *Behavior Therapist, 8,* 9–12.

Kelley, S. J., Brant, R., and Waterman, J. 1993. Sexual abuse of children in day care centers. *Child Abuse and Neglect, 17,* 71–89.

Kempe, C. H., Silverman, F. N., Steele, B. F., Droegemueller, W., and Silver, H. K. 1962. The battered-child syndrome. *JAMA, 181,* 17–24.

Kendall-Tackett, K. A., Williams, L. M., and Finkelhor, D. 1993. Impact of sexual abuse on children: A review and synthesis of recent empirical studies. *Psychological Bulletin, 113,* 164–180.

Kendler, K. S., Bulik, C. M., Silberg, J., Hettema, J. M., Myers, J., and Prescott, C. A. 2000. Childhood sexual abuse and adult psychiatric and substance use disorders in women: An epidemiological and cotwin control analysis. *Archives of General Psychiatry, 57,* 953–959.

Keppel, R. D., and Birnes, W. J. 1997. *Signature killers: Interpreting the calling cards of the serial murderer*. New York: Pocket Books.

Kernberg, O. 2002. Discussion. In H. I. Lief, chair, *Traumatic memories and their effect on psychoanalysis and psychotherapy*. Symposium held at the meeting of the American Academy of Psychoanalysis, Philadelphia, May.

Kessler, R. C., Sonnega, A., Bromet, E., Hughes, M., and Nelson, C. B. 1995. Posttraumatic stress disorder in the National Comorbidity Survey. *Archives of General Psychiatry, 52*, 1048–60.

Kihlstrom, J. F. 1987. The cognitive unconscious. *Science, 237*, 1445–52.

———— 1995. The trauma-memory argument. *Consciousness and Cognition, 4*, 63–67.

———— 1997a. Hypnosis, memory and amnesia. *Philosophical Transactions of the Royal Society: Biological Sciences, 352*, 1727–32.

———— 1997b. Suffering from reminiscences: Exhumed memory, implicit memory, and the return of the repressed. In M. A. Conway, ed., *Recovered memories and false memories*, 100–117. Oxford: Oxford University Press.

———— 1998. Exhumed memory. In S. J. Lynn and K. M. McConkey, eds., *Truth in memory*, 3–31. New York: Guilford.

Kihlstrom, J. F., and Harackiewicz, J. M. 1982. The earliest recollection: A new survey. *Journal of Personality, 50*, 134–148.

Kihlstrom, J. F., and Schacter, D. L. 2000. Functional amnesia. In F. Boller and J. Grafman, eds., *Handbook of neuropsychology*, 2nd ed., vol. 2, 409–427. Amsterdam: Elsevier Science.

King, D. W., King, L. A., Erickson, D. J., Huang, M. T., Sharkansky, E. J., and Wolfe, J. 2000. Posttraumatic stress disorder and retrospectively reported stressor exposure: A longitudinal prediction model. *Journal of Abnormal Psychology, 109*, 624–633.

King, D. W., King, L. A., Foy, D. W., and Gudanowski, D. M. 1996. Prewar factors in combat-related posttraumatic stress disorder: Structural equation modeling with a national sample of female and male Vietnam veterans. *Journal of Consulting and Clinical Psychology, 64*, 520–531.

King, D. W., King, L. A., Gudanowski, D. M., and Vreven, D. L. 1995. Alternative representations of war zone stressors: Relationships to posttraumatic stress disorder in male and female Vietnam veterans. *Journal of Abnormal Psychology, 104,* 184–196.

King, N. S. 2001. "Affect without recollection" in post-traumatic stress disorder where head injury causes organic amnesia for the event. *Behavioural and Cognitive Psychotherapy, 29,* 501–504.

Kinzie, J. D. 1993. Posttraumatic effects and their treatment among Southeast Asian refugees. In J. P. Wilson and B. Raphael, eds., *International handbook of traumatic stress syndromes,* 311–319. New York: Plenum.

Kinzie, J. D., Sack, W. H., Angell, R. H., Manson, S., and Rath, B. 1986. The psychiatric effects of massive trauma on Cambodian children: I. The children. *Journal of the American Academy of Child Psychiatry, 25,* 370–376.

Kirschbaum, C., Wolf, O. T., May, M., Wippich, W., and Hellhammer, D. H. 1996. Stress- and treatment-induced elevations of cortisol levels associated with impaired declarative memory in healthy adults. *Life Sciences, 58,* 1475–83.

Kluft, R. P. 1991. Hospital treatment of multiple personality disorder: An overview. *Psychiatric Clinics of North America, 14,* 695–719.

—— 1997. The argument for the reality of delayed recall of trauma. In P. S. Appelbaum, L. A. Uyehara, and M. R. Elin, eds., *Trauma and memory: Clinical and legal controversies,* 25–57. New York: Oxford University Press.

Koopman, C., Gore-Felton, C., and Spiegel, D. 1997. Acute stress disorder symptoms among female sexual abuse survivors seeking treatment. *Journal of Child Sexual Abuse, 6,* 65–85.

Kopelman, M. D. 1987. Amnesia: Organic and psychogenic. *British Journal of Psychiatry, 150,* 428–442.

—— 1995. The assessment of psychogenic amnesia. In A. D. Baddeley, B. A. Wilson, and F. N. Watts, eds., *Handbook of memory disorders,* 427–448. Chichester, UK: Wiley.

Kopelman, M. D., Christensen, H., Puffett, A., and Stanhope, N. 1994. The great escape: A neuropsychological study of psychogenic amnesia. *Neuropsychologia, 32,* 675–691.

Kopelman, M. D., Green, R. E. A., Guinan, E. M., Lewis, P. D. R., and Stanhope, N. 1994. The case of the amnesic intelligence officer. *Psychological Medicine, 24,* 1037–45.

Korfine, L., and Hooley, J. M. 2000. Directed forgetting of emotional stimuli in borderline personality disorder. *Journal of Abnormal Psychology*, 109, 214–221.

Koriat, A., Goldsmith, M., and Pansky, A. 2000. Toward a psychology of memory accuracy. *Annual Review of Psychology*, 51, 481–537.

Koss, M. P., Figueredo, A. J., Bell, I., Tharan, M., and Tromp, S. 1996. Traumatic memory characteristics: A cross-validated mediational model of response to rape among employed women. *Journal of Abnormal Psychology*, 105, 421–432.

Koutstaal, W., and Schacter, D. L. 1997. Gist-based false recognition of pictures in older and younger adults. *Journal of Memory and Language*, 37, 555–583.

Krafft-Ebing, R. von. 1886. *Psychopathia sexualis: A medico-forensic study*, trans. H. E. Wedeck. New York: Putnam, 1965.

Kramer, T. H., Buckhout, R., Fox, P., Widman, E., and Tusche, B. 1991. Effects of stress on recall. *Applied Cognitive Psychology*, 5, 483–488.

Krikorian, R., and Layton, B. S. 1998. Implicit memory in posttraumatic stress disorder with amnesia for the traumatic event. *Journal of Neuropsychiatry and Clinical Neurosciences*, 10, 359–362.

Kubie, L. S. 1943. Manual of emergency treatment for acute war neuroses. *War Medicine*, 4, 582–598.

Kuch, K., and Cox, B. J. 1992. Symptoms of PTSD in 124 survivors of the Holocaust. *American Journal of Psychiatry*, 149, 337–340.

Kulka, R. A., Schlenger, W. E., Fairbank, J. A., Hough, R. L., Jordan, B. K., Marmar, C. R., and Weiss, D. S. 1990. *Trauma and the Vietnam war generation: Report of findings from the National Vietnam Veterans Readjustment Study*. New York: Brunner/Mazel.

Kuyken, W., and Brewin, C. R. 1995. Autobiographical memory functioning in depression and reports of early abuse. *Journal of Abnormal Psychology*, 104, 585–591.

La Fontaine, J. S. 1998. *Speak of the devil: Tales of satanic abuse in contemporary England*. Cambridge: Cambridge University Press.

Lampinen, J. M., and Schwartz, R. M. 2000. The impersistence of false memory persistence. *Memory*, 8, 393–400.

Lang, P. J. 1985. The cognitive psychophysiology of emotion: Fear and anxiety. In A. H. Tuma and J. D. Maser, eds., *Anxiety and the anxiety disorders*, 131–170. Hillsdale, NJ: Erlbaum.

Langer, L. L. 1991. *Holocaust testimonies: The ruins of memory*. New Haven: Yale University Press.

Lanius, R. A., Williamson, P. C., Densmore, M., Boksman, K., Gupta, M. A., Neufeld, R. W., Gati, J. S., and Menon, R. S. 2001. Neural correlates of traumatic memories in posttraumatic stress disorder: A functional MRI investigation. *American Journal of Psychiatry, 158,* 1920–22.

Lanning, K. V. 1991. Ritual abuse: A law enforcement view or perspective. *Child Abuse and Neglect, 15,* 171–173.

———— 1992. A law-enforcement perspective on allegations of ritual abuse. In Sakheim and Devine, eds., 1992.

Laor, N., Wolmer, L., Wiener, Z., Reiss, A., Muller, U., Weizman, R., and Ron, S. 1998. The function of image control in the psychophysiology of posttraumatic stress disorder. *Journal of Traumatic Stress, 11,* 679–696.

Lavie, P. 2001. Sleep disturbances in the wake of traumatic events. *New England Journal of Medicine, 345,* 1825–32.

Lavie, P., Hefez, A., Halperin, G., and Enoch, D. 1979. Long-term effects of traumatic war-related events on sleep. *American Journal of Psychiatry, 136,* 175–178.

Lawrence, K. J., Cozolino, L., and Foy, D. W. 1995. Psychological sequelae in adult females reporting childhood ritualistic abuse. *Child Abuse and Neglect, 19,* 975–984.

Lazarus, R. S., DeLongis, A., Folkman, S., and Gruen, R. 1985. Stress and adaptational outcomes: The problem of confounded measures. *American Psychologist, 40,* 770–779.

Leavitt, F. 1997. False attribution of suggestibility to explain recovered memory of childhood sexual abuse following extended amnesia. *Child Abuse and Neglect, 21,* 265–272.

Leavitt, F., and Labott, S. M. 1998. Revision of the word association test for assessing associations of patients reporting satanic ritual abuse in childhood. *Journal of Clinical Psychology, 54,* 933–943.

LeDoux, J. E. 1996. *The emotional brain: The mysterious underpinnings of emotional life*. New York: Simon and Schuster.

——— 2000. Emotion circuits in the brain. *Annual Review of Neuroscience, 23*, 155–184.

LeDoux, J. E., Romanski, L., and Xagoraris, A. 1989. Indelibility of subcortical emotional memories. *Journal of Cognitive Neuroscience, 1*, 238–243.

Lees-Haley, P. R. 1999. Pseudo posttraumatic stress disorder: An update. *Hippocrates' Lantern, 6*, 1–9.

Leichtman, M. D., and Ceci, S. J. 1995. The effects of stereotypes and suggestions on preschoolers' reports. *Developmental Psychology, 31*, 568–578.

Lemieux, A. M., and Coe, C. L. 1995. Abuse-related posttraumatic stress disorder: Evidence for chronic neuroendocrine activation in women. *Psychosomatic Medicine, 57*, 105–115.

Leopold, R. L., and Dillon, H. 1963. Psycho-anatomy of a disaster: A long-term study of post-traumatic neuroses in survivors of a marine explosion. *American Journal of Psychiatry, 119*, 913–921.

Lerch, I. 1999. Letter from the chair of the American Association for the Advancement of Science's Committee on Scientific Freedom and Responsibility to Richard McCarty, Executive Director of Science, American Psychological Association. *Psychological Science Agenda, 12* (6) (Nov.-Dec.), 2–3.

Lewis, D. O., Yeager, C. A., Swica, Y., Pincus, J. H., and Lewis, M. 1997. Objective documentation of child abuse and dissociation in 12 murderers with dissociative identity disorder. *American Journal of Psychiatry, 154*, 1703–10.

Lewontin, R. C. 1998. The evolution of cognition: Questions we will never answer. In D. Scarborough and S. Sternberg, eds., *An invitation to cognitive science*, vol. 4: *Methods, models, and conceptual issues*, 2nd ed., 105–132. Cambridge, MA: MIT Press.

Lewy, G. 1978. *America in Vietnam*. Oxford: Oxford University Press.

Liberzon, I., Taylor, S. F., Amdur, R., Jung, T. D., Chamberlain, K. R., Minoshima, S., Koeppe, R. A., and Fig, L. M. 1999. Brain activation in PTSD in response to trauma-related stimuli. *Biological Psychiatry, 45*, 817–826.

Liberzon, I., Taylor, S. F., Fig, L. M., and Koeppe, R. A. 1996/1997. Alterations of corticothalamic perfusion ratios during a PTSD flashback. *Depression and Anxiety, 4,* 146–150.

Lidz, T. 1946a. Nightmares and combat neuroses. *Psychiatry, 9,* 37–49.

———— 1946b. Psychiatric casualties from Guadalcanal: A study of reactions to extreme stress. *Psychiatry, 9,* 193–213.

Lie, E., and Newcombe, N. S. 1999. Elementary school children's explicit and implicit memory for faces of preschool classmates. *Developmental Psychology, 35,* 102–112.

Lief, H. I., Fetkewicz, J. 1995. Retractors of false memories: The evolution of pseudo-memories. *Journal of Psychiatry and Law, 23,* 411–435.

Lifton, R. J. 1973. *Home from the war: Vietnam veterans: Neither victims nor executioners.* New York: Touchstone.

Lilienfeld, S. O. 2002a. When worlds collide: Social science, politics, and the Rind et al. (1998) child sexual abuse meta-analysis. *American Psychologist, 57,* 176–188.

———— 2002b. A funny thing happened on the way to my *American Psychologist* publication. *American Psychologist, 57,* 225–227.

Lilienfeld, S. O., and Loftus, E. F. 1998. Repressed memories and World War II: Some cautionary notes. *Professional Psychology: Research and Practice, 29,* 471–475.

Lilienfeld, S. O., Lynn, S. J., Kirsch, I., Chaves, J. F., Sarbin, T. R., Ganaway, G. K., and Powell, R. A. 1999. Dissociative identity disorder and the sociocognitive model: Recalling the lessons of the past. *Psychological Bulletin, 125,* 507–523.

Lindsay, D. S. 1990. Misleading suggestions can impair eyewitnesses' ability to remember event details. *Journal of Experimental Psychology: Learning, Memory, and Cognition, 16,* 1077–83.

Lindsay, D. S., and Johnson, M. K. 1989. The eyewitness suggestibility effect and memory for source. *Memory and Cognition, 17,* 349–358.

Lindsay, D. S., and Poole, D. A. 1998. The Poole et al. (1995) surveys of therapists: Misinterpretations by both sides of the recovered memories controversy. *Journal of Psychiatry and Law, 26,* 383–399.

Lindsay, D. S., and Read, J. D. 1994. Psychotherapy and memories of childhood sexual abuse: A cognitive perspective. *Applied Cognitive Psychology*, 8, 281–338.

Linton, M. 1986. Ways of searching and the contents of memory. In D. C. Rubin, ed., *Autobiographical memory*, 50–67. Cambridge: Cambridge University Press.

Lipinski, J. F., Jr., and Pope, H. G., Jr. 1994. Do "flashbacks" represent obsessional imagery? *Comprehensive Psychiatry*, 35, 245–247.

Lipton, A. 1999. Recovered memories in the courts. In S. Taub, ed., *Recovered memories of child sexual abuse: Psychological, social, and legal perspectives on a contemporary mental health controversy*, 165–210. Springfield, IL: Charles C. Thomas.

Litz, B. T., Weathers, F. W., Monaco, V., Herman, D. S., Wulfsohn, M., Marx, B., and Keane, T. M. 1996. Attention, arousal, and memory in posttraumatic stress disorder. *Journal of Traumatic Stress*, 9, 497–519.

Loftus, E. F. 1975. Leading questions and the eyewitness report. *Cognitive Psychology*, 7, 560–572.

——— 1979. *Eyewitness testimony*. Cambridge, MA: Harvard University Press.

——— 1993. Desperately seeking memories of the first few years of childhood: The reality of early memories. *Journal of Experimental Psychology: General*, 122, 274–277.

——— 1999. Lost in the mall: Misrepresentations and misunderstandings. *Ethics and Behavior*, 9, 51–60.

Loftus, E. F., and Burns, T. E. 1982. Mental shock can produce retrograde amnesia. *Memory and Cognition*, 10, 318–323.

Loftus, E. F., Donders, K., Hoffman, H. G., and Schooler, J. W. 1989. Creating new memories that are quickly accessed and confidently held. *Memory and Cognition*, 17, 607–616.

Loftus, E. F., Garry, M., and Feldman, J. 1994. Forgetting sexual trauma: What does it mean when 38% forget? *Journal of Consulting and Clinical Psychology*, 62, 1177–81.

Loftus, E. F., and Guyer, M. J. 2002a. Who abused Jane Doe? The hazards of the single case history. Part I. *Skeptical Inquirer*, 26(3), 24–32.

———— 2002b. Who abused Jane Doe? The hazards of the single case history. Part II. *Skeptical Inquirer, 26(4)*, 37–40, 44.

Loftus, E. F., and Hoffman, H. G. 1989. Misinformation and memory: The creation of new memories. *Journal of Experimental Psychology: General, 118,* 100–104.

Loftus, E., and Ketcham, K. 1994. *The myth of repressed memory: False memories and allegations of sexual abuse.* New York: St. Martin's Griffin.

Loftus, E. F., and Loftus, G. R. 1980. On the permanence of stored information in the human brain. *American Psychologist, 35,* 409–420.

Loftus, E. F., Loftus, G. R., and Messo, J. 1987. Some facts about "weapon focus." *Law and Human Behavior, 11,* 55–62.

Loftus, E. F., Miller, D. G., and Burns, H. J. 1978. Semantic integration of verbal information into a visual memory. *Journal of Experimental Psychology: Human Learning and Memory, 4,* 19–31.

Loftus, E. F., Milo, E. M., and Paddock, J. R. 1995. The accidental executioner: Why psychotherapy must be informed by science. *Counseling Psychologist, 23,* 300–309.

Loftus, E. F., and Palmer, J. C. 1974. Reconstruction of automobile destruction: An example of the interaction between language and memory. *Journal of Verbal Learning and Verbal Behavior, 13,* 585–589.

Loftus, E. F., and Pickrell, J. E. 1995. The formation of false memories. *Psychiatric Annals, 25,* 720–725.

Loftus, E. F., Polonsky, S., and Fullilove, M. T. 1994. Memories of childhood sexual abuse: Remembering and repressing. *Psychology of Women Quarterly, 18,* 67–84.

Loftus, E. F., Schooler, J. W., Boone, S. M., and Kline, D. 1987. Time went by so slowly: Overestimation of event duration by males and females. *Applied Cognitive Psychology, 1,* 3–13.

Loftus, E. F., and Zanni, G. 1975. Eyewitness testimony: The influence of the wording of a question. *Bulletin of the Psychonomic Society, 5,* 86–88.

Lovibond, P. F., and Shanks, D. R. 2002. The role of awareness in Pavlovian conditioning: Empirical evidence and theoretical implications. *Journal of Experimental Psychology: Animal Behavior Processes, 28,* 3–26.

Lucchelli, F., Muggia, S., and Spinnler, H. 1995. The "Petites Madeleines" phenomenon in two amnesic patients: Sudden recovery of forgotten memories. *Brain, 118*, 167–183.

Lupien, S. J., de Leon, M., de Santi, S., Convit, A., Tarshish, C., Nair, N. P. V., Thakur, M., McEwen, B. S., Hauger, R. L., and Meaney, M. J. 1998. Cortisol levels during human aging predict hippocampal atrophy and memory deficits. *Nature Neuroscience, 1*, 69–73.

Lupien, S. J., and McEwen, B. S. 1997. The acute effects of corticosteroids on cognition: Integration of animal and human model studies. *Brain Research Reviews, 24*, 1–27.

Lustig, C., and Hasher, L. 2001. Implicit memory is not immune to interference. *Psychological Bulletin, 127*, 618–628.

Lynn, S. J., Lock, T. G., Myers, B., and Payne, D. G. 1997. Recalling the unrecallable: Should hypnosis be used to recover memories in psychotherapy? *Current Directions in Psychological Science, 6*, 79–83.

Lyon, T. D. 1999. The new wave in children's suggestibility research: A critique. *Cornell Law Review, 84*, 1004–87.

Lyons, D. M., Yang, C., Sawyer-Glover, A. M., Moseley, M. E., and Schatzberg, A. F. 2001. Early life stress and inherited variation in monkey hippocampal volumes. *Archives of General Psychiatry, 58*, 1145–51.

Mabry, T. R., Gold, P. E., and McCarty, R. 1995. Age-related changes in plasma catecholamine responses to acute swim stress. *Neurobiology of Learning and Memory, 63*, 260–268.

MacCurdy, J. T. 1918. *War neuroses.* Cambridge: Cambridge University Press.

MacFarlane, K. 1985. Diagnostic evaluations and the use of videotapes in child sexual abuse cases. *University of Miami Law Review, 40*, 135–165.

Mack, J. E. 1994. *Abduction: Human encounters with aliens,* rev. ed. New York: Ballantine.

Macklin, M. L., Metzger, L. J., Litz, B. T., McNally, R. J., Lasko, N. B., Orr, S. P., and Pitman, R. K. 1998. Lower pre-combat intelligence is a risk factor for posttraumatic stress disorder. *Journal of Consulting and Clinical Psychology, 66*, 323–326.

MacLeod, C. M. 1991a. Half a century of research on the Stroop effect: An integrative review. *Psychological Bulletin, 109,* 163–203.

——— 1991b. John Ridley Stroop: Creator of a landmark cognitive task. *Canadian Psychology, 32,* 521–524.

MacMillan, H. L., Fleming, J. E., Streiner, D. L., Lin, E., Boyle, M. H., Jamieson, E., Duku, E. K., Walsh, C. A., Wong, M. Y.-Y., and Beardslee, W. R. 2001. Childhood abuse and lifetime psychopathology in a community sample. *American Journal of Psychiatry, 158,* 1878–83.

Macmillan, M. 1997. *Freud evaluated: The completed arc.* Cambridge, MA: MIT Press.

Madakasira, S., and O'Brien, K. F. 1987. Acute posttraumatic stress disorder in victims of a natural disaster. *Journal of Nervous and Mental Disease, 175,* 286–290.

Maher, B. A. 1999. Anomalous experience in everyday life: Its significance for psychopathology. *Monist, 82,* 547–570.

Mai, F. M. 1995. Psychiatrists' attitudes to multiple personality disorder: A questionnaire study. *Canadian Journal of Psychiatry, 40,* 154–157.

Malcolm, J. 1984. *In the Freud Archives.* New York: Knopf.

Malloy, P. F., Fairbank, J. A., and Keane, T. M. 1983. Validation of a multimethod assessment of posttraumatic stress disorders in Vietnam veterans. *Journal of Consulting and Clinical Psychology, 51,* 488–494.

Malmquist, C. P. 1986. Children who witness parental murder: Posttraumatic aspects. *Journal of the American Academy of Child Psychiatry, 25,* 320–325.

Malpass, R. S., and Devine, P. G. 1981. Guided memory in eyewitness identification. *Journal of Applied Psychology, 66,* 343–350.

Manchester, W. 1979. *Goodbye, darkness: A memoir of the Pacific War.* Boston: Little, Brown.

Manns, J. R., Clark, R. E., and Squire, L. R. 2002. Standard delay eyeblink classical conditioning is independent of awareness. *Journal of Experimental Psychology: Animal Behavior Processes, 28,* 32–37.

March, J. S. 1993. What constitutes a stressor? The "Criterion A" issue. In J. R. T. Davidson and E. B. Foa, eds., *Posttraumatic stress disorder: DSM-IV and beyond,* 37–54. Washington: American Psychiatric Press.

Markowitsch, H. J. 1999. Functional neuroimaging correlates of functional amnesia. *Memory*, 7, 561–583.

Markowitsch, H. J., Fink, G. R., Thöne, A., Kessler, J., and Heiss, W.-D. 1997. A PET study of persistent psychogenic amnesia covering the whole life span. *Cognitive Neuropsychiatry*, 2, 135–158.

Markowitsch, H. J., Kessler, J., van der Ven, C., Weber-Luxenburger, G., Albers, M., and Heiss, W.-D. 1998. Psychic trauma causing grossly reduced brain metabolism and cognitive deterioration. *Neuropsychologia*, 36, 77–82.

Marks, J. 1979. *The search for the "Manchurian candidate."* New York: Norton.

Marlar, R. A., Leonard, B. L., Billman, B. R., Lambert, P. M., and Marlar, J. E. 2000. Biochemical evidence of cannibalism at a prehistoric Puebloan site in southwestern Colorado. *Nature*, 407, 74–78.

Marshall, R. D., Spitzer, R., Liebowitz, M. R. 1999. Review and critique of the new DSM-IV diagnosis of acute stress disorder. *American Journal of Psychiatry*, 156, 1677–85.

Mason, J. W., Giller, E. L., Kosten, T. R., Ostroff, R. B., and Podd, L. 1986. Urinary free-cortisol levels in posttraumatic stress disorder patients. *Journal of Nervous and Mental Disease*, 174, 145–149.

Mason, J. W., Wang, S., Yehuda, R., Riney, S., Charney, D. S., and Southwick, S. M. 2001. Psychogenic lowering of urinary cortisol levels linked to increased emotional numbing and a shame-depressive syndrome in combat-related posttraumatic stress disorder. *Psychosomatic Medicine*, 63, 387–401.

Masson, J. M. 1984. *The assault on truth: Freud's suppression of the seduction theory.* New York: Farrar, Straus and Giroux.

Mather, M., Henkel, L. A., and Johnson, M. K. 1997. Evaluating characteristics of false memories: Remember/know judgments and memory characteristics questionnaire compared. *Memory and Cognition*, 25, 826–837.

Mathews, A., and MacLeod, C. 1985. Selective processing of threat cues in anxiety states. *Behaviour Research and Therapy*, 23, 563–569.

Mayer, P., and Pope, H. G., Jr. 1997. Unusual flashbacks in a Vietnam veteran. *American Journal of Psychiatry*, 154, 713.

Mayou, R. A., Black, J., and Bryant, B. 2000. Unconsciousness, amnesia and psychiatric symptoms following road traffic accident injury. *British Journal of Psychiatry, 177*, 540–545.

Mayou, R., Bryant, B., and Ehlers, A. 2001. Prediction of psychological outcomes one year after a motor vehicle accident. *American Journal of Psychiatry, 158*, 1231–38.

Mazor, A., Gampel, Y., Enright, R. D., and Orenstein, R. 1990. Holocaust survivors: Coping with post-traumatic memories in childhood and 40 years later. *Journal of Traumatic Stress, 3*, 1–14.

Mazzoni, G. A. L., Loftus, E. F., and Kirsch, I. 2001. Changing beliefs about implausible autobiographical events: A little plausibility goes a long way. *Journal of Experimental Psychology: Applied, 7*, 51–59.

Mazzoni, G. A. L., Lombardo, P., Malvagia, S., and Loftus, E. F. 1999. Dream interpretation and false beliefs. *Professional Psychology: Research and Practice, 30*, 45–50.

McCloskey, M., Wible, C. G., and Cohen, N. J. 1988. Is there a special flashbulb-memory mechanism? *Journal of Experimental Psychology: General, 117*, 171–181.

McCloskey, M., and Zaragoza, M. 1985. Misleading postevent information and memory for events: Arguments and evidence against memory impairment hypotheses. *Journal of Experimental Psychology: General, 114*, 1–16.

McDermott, K. B. 1996. The persistence of false memories in list recall. *Journal of Memory and Language, 35*, 212–230.

McDermott, K. B., and Roediger, H. L., III. 1998. Attempting to avoid illusory memories: Robust false recognition of associates persists under conditions of explicit warnings and immediate testing. *Journal of Memory and Language, 39*, 508–520.

McDonagh-Coyle, A., McHugo, G. J., Friedman, M. J., Schnurr, P. P., Zayfert, C., and Descamps, M. 2001. Psychophysiological reactivity in female sexual abuse survivors. *Journal of Traumatic Stress, 14*, 667–683.

McDonough, L., and Mandler, J. M. 1994. Very long-term recall in infants: Infantile amnesia reconsidered. *Memory, 2*, 339–352.

McDonough, L., Mandler, J. M., McKee, R. D., and Squire, L. R. 1995. The deferred imitation task as a nonverbal measure of declarative memory. *Proceedings of the National Academy of Sciences, 92*, 7580–84.

McFarlane, A. C. 1988a. The phenomenology of posttraumatic stress disorders following a natural disaster. *Journal of Nervous and Mental Disease*, *176*, 22–29.

—— 1988b. The longitudinal course of posttraumatic morbidity: The range of outcomes and their predictors. *Journal of Nervous and Mental Disease*, *176*, 30–39.

—— 1989. The aetiology of post-traumatic morbidity: Predisposing, precipitating and perpetuating factors. *British Journal of Psychiatry*, *154*, 221–228.

McFarlane, A. C., Atchison, M., and Yehuda, R. 1997. The acute stress response following motor vehicle accidents and its relation to PTSD. *Annals of the New York Academy of Sciences*, *821*, 437–441.

McGaugh, J. L. 1990. Significance and remembrance: The role of neuromodulatory systems. *Psychological Science*, *1*, 15–25.

McGaugh, J. L., Ferry, B., Vazdarjanova, A., and Roozendaal, B. 2000. Amygdala: Role in modulation of memory storage. In J. P. Aggleton, ed., *The amygdala: A functional analysis*, 2nd ed., 391–423. Oxford: Oxford University Press.

McGinnis, D., and Roberts, P. 1996. Qualitative characteristics of vivid memories attributed to real and imagined experiences. *American Journal of Psychology*, *109*, 59–77.

McGrath, J. M., and Frueh, B. C. 2002. Fraudulent claims of combat heroics within the VA? *Psychiatric Services*, *53*, 345.

McHugh, P. R. 1992. Psychiatric misadventures. *American Scholar*, *61*, 497–510.

McMillan, T. M. 1996. Post-traumatic stress disorder following minor and severe closed head injury: 10 single cases. *Brain Injury*, *10*, 749–758.

McNally, R. J. 1991. Assessment of posttraumatic stress disorder in children. *Psychological Assessment*, *3*, 531–537.

—— 1993. Stressors that produce posttraumatic stress disorder in children. In J. R. T. Davidson and E. B. Foa, eds., *Posttraumatic stress disorder: DSM-IV and beyond*, 57–74. Washington: American Psychiatric Press.

—— 1994. *Panic disorder: A critical analysis*. New York: Guilford.

—— 1995. Automaticity and the anxiety disorders. *Behaviour Research and Therapy*, *33*, 747–754.

———— 1996. Cognitive bias in the anxiety disorders. *Nebraska Symposium on Motivation, 43,* 211–250.

———— 1998. Experimental approaches to cognitive abnormality in posttraumatic stress disorder. *Clinical Psychology Review, 18,* 971–982.

———— 1999a. Posttraumatic stress disorder. In T. Millon, P. H. Blaney, and Roger D. Davis, eds., *Oxford textbook of psychopathology,* 144–165. Oxford: Oxford University Press.

———— 1999b. On the experimental induction of panic. *Behavior Therapy, 30,* 333–339.

———— 2001a. On Wakefield's harmful dysfunction analysis of mental disorder. *Behaviour Research and Therapy, 39,* 309–314.

———— 2001b. Vulnerability to anxiety disorders in adulthood. In R. E. Ingram and J. M. Price, eds., *Vulnerability to psychopathology: Risk across the lifespan,* 304–321. New York: Guilford.

———— 2001c. On the scientific status of cognitive appraisal models of anxiety disorder. *Behaviour Research and Therapy, 39,* 513–521.

———— 2001d. The cognitive psychology of repressed and recovered memories of childhood sexual abuse: Clinical implications. *Psychiatric Annals, 31,* 509–514.

———— 2003. Progress and controversy in the study of posttraumatic stress disorder. *Annual Review of Psychology, 54,* 229–252.

McNally, R. J., and Amir, N. 1996. Perceptual implicit memory for trauma-related information in post-traumatic stress disorder. *Cognition and Emotion, 10,* 551–556.

McNally, R. J., Amir, N., and Lipke, H. J. 1996. Subliminal processing of threat cues in posttraumatic stress disorder? *Journal of Anxiety Disorders, 10,* 115–128.

McNally, R. J., Clancy, S. A., and Schacter, D. L. 2001. Directed forgetting of trauma cues in adults reporting repressed or recovered memories of childhood sexual abuse. *Journal of Abnormal Psychology, 110,* 151–156.

McNally, R. J., Clancy, S. A., Schacter, D. L., and Pitman, R. K. 2000a. Personality profiles, dissociation, and absorption in women reporting repressed, recovered, or continuous memories of childhood sexual abuse. *Journal of Consulting and Clinical Psychology, 68,* 1033–37.

———— 2000b. Cognitive processing of trauma cues in adults reporting repressed, recovered, or continuous memories of childhood sexual abuse. *Journal of Abnormal Psychology, 109,* 355–359.

McNally, R. J., English, G. E., and Lipke, H. J. 1993. Assessment of intrusive cognition in PTSD: Use of the modified Stroop paradigm. *Journal of Traumatic Stress, 6,* 33–41.

McNally, R. J., Kaspi, S. P., Riemann, B. C., and Zeitlin, S. B. 1990. Selective processing of threat cues in posttraumatic stress disorder. *Journal of Abnormal Psychology, 99,* 398–402.

McNally, R. J., Lasko, N. B., Clancy, S. A., Macklin, M. L., Pitman, R. K., and Orr, S. P. 2002. Psychophysiologic responding during script-driven imagery in people reporting abduction by space aliens. Manuscript submitted for publication.

McNally, R. J., Lasko, N. B., Macklin, M. L., and Pitman, R. K. 1995. Autobiographical memory disturbance in combat-related posttraumatic stress disorder. *Behaviour Research and Therapy, 33,* 619–630.

McNally, R. J., Litz, B. T., Prassas, A., Shin, L. M., and Weathers, F. W. 1994. Emotional priming of autobiographical memory in post-traumatic stress disorder. *Cognition and Emotion, 8,* 351–367.

McNally, R. J., Luedke, D. L., Besyner, J. K., Peterson, R. A., Bohm, K., and Lips, O. J. 1987. Sensitivity to stress-relevant stimuli in posttraumatic stress disorder. *Journal of Anxiety Disorders, 1,* 105–116.

McNally, R. J., and Lukach, B. M. 1992. Are panic attacks traumatic stressors? *American Journal of Psychiatry, 149,* 824–826.

McNally, R. J., Metzger, L. J., Lasko, N. B., Clancy, S. A., and Pitman, R. K. 1998. Directed forgetting of trauma cues in adult survivors of childhood sexual abuse with and without posttraumatic stress disorder. *Journal of Abnormal Psychology, 107,* 596–601.

McNally, R. J., Otto, M. W., Yap, L., Pollack, M. H., and Hornig, C. D. 1999. Is panic disorder linked to cognitive avoidance of threatening information? *Journal of Anxiety Disorders, 13,* 335–348.

McNally, R. J., and Ricciardi, J. N. 1996. Suppression of negative and neutral thoughts. *Behavioural and Cognitive Psychotherapy, 24,* 17–25.

McNally, R. J., Riemann, B. C., and Kim, E. 1990. Selective processing of threat cues in panic disorder. *Behaviour Research and Therapy, 28*, 407–412.

McNally, R. J., and Shin, L. M. 1995. Association of intelligence with severity of posttraumatic stress disorder symptoms in Vietnam combat veterans. *American Journal of Psychiatry, 152*, 936–938.

McNally, R. J., and Steketee, G. S. 1985. The etiology and maintenance of severe animal phobias. *Behaviour Research and Therapy, 23*, 431–435.

Means, B., and Loftus, E. F. 1991. When personal history repeats itself: Decomposing memories for recurring events. *Applied Cognitive Psychology, 5*, 297–318.

Meesters, C., Merckelbach, H., Muris, P., and Wessel, I. 2000. Autobiographical memory and trauma in adolescents. *Journal of Behavior Therapy and Experimental Psychiatry, 31*, 29–39.

Melchert, T. P. 1996. Childhood memory and a history of different forms of abuse. *Professional Psychology: Research and Practice, 27*, 438–446.

——— 1999. Relations among childhood memory, a history of abuse, dissociation, and repression. *Journal of Interpersonal Violence, 14*, 1172–92.

Melchert, T. P., and Parker, R. L. 1997. Different forms of childhood abuse and memory. *Child Abuse and Neglect, 21*, 125–135.

Mellman, T. A., David, D., Bustamante, V., Torres, J., and Fins, A. 2001. Dreams in the acute aftermath of trauma and their relationship to PTSD. *Journal of Traumatic Stress, 14*, 241–247.

Mellman, T. A., and Davis, G. C. 1985. Combat-related flashbacks in posttraumatic stress disorder: Phenomenology and similarity to panic attacks. *Journal of Clinical Psychiatry, 46*, 379–382.

Mellman, T. A., Kulick-Bell, R., Ashlock, L. E., and Nolan, B. 1995. Sleep events among veterans with combat-related posttraumatic stress disorder. *American Journal of Psychiatry, 152*, 110–115.

Meltzoff, A. N. 1985. Immediate and deferred imitation in fourteen- and twenty-four-month-old infants. *Child Development, 56*, 62–72.

——— 1995. What infant memory tells us about infantile amnesia: Long-term recall and deferred imitation. *Journal of Experimental Child Psychology, 59*, 497–515.

Menzies, R. G., and Clarke, J. C. 1995. The etiology of phobias: A nonassociative account. *Clinical Psychology Review, 15,* 23–48.

Merckelbach, H., Muris, P., Horselenberg, R., and Rassin, E. 1998. Traumatic intrusions as "worse case scenarios." *Behaviour Research and Therapy, 36,* 1075–79.

Merckelbach, H., Wiers, R., Horselenberg, R., and Wessel, I. 2001. Effects of retrieving childhood events on metamemory judgments depend on the questions you ask. *British Journal of Clinical Psychology, 40,* 215–220.

Metzger, L. J., Orr, S. P., Lasko, N. B., McNally, R. J., and Pitman, R. K. 1997. Seeking the source of emotional Stroop interference effects in PTSD: A study of P3s to traumatic words. *Integrative Physiological and Behavioral Science, 32,* 43–51.

Miller, A. 1997. *The drama of the gifted child: The search for the true self* (1979), rev. ed., trans. R. Ward. New York: Basic Books.

Miller, M. B., and Gazzaniga, M. S. 1998. Creating false memories for visual scenes. *Neuropsychologia, 36,* 513–520.

Milner, B. 1966. Amnesia following operation on the temporal lobes. In C. W. M. Whitty and O. L. Zangwill, eds., *Amnesia,* 109–133. New York: Appleton-Century-Crofts.

Mitchell, K. J., and Johnson, M. K. 2000. Source monitoring: Attributing mental experiences. In Tulving and Craik, eds., 2000, 179–195.

Mitchell, K. J., and Zaragoza, M. S. 1996. Repeated exposure to suggestion and false memory: The role of contextual variability. *Journal of Memory and Language, 35,* 246–260.

Mollon, P. 2000. *Freud and False Memory Syndrome.* New York: Totem Books.

Mori, E., Ikeda, M., Hirono, N., Kitagaki, H., Imamura, T., and Shimomura, T. 1999. Amygdalar volume and emotional memory in Alzheimer's Disease. *American Journal of Psychiatry, 156,* 216–222.

Morrison, P. D., Allardyce, J., and McKane, J. P. 2002. Fear knot: Neurobiological disruption of long-term fear memory. *British Journal of Psychiatry, 180,* 195–197.

Mossman D. 1994. At the VA, it pays to be sick. *Public Interest, 114* (Winter), 35–47.

Moulds, M. L., and Bryant, R. A. 2002. Directed forgetting in acute stress disorder. *Journal of Abnormal Psychology*, *111*, 175–179.

Mulder, R. T., Beautrais, A. L., Joyce, P. R., and Fergusson, D. M. 1998. Relationship between dissociation, childhood sexual abuse, childhood physical abuse, and mental illness in a general population sample. *American Journal of Psychiatry*, *155*, 806–811.

Mulhern, S. A. 1991. Satanism and psychotherapy: A rumor in search of an Inquisition. In J. T. Richardson, J. Best, and D. G. Bromley, eds., *The satanism scare*, 145–172. New York: Aldine de Gruyter.

———— 1992. Ritual abuse: Defining a syndrome versus defending a belief. *Journal of Psychology and Theology*, *20*, 230–232.

———— 1997. Commentary on "The Logical Status of Case Histories." In Read and Lindsay, eds., 1997, 126–142.

Myers, C. S. 1915. A contribution to the study of shell shock: Being an account of three cases of loss of memory, vision, smell, and taste, admitted into the Duchess of Westminster's Hospital, Le Touquet. *Lancet*, 93rd year (Feb. 13), 316–320.

Myers, N. A., Clifton, R. K., and Clarkson, M. G. 1987. When they were very young: Almost-threes remember two years ago. *Infant Behavior and Development*, *10*, 123–132.

Nadel, L., and Zola-Morgan, S. 1984. Infantile amnesia: A neurobiological perspective. In M. Moscovitch, ed., *Infant memory: Its relation to normal and pathological memory in humans and other animals*, 145–172. New York: Plenum.

Nadelson, T. 1992. Attachment to killing. *Journal of the American Academy of Psychoanalysis*, *20*, 130–141.

Nader, K., Schafe, G. E., and LeDoux, J. E. 2000. Fear memories require protein synthesis in the amygdala for reconsolidation after retrieval. *Nature*, *406*, 722–726.

Nadler, A., and Ben-Shushan, D. 1989. Forty years later: Long-term consequences of massive traumatization as manifested by Holocaust survivors from the city and the kibbutz. *Journal of Consulting and Clinical Psychology*, *57*, 287–293.

Najarian, L. M., Goenjian, A. K., Pelcovitz, D., Mandel, F., and Najarian, B. 1996. Relocation after a disaster: Posttraumatic stress disorder in Armenia after the earthquake. *Journal of the American Academy of Child and Adolescent Psychiatry, 35,* 374–383.

Nash, M. 1987. What, if anything, is regressed about hypnotic age regression? A review of the empirical literature. *Psychological Bulletin, 102,* 42–52.

———— 1994. Memory distortion and sexual trauma: The problem of false negatives and false positives. *International Journal of Clinical and Experimental Hypnosis, 42,* 346–362.

Nash, M. R., Hulsey, T. L., Sexton, M. C., Harralson, T. L., and Lambert, W. 1993. Long-term sequelae of childhood sexual abuse: Perceived family environment, psychopathology, and dissociation. *Journal of Consulting and Clinical Psychology, 61,* 276–283.

Nathan, D. 1991. Satanism and child molestation: Constructing the ritual abuse scare. In J. T. Richardson, J. Best, and D. G. Bromley, eds., *The satanism scare,* 75–94. New York: Aldine de Gruyter.

Nathan, D., and Snedeker, M. 1995. *Satan's silence: Ritual abuse and the making of a modern American witch hunt.* New York: Basic Books.

Neisser, U. 1981. John Dean's memory: A case study. *Cognition, 9,* 1–22.

Neisser, U., and Harsch, N. 1992. Phantom flashbulbs: False recollections of hearing the news about *Challenger.* In E. Winograd and U. Neisser, eds., *Affect and accuracy in recall: Studies of "flashbulb" memories,* 9–31. Cambridge: Cambridge University Press.

Neisser, U., Winograd, E., Bergman, E. T., Schreiber, C. A., Palmer, S. E., and Weldon, M. S. 1996. Remembering the earthquake: Direct experience *vs.* hearing the news. *Memory, 4,* 337–357.

Nelson, E. C., Heath, A. C., Madden, P. A. F., Cooper, M. L., Dinwiddie, S. H., Bucholz, K. K., Glowinski, A., McLaughlin, T., Dunne, M. P., Stathan, D. J., and Martin, N. G. 2002. Association between self-reported childhood sexual abuse and adverse psychosocial outcomes: Results from a twin study. *Archives of General Psychiatry, 59,* 139–145.

Nelson, E. L., and Simpson, P. 1994. First glimpse: An initial examination of subjects who have rejected their recovered visualizations as false memories. *Issues in Child Abuse Accusations, 6,* 123–133.

Nelson, K. 1994. Long-term retention of memory for preverbal experience: Evidence and implications. *Memory, 2,* 467–475.

Newcombe, N. S., Drummey, A. B., Fox, N. A., Lie, E., and Ottinger-Alberts, W. 2000. Remembering early childhood: How much, how, and why (or why not). *Current Directions in Psychological Science, 9,* 55–58.

Newcomer, J. W., Selke, G., Melson, A. K., Hershey, T., Craft, S., Richards, K., and Alderson, A. L. 1999. Decreased memory performance in healthy humans induced by stress-level cortisol treatment. *Archives of General Psychiatry, 56,* 527–533.

Neylan, T. C., Marmar, C. R., Metzler, T. J., Weiss, D. S., Zatzick, D. F., Delucchi, K. L., Wu, R. M., and Schoenfeld, F. B. 1998. Sleep disturbances in the Vietnam generation: Findings from a nationally representative sample of male Vietnam veterans. *American Journal of Psychiatry, 155,* 929–933.

Nice, D. S., Garland, C. F., Hilton, S. M., Baggett, J. C., and Mitchell, R. E. 1996. Long-term health outcomes and medical effects of torture among US Navy prisoners of war in Vietnam. *JAMA, 276,* 375–381.

Nietzsche, F. 1888. Twilight of the idols: Or, how one philosophizes with a hammer. In W. Kaufmann, ed. and trans., *The portable Nietzsche,* 463–563. New York: Viking, 1954.

Nishith, P., Mechanic, M. B., and Resick, P. A. 2000. Prior interpersonal trauma: The contribution to current PTSD symptoms in female rape victims. *Journal of Abnormal Psychology, 109,* 20–25.

Nissen, M. J., Ross, J. L., Willingham, D. B., Mackenzie, T. B., and Schacter, D. L. 1988. Memory and awareness in a patient with multiple personality disorder. *Brain and Cognition, 8,* 117–134.

Noblitt, J. R., and Perskin, P. S. 2000. *Cult and ritual abuse: Its history, anthropology, and recent discovery in contemporary America,* rev. ed. Westport, CT: Praeger.

Noll, R. 1989. Satanism, UFO abductions, historians and clinicians: Those who do not remember the past . . . *Dissociation, 2,* 251–253.

Norman, K. A., and Schacter, D. L. 1997. False recognition in younger and older adults: Exploring the characteristics of illusory memories. *Memory and Cognition, 25,* 838–848.

North, C. S., Nixon, S. J., Shariat, S., Mallonee, S., McMillen, J. C., Spitznagel, E. L., and Smith, E. M. 1999. Psychiatric disorders among survivors of the Oklahoma City bombing. *JAMA, 282,* 755–762.

Noyes, R., Jr., and Kletti, R. 1976. Depersonalization in the face of life-threatening danger: A description. *Psychiatry, 39,* 19–27.

———— 1977. Depersonalization in response to life-threatening danger. *Comprehensive Psychiatry, 18,* 375–384.

Obermeyer, C. M. 1999. Female genital surgeries: The known, the unknown, and the unknowable. *Medical Anthropology Quarterly, 13,* 79–106.

O'Carroll, R. E., Drysdale, E., Cahill, L., Shajahan, P., and Ebmeier, K. P. 1999a. Memory for emotional material: A comparison of central versus peripheral beta blockade. *Journal of Psychopharmacology, 13,* 32–39.

———— 1999b. Stimulation of the noradrenergic system enhances and blockade reduces memory for emotional material in man. *Psychological Medicine, 29,* 1083–88.

O'Donnell, P. K. 2002. *Into the rising sun: In their own words, World War II's Pacific veterans reveal the heart of combat.* New York: Free Press.

Offer, D., Kaiz, M., Howard, K. I., and Bennett, E. S. 2000. The altering of reported experiences. *Journal of the American Academy of Child and Adolescent Psychiatry, 39,* 735–742.

Ofshe, R. J. 1992. Inadvertent hypnosis during interrogation: False confession due to dissociative state; mis-identified multiple personality and the satanic cult hypothesis. *International Journal of Clinical and Experimental Hypnosis, 40,* 125–156.

Ofshe, R. 1994. Making grossly damaging but avoidable errors: The pitfalls of the Olio/Cornell thesis. *Journal of Child Sexual Abuse, 3,* 95–108.

Ofshe, R., and Watters, E. 1994. *Making monsters: False memories, psychotherapy, and sexual hysteria.* Berkeley: University of California Press.

Olio, K. A. 1989. Memory retrieval in the treatment of adult survivors of sexual abuse. *Transactional Analysis Journal, 19,* 93–100.

———— 1994. Truth in memory. *American Psychologist, 49,* 442–443.

Olio, K. A., and Cornell, W. F. 1998. The facade of scientific documentation: A case study of Richard Ofshe's analysis of the Paul Ingram case. *Psychology, Public Policy, and Law, 4,* 1182–97.

Ondersma, S. J., Chaffin, M., Berliner, L., Cordon, I., Goodman, G. S., and

Barnett, D. 2001. Sex with children is abuse: Comment on Rind et al. 1998. *Psychological Bulletin, 127*, 707–714.

Ornstein, P. A., Ceci, S. J., and Loftus, E. F. 1998a. Comment on Alpert, Brown, and Courtois (1998): The science of memory and the practice of psychotherapy. *Psychology, Public Policy, and Law, 4*, 996–1010.

———— 1998b. Adult recollections of childhood abuse: Cognitive and developmental perspectives. *Psychology, Public Policy, and Law, 4*, 1025–51.

———— 1998c. More on the repressed memory debate: A reply to Alpert, Brown, and Courtois 1998. *Psychology, Public Policy, and Law, 4*, 1068–78.

Orr, S. P., Lasko, N. B., Metzger, L. J., Berry, N. J., Ahern, C. E., and Pitman, R. K. 1998. Psychophysiologic assessment of women with posttraumatic stress disorder resulting from childhood sexual abuse. *Journal of Consulting and Clinical Psychology, 66*, 906–913.

Orr, S. P., Metzger, L. J., and Pitman, R. K. 2002. Psychophysiology of posttraumatic stress disorder. *Psychiatric Clinics of North America, 25*, 271–293.

Orr, S. P., Pitman, R. K., Lasko, N. B., and Herz, L. R. 1993. Psychophysiological assessment of posttraumatic stress disorder imagery in World War II and Korean combat veterans. *Journal of Abnormal Psychology, 102*, 152–159.

Osborn, W. M. 2000. *The wild frontier: Atrocities during the American-Indian war from Jamestown Colony to Wounded Knee*. New York: Random House.

Ost, J., Costall, A., and Bull, R. 2002. A perfect symmetry? A study of retractors' experiences of making and then repudiating claims of early sexual abuse. *Psychology, Crime and Law, 8*, 155–181.

Ost, J., Vrij, A., Costall, A., and Bull, R. 2002. Crashing memories and reality monitoring: Distinguishing between perceptions, imaginations and "false memories." *Applied Cognitive Psychology, 16*, 125–134.

Pallmeyer, T. P., Blanchard, E. B., and Kolb, L. C. 1986. The psychophysiology of combat-induced post-traumatic stress disorder in Vietnam veterans. *Behaviour Research and Therapy, 24*, 645–652.

Parfitt, D. N., and Carlyle Gall, C. M. 1944. Psychogenic amnesia: The refusal to remember. *Journal of Mental Science, 90*, 511–531.

Parkin, A. J. 1996. H.M.: The medial temporal lobes and memory. In C. Code,

C.-W. Wallesch, Y. Joanette, and A. R. Lecours, eds., *Classic cases in neuropsychology*, 337–347. East Sussex, UK: Psychology Press.

——— 1998. The central executive does not exist. *Journal of the International Neuropsychological Society*, 4, 518–522.

Parks, E. D., and Balon, R. 1995. Autobiographical memory for childhood events: Patterns of recall in psychiatric patients with a history of alleged trauma. *Psychiatry*, 58, 199–208.

Payne, D. G. 1987. Hypermnesia and reminiscence in recall: A historical and empirical review. *Psychological Bulletin*, 101, 5–27.

Payne, D. G., Elie, C. J., Blackwell, J. M., and Neuschatz, J. S. 1996. Memory illusions: Recalling, recognizing, and recollecting events that never occurred. *Journal of Memory and Language*, 35, 261–285.

Payne, J. D., Nadel, L., Allen, J. J. B., Thomas, K. G. F., and Jacobs, W. J. 2002. The effects of experimentally induced stress on false recognition. *Memory*, 10, 1–6.

Pearson, J. L. 2001. *Belly of the beast: A POW's inspiring true story of faith, courage, and survival aboard the infamous WWII Japanese hell ship Oryoku Maru*. New York: New American Library.

Pelcovitz, D., Kaplan, S., Goldenberg, B., Mandel, F., Lehane, J., and Guarrera, J. 1994. Post-traumatic stress disorder in physically abused adolescents. *Journal of the American Academy of Child and Adolescent Psychiatry*, 33, 305–312.

Pendergrast, M. 1996. *Victims of memory: Incest accusations and shattered lives*, rev. ed. London: HarperCollins.

——— 1998. Response to Karon and Widener 1997. *Professional Psychology: Research and Practice*, 29, 479–481.

——— 1999. Smearing in the name of scholarship. *Professional Psychology: Research and Practice*, 30, 623–625.

Penfield, W. 1955. The permanent record of the stream of consciousness. *Acta Psychologica*, 11, 47–69.

——— 1969. Consciousness, memory, and Man's conditioned reflexes. In K. H. Pribram, ed., *On the biology of learning*, 127–168. New York: Harcourt, Brace and World.

Penfield, W., and Perot, P. 1963. The brain's record of auditory and visual experience: A final summary and discussion. *Brain, 86*, 595–696.

Perry, C. 1999. [Review of *Memory, trauma treatment, and the law*]. *International Journal of Clinical and Experimental Hypnosis, 47*, 366–374.

Perry, S., Difede, J., Musgni, G., Frances, A. J., and Jacobsberg, L. 1992. Predictors of posttraumatic stress disorder after burn injury. *American Journal of Psychiatry, 149*, 931–935.

Person, E. S., and Klar, H. 1994. Establishing trauma: The difficulty distinguishing between memories and fantasies. *Journal of the American Psychoanalytic Association, 42*, 1055–81.

Peters, M. L., Uyterlinde, S. A., Consemulder, J., and van der Hart, O. 1998. Apparent amnesia on experimental memory tests in dissociative identity disorder: An exploratory study. *Consciousness and Cognition, 7*, 27–41.

Peterson, C., and Bell, M. 1996. Children's memory for traumatic injury. *Child Development, 67*, 3045–70.

Peterson, C., and Biggs, M. 1997. Interviewing children about trauma: Problems with "specific" questions. *Journal of Traumatic Stress, 10*, 279–290.

Peterson, C., and Rideout, R. 1998. Memory for medical emergencies experienced by 1- and 2-year-olds. *Developmental Psychology, 34*, 1059–72.

Peterson, C., and Whalen, N. 2001. Five years later: Children's memory for medical emergencies. *Applied Cognitive Psychology, 15*, S7–S24.

Pezdek, K., Finger, K., and Hodge, D. 1997. Planting false childhood memories: The role of event plausibility. *Psychological Science, 8*, 437–441.

Philbrick, N. 2000. *In the heart of the sea: The tragedy of the whaleship Essex.* New York: Penguin.

Pickering, M. 1999. Consuming doubts: What some people ate? Or what some people swallowed? In L. R. Goldman, ed., *The anthropology of cannibalism*, 51–74. Westport, CT: Bergin and Garvey.

Pillemer, D. B. 1984. Flashbulb memories of the assassination attempt on President Reagan. *Cognition, 16*, 63–80.

Piper, A., Jr. 1993. "Truth serum" and "recovered memories" of sexual abuse: A review of the evidence. *Journal of Psychiatry and Law, 21*, 447–471.

———— 1998. Repressed memories from World War II: Nothing to forget. Examining Karon and Widener's (1997) claim to have discovered evidence for repression. *Professional Psychology: Research and Practice, 29,* 476–478.

———— 1999. A skeptic considers, then responds to Cheit. *Ethics and Behavior, 9,* 277–293.

Piper, A., Jr., Pope, H. G., Jr., and Borowiecki, J. J., III. 2000. Custer's last stand: Brown, Scheflin, and Whitfield's latest attempt to salvage "dissociative amnesia." *Journal of Psychiatry and Law, 28,* 149–213.

Pitman, R. K. 2001. Hippocampal diminution in PTSD: More (or less?) than meets the eye. *Hippocampus, 11,* 73–74.

Pitman, R. K., Altman, B., Greenwald, E., Longpre, R. E., Macklin, M. L., Poiré, R. E., and Steketee, G. S. 1991. Psychiatric complications during flooding therapy for posttraumatic stress disorder. *Journal of Clinical Psychiatry, 52,* 17–20.

Pitman, R. K., and Orr, S. P. 1990. Twenty-four hour urinary cortisol and catecholamine excretion in combat-related posttraumatic stress disorder. *Biological Psychiatry, 27,* 245–247.

Pitman, R. K., Orr, S. P., Forgue, D. F., Altman, B., de Jong, J. B., and Herz, L. R. 1990. Psychophysiologic responses to combat imagery of Vietnam veterans with posttraumatic stress disorder versus other anxiety disorders. *Journal of Abnormal Psychology, 99,* 49–54.

Pitman, R. K., Orr, S. P., Forgue, D. F., de Jong, J. B., and Claiborn, J. M. 1987. Psychophysiologic assessment of posttraumatic stress disorder imagery in Vietnam combat veterans. *Archives of General Psychiatry, 44,* 970–975.

Pitman, R. K., Orr, S. P., Lowenhagen, M. J., Macklin, M. L., and Altman, B. 1991. Pre-Vietnam contents of posttraumatic stress disorder veterans' service medical and personnel records. *Comprehensive Psychiatry, 32,* 416–422.

Pitman, R. K., Sanders, K. M., Zusman, R. M., Healy, A. R., Cheema, F., Lasko, N. B., Cahill, L., and Orr, S. P. 2002. Pilot study of secondary prevention of posttraumatic stress disorder with propranolol. *Biological Psychiatry, 51,* 189–192.

Pitman, R. K., Shalev, A. Y., and Orr, S. P. 2000. Posttraumatic stress disorder: Emotion, conditioning, and memory. In M. S. Gazzaniga, ed., *The new cognitive neurosciences,* 2nd ed., 1133–47. Cambridge, MA: MIT Press.

Polusny, M. A., and Follette, V. M. 1996. Remembering childhood sexual abuse: A national survey of psychologists' clinical practices, beliefs, and personal experiences. *Professional Psychology: Research and Practice, 27,* 41–52.

Poole, D. A., Lindsay, D. S., Memon, A., and Bull, R. 1995. Psychotherapy and the recovery of memories of childhood sexual abuse: U.S. and British practitioners' opinions, practices, and experiences. *Journal of Consulting and Clinical Psychology, 63,* 426–437.

Pope, H. G., Jr. 1997. *Psychology astray: Fallacies in studies of "repressed memory" and childhood trauma.* Boca Raton, FL: Upton Books.

Pope, H. G., Jr., Hudson, J. I., Bodkin, J. A., and Oliva, P. 1998. Questionable validity of "dissociative amnesia" in trauma victims. *British Journal of Psychiatry, 172,* 210–215.

Pope, H. G., Jr., Oliva, P. S., and Hudson, J. I. 1999. Repressed memories: The scientific status. In D. L. Faigman, D. H. Kaye, M. J. Saks, and J. Sanders, eds., *Modern scientific evidence: The law and science of expert testimony,* vol. 1, Pocket part, 115–155. St. Paul: West Publishing.

Pope, H. G., Jr., Oliva, P. S., Hudson, J. I., Bodkin, J. A., and Gruber, A. J. 1999. Attitudes toward DSM-IV dissociative disorders diagnoses among board-certified American psychiatrists. *American Journal of Psychiatry, 156,* 321–323.

Pope, K. S. 1995. What psychologists better know about recovered memories, research, lawsuits, and the pivotal experiment. [Review of *The myth of repressed memory: False memories and allegations of sexual abuse*]. *Clinical Psychology: Science and Practice, 2,* 304–315.

——— 1996. Memory, abuse, and science: Questioning claims about the False Memory Syndrome epidemic. *American Psychologist, 51,* 957–974.

——— 1998. Pseudoscience, cross-examination, and scientific evidence in the recovered memory controversy. *Psychology, Public Policy, and Law, 4,* 1160–81.

Porter, S., Birt, A. R., Yuille, J. C., and Hervé, H. F. 2001. Memory for murder: A psychological perspective on dissociative amnesia in legal contexts. *International Journal of Law and Psychiatry, 24,* 23–42.

Porter, S., Yuille, J. C., and Lehman, D. R. 1999. The nature of real, implanted, and fabricated memories for emotional childhood events: Implications for the recovered memory debate. *Law and Human Behavior, 23,* 517–537.

Putnam, F. W. 1991a. Recent research on multiple personality disorder. *Psychiatric Clinics of North America, 14,* 489–502.

——— 1991b. The satanic ritual abuse controversy. *Child Abuse and Neglect, 15,* 175–179.

Putnam, F. W., Guroff, J. J., Silberman, E. K., Barban, L., and Post, R. M. 1986. The clinical phenomenology of multiple personality disorder: Review of 100 recent cases. *Journal of Clinical Psychiatry, 47,* 285–293.

Putnam, F. W., and Loewenstein, R. J. 1993. Treatment of multiple personality disorder: A survey of current practices. *American Journal of Psychiatry, 150,* 1048–52.

Pynoos, R. S., Goenjian, A., Tashjian, M., Karakashian, M., Manjikian, R., Manoukian, G., Steinberg, A. M., and Fairbanks, L. A. 1993. Post-traumatic stress reactions in children after the 1988 Armenian earthquake. *British Journal of Psychiatry, 163,* 239–247.

Pynoos, R. S., and Nader, K. 1988. Children who witness the sexual assaults of their mothers. *Journal of the American Academy of Child and Adolescent Psychiatry, 27,* 567–572.

——— 1989. Children's memory and proximity to violence. *Journal of the American Academy of Child and Adolescent Psychiatry, 28,* 236–241.

Qin, J., Goodman, G. S., Bottoms, B. L., and Shaver, P. R. 1998. Repressed memories of ritualistic and religion-related child abuse. In S. J. Lynn and K. M. McConkey, eds., *Truth in memory,* 260–283. New York: Guilford.

Quas, J. A., Goodman, G. S., Bidrose, S., Pipe, M.-E., Craw, S., and Ablin, D. S. 1999. Emotion and memory: Children's long-term remembering, forgetting, and suggestibility. *Journal of Experimental Child Psychology, 72,* 235–270.

Rainey, J. M., Jr., Aleem, A., Ortiz, A., Yeragani, V., Pohl, R., and Berchou, R. 1987. A laboratory procedure for the induction of flashbacks. *American Journal of Psychiatry, 144,* 1317–19.

Rangell, L. 1976. Discussion of the Buffalo Creek disaster: The course of psychic trauma. *American Journal of Psychiatry, 133,* 313–316.

Rauch, S. L., van der Kolk, B. A., Fisler, R. E., Alpert, N. M., Orr, S. P., Savage, C. R., Fischman, A. J., Jenike, M. A., and Pitman, R. K. 1996. A symptom provocation study of posttraumatic stress disorder using positron emission tomography and script-driven imagery. *Archives of General Psychiatry, 53,* 380–387.

Rauch, S. L., Whalen, P. J., Shin, L. M., McInerney, S. C., Macklin, M. L., Lasko, N. B., Orr, S. P., and Pitman, R. K. 2000. Exaggerated amygdala response to masked facial stimuli in posttraumatic stress disorder: A functional MRI study. *Biological Psychiatry, 47,* 769–776.

Read, J. D. 1996. From a passing thought to a false memory in 2 minutes: Confusing real and illusory events. *Psychonomic Bulletin and Review, 3,* 105–111.

———— 1997. Memory issues in the diagnosis of unreported trauma. In Read and Lindsay, eds., 1997, 79–100.

Read, J. D., and Lindsay, D. S. 1994. Moving toward a middle ground on the "false memory debate": Reply to commentaries on Lindsay and Read. *Applied Cognitive Psychology, 8,* 407–435.

————, eds. 1997. *Recollections of trauma: Scientific evidence and clinical practice.* New York: Plenum.

———— 2000. "Amnesia" for summer camps and high school graduation: Memory work increases reports of prior periods of remembering less. *Journal of Traumatic Stress, 13,* 129–147.

Reagan, R. T. 1999. Scientific consensus on memory repression and recovery. *Rutgers Law Review, 51,* 275–321.

Realmuto, G. M., Jensen, J. B., and Wescoe, S. 1990. Specificity and sensitivity of sexually anatomically correct dolls in substantiating abuse: A pilot study. *Journal of the American Academy of Child and Adolescent Psychiatry, 29,* 743–746.

Realmuto, G. M., Masten, A., Carole, L. F., Hubbard, J., Groteluschen, A., and Chhun, B. 1992. Adolescent survivors of massive childhood trauma in Cambodia: Life events and current symptoms. *Journal of Traumatic Stress, 5,* 589–599.

Realmuto, G. M., Wagner, N., and Bartholow, J. 1991. The Williams pipeline disaster: A controlled study of a technological accident. *Journal of Traumatic Stress, 4,* 469–479.

Realmuto, G. M., and Wescoe, S. 1992. Agreement among professionals about a child's sexual abuse status: Interviews with sexually anatomically correct dolls as indicators of abuse. *Child Abuse and Neglect, 16*, 719–725.

Resnick, H. S., Yehuda, R., Pitman, R. K., and Foy, D. W. 1995. Effect of previous trauma on acute plasma cortisol level following rape. *American Journal of Psychiatry, 152*, 1675–77.

Reviere, S. L., and Bakeman, R. 2001. The effects of early trauma on autobiographical memory and schematic self-representation. *Applied Cognitive Psychology, 15*, S89–S100.

Riemann, B. C., and McNally, R. J. 1995. Cognitive processing of personally relevant information. *Cognition and Emotion, 9*, 325–340.

Rind, B., Bauserman, R., and Tromovitch, P. 2000a. Science versus orthodoxy: Anatomy of the congressional condemnation of a scientific article and reflections on remedies for future ideological attacks. *Applied and Preventive Psychology, 9*, 211–225.

——— 2000b. Debunking the false allegations of "statistical abuse": A reply to Spiegel. *Sexuality and Culture, 4*, 101–111.

Rind, B., and Tromovitch, P. 1997. A meta-analytic review of findings from national samples on psychological correlates of child sexual abuse. *Journal of Sex Research, 34*, 237–255.

Rind, B., Tromovitch, P., and Bauserman, R. 1998. A meta-analytic examination of assumed properties of child sexual abuse using college samples. *Psychological Bulletin, 124*, 22–53.

——— 2000. Condemnation of a scientific article: A chronology and refutation of the attacks and a discussion of threats to the integrity of science. *Sexuality and Culture, 4*, 1–61.

——— 2001. The validity and appropriateness of methods, analyses, and conclusions in Rind et al. (1998): A rebuttal of victimological critique from Ondersma et al. (2001) and Dallam et al. (2001). *Psychological Bulletin, 127*, 734–758.

Rivers, W. H. R. 1918. The repression of war experience. *Lancet*, 96th year (Feb. 2), 173–177.

Roberts, G., and Owen, J. 1988. The near-death experience. *British Journal of Psychiatry, 153*, 607–617.

Robinson, K. J., and Roediger, H. L., III. 1997. Associative processes in false recall and false recognition. *Psychological Science, 8,* 231–237.

Robinson, S., Rapaport, J., Durst, R., Rapaport, M., Rosca, P., Metzer, S., and Zilberman, L. 1990. The late effects of Nazi persecution among elderly Holocaust survivors. *Acta Psychiatrica Scandinavica, 82,* 311–315.

Robinson, S., Rapaport-Bar-Sever, M., and Rapaport, J. 1994. The present state of people who survived the holocaust as children. *Acta Psychiatrica Scandinavica, 89,* 242–245.

Rodriguez, N., Ryan, S. W., Vande Kemp, H., and Foy, D. W. 1997. Posttraumatic stress disorder in adult female survivors of childhood sexual abuse: A comparison study. *Journal of Consulting and Clinical Psychology, 65,* 53–59.

Roe, C. M., and Schwartz, M. F. 1996. Characteristics of previously forgotten memories of sexual abuse: A descriptive study. *Journal of Psychiatry and Law, 24,* 189–206.

Roediger, H. L., III, and Bergman, E. T. 1998. The controversy over recovered memories. *Psychology, Public Policy, and Law, 4,* 1091–1109.

Roediger, H. L., III, and Guynn, M. J. 1996. Retrieval processes. In E. L. Bjork and R. A. Bjork, eds., *Memory,* 197–236. San Diego: Academic Press.

Roediger, H. L., III, Jacoby, J. D., and McDermott, K. D. 1996. Misinformation effects in recall: Creating false memories through repeated retrieval. *Journal of Memory and Language, 35,* 300–318.

Roediger, H. L., III, and McDermott, K. B. 1995. Creating false memories: Remembering words not presented in lists. *Journal of Experimental Psychology: Learning, Memory, and Cognition, 21,* 803–814.

——— 1996. False perceptions of false memories. *Journal of Experimental Psychology: Learning, Memory, and Cognition, 22,* 814–816.

——— 2000. Distortions of memory. In Tulving and Craik, eds., 2000, 149–162.

Roemer, L., Litz, B. T., Orsillo, S. M., Ehlich, P. J., and Friedman, M. J. 1998. Increases in retrospective accounts of war-zone exposure over time: The role of PTSD symptom severity. *Journal of Traumatic Stress, 11,* 597–605.

Roesler, T. A., and Wind, T. W. 1994. Telling the secret: Adult women describe their disclosures of incest. *Journal of Interpersonal Violence, 9,* 327–338.

Rosen, G. M. 1995. The Aleutian Enterprise sinking and posttraumatic stress disorder: Misdiagnosis in clinical and forensic settings. *Professional Psychology: Research and Practice, 26,* 82–87.

Rosen, H., and Myers, H. J. 1947. Abreaction in the military setting. *Archives of Neurology and Psychiatry, 57,* 161–172.

Rosen, V. H. 1955. The reconstruction of a traumatic childhood event in a case of derealization. *Journal of the American Psychoanalytic Association, 3,* 211–221.

Ross, C. A. 1995. *Satanic ritual abuse: Principles of treatment.* Toronto: University of Toronto Press.

Ross, C. A., Miller, S. D., Reagor, P., Bjornson, L., Fraser, G. A., and Anderson, G. 1990. Structured interview data on 102 cases of multiple personality disorder from four centers. *American Journal of Psychiatry, 147,* 596–601.

Ross, R. J., Ball, W. A., Sullivan, K. A., and Caroff, S. N. 1989. Sleep disturbance as the hallmark of posttraumatic stress disorder. *American Journal of Psychiatry, 146,* 697–707.

Rubenstein, R., and Newman, R. 1954. The living out of "future" experiences under hypnosis. *Science, 119,* 472–473.

Rubin, D. C. 2000. The distribution of early childhood memories. *Memory, 8,* 265–269.

Rubin, D. C., and Kozin, M. 1984. Vivid memories. *Cognition, 16,* 81–95.

Rubin, L. J. 1996. Childhood sexual abuse: Whose memories are faulty? *Counseling Psychologist, 24,* 140–143.

Rush, F. 1977. The Freudian cover-up. *Chrysalis, 1,* 31–45.

Russell, D. E. H. 1986. *The secret trauma: Incest in the lives of girls and women,* rev. ed. New York: Basic Books, 1999.

Rynearson, E. K., and McCreery, J. M. 1993. Bereavement after homicide: A synergism of trauma and loss. *American Journal of Psychiatry, 150,* 258–261.

Sack, W. H., Him, C., and Dickason, D. 1999. Twelve-year follow-up study of Khmer youths who suffered massive war trauma as children. *Journal of the American Academy of Child and Adolescent Psychiatry, 38,* 1173–79.

Saigh, P. A. 1991. The development of posttraumatic stress disorder following four different types of traumatization. *Behaviour Research and Therapy, 29,* 213–216.

Sakheim, D. K., and Devine, S. E. 1992. Introduction: The phenomenon of satanic ritual abuse. In Sakheim and Devine, eds., 1992.

———, eds. 1992. *Out of darkness: Exploring satanism and ritual abuse.* New York: Lexington Books.

Sapolsky, R. M. 1996. Why stress is bad for your brain. *Science, 273,* 749–750.

——— 1998. *Why zebras don't get ulcers: An updated guide to stress, stress-related disease, and coping.* New York: Freeman.

——— 2000. Glucocorticoids and hippocampal atrophy in neuropsychiatric disorders. *Archives of General Psychiatry, 57,* 925–935.

Sapolsky, R. M., Krey, L. C., and McEwen, B. S. 1985. Prolonged glucocorticoid exposure reduces hippocampal neuron number: Implications for aging. *Journal of Neuroscience, 5,* 1222–27.

Sapolsky, R. M., and Pulsinelli, W. A. 1985. Glucocorticoids potentiate ischemic injury to neurons: Therapeutic implications. *Science, 229,* 1397–1400.

Sapolsky, R. M., Uno, H., Rebert, C. S., and Finch, C. E. 1990. Hippocampal damage associated with prolonged glucocorticoid exposure in primates. *Journal of Neuroscience, 10,* 2897–2902.

Sargant, W., and Slater, E. 1940, July 6. Acute war neuroses. *Lancet, 239,* 1–2.

——— 1941. Amnesic syndromes in war. *Proceedings of the Royal Society of Medicine, 34,* 757–764.

Saufley, W. H., Jr., Otaka, S. R., and Bavaresco, J. L. 1985. Context effects: Classroom tests and context independence. *Memory and Cognition, 13,* 522–528.

Savin, D., Sack, W. H., Clarke, G. N., Meas, N., and Richart, I. 1996. The Khmer adolescent project: III. A study of trauma from Thailand's Site II refugee camp. *Journal of the American Academy of Child and Adolescent Psychiatry, 35,* 384–391.

Saywitz, K. J., Goodman, G. S., Nicholas, E., and Moan, S. F. 1991. Children's memories of a physical examination involving genital touch: Implications for reports of child sexual abuse. *Journal of Consulting and Clinical Psychology, 59,* 682–691.

Sbordone, R. J., and Liter, J. C. 1995. Mild traumatic brain injury does not produce post-traumatic stress disorder. *Brain Injury, 9*, 405–412.

Schacter, D. L. 1986. Amnesia and crime: How much do we really know? *American Psychologist, 41*, 286–295.

——— 1987. Implicit memory: History and current status. *Journal of Experimental Psychology: Learning, Memory, and Cognition, 13*, 501–518.

———, ed. 1995. *Memory distortion: How minds, brains, and societies reconstruct the past.* Cambridge, MA: Harvard University Press.

——— 1996. *Searching for memory: The brain, the mind, and the past.* New York: Basic Books.

——— 2001. *The seven sins of memory: How the mind forgets and remembers.* Boston: Houghton Mifflin.

Schacter, D. L., Israel, L., and Racine, C. 1999. Suppressing false recognition in younger and older adults: The distinctiveness heuristic. *Journal of Memory and Language, 40*, 1–24.

Schacter, D. L., Kihlstrom, J. F., Kihlstrom, L. C., and Berren, M. B. 1989. Autobiographical memory in a case of multiple personality disorder. *Journal of Abnormal Psychology, 98*, 508–514.

Schacter, D. L., Reiman, E., Curran, T., Yun, L. S., Bandy, D., McDermott, K. B., and Roediger, H. L., III. 1996. Neuroanatomical correlates of veridical and illusory recognition memory: Evidence from positron emission tomography. *Neuron, 17*, 267–274.

Schacter, D. L., Verfaellie, M., and Pradere, D. 1996. The neuropsychology of memory illusions: False recall and recognition in amnesia. *Journal of Memory and Language, 35*, 319–334.

Schacter, D. L., Wagner, A. D., and Buckner, R. L. 2000. Memory systems of 1999. In Tulving and Craik, eds., 2000, 627–643.

Schacter, D. L., Wang, P. L., Tulving, E., and Freedman, M. 1982. Functional retrograde amnesia: A quantitative case study. *Neuropsychologia, 20*, 523–532.

Schaffer, R. E., and Cozolino, L. J. 1992. Adults who report childhood ritualistic abuse. *Journal of Psychology and Theology, 20*, 188–193.

Schelach, L., and Nachson, I. 2001. Memory of Auschwitz survivors. *Applied Cognitive Psychology, 15*, 119–132.

Schimek, J. G. 1987. Fact and fantasy in the seduction theory: A historical review. *Journal of the American Psychoanalytic Association, 35,* 937–965.

Schlosberg, A., and Benjamin, M. 1978. Sleep patterns in three acute combat fatigue cases. *Journal of Clinical Psychiatry, 39,* 546–549.

Schmidt, S. R. 2002. Outstanding memories: The positive and negative effects of nudes on memory. *Journal of Experimental Psychology: Learning, Memory, and Cognition, 28,* 353–361.

Schmidt, S. R., and Bohannon, J. N., III. 1988. In defense of the flashbulb-memory hypothesis: A comment on McCloskey, Wible, and Cohen 1988. *Journal of Experimental Psychology: General, 117,* 332–335.

Schmolck, H., Buffalo, E. A., and Squire, L. R. 2000. Memory distortions develop over time: Recollections of the O. J. Simpson trial verdict after 15 and 32 months. *Psychological Science, 11,* 39–45.

Schnurr, P. P., Friedman, M. J., and Rosenberg, S. D. 1993. Premilitary MMPI scores as predictors of combat-related PTSD symptoms. *American Journal of Psychiatry, 150,* 479–483.

Schnurr, P. P., Rosenberg, S. D., and Friedman, M. J. 1993. Change in MMPI scores from college to adulthood as a function of military service. *Journal of Abnormal Psychology, 102,* 288–296.

Schnyder, U., Moergeli, H., Klaghofer, R., and Buddeberg, C. 2001. Incidence and prediction of posttraumatic stress disorder symptoms in severely injured accident victims. *American Journal of Psychiatry, 158,* 594–599.

Schooler, J. W., Bendiksen, M., and Ambadar, Z. 1997. Taking the middle line: Can we accommodate both fabricated and recovered memories of sexual abuse? In M. A. Conway, ed., *Recovered memories and false memories,* 251–292. Oxford: Oxford University Press.

Schrader, H., Obelieniene, D., Bovim, G., Surkiene, D., Mickeviciene, D., Miseviciene, I., and Sand, T. 1996. Natural evolution of late whiplash syndrome outside the medicolegal context. *Lancet, 347,* 1207–11.

Schreiber, F. R. 1973. *Sybil.* New York: Warner Books.

Schreuder, B. J. N., Kleijn, W. C., and Rooijmans, H. G. M. 2000. Nocturnal reexperiencing more than forty years after war trauma. *Journal of Traumatic Stress, 13,* 453–463.

Schreuder, B. J. N., van Egmond, M., Kleijn, W. C., and Visser, A. T. 1998. Daily reports of posttraumatic nightmares and anxiety dreams in Dutch war victims. *Journal of Anxiety Disorders, 12*, 511–524.

Schroeder, P. 1994. Female genital mutilation—A form of child abuse. *New England Journal of Medicine, 331*, 739–740.

Schuster, M. A., Stein, B. D., Jaycox, L. H., Collins, R. L., Marshall, G. N., Elliott, M. N., Zhou, A. J., Kanouse, D. E., Morrison, J. L., and Berry, S. H. 2001. A national survey of stress reactions after the September 11, 2001, terrorist attacks. *New England Journal of Medicine, 345*, 1507–12.

Schwarz, E. D., and Kowalski, J. M. 1991. Posttraumatic stress disorder after a school shooting: Effects of symptom threshold selection and diagnosis by DSM-III, DSM-III-R, or proposed DSM-IV. *American Journal of Psychiatry, 148*, 592–597.

Schwarz, E. D., Kowalski, J. M., and McNally, R. J. 1993. Malignant memories: Post-traumatic changes in memory in adults after a school shooting. *Journal of Traumatic Stress, 6*, 545–553.

Scott, S. 2001. *The politics and experience of ritual abuse: Beyond disbelief.* Buckingham, UK: Open University Press.

Scott, W. J. 1990. PTSD in DSM-III: A case in the politics of diagnosis and disease. *Social Problems, 37*, 294–310.

Scoville, W. B. 1954. The limbic lobe in man. *Journal of Neurosurgery, 11*, 64–66.

Scoville, W. B., and Milner, B. 1957. Loss of recent memory after bilateral hippocampal lesions. *Journal of Neurology, Neurosurgery, and Psychiatry, 20*, 11–21.

Scrivner, E., and Safer, M. A. 1988. Eyewitnesses show hypermnesia for details about a violent event. *Journal of Applied Psychology, 73*, 371–377.

Sengupta, S. N., Jena, S., and Saxena, S. 1993. Generalised dissociative amnesia. *Australian and New Zealand Journal of Psychiatry, 27*, 699–700.

Shalev, A. Y., Orr, S. P., and Pitman, R. K. 1993. Psychophysiologic assessment of traumatic imagery in Israeli civilian patients with posttraumatic stress disorder. *American Journal of Psychiatry, 150*, 620–624.

Shalev, A. Y., Peri, T., Canetti, L., and Schreiber, S. 1996. Predictors of PTSD in injured trauma survivors: A prospective study. *American Journal of Psychiatry,* *153,* 219–225.

Shalev, A. Y., Sahar, T., Freedman, S., Peri, T., Glick, N., Brandes, D., Orr, S. P., and Pitman, R. K. 1998. A prospective study of heart rate response following trauma and the subsequent development of posttraumatic stress disorder. *Archives of General Psychiatry, 55,* 553–559.

Shanks, D. R., and Lovibond, P. F. 2002. Autonomic and eyeblink conditioning are closely related to contingency awareness: Reply to Wiens and Öhman (2002), Manns et al. (2002). *Journal of Experimental Psychology: Animal Behavior Processes, 28,* 38–42.

Shatan, C. F. 1973. The grief of soldiers: Vietnam combat veterans' self-help movement. *American Journal of Orthopsychiatry, 43,* 640–653.

Shay, J. 1994. *Achilles in Vietnam: Combat trauma and the undoing of character.* New York: Atheneum.

Sheiman, J. A. 1993. "I've always wondered if something happened to me": Assessment of child sexual abuse survivors with amnesia. *Journal of Child Sexual Abuse, 2,* 13–21.

Sheingold, K., and Tenney, Y. J. 1982. Memory for a salient childhood event. In U. Neisser, ed., *Memory observed: Remembering in natural contexts,* 201–212. San Francisco: Freeman.

Shengold, L. 1980. Some reflections on a case of mother/adolescent son incest. *International Journal of Psycho-Analysis, 61,* 461–476.

Shephard, B. 2001. *A war of nerves: Soldiers and psychiatrists in the twentieth century.* Cambridge, MA: Harvard University Press.

Sher, K. J., and Eisenberg, N. 2002. Publication of Rind et al. (1998): The editors' perspective. *American Psychologist, 57,* 206–210.

Shin, L. M., Kosslyn, S. M., McNally, R. J., Alpert, N. M., Thompson, W. L., Rauch, S. L., Macklin, M. L., and Pitman, R. K. 1997. Visual imagery and perception in posttraumatic stress disorder: A positron emission tomographic investigation. *Archives of General Psychiatry, 54,* 233–241.

Shin, L. M., McNally, R. J., Kosslyn, S. M., Thompson, W. L., Rauch, S. L., Alpert, N. M., Metzger, L. J., Lasko, N. B., Orr, S. P., and Pitman, R. K. 1999. Regional cerebral blood flow during script-driven imagery in childhood sexual abuse-related PTSD: A PET investigation. *American Journal of Psychiatry, 156,* 575–584.

Shipherd, J. C., and Beck, J. G. 1999. The effects of suppressing trauma-related thoughts on women with rape-related posttraumatic stress disorder. *Behaviour Research and Therapy, 37,* 99–112.

Shobe, K. K., and Kihlstrom, J. F. 1997. Is traumatic memory special? *Current Directions in Psychological Science, 6,* 70–74.

Shore, J. H., Tatum, E. L., and Vollmer, W. M. 1986. Psychiatric reactions to disaster: The Mount St. Helens experience. *American Journal of Psychiatry, 143,* 590–595.

Showalter, E. 1997. *Hystories.* New York: Columbia University Press.

Shrestha, N. M., Sharma, B., van Ommeren, M., Regmi, S., Makaju, R., Komproe, I., Shrestha, G. B., and de Jong, J. T. V. M. 1998. Impact of torture on refugees displaced within the developing world: Symptomatology among Bhutanese refugees in Nepal. *JAMA, 280,* 443–448.

Shweder, R. A. 2000. What about "female genital mutilation"? And why understanding culture matters in the first place. *Daedalus, 129* (4), 209–232.

Sierra, M., and Berrios, G. E. 1999. Flashbulb memories and other repetitive images: A psychiatric perspective. *Comprehensive Psychiatry, 40,* 115–125.

Silber, A. 1979. Childhood seduction, parental pathology and hysterical symptomatology: The genesis of an altered state of consciousness. *International Journal of Psycho-Analysis, 60,* 109–116.

Silva, R. R., Alpert, M., Munoz, D. M., Singh, S., Matzner, F., and Dummitt, S. 2000. Stress and vulnerability to posttraumatic stress disorder in children and adolescents. *American Journal of Psychiatry, 157,* 1229–35.

Simon, B. 1992. "Incest—see under Oedipus complex": The history of an error in psychoanalysis. *Journal of the American Psychoanalytic Association, 40,* 955–988.

Sivan, A. B., Schor, D. P., Koeppl, G. K., and Noble, L. D. 1988. Interaction of normal children with anatomical dolls. *Child Abuse and Neglect, 12,* 295–304.

Skinner, L. J., and Berry, K. K. 1993. Anatomically detailed dolls and the evaluation of child sexual abuse allegations: Psychometric considerations. *Law and Human Behavior, 17,* 399–421.

Skues, R. 1987. Jeffrey Masson and the assault on Freud. *British Journal of Psychotherapy, 3*, 305–314.

———— 1998. The first casualty: The war over psychoanalysis and the poverty of historiography. *History of Psychiatry, 9*, 151–177.

Sledge, W. H., Boydstun, J. A., and Rabe, A. J. 1980. Self-concept changes related to war captivity. *Archives of General Psychiatry, 37*, 430–443.

Slovenko, R. 1999. The production of multiple personalities. *Journal of Psychiatry and Law, 27*, 215–253.

Smith, B. S., Ratner, H. H., and Hobart, C. J. 1987. The role of cuing and organization in children's memory for events. *Journal of Experimental Child Psychology, 44*, 1–24.

Smith, E. M., North, C. S., McCool, R. E., and Shea, J. M. 1990. Acute postdisaster psychiatric disorders: Identification of persons at risk. *American Journal of Psychiatry, 147*, 202–206.

Smith, E. R., and Hunt, R. R. 1998. Presentation modality affects false memory. *Psychonomic Bulletin and Review, 5*, 710–715.

Smith, M., and Pazder, L. 1980. *Michelle remembers*. New York: Pocket Books.

Snow, B., and Sorensen, T. 1990. Ritualistic child abuse in a neighborhood setting. *Journal of Interpersonal Violence, 5*, 474–487.

Solomon, Z., Mikulincer, M., and Avitzur, E. 1988. Coping, locus of control, social support, and combat-related posttraumatic stress disorder: A prospective study. *Journal of Personality and Social Psychology, 55*, 279–285.

Solomon, Z., Neria, Y., Ohry, A., Waysman, M., and Ginzburg, K. 1994. PTSD among Israeli former prisoners of war and soldiers with combat stress reaction: A longitudinal study. *American Journal of Psychiatry, 151*, 554–559.

Sorensen, T., and Snow, B. 1991. How children tell: The process of disclosure in child sexual abuse. *Child Welfare, 70*, 3–15.

Southwick, S. M., Krystal, J. H., Bremner, J. D., Morgan, C. A., III, Nicolaou, A. L., Nagy, L. M., Johnson, D. R., Heninger, G. R., and Charney, D. S. 1997. Noradrenergic and serotonergic function in posttraumatic stress disorder. *Archives of General Psychiatry, 54*, 749–758.

Southwick, S. M., Krystal, J. H., Morgan, C. A., Johnson, D., Nagy, L. M., Nicolaou, A., Heninger, G. R., and Charney, D. S. 1993. Abnormal noradrenergic function in posttraumatic stress disorder. *Archives of General Psychiatry, 50,* 266–274.

Southwick, S. M., Morgan, C. A. III, Nicolaou, A. L., and Charney, D. S. 1997. Consistency of memory for combat-related traumatic events in veterans of Operation Desert Storm. *American Journal of Psychiatry, 154,* 173–177.

Spanos, N. P. 1994. Multiple identity enactments and multiple personality disorder: A sociocognitive perspective. *Psychological Bulletin, 116,* 143–165.

Spanos, N. P., Burgess, C. A., Burgess, M. F., Samuels, C., and Blois, W. O. 1999. Creating false memories of infancy with hypnotic and non-hypnotic procedures. *Applied Cognitive Psychology, 13,* 201–218.

Spanos, N. P., Menary, E., Gabora, N. J., DuBreuil, S. C., and Dewhirst, B. 1991. Secondary identity enactments during hypnotic past-life regression: A sociocognitive perspective. *Journal of Personality and Social Psychology, 61,* 308–320.

Sparr, L., and Pankratz, L. D. 1983. Factitious posttraumatic stress disorder. *American Journal of Psychiatry, 140,* 1016–19.

Sperling, G. 1960. The information available in brief visual presentations. *Psychological Monographs: General and Applied, 74* (11, whole no. 498).

Spiegel, D. 2000. The price of abusing children and numbers. *Sexuality and Culture, 4,* 63–66.

Spiegel, H. 1974. The Grade-5 Syndrome: The highly hypnotizable person. *International Journal of Clinical and Experimental Hypnosis, 22,* 303–319.

Spinrad, P. S. 1995. Hotspur in Massachusetts: The problem with Achilles in Vietnam. *Viet Nam Generation, 6,* 193–196.

Squire, L. R. 1994. Declarative and nondeclarative memory: Multiple brain systems supporting learning and memory. In D. L. Schacter and E. Tulving, eds., *Memory systems 1994,* 203–231. Cambridge, MA: MIT Press.

Stanley, L. A. 1989. The child porn myth. *Cardozo Arts and Entertainment Law Journal, 7,* 295–358.

Starkman, M. N., Gebarski, S. S., Berent, S., and Schteingart, D. E. 1992. Hippocampal formation volume, memory dysfunction, and cortisol levels in patients with Cushing's Syndrome. *Biological Psychiatry, 32,* 756–765.

Starkman, M. N., Giordani, B., Berent, S., Schork, M. A., and Schteingart, D. E.

2001. Elevated cortisol levels in Cushing's Disease are associated with cognitive decrements. *Psychosomatic Medicine, 63,* 985–993.

Starkman, M. N., Giordani, B., Gebarski, S. S., Berent, S., Schork, M. A., and Schteingart, D. E. 1999. Decrease in cortisol reverses human hippocampal atrophy following treatment of Cushing's disease. *Biological Psychiatry, 46,* 1595–1602.

Steblay, N. M., and Bothwell, R. K. 1994. Evidence for hypnotically refreshed testimony: The view from the laboratory. *Law and Human Behavior, 18,* 635–651.

Stein, M. B., Hanna, C., Vaerum, V., and Koverola, C. 1999. Memory functioning in adult women traumatized by childhood sexual abuse. *Journal of Traumatic Stress, 12,* 527–534.

Stein, M. B., Koverola, C., Hanna, C., Torchia, M. G., and McClarty, B. 1997. Hippocampal volume in women victimized by childhood sexual abuse. *Psychological Medicine, 27,* 951–959.

Stender, W. W., and Walker, E. 1974. The National Personnel Records Center fire: A study in disaster. *American Archivist, 37,* 521–549.

Stengel, E. 1941. On the aetiology of the fugue states. *Journal of Mental Science, 87,* 572–599.

Sterlini, G. L., and Bryant, R. A. 2002. Hyperarousal and dissociation: A study of novice skydivers. *Behaviour Research and Therapy, 40,* 431–437.

Stevenson, I. 1994. A case of the Psychotherapist's Fallacy: Hypnotic regression to "previous lives." *American Journal of Clinical Hypnosis, 36,* 188–193.

Stewart, G. R. 1960. *Ordeal by hunger: The story of the Donner Party,* rev. ed. Boston: Houghton Mifflin.

Stine, S. A. 1999. The snuff film: The making of an urban legend. *Skeptical Inquirer, 23(3)* (May/June), 29–33.

Strom, A., Refsum, S. B., Eitinger, L., Gronvik, O., Lonnum, A., Engeset, A., Osvik, K., and Rogan, B. 1962. Examination of Norwegian ex-concentration-camp prisoners. *Journal of Neuropsychiatry, 4,* 43–62.

Stroop, J. R. 1935. Studies of interference in serial verbal reactions. *Journal of Experimental Psychology, 18,* 643–661.

Suengas, A. G., and Johnson, M. K. 1988. Qualitative effects of rehearsal on memories for perceived and imagined complex events. *Journal of Experimental Psychology: General, 117,* 377–389.

Sugar, M. 1992. Toddlers' traumatic memories. *Infant Mental Health Journal, 13,* 245–251.

Summerfield, D. 1999. A critique of seven assumptions behind psychological programmes in war-affected areas. *Social Science and Medicine, 48,* 1449–62.

——— 2000. War and mental health: A brief overview. *BMJ, 321,* 232–235.

——— 2001. The invention of post-traumatic stress disorder and the social usefulness of a psychiatric category. *BMJ, 332,* 95–98.

Summit, R. C. 1983. The child sexual abuse accommodation syndrome. *Child Abuse and Neglect, 7,* 177–193.

Sutker, P. B., Allain, A. N., Jr., and Winstead, D. K. 1993. Psychopathology and psychiatric diagnoses of World War II Pacific Theater prisoner of war survivors and combat veterans. *American Journal of Psychiatry, 150,* 240–245.

Sutker, P. B., Galina, Z. H., West, J. A., and Allain, A. N. 1990. Trauma-induced weight loss and cognitive deficits among former prisoners of war. *Journal of Consulting and Clinical Psychology, 58,* 323–328.

Sutker, P. B., Uddo, M., Brailey, K., Vasterling, J. J., and Errera, P. 1994. Psychopathology in war-zone deployed and nondeployed Operation Desert Storm troops assigned graves registration duties. *Journal of Abnormal Psychology, 103,* 383–390.

Sutker, P. B., Vasterling, J. J., Brailey, K., and Allain, A. N., Jr. 1995. Memory, attention, and executive deficits in POW survivors: Contributing biological and psychological factors. *Neuropsychology, 9,* 118–125.

Sutker, P. B., Winstead, D. K., Galina, Z. H., and Allain, A. N. 1991. Cognitive deficits and psychopathology among former prisoners of war and combat veterans of the Korean Conflict. *American Journal of Psychiatry, 148,* 67–72.

Swihart, G., Yuille, J., and Porter, S. 1999. The role of state-dependent memory in "red-outs." *International Journal of Law and Psychiatry, 22,* 199–212.

Szajnberg, N. M. 1993. Recovering a repressed memory, and representational shift in an adolescent. *Journal of the American Psychoanalytic Association*, *41*, 711–727.

Takahashi, Y. 1988. Aokigahara-jukai: Suicide and amnesia in Mt. Fuji's Black Forest. *Suicide and Life-Threatening Behavior*, *18*, 164–175.

Talbot, M. 1999. Against innocence: The truth about child abuse and the truth about children. *New Republic*, *220* (March 15), 27–38.

Taub, S. 1996. The legal treatment of recovered memories of child sexual abuse. *Journal of Legal Medicine*, *17*, 183–214.

Tavris, C. 1993. Beware the incest-survivor machine. *New York Times Book Review* (Jan. 3), 1, 16–17.

———— 2000. The uproar over sexual abuse research and its findings. *Society*, *37* (May/June), 15–17.

Tellegen, A. 1982. *Brief manual for the Differential Personality Questionnaire*. Department of Psychology, University of Minnesota, Minneapolis.

Tellegen, A., and Atkinson, G. 1974. Openness to absorbing and self-altering experiences ("absorption"), a trait related to hypnotic susceptibility. *Journal of Abnormal Psychology*, *83*, 268–277.

Terr, L. C. 1979. Children of Chowchilla: A study of psychic trauma. *Psychoanalytic Study of the Child*, *34*, 547–623.

———— 1981. "Forbidden games": Post-traumatic child's play. *Journal of the American Academy of Child Psychiatry*, *20*, 741–760.

———— 1983. Chowchilla revisited: The effects of psychic trauma four years after a school-bus kidnapping. *American Journal of Psychiatry*, *140*, 1543–50.

———— 1988. What happens to early memories of trauma? A study of twenty children under age five at the time of documented traumatic events. *Journal of the American Academy of Child and Adolescent Psychiatry*, *27*, 96–104.

———— 1989. Terror writing by the formerly terrified: A look at Stephen King. *Psychoanalytic Study of the Child*, *44*, 369–390.

———— 1991. Childhood traumas: An outline and overview. *American Journal of Psychiatry*, *148*, 10–20.

Thigpen, C. H., and Cleckley, H. 1954. A case of multiple personality. *Journal of Abnormal and Social Psychology*, *49*, 135–151.

————— 1984. On the incidence of multiple personality disorder: A brief communication. *International Journal of Clinical and Experimental Hypnosis, 32,* 63–66.

Thom, D. A., and Fenton, N. 1920. Amnesias in war cases. *American Journal of Insanity, 76,* 437–448.

Thrasher, S. M., Dalgleish, T., and Yule, W. 1994. Information processing in post-traumatic stress disorder. *Behaviour Research and Therapy, 32,* 247–254.

Thyer, B. A., and Curtis, G. C. 1983. The repeated pretest-posttest single-subject experiment: A new design for empirical clinical practice. *Journal of Behavior Therapy and Experimental Psychiatry, 14,* 311–315.

Toglia, M. P., Neuschatz, J. S., and Goodwin, K. A. 1999. Recall accuracy and illusory memories: When more is less. *Memory, 7,* 233–256.

Torrie, A. 1944. Psychosomatic casualties in the Middle East. *Lancet, 246* (Jan. 29), 139–143.

Trandel, D. V., and McNally, R. J. 1987. Perception of threat cues in post-traumatic stress disorder: Semantic processing without awareness? *Behaviour Research and Therapy, 25,* 469–476.

Tromp, S., Koss, M. P., Figueredo, A. J., and Tharan, M. 1995. Are rape memories different? A comparison of rape, other unpleasant, and pleasant memories among employed women. *Journal of Traumatic Stress, 8,* 607–627.

True, W. R., and Lyons, M. J. 1999. Genetic risk factors for PTSD: A twin study. In R. Yehuda, ed., *Risk factors for posttraumatic stress disorder,* 61–78. Washington: American Psychiatric Press.

Tulving, E. 1985a. How many memory systems are there? *American Psychologist, 40,* 385–398.

————— 1985b. Memory and consciousness. *Canadian Psychology, 26,* 1–12.

————— 1999. Study of memory: Processes and systems. In J. K. Foster and M. Jelicic, eds., *Memory: Systems, process, or function?* 11–30. Oxford: Oxford University Press.

Tulving, E., and Craik, F. I. M., eds. 2000. *The Oxford handbook of memory.* Oxford: Oxford University Press.

Tulving, E., and Pearlstone, Z. 1966. Availability versus accessibility of information in memory for words. *Journal of Verbal Learning and Verbal Behavior, 5*, 381–391.

Tulving, E., Schacter, D. L., and Stark, H. A. 1982. Priming effects in word-fragment completion are independent of recognition memory. *Journal of Experimental Psychology: Learning, Memory, and Cognition, 8*, 336–342.

Tulving, E., and Thomson, D. M. 1973. Encoding specificity and retrieval processes in episodic memory. *Psychological Review, 80*, 352–373.

Tussing, A. A., and Greene, R. L. 1997. False recognition of associates: How robust is the effect? *Psychonomic Bulletin and Review, 4*, 572–576.

Underwood, B. J. 1965. False recognition produced by implicit verbal responses. *Journal of Experimental Psychology, 70*, 122–129.

Uno, H., Lohmiller, L., Thieme, C., Kemnitz, J. W., Engle, M. J., Roecker, E. B., and Farrell, P. M. 1990. Brain damage induced by prenatal exposure to dexamethasone in fetal rhesus macaques. I. Hippocampus. *Developmental Brain Research, 53*, 157–167.

Uno, H., Tarara, R., Else, J. G., Suleman, M. A., and Sapolsky, R. M. 1989. Hippocampal damage associated with prolonged and fatal stress in primates. *Journal of Neuroscience, 9*, 1705–11.

Ursano, R. J., Fullerton, C. S., Epstein, R. S., Crowley, B., Vance, K., Kao, T.-C., and Baum, A. 1999. Peritraumatic dissociation and posttraumatic stress disorder following motor vehicle accidents. *American Journal of Psychiatry, 156*, 1808–10.

U.S. House of Representatives. 1999. *Concurrent resolution 107 of the 106th Congress*. July 12.

Usher, J. A., and Neisser, U. 1993. Childhood amnesia and the beginnings of memory for four early life events. *Journal of Experimental Psychology: General, 122*, 155–165.

Uttal, W. R. 2001. *The new phrenology: The limits of localizing cognitive processes in the brain*. Cambridge, MA: MIT Press.

van der Hart, O. 1996. Ian Hacking on Pierre Janet: A critique with further observations. *Dissociation, 9*, 80–84.

van der Hart, O., and Brom, D. 2000. When the victim forgets: Trauma-induced amnesia and its assessment in Holocaust survivors. In A. Y. Shalev,

R. Yehuda, and McFarlane, A. C., eds., *International handbook of human response to trauma*, 233–248. New York: Kluwer Academic/Plenum.

van der Hart, O., Brown, P., and Graafland, M. 1999. Trauma-induced dissociative amnesia in World War I combat soldiers. *Australian and New Zealand Journal of Psychiatry, 33,* 37–46.

van der Hart, O., and Friedman, B. 1989. A reader's guide to Pierre Janet on dissociation: A neglected intellectual heritage. *Dissociation, 2,* 3–16.

van der Hart, O., Lierens, R., and Goodwin, J. 1996. Jeanne Fery: A sixteenth-century case of dissociative identity disorder. *Journal of Psychohistory, 24,* 18–35.

van der Hart, O., and Steele, K. 1999. Relieving or reliving childhood trauma? A commentary on Miltenburg and Singer 1997. *Theory and Psychology, 9,* 533–540.

van der Kolk, B. A. 1994. The body keeps the score: Memory and the evolving psychobiology of posttraumatic stress. *Harvard Review of Psychiatry, 1,* 253–265.

van der Kolk, B., Blitz, R., Burr, W., Sherry, S., and Hartmann, E. 1984. Nightmares and trauma: A comparison of nightmares after combat with lifelong nightmares in veterans. *American Journal of Psychiatry, 141,* 187–190.

van der Kolk, B. A., and Fisler, R. 1995. Dissociation and the fragmentary nature of traumatic memories: Overview and exploratory study. *Journal of Traumatic Stress, 8,* 505–525.

van der Kolk, B., Greenberg, M., Boyd, H., and Krystal, J. 1985. Inescapable shock, neurotransmitters, and addiction to trauma: Toward a psychobiology of post traumatic stress. *Biological Psychiatry, 20,* 314–325.

van der Kolk, B. A., and Kadish, W. 1987. Amnesia, dissociation, and the return of the repressed. In van der Kolk, *Psychological trauma,* 173–190. Washington: American Psychiatric Press.

van der Kolk, B. A., and van der Hart, O. 1989. Pierre Janet and the breakdown of adaptation in psychological trauma. *American Journal of Psychiatry, 146,* 1530–1540.

——— 1991. The intrusive past: The flexibility of memory and the engraving of trauma. *American Imago, 48,* 425–454.

Vandermaas, M. O., Hess, T. M., and Baker-Ward, L. 1993. Does anxiety affect children's reports of memory for a stressful event? *Applied Cognitive Psychology*, 7, 109–127.

van Stegeren, A. H., Everaerd, W., Cahill, L., McGaugh, J. L., and Gooren, L. J. G. 1998. Memory for emotional events: Differential effects of centrally versus peripherally acting ß-blocking agents. *Psychopharmacology*, *138*, 305–310.

Vasterling, J. J., Brailey, K., Constans, J. I., Borges, A., and Sutker, P. B. 1997. Assessment of intellectual resources in Gulf War veterans: Relationship to PTSD. *Assessment*, *1*, 51–59.

Vasterling, J. J., Brailey, K., Constans, J. I., and Sutker, P. B. 1998. Attention and memory dysfunction in posttraumatic stress disorder. *Neuropsychology*, *12*, 125–133.

Vasterling, J. J., Duke, L. M., Brailey, K., Constans, J. I., Allain, A. N., Jr., and Sutker, P. B. 2002. Attention, learning, and memory performances and intellectual resources in Vietnam veterans: PTSD and no disorder comparisons. *Neuropsychology*, *16*, 5–14.

Victor, J. S. 1993. *Satanic panic: The creation of a contemporary legend*. Chicago: Open Court.

——— 1998. Moral panics and the social construction of deviant behavior: A theory and application to the case of ritual child abuse. *Sociological Perspectives*, *41*, 541–565.

Viederman, M. 1995. The reconstruction of a repressed sexual molestation fifty years later. *Journal of the American Psychoanalytic Association*, *43*, 1169–95.

Vines, J. K., and Cohen, W. M. 2002. Clarksville man enters plea of guilty to scheme to defraud the Department of Veterans Affairs. Press release. U.S. Department of Justice, Office of the United States Attorney, Middle District of Tennessee. March 4.

Vrana, S. R., Roodman, A., and Beckham, J. C. 1995. Selective processing of trauma-relevant words in posttraumatic stress disorder. *Journal of Anxiety Disorders*, *9*, 515–530.

Vreven, D. L., Gudanowski, D. M., King, L. A., and King, D. W. 1995. The civilian version of the Mississippi PTSD Scale: A psychometric evaluation. *Journal of Traumatic Stress*, *8*, 91–109.

Wagenaar, W. A. 1997. The logical status of case histories. In Read and Lindsay, eds., 1997, 109–126.

Wagenaar, W. A., and Groeneweg, J. 1990. The memory of concentration camp survivors. *Applied Cognitive Psychology, 4,* 77–87.

Wakefield, J. C. 1996. DSM-IV: Are we making diagnostic progress? *Contemporary Psychology, 41,* 646–652.

Wakefield, J. C., and Spitzer, R. L. 2002. Lowered estimates—but of what? *Archives of General Psychiatry, 59,* 129–130.

Waldfogel, S. 1948. The frequency and affective character of childhood memories. *Psychological Monographs, 62* (4, whole no. 291).

Warren, A. R., and Swartwood, J. N. 1992. Developmental issues in flashbulb memory research: Children recall the *Challenger* event. In E. Winograd and U. Neisser, eds., *Affect and accuracy in recall: Studies of "flashbulb" memories,* 95–120. Cambridge: Cambridge University Press.

Warrington, E. K., and Weiskrantz, L. 1970. Amnesic syndrome: Consolidation or retrieval? *Nature, 228,* 628–630.

Watters, E., and Ofshe, R. 1999. *Therapy's delusions: The myth of the unconscious and the exploitation of today's walking worried.* New York: Scribner.

Weaver, C. A., III. 1993. Do you need a "flash" to form a flashbulb memory? *Journal of Experimental Psychology: General, 122,* 39–46.

Wegner, D. M. 1994. Ironic processes of mental control. *Psychological Review, 101,* 34–52.

Weine, S. M., Becker, D. F., McGlashan, T. H., Laub, D., Lazrove, S., Vojvoda, D., and Hyman, L. 1995. Psychiatric consequences of "ethnic cleansing": Clinical assessments and trauma testimonies of newly resettled Bosnian refugees. *American Journal of Psychiatry, 152,* 536–542.

Weine, S., Becker, D. F., McGlashan, T. H., Vojvoda, D., Hartman, S., and Robbins, J. P. 1995. Adolescent survivors of "ethnic cleansing": Observations on the first year in America. *Journal of the American Academy of Child and Adolescent Psychiatry, 34,* 1153–59.

Weir, I. K., and Wheatcroft, M. S. 1995. Allegations of children's involvement in ritual sexual abuse: Clinical experience of 20 cases. *Child Abuse and Neglect, 19,* 491–505.

Weisæth, L. 1989. Torture of a Norwegian ship's crew: The torture, stress reactions and psychiatric after-effects. *Acta Psychiatrica Scandinavica, 80* (Suppl. 355), 63–72.

Weiskrantz, L., and Warrington, E. K. 1979. Conditioning in amnesic patients. *Neuropsychologia, 17,* 187–194.

Wells, G. L., and Leippe, M. R. 1981. How do triers of fact infer the accuracy of eye-witness identifications? Using memory for peripheral detail can be misleading. *Journal of Applied Psychology, 66,* 682–687.

Wessel, I., Meeren, M., Peeters, F., Arntz, A., and Merckelbach, H. 2001. Correlates of autobiographical memory specificity: The role of depression, anxiety and childhood trauma. *Behaviour Research and Therapy, 39,* 409–421.

Wessel, I., Merckelbach, H., and Dekkers, T. 2002. Autobiographical memory specificity, intrusive memory, and general memory skills in Dutch-Indonesian survivors of the World War II era. *Journal of Traumatic Stress, 15,* 227–234.

Westen, D. 1998. The scientific legacy of Sigmund Freud: Toward a psychodynamically informed psychological science. *Psychological Bulletin, 124,* 333–371.

Westerhof, Y., Woertman, L., van der Hart, O., and Nijenhuis, E. 2000. Forgetting child abuse: Feldman-Summers and Pope's (1994) study replicated among Dutch psychologists. *Clinical Psychology and Psychotherapy, 7,* 220–229.

Whalen, P. J. 1998. Fear, vigilance, and ambiguity: Initial neuroimaging studies of the human amygdala. *Current Directions in Psychological Science, 7,* 177–188.

Whipple, G. M. 1909. The observer as reporter: A survey of the "psychology of testimony." *Psychological Bulletin, 6,* 153–170.

White, S., Strom, G. A., Santilli, G., and Halpin, B. M. 1986. Interviewing young sexual abuse victims with anatomically correct dolls. *Child Abuse and Neglect, 10,* 519–529.

White, S. H., and Pillemer, D. B. 1979. Childhood amnesia and the development of a socially accessible memory system. In J. F. Kihlstrom and F. J. Evans, eds., *Functional disorders of memory,* 29–73. Hillsdale, NJ: Erlbaum.

Whitfield, C. L. 1997. Traumatic amnesia: The evolution of our understanding from a clinical and legal perspective. *Sexual Addiction and Compulsivity, 4,* 107–133.

Whittington, W. L., Rice, R. J., Biddle, J. W., and Knapp, J. S. 1988. Incorrect identification of *Neisseria gonorrhoeae* from infants and children. *Pediatric Infectious Disease Journal, 7,* 3–10.

Widom, C. S., and Morris, S. 1997. Accuracy of adult recollections of childhood victimization: Part 2. Childhood sexual abuse. *Psychological Assessment, 9,* 34–46.

Widom, C. S., and Shepard, R. L. 1996. Accuracy of adult recollections of childhood victimization: Part 1. Childhood physical abuse. *Psychological Assessment, 8,* 412–421.

Wiens, S., and Öhman, A. 2002. Unawareness is more than a chance event: Comment on Lovibond and Shanks (2002). *Journal of Experimental Psychology: Animal Behavior Processes, 28,* 27–31.

Wilhelm, S., McNally, R. J., Baer, L., and Florin, I. 1996. Directed forgetting in obsessive-compulsive disorder. *Behaviour Research and Therapy, 34,* 633–641.

———— 1997. Autobiographical memory in obsessive-compulsive disorder. *British Journal of Clinical Psychology, 36,* 21–31.

Wilkinson, C. B. 1983. Aftermath of a disaster: The collapse of the Hyatt Regency Hotel skywalks. *American Journal of Psychiatry, 140,* 1134–39.

Williams, J. M. G., and Broadbent, K. 1986. Autobiographical memory in suicide attempters. *Journal of Abnormal Psychology, 95,* 144–149.

Williams, J. M. G., Mathews, A., and MacLeod, C. 1996. The emotional Stroop task and psychopathology. *Psychological Bulletin, 120,* 3–24.

Williams, J. M. G., and Scott, J. 1988. Autobiographical memory in depression. *Psychological Medicine, 18,* 689–695.

Williams, J. M. G., Watts, F. N., MacLeod, C., and Mathews, A. 1997. *Cognitive psychology and emotional disorders,* 2nd ed. Chichester, UK: Wiley.

Williams, L. M. 1994a. Recall of childhood trauma: A prospective study of women's memories of child sexual abuse. *Journal of Consulting and Clinical Psychology, 62,* 1167–76.

———— 1994b. What does it mean to forget child sexual abuse? A reply to Loftus,

Garry, and Feldman (1994). *Journal of Consulting and Clinical Psychology*, *62*, 1182–86.

——— 1995. Recovered memories of abuse in women with documented child sexual victimization histories. *Journal of Traumatic Stress*, *8*, 649–673.

Williams, L. M., and Banyard, V. L. 1997. Gender and recall of child sexual abuse: A prospective study. In Read and Lindsay, eds., 1997, 371–377.

Williams, M. 1987. Reconstruction of an early seduction and its aftereffects. *Journal of the American Psychoanalytic Association*, *35*, 145–163.

Williams, M. R. 1996. Suits by adults for childhood sexual abuse: Legal origins of the "repressed memory" controversy. *Journal of Psychiatry and Law*, *24*, 207–228.

Wilson, G., Rupp, C., and Wilson, W. W. 1950. Amnesia. *American Journal of Psychiatry*, *106*, 481–485.

Wilson, J. P. 1994. The historical evolution of PTSD diagnostic criteria: From Freud to DSM-IV. *Journal of Traumatic Stress*, *7*, 681–698.

Wilson, S. C., and Barber, T. X. 1978. The Creative Imagination Scale as a measure of hypnotic responsiveness: Applications to experimental and clinical hypnosis. *American Journal of Clinical Hypnosis*, *20*, 235–249.

Winkielman, P., Schwarz, N., and Belli, R. F. 1998. The role of ease of retrieval and attribution in memory judgments: Judging your memory as worse despite recalling more events. *Psychological Science*, *9*, 124–126.

Winograd, E., and Killinger, W. A., Jr. 1983. Relating age at encoding in early childhood to adult recall: Development of flashbulb memories. *Journal of Experimental Psychology: General*, *112*, 413–422.

Wittgenstein, L. 1966. *Lectures and conversations on aesthetics, psychology and religious belief*, ed. C. Barrett. Berkeley: University of California Press.

Wolf, E. K., and Alpert, J. L. 1991. Psychoanalysis and child sexual abuse: A review of the post-Freudian literature. *Psychoanalytic Psychology*, *8*, 305–327.

Wolfner, G., Faust, D., and Dawes, R. M. 1993. The use of anatomically detailed dolls in sexual abuse evaluations: The state of the science. *Applied and Preventive Psychology*, *2*, 1–11.

Wood, J. M., and Bootzin, R. R. 1990. The prevalence of nightmares and their independence from anxiety. *Journal of Abnormal Psychology*, *99*, 64–68.

Woolley, C. S., Gould, E., and McEwen, B. S. 1990. Exposure to excess glucocorticoids alters dendritic morphology of adult hippocampal pyramidal neurons. *Brain Research, 531,* 225–231.

Wright, D. B. 1993. Recall of the Hillsborough disaster over time: Systematic biases of "flashbulb" memories. *Applied Cognitive Psychology, 7,* 129–138.

Wright, D. B., Gaskell, G. D., and O'Muircheartaigh, C. A. 1998. Flashbulb memory assumptions: Using national surveys to explore cognitive phenomena. *British Journal of Psychology, 89,* 103–121.

Wright, L. 1994. *Remembering Satan.* New York: Knopf.

Yapko, M. D. 1994a. Suggestibility and repressed memories of abuse: A survey of psychotherapists' beliefs. *American Journal of Clinical Hypnosis, 36,* 163–171.

—— 1994b. Response to comments. *American Journal of Clinical Hypnosis, 36,* 185–187.

Yehuda, R. 1997. Sensitization of the hypothalamic-pituitary-adrenal axis in posttraumatic stress disorder. *Annals of the New York Academy of Science, 821,* 57–75.

——, ed. 1999. *Risk factors for posttraumatic stress disorder.* Washington: American Psychiatric Press.

—— 2001. Are glucocorticoids responsible for putative hippocampal damage in PTSD? How and when to decide. *Hippocampus, 11,* 85–89.

—— 2002. Post-traumatic stress disorder. *New England Journal of Medicine, 346,* 108–114.

Yehuda, R., Kahana, B., Binder-Brynes, K., Southwick, S. M., Mason, J. W., and Giller, E. L. 1995. Low urinary cortisol excretion in Holocaust survivors with posttraumatic stress disorder. *American Journal of Psychiatry, 152,* 982–986.

Yehuda, R., Keefe, R. S. E., Harvey, P. D., Levengood, R. A., Gerber, D. K., Geni, J., and Siever, L. J. 1995. Learning and memory in combat veterans with posttraumatic stress disorder. *American Journal of Psychiatry, 152,* 137–139.

Yehuda, R., and McFarlane, A. C. 1995. Conflict between current knowledge about posttraumatic stress disorder and its original conceptual basis. *American Journal of Psychiatry, 152,* 1705–13.

Yehuda, R., Schmeidler, J., Siever, L. J., Binder-Brynes, K., and Elkin, A. 1997. Individual differences in posttraumatic stress disorder symptom profiles in Holocaust survivors in concentration camps or in hiding. *Journal of Traumatic Stress, 10,* 453–463.

Yehuda, R., Southwick, S. M., and Giller, E. L., Jr. 1992. Exposure to atrocities and severity of chronic posttraumatic stress disorder in Vietnam combat veterans. *American Journal of Psychiatry, 149,* 333–336.

Yehuda, R., Southwick, S. M., Nussbaum, G., Wahby, V., Giller, E. L., Jr., and Mason, J. W. 1990. Low urinary cortisol excretion in patients with posttraumatic stress disorder. *Journal of Nervous and Mental Disease, 178,* 366–369.

Yehuda, R., Teicher, M. H., Trestman, R. L., Levengood, R. A., and Siever, L. J. 1996. Cortisol regulation in posttraumatic stress disorder and major depression: A chronobiological analysis. *Biological Psychiatry, 40,* 79–88.

Yerkes, R. M., and Dodson, J. D. 1908. The relation of strength of stimulus to rapidity of habit-formation. *Journal of Comparative Neurology and Psychology, 18,* 459–482.

Young, A. 1995. *The harmony of illusions: Inventing post-traumatic stress disorder.* Princeton: Princeton University Press.

Young, W. C. 1992. Recognition and treatment of survivors reporting ritual abuse. In Sakheim and Devine, eds., 1992.

Young, W. C., Sachs, R. G., Braun, B. G., and Watkins, R. T. 1991. Patients reporting ritual abuse in childhood: A clinical syndrome. Report of 37 cases. *Child Abuse and Neglect, 15,* 181–189.

Yuille, J. C., and Cutshall, J. L. 1986. A case study of eyewitness memory of a crime. *Journal of Applied Psychology, 71,* 291–301.

Zalewski, C., Thompson, W., and Gottesman, I. 1994. Comparison of neuropsychological test performance in PTSD, generalized anxiety disorder, and control Vietnam veterans. *Assessment, 1,* 133–142.

Zander, J. R., and McNally, R. J. 1988. Bio-informational processing in agoraphobia. *Behaviour Research and Therapy, 26,* 421–429.

Zaragoza, M. S., and Mitchell, K. J. 1996. Repeated exposure to suggestion and the creation of false memories. *Psychological Science, 7,* 294–300.

Zeanah, C. H. 1988. Atypical panic attacks and lack of resolution of mourning. *General Hospital Psychiatry*, 10, 373–377.

Zoellner, L. A., Foa, E. B., Brigidi, B. D., and Przeworski, A. 2000. Are trauma victims susceptible to "false memories"? *Journal of Abnormal Psychology*, 109, 517–524.

Zola, S. M. 1997. The neurobiology of recovered memory. *Journal of Neuropsychiatry and Clinical Neurosciences*, 9, 449–459.

ACKNOWLEDGMENTS

I thank Steven Reiss for suggesting that I tackle the topic of trauma and memory in a book. *Remembering Trauma* has been greatly improved by the thoughtful critiques of several people. Dan Schacter read an early version, and Carol Tavris's incisive comments on several chapters enhanced all of them. Harvard University Press sent the manuscript to three peer reviewers who represented the full spectrum of opinion on the recovered memory controversy. I am grateful for their substantive suggestions. One peer reviewer, John Kihlstrom, signed his critique, enabling me to thank him personally. The readability of the manuscript was vastly improved by the detailed comments of Elizabeth Knoll, Camille Smith, Heidi Barrett, and my wife, Peggy McNally. Elizabeth and Camille have made working with Harvard University Press a real pleasure. But it is to my wife that I owe my biggest debt of gratitude. I am not only grateful for her penetrating critiques of two versions of the manuscript, but also deeply appreciative of her understanding and support while I was preoccupied with this project.

ACKNOWLEDGMENTS

INDEX

ASD = acute stress disorder; CSA = childhood sexual abuse;
MPD = multiple personality disorder; PTSD = posttraumatic stress disorder

Torture, 10, 78, 80–81, 85–87, 97, 98, 100,
243, 244, 282; amnesia for, 211–213, 307–
308n17
Trauma, 4–5, 6, 86, 156; symptoms of, 8–9,
100–103; repression/recovery of memory
of, 19, 260, 307n13; types of, 36;
definition of, 78, 79, 97, 279–280, 281;
duration of exposure to, 81, 175; frequency
of exposure to, 81; self-reports of, 81–83,
84, 92, 103, 114, 123, 157; risk factors for,
89–90; reexperience of, 105, 120–123,
177; forgetting of, 149–152, 197; and science and advocacy, 284–285; biological
consequences of, 285; denial of, 307n13
Trauma scripts, 118–119, 120, 153, 154, 156,
157, 272–273
Traumatic amnesia, 2, 42, 140, 183, 186–
189, 275; for sexual abuse, 5, 196–209; for
homicide, 13, 210–211; for disasters/acci-
dents, 120–121, 193–194, 210, 214–215;
and brain damage, 141, 190; for CSA, 172,
189, 196–209, 210; and repression of
memory, 172; elements of, 183; mechanisms of, 183–185; triggers for, 186; psychogenic, 189–190, 210, 228; theory of,
190–191; evidence of, 190–196, partial/
incomplete, 195–196, 204–205, 303n14;
duration of, 203–204; for genocide and
torture, 211–213; for combat, 215–219;
retrospective, 216. *See also* Amnesia;
Dissociative (psychogenic) amnesia
Twin studies, 94–95, 144

Unconscious, 161, 169
Unconsciousness, 120–121, 122–123, 124,
194, 216
Urbach-Wiethe disease, 64
U.S. Congress, and CSA controversy, 1, 22–
26, 284–285

Venereal disease, 102
"Victim" terminology, 2
Vietnam war, 1, 9, 85, 89, 90, 98; and PTSD,
78, 80, 95, 119–120, 132, 133, 139, 140,
276–279; and nightmares, 105–106, 108,
109; and symptoms experienced by veterans, 114, 115, 126, 132; information processing in veterans, 148–149; atrocity narratives, 294n3. *See also* Combat; POWs
Violence: domestic, 4, 201; community, 175;
institutionalized, 282
Visualization studies, 153–155

Whiplash, 281–282
Witchcraft, 243

Yohimbine, 65, 114–115